THE COLORED PENCIL MANUAL

Step-by-Step Instructions & Techniques

Veronica Winters

DOVER PUBLICATIONS
Garden City, New York

The following trademarked products are mentioned in this book. References to these trademarks have not been licensed from or approved by the individual trademark holders.

Adobe® Photoshop®
Arches® Velin BFK Rives® Papers
Arches® Watercolour Papers
Canson® Colorline Art Papers
Caran d'Ache® Full Blender Pencils
Caran d'Ache® Luminance® Colored Pencils
Caran d'Ache® Neocolor II® Water-Soluble Pencils
Caran d'Ache® Pablo® Colored Pencils
Clairefontaine® Pastelmat®
Crescent RagMat® Matboard
Derwent Coloursoft Pencils
Faber-Castell® Albrecht Dürer Watercolor Pencils
Faber-Castell® Artist Brush Pen
Faber-Castell® Kneaded Eraser
Faber-Castell® Polychromos Colored Pencils
Finesse™ Blender Pen for Colored Pencils
Gamblin® Gamsol™
General's® All Art® Pencil Sharpener
Grumbacher® Final Fixative
Icarus Drawing Board®
Koh-I-Noor® Black Drawing Pads
Koh-I-Noor® Bristol Smooth Paper Pads
Koh-I-Noor® Bristol Vellum Paper Pads
Koh-I-Noor® Polycolor Colored Pencils
Koh-I-Noor® Woodless Colour Pencils
Legion Somerset® Printmaking Papers
Legion Stonehenge® Paper and Drawing Paper Pads
Lyra Rembrandt Splender Blender
Molotow™ Acrylic Pen
Mylar® (Dupont Teijin Films) Film Sheet
OttLite® Desk Lamp
PanPastel® Colorless Blender
Premier Illustration markers
Prismacolor® Colorless Blender Pencils
Prismacolor® Premier® Colored Pencils
Prismacolor® Premier® Markers
Prismacolor® Scholar® Pencil Sharpener
Prismacolor® Verithin® Colored Pencils
Prismacolor® Watercolor Pencils
Sakura® Pen-touch™ Paint Markers
Strathmore® Artagain® Drawing Paper
Strathmore® Bristol Vellum Paper Pads
Strathmore® Paper and Drawing Paper Pads
Strathmore® Premium Paper
Turpenoid® Natural
Winsor & Newton Pigment Marker™ Pads
Zest-it® Solvent (Citrus Free)

Bibliographical Note

The Colored Pencil Manual: Step-by-Step Instructions and Techniques is a new work, first published by Dover Publications in 2018.

Library of Congress Cataloging-in-Publication Data

Names: Winters, Veronica, author.
Title: The colored pencil manual : step-by-step instructions and techniques / Veronica Winters.
Description: Garden City, New York : Dover Publications, 2018.
Identifiers: LCCN 2018020456| ISBN 9780486822969 (paperback) | ISBN 0486822966
Subjects: LCSH: Colored pencil drawing—Technique. | BISAC: ART / Techniques / Drawing. | ART / Techniques / Color. | ART / Techniques / Pencil Drawing. | ART / Techniques / General. | ART / Subjects & Themes / Portraits. | ART / Subjects & Themes / Plants & Animals. | ART / Color Theory.
Classification: LCC NC892 .W555 2018 | DDC 741.2/4—dc23
LC record available at https://lccn.loc.gov/2018020456

Printed in China by Chang Jiang Printing Media Co., Ltd.
82296605 2023
www.doverpublications.com

Contents

Introduction v

Materials 1

Chapter 1: The Importance of Light and a Setup 11

Chapter 2: Composition and the Focal Point 22

Chapter 3: How to Turn the Form 33

Chapter 4: How to Create Volume 48

Chapter 5: How to Blend Colored Pencils 59

Chapter 6: Color Theory in Practice 72

Chapter 7: How to Draw Fabric 95

Chapter 8: How to Create Symmetrical Shapes 105

Chapter 9: How to Draw Metal, Reflective Surfaces, and Crystal. 117

Chapter 10: How to Draw Textures. 135

Troubleshooting 169

Introduction

This book is designed for beginners in colored pencil art but not for an absolute beginner in drawing. You will need some understanding of basic concepts and practice with drawing in pencil before switching to color.

It is important that you have an open mind when reading the material, and you should take it as a compass rather than a rule. This book contains many art fundamentals that are applicable to any form of realist art, whether it's painting, drawing, acrylic, oil, pencil, or colored pencil.

This is a book that is hands on, in which you'll see lots of condensed information so that it is easy to follow. There are step-by-step instructions demonstrating particular techniques, action steps for you to apply what you have learned, sidebars, and helpful tips. I'd like to say that I teach the approach to drawing, not painting by numbers, so you'll be learning to make decisions on your own in terms of color, as opposed to just following the given colors.

This book is intended for those serious at mastering the medium. Therefore, don't skip through the beginning chapters, but take the time to read the entire book first, absorb the information, and then start working on your projects.

I hope this book serves as an inspirational guide for your creative endeavors. I offer my sincere gratitude and salute you for accepting this challenge. Let's bring your art to the next level!

Artfully,
Veronica

Note: Students can download the outlines for the projects in this book from:
www.veronicasart.com

Materials

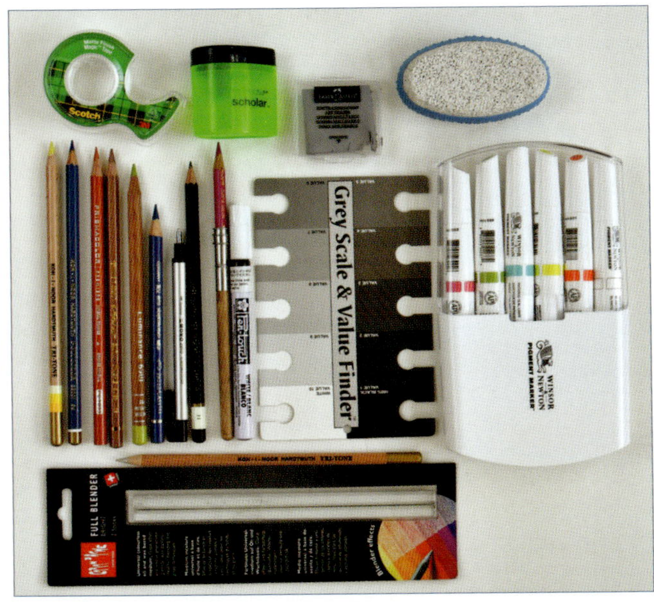

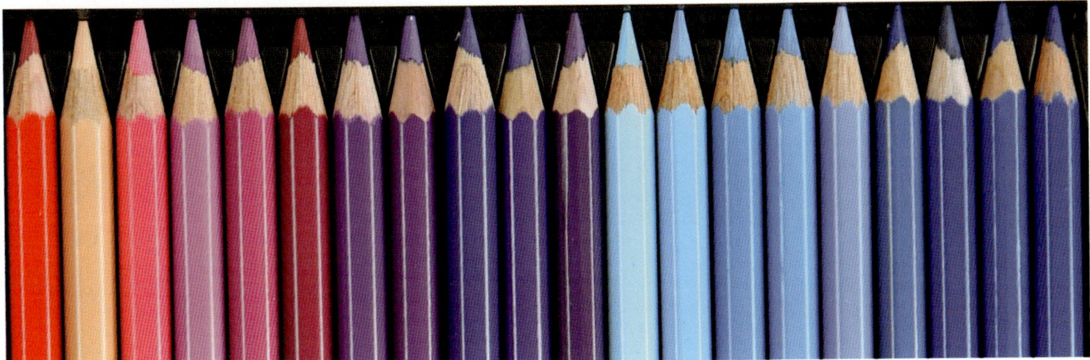

PENCILS

There are numerous varieties of colored pencils available on the market. While many sell as open stock, most sell in boxes and packages ranging from 24 to 132 colors. There is a very big difference in drawing quality between the generic brands and artist-quality, professional colored pencils.

Generics are good for child-like sketching and for taking notes, but you won't be able to achieve the same beautiful results with them as other artists do working with the professional brands, assuming all other variables are kept equal. Let's look at key features that contribute to the quality of a professional colored pencil. These qualities are the lead's durability, lightfastness, softness, and base.

In essence all colored pencils are wax-based, but some brands have a lot more wax in them and they are categorized as "wax-based," while the rest have different percentages of wax in them and are usually referred to as "oil-based." While this separation seems confusing, these terms are mainly used to describe the layering properties of the pencils. Soft, wax-based colored pencils adhere to the paper's tooth (the surface feel or texture) more than the "oil-based" colored pencils, which leads to different blending techniques. Oil-based pencils behave more like soft pastels, and artists often match the surfaces and tools applicable to these pencils such as drawing on sanded papers and using the PanPastel blenders. Besides the percentage of wax present in every pencil, colored pencils also consist of binders, hardeners, fillers, and colorants, which all contribute to color intensity.

Wax-based colored pencils with wax-based colorless blender

Brands: Caran d'Ache Luminance, Prismacolor Premier, Koh-I-Noor Woodless Colour Pencils, Derwent Coloursoft, Prismacolor Colorless Blender, Caran d'Ache Full Blender

Wax-based colored pencils offer superior coverage and easy application and blending due to their softness. The disadvantages of such pencils include wax bloom and a fairly easy breakdown of a pencil; also the core's softness leads to faster use of a pencil.

Oil-based colored pencils with oil-based colorless blender

Brands: Faber-Castell Polychromos, Caran d'Ache Pablo, Koh-I-Noor Polycolor, Prismacolor Verithin, Lyra Splender Blender

Oil-based colored pencils have much less wax in them; therefore they're less soft and more durable. While oil-based pencils don't break or bloom, lasting longer, they are harder than the wax-based pencils and layering feels different, depending on the brand. In general, they are great for working on details (Caran d'Ache Pablo, Koh-I-Noor Polycolor) and not so great layering in the background because of the harder lead. However, pastel-like pencils such as the Faber-Castell Polychromos work well in backgrounds and on sanded surfaces with PanPastel blenders.

Among all oil-based pencils, Faber-Castell Polychromos Pencils are truly amazing, waterproof, and lightfast colored pencils that are highly pigmented, don't break, and last a long time. They offer a great alternative to Luminance.

Water-soluble colored pencils

Brands: Caran d'Ache Neocolor II Watersoluble, Prismacolor Watercolor, Faber-Castell Albrecht Dürer

Many artists confuse these pencils with the ones mentioned above. Their key feature is that they are diluted with water, for painting large and small areas. Many artists underpaint with water-soluble colored pencils and then continue shading with regular colored pencils over them. The use of either permanent markers or water-soluble colored pencils speeds up the drawing process greatly, layering a solid foundation for the drawing. Wet pigment becomes smoother and darker, so test your supplies on a separate piece of paper to understand their properties.

Water-soluble colored pencils differ slightly among brands in the core's hardness, chalkiness, or brightness of a diluted color, and in the amount of undiluted grain left. Faber-Castell Albrecht Dürer pencils dilute with water completely. Caran d'Ache Neocolors have the highest pigmentation among the watercolor pencils and therefore last a very long time. They come in a crayon shape, however, and you can't sharpen them with a regular pencil sharpener. The artist often uses a watercolor brush charged with water to take pigment off the crayon and to paint on paper.

It will be your personal preference and experience that defines the use of either oil-based or wax-based colored pencils. In this book the artist uses wax-based colored pencils most often with the blending techniques applicable to these pencils.

Durability, lightfastness, softness

The best professional colored pencils that match all the parameters in softness, lightfastness, and durability are the wax-based Caran d'Ache Luminance pencils. Their core is very soft with unbreakable casting, which leads to top performance in shading and coverage. Their pigments are 100% lightfast, which means that colors don't fade off the drawing paper unlike so many other pencils available. These incredibly well-crafted pencils are also the most expensive, sell in boxes and as open stock, and become the ultimate dream of every professional colored pencil artist!

The oil-based Faber-Castell Polychromos colored pencils from Germany have a great saturation, durability, and softness. They also layer smoothly, but differ from Prismacolor or Luminance pencils because their core is somewhat similar to soft pastels. They are water resistant and have three grades of lightfastness. They offer a great alternative to Luminance.

Sanford Prismacolor Premier colored pencils are the favorites of so many artists because of their ultimate softness, which makes it easy to shade, blend, and achieve smooth vividness in drawings. They are also priced competitively, have the widest color range, and sell in boxes and as open stock. They are less durable, however, because of their high wax content, and their lightfastness varies greatly. Some colors, such as the blues and greens, fade off the paper quite quickly without even a considerable exposure to UV light. Prismacolor has its own downloadable lightfastness reference chart where an artist can look up every color to see its lightfastness rating. Stay away from LF-III and LF-IV colors because they fade quickly. Throughout this book, you'll see the artist using particular colors by Prismacolor chosen for their highest lightfastness rating, not just the hue. You can also try drawing with wax-based Derwent Coloursoft as an alternative to Prismacolor Premier colored pencils. Coloursoft pencils are even softer than the Prismacolors but seem to be quite chalky.

It often happens that artists use a combination of colored pencils, using the softest ones in the initial layering or underpainting, and then switching to the harder ones to draw the details. It becomes crucial when you work small and can't produce the tiniest detail with a very soft pencil like Prismacolor Premier. Therefore you can switch to Swiss-made Caran d'Ache Pablo colored pencils that are harder and thus keep the finest point for quite some time. Very durable, they are less soft and less pigmented. Sold for much less than the Caran d'Ache Luminance, note that not all Pablos are equally lightfast. Once again, check for the manufacturer's lightfastness rating chart to pick your pencils if you draw professionally. You can also try Koh-I-Noor Polycolor and Koh-I-Noor Woodless colored pencils for detail work, which sell at a great price point. Their lightfastness ratings also vary.

Note that you can mix oil-based and wax-based colored pencils in one drawing, just as you can underpaint with markers or watercolor pencils before working in colored pencil. Because professional grade colored pencils are a considerable investment, buy colored pencils by various brands as open stock to understand which qualities matter the most to you and work best with your drawing technique and style.

PAPER

Just as important as the choice of colored pencils, the right choice of paper is critical to your success. You won't go far drawing on poor-quality sketch paper or a generic brand drawing paper. These papers wear out quickly; erasing makes permanent change to the surface; and they are not able to hold extensive layering, solvent blending, and burnishing. Therefore, the result is below average. Because there are countless brands of paper available, here we focus on the most basic and versatile papers applicable to colored pencil drawing only.

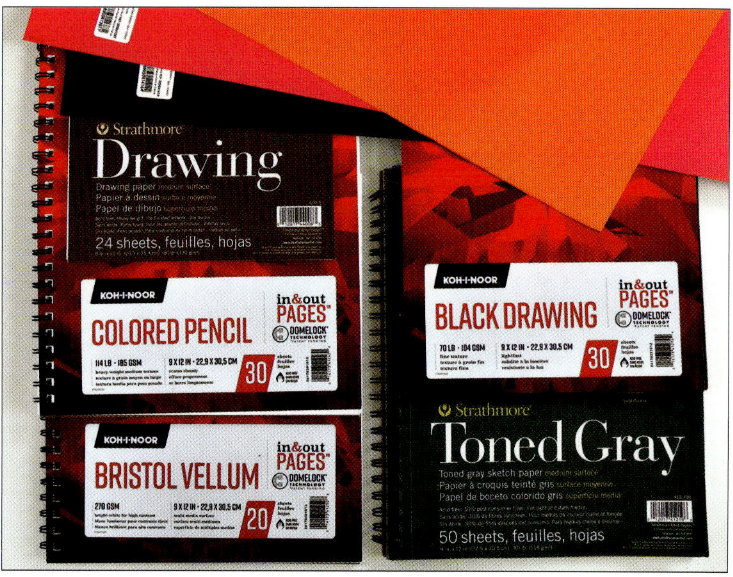

With practice you will learn to match specific colored pencils with specific papers that the pencils work best on. For instance Faber-Castell Polychromos pencils perform well on pastel paper (Pastelmat) and boards, while Prismacolor Premier pencils work great on Bristol vellum surfaces (Koh-I-Noor Bristol Vellum or Stonehenge paper pads). If you do underpainting with pigment markers, test the specific paper designed for markers (Winsor & Newton pigment markers work great on Winsor & Newton pigment marker paper that's bleed-proof and offers superior blending and color vibrancy despite its rather thin pages). If you underpaint with water-soluble pencils, use professional hot pressed watercolor paper such as Arches.

The ideal colored paper for colored pencil drawing should be thick, smooth, and come in a variety of colors. There are three characteristics to drawing paper: color, texture, and weight. They are usually noted right on the paper's cover, but if you are a newbie, you can go to a craft store to touch and feel the paper to understand its parameters. These features affect blending, time spent shading, and overall look of your art. All professional drawing papers are archival (acid-free) these days, so it's not included as a separate parameter here.

Weight or thickness

On average, the thicker the paper, the better it is for your drawing in any media due to its flatness and stability. Try not to buy a very thin paper that is under 80 lb. in weight unless it is especially formulated to hold markers or colored pencils. On average, thick (100–300 lb.) paper withstands solvent washes and watercolor underpainting, is easy to store, and easy to frame as well. Many artists draw on boards with the same properties as paper; the only difference is their thickness.

Sketch papers with thin (50 lb.) pages are good for sketching only. Please don't use sketch paper for your colored pencil drawing! Use sketch paper to create the outlines that you can transfer onto a fine drawing paper.

Brands: Legion Stonehenge paper pads, Strathmore drawing paper pads, 80 lb., medium surface; or Strathmore Premium Recycled, Strathmore Bristol Smooth, 100 lb.; Strathmore Bristol Board, 100 lb.; Museum Grade, 1.4mm thick (4-ply) matboards such as Crescent RagMat Matboard; Koh-I-Noor Bristol Smooth and Koh-I-Noor Bristol Vellum, 270 gsm; Koh-I-Noor Colored Pencil and Koh-I- Noor Black Drawing pads

Texture or paper's tooth

Paper tooth lets your colored pencil adhere to a surface. Think of it as a wave. The higher the wave is, the more texture it has and the more layering your paper accepts.

While textured papers are great for work in pastel, charcoal, or conte, texture is the most serious impediment to a smooth colored pencil layering and blending. It also "eats" up soft colored pencils. Stay away from textured surfaces at all costs. A slight texture is a plus, however, because there is enough paper tooth for a colored pencil to grab. While some artists stick to Strathmore Bristol smooth papers that have zero texture and colored pencils seem to blend on their own, these papers are very challenging for a beginner because pencil layering is limited to two layers.

Therefore, a medium-textured paper such as the Legion Stonehenge is the absolute favorite of most colored pencil artists. Its texture and fair thickness produce very smooth shading that often needs no additional blending. Somerset and BFK Rives printmaking papers have similar properties to Stonehenge. New paper by Koh-I-Noor is surprisingly high quality. Their Bristol Smooth, Bristol Vellum, Colored Pencil, and Black Drawing pads all feature "in & out" pages, meaning you can take the pages out and put them back in for easy storage and folio view.

Brands: Legion Stonehenge Paper, Vellum, 90 lb.; Koh-I-Noor Bristol Smooth and Bristol Vellum, and Koh-I-Noor Colored Pencil and Black Drawing pads; Winsor & Newton Pigment Marker Paper, 47 lb.; Arches hot pressed watercolor paper; Somerset, 100 lb., printmaking papers; BFK Rives, 100 lb., printmaking paper; 1.4mm thick matboards such as Crescent RagMat Matboard

COLOR

Colored paper or toned paper is the author's favorite because it adds a novel dimension to drawing in color. The same colors "react" differently to colored surfaces, giving new color combinations and vividness that is often impossible to achieve on a white drawing paper. It's also fun to create highlights using white colored pencil on toned paper. Note that color construction paper is not suitable for professional drawing.

Strathmore's toned grey sketch paper is good for sketching and studies in two, black and white, colors but seems to be quite thin for professional drawing that involves multiple layering.

Brands: Legion Stonehenge paper (light shades); Crescent RagMat Matboard (a variety of colors are available, ranging from very dark, strong ones to light, subtle shades); Canson Colorline papers; Koh-I-Noor Black Drawing pads

Colored paper vs. white paper

White paper is not quite white and has its own gradations of color temperature and tone. Usually it is a personal preference for which paper you like to work with. Stark white or yellowish white? Cool, bluer white or a warmer white? Printmaking papers mentioned above also have their variations in color, ranging from pure white to a light grey.

The bottom line is to get inexpensive practice paper such as Strathmore Drawing, medium surface, for general drawing; Stonehenge or Koh-I-Noor Bristol Vellum papers for refined, professional, or commissioned drawings; or 4-ply museum boards with the highest thickness for professional drawings.

To store your paper, use acid-free space in a drawer. To create a barrier between the wood and the drawings or paper, use sheets of Mylar film or acid-free boards or paper. As with any artwork, changing high temperature and high humidity levels lead to fast deterioration of your art and materials, especially in the warm and humid climates of the South, like Florida.

OTHER SUPPLIES

Colored pencils must be sharp at all times. Because wax-based colored pencils may be brittle, the right **pencil sharpener** is a crucial tool to keep a pencil's point needle sharp. There are electric sharpeners, battery operated pencil sharpeners, and manual sharpeners. While electric sharpeners sharpen the pencils very quickly and can last for quite some time, they can also "eat" your pencils as the blade will need a replacement at some point. The author's preference is a single manual German-blade sharpener. It will give the most gentle and perfect sharpening and will fit in your pencil pouch.

Brands: Prismacolor Scholar Pencil Sharpener or the General's All-Art Pencil Sharpener. The electric pencil sharpener by Panasonic is also good.

The author uses two types of **erasers** throughout the book: a kneaded eraser and the Japanese brand Tombow Mono Zero eraser. The kneaded eraser lifts out pigment and pencil residue softly, leaving no grease or residue on the paper, which is vital to the clean appearance of your artwork. The Tombow eraser, which has a small, pencil-like point, is wonderful for erasing mistakes in tiny places that are unreachable with any other kind of eraser. There are electric erasers that could do the job, but they may be harder to control in delicate areas. For a more aggressive erasing you can use the white vinyl erasers; however, they do leave debris. Also consider the pigment lifting out technique by using magic tape and mounting putty.

Brands: Faber-Castell kneaded art eraser comes with a handy plastic case to ensure clean storage; Tombow Mono Zero Elastomer Eraser, ultra fine, 2.3mm.

When a pencil gets short, a **pencil extender** will allow you to hold it easier. A **ruler** will help you draw straight lines. A **drafting brush** will keep your drawing clean from pencil fleck. A **light box** may help to transfer the outlines right from your photo to your drawing paper, if your paper is not very thick. **Graphite transfer pape**r works well to transfer the outlines if you have no light box, the paper is very thick, or you simply prefer hand sketching as opposed to a light box transferal process. You can also buy an OttLite desk lamp, but the artist finds that working during the day in a natural light is the best for a colored pencil artist.

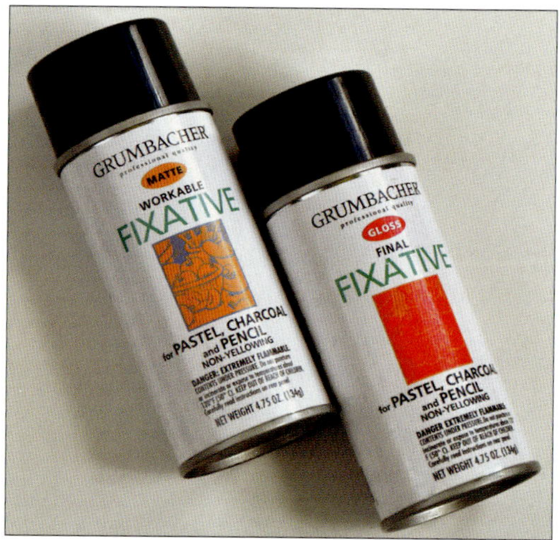

You will also need two types of **fixatives**: workable and a final one for dry media. Make sure the fixative is not for oil painting, but for pastel, charcoal, and pencil artwork. Artists use a workable fixative to spray drawings between the layers when the paper tooth is filled and doesn't accept any more layering. Another use is to spray it when working on black paper. The subsequently added colors become much brighter when they are applied over the sprayed layer. The final fixative protects art from UV rays and humidity; it also evens out the surface if you have wax bloom. The artist recommends a professional spray such as Grumbacher Matte Final Fixative.

BLENDING SUPPLIES

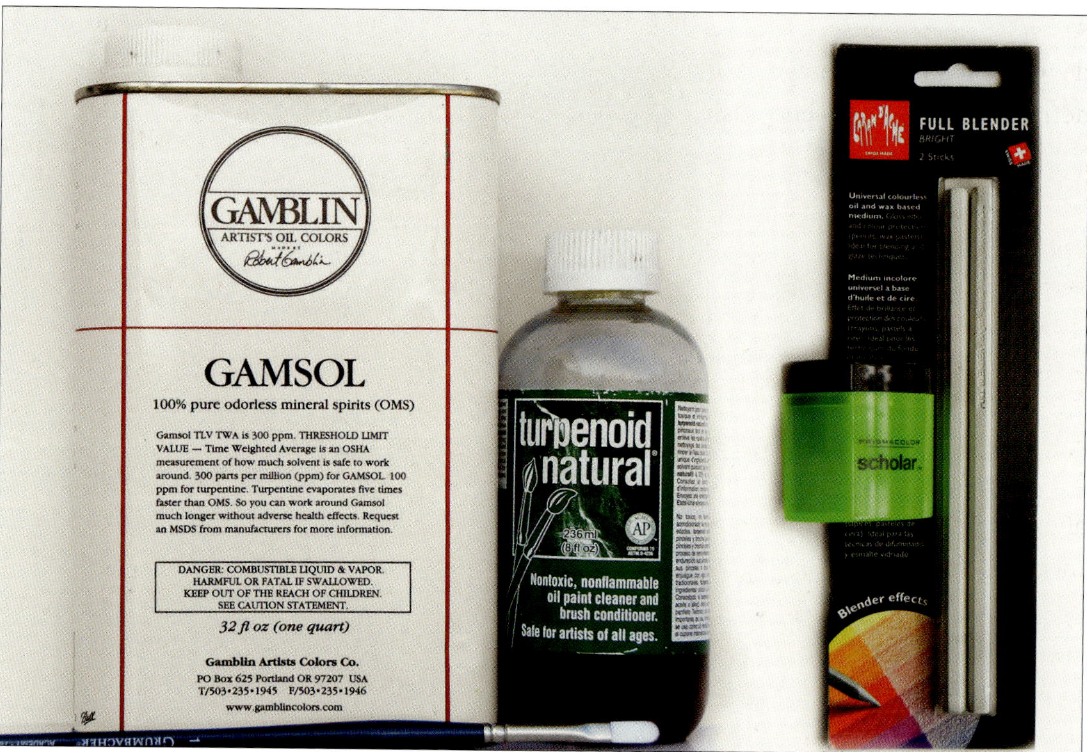

Most colored pencil art requires some kind of blending to achieve a smooth, glass-like appearance of the surface. There are two types of blending techniques you can use: solvents and pencils.

Solvents melt the binder in the pencil, producing a rich, uniform surface, which eliminates pencil strokes. Solvents include paint thinners, rubbing alcohol, mineral oil, and even vodka. Even nontoxic solvents should be handled with care. Store a small amount of a solvent in a glass jar with a lid for easy access. Don't inhale the solvent or touch it with your hands. When painting with a solvent, move the pigment in your drawing with either a cotton-tipped swab or a cheap synthetic brush that can hold a fine point.

Brands: Gamsol blends both wax-based and oil-based pencils. A good alternative to Gamsol is Zest-it (citrus-based solvent that works with both types of pencils). Finesse™ Blender Pen for Colored Pencils is a unique product that is solvent-based, has two points, works well with wax-based pencils, and comes in a pencil form. The downside to it is that it doesn't last for very long.

To blend drawings with pencils you may use colorless blenders that are not messy, but very time-consuming to work with, especially if you work large. These have no pigment in them but move the pigment in the drawing to get rid of the pencil strokes. Pencils are necessary to smooth out the edges or to blend the entire area. The surface becomes smooth and vivid, though differently from using a solvent.

Artists may combine two methods of blending, or prefer using one over the other, depending on the image. Sometimes blending with a solvent is too aggressive and detracts from the unblended drawing. It is vital to practice this technique on scrap paper to see how the solvent affects colors. There are a few colors in the Prismacolor line that blend differently from the rest. The author's favorite pencil blender is Caran d'Ache Full Blender because it's 100% colorless, blends exceptionally well, and even creates a barrier against UV light.

Brands: Caran d'Ache Full Blender Bright, Prismacolor Colorless Blender, Lyra Rembrandt Splender Colorless Blender

Many artists find the Icarus Board as a great alternative to the blending methods mentioned above. The Icarus Board is a portable, electrically heated drawing board for all wax-based media, particularly colored pencils, artist crayons, and wax pastels. This technique is based on the principle that when a wax-based medium is exposed to heat, it becomes softer or even melts; when returned to room temperature it quickly solidifies. With the dial set at a desired temperature, the heat of the board transfers onto the substrate, softening the pigments and greatly speeding up the blending and burnishing. There are two types of boards available: the Icarus Drawing Board, designed to be used horizontally on a desk, and the Icarus Painting Board, designed to be used vertically on an easel. For more information, please visit this website: www.icarusart.net

Other tools: For minor highlights: Molotow Acrylic Pen, Faber-Castell Artist Brush Pen, or Sakura Pen-Touch, extra fine; tracing paper for paper indenting; transfer paper to transfer outlines onto drawing paper

To complete the underpainting in some of your drawings, the author recommends trying the Winsor & Newton pigment markers. Premier double-ended art markers have dye-based nontoxic ink and come in 156 colors. Premier Illustration markers contain lightfast and archival nontoxic ink and come in three tips—fine, chisel, and brush tip.

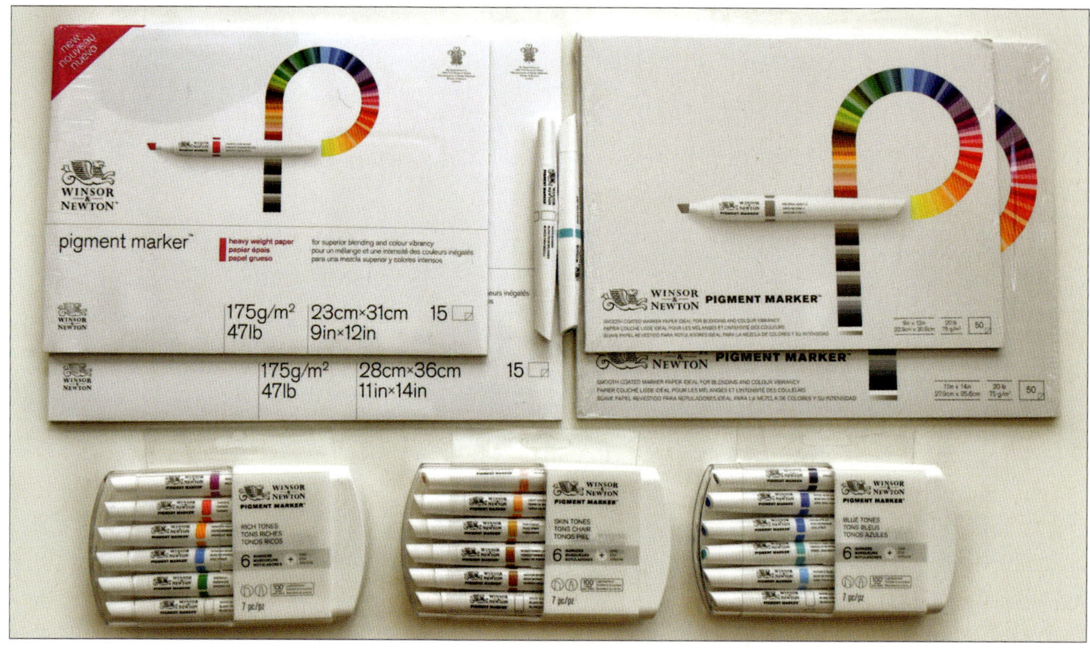

Action Step: Take samples of various papers and make a few color swatches on each of them to see how the individual paper's texture and color affect your shading. You'll learn which paper feels right for you.

Chapter 1

The Importance of Light and a Setup

How to take great pictures suitable for colored pencil drawing

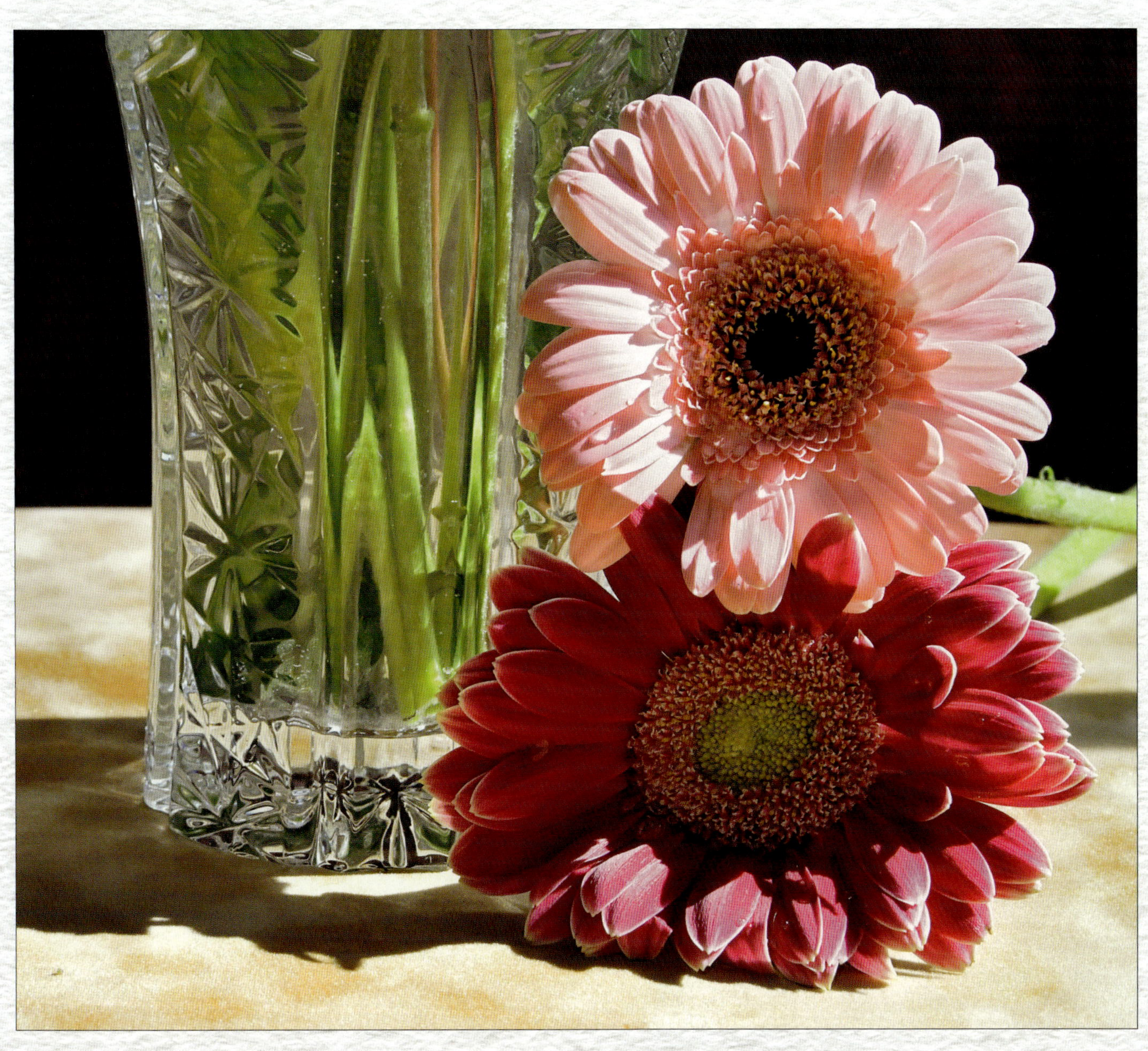

REFERENCE PHOTOGRAPHY

Because colored pencil drawing is such a slow medium to work in, almost all artists rely on their references to create art as opposed to drawing from life. Sometimes it takes weeks to complete one colored pencil drawing, and we have to rely on our photo reference to capture story, composition, design, color, and details. Unless you draw from life in colored pencils, great photography becomes key to artistic success, which leaves you with no excuse not to master it.

Advantages of Mastering Photography:

- It develops your originality and vision.
- It forces you to extrapolate and focus on what's important or to find the center of interest in busy environments.
- It teaches you to see how light shapes the form that you copy on paper in 3-D.
- It makes you the sole creator of your art. You don't have to worry about a copyright or entering a juried art contest.
- It's a forgiving medium, giving you many chances to practice at all times. You become attuned to cropping and balancing techniques that artists traditionally use in their paintings.

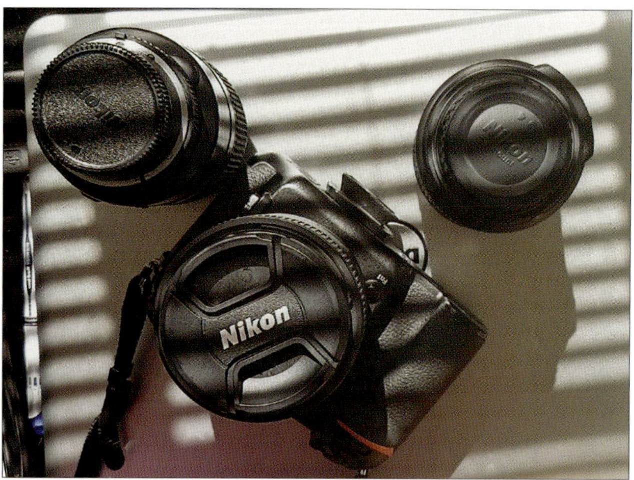

Disadvantages of Using Photography:

- It often flattens out the form to such a degree that you have a hard time re-creating the volume. That's why it is best to start taking pictures with one directional light source that gives you definite lights and shadows.
- Camera makes its choice. Even the best cameras don't capture what you see as an artist, which involves emotion. By working from a picture, artists analyze the subject rather than respond to it freely.
- There is a lot of distortion in the images depending on the lens and camera you use that is obvious in cityscape photography or in pictures of geometric objects. The same distortion is present in pictures of people or fruit, or whatever subject you have, but our eye doesn't catch those distortions as quickly as we notice those in linear and geometric forms. Those "unseen" distortions will travel to a student's drawing when the artist transfers the outlines rather than learns to sketch freehand from his reference.

- You may also have problems with exposure, depending on the lighting conditions. Use the HDR (high dynamic range) function on your phone to level out the exposure. HDR combines two or three pictures into one automatically, giving you a single balanced shot. HDR function is very handy when the sky looks too bright or the background is so light that it makes your subject appear too dark.
- You can take good pictures with your phone, although the quality won't be the same as shooting with a DSLR (digital single lens reflex) camera. If you shoot with your phone, zoom in on your object as closely as you can. That will blur the background, giving your subject a boost in color and texture.

If you decide that photography is not right for you, you always have three options:

- Browse the stock photo websites that have vast collections of images such as iStockphoto and Shutterstock.
- Look at websites that offer creative common (copyright free) images as well, like Pixabay or Flickr.
- You can also contact the photographer directly, explaining the reason for using their image and asking for permission to use it in your art. Websites such as Flickr have images with free and copyright-restricted pictures. Just know that contests don't allow artists to enter drawings done from someone else's reference. The artist is the sole designer and creator of artwork beginning from the very first step of photography.

SUBJECTS

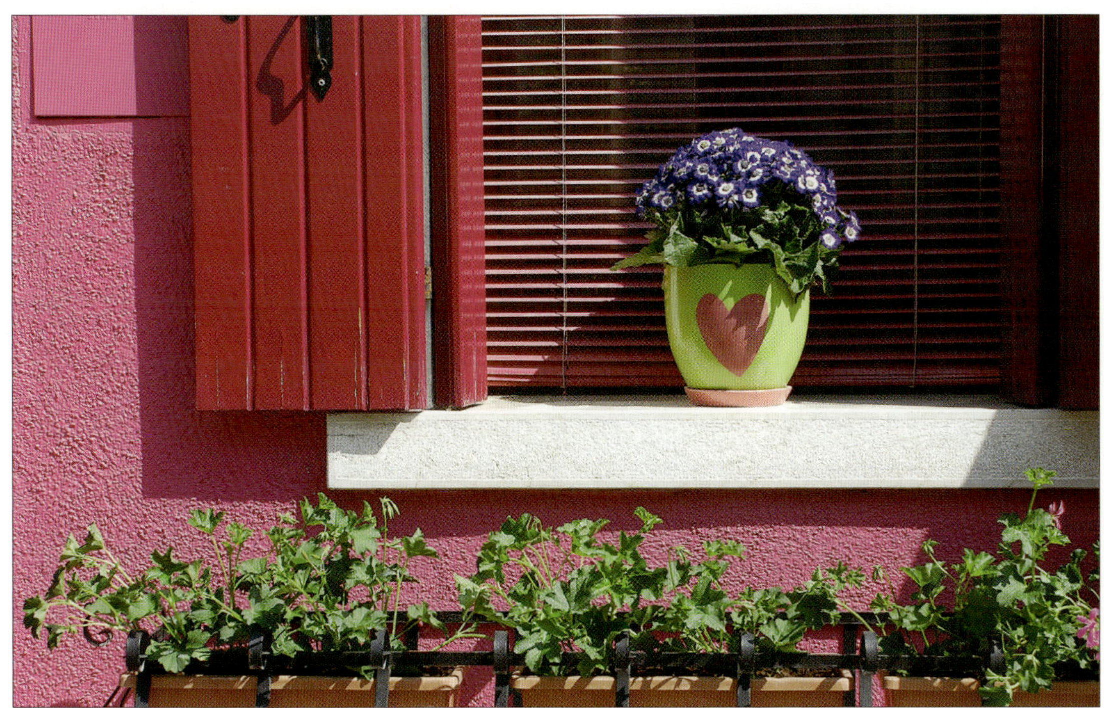

If you feel stuck and don't know what to draw, just look at images in art magazines or on Pinterest, Pixabay, or Facebook drawing groups for ideas. Below you'll find several groups of subjects to consider for drawing:

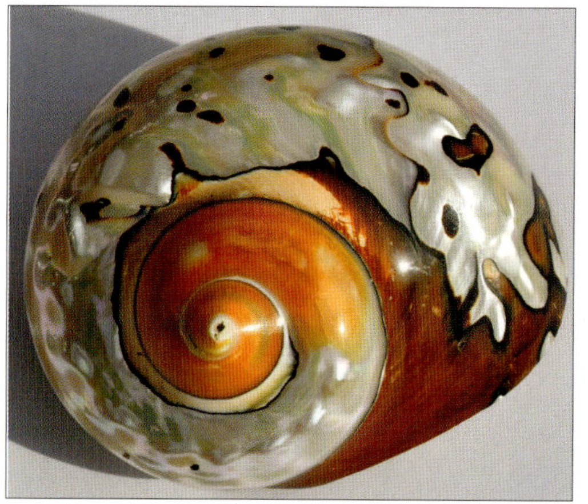

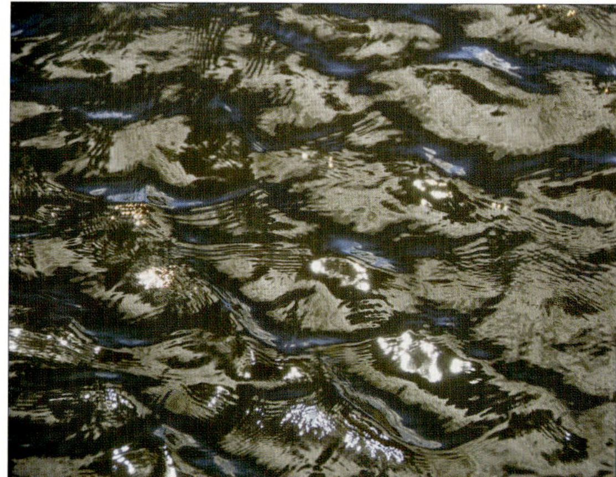

Close-ups of textured subjects—these can be the most fun, unpredictable subjects for your photography and art. They can be reflective surfaces and reflections, fabric patterns and lace, rusted door locks, wood grain, colorful feathers, candy, sliced fruit, marbles, flowers, kitchen utensils or tools, and even mechanical parts of clocks.

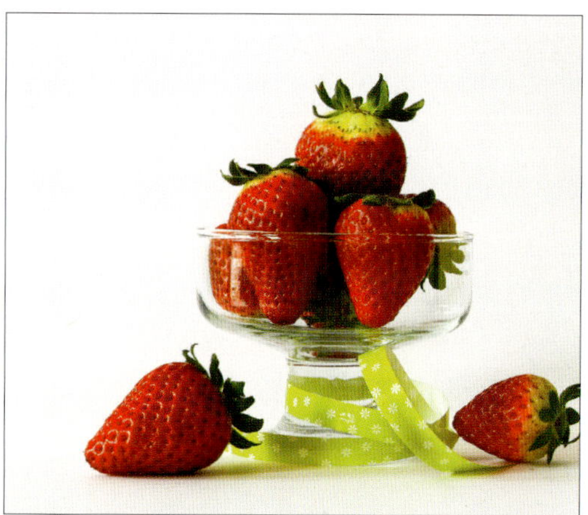

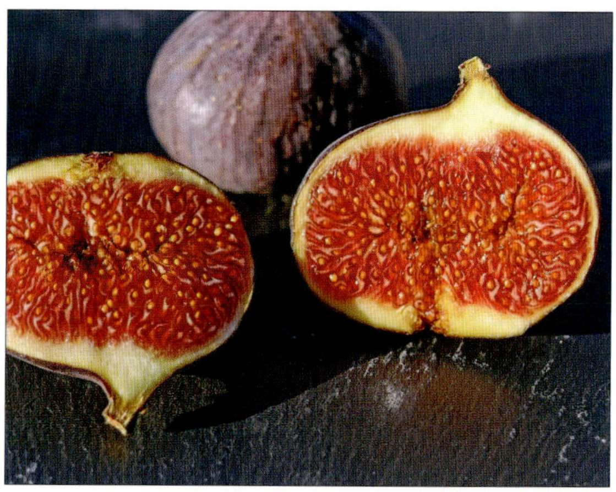

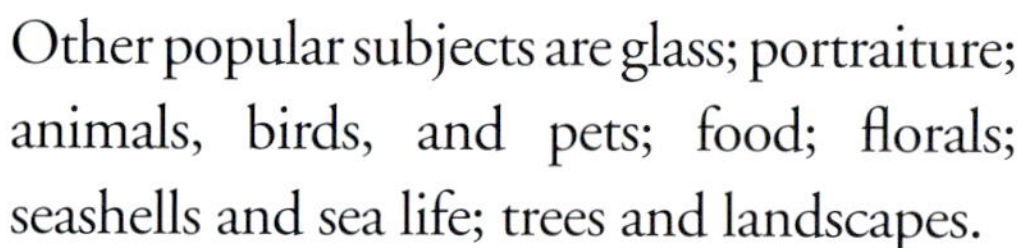

Other popular subjects are glass; portraiture; animals, birds, and pets; food; florals; seashells and sea life; trees and landscapes.

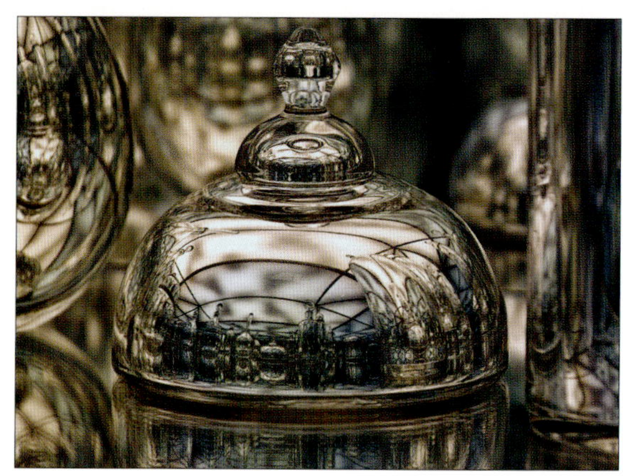

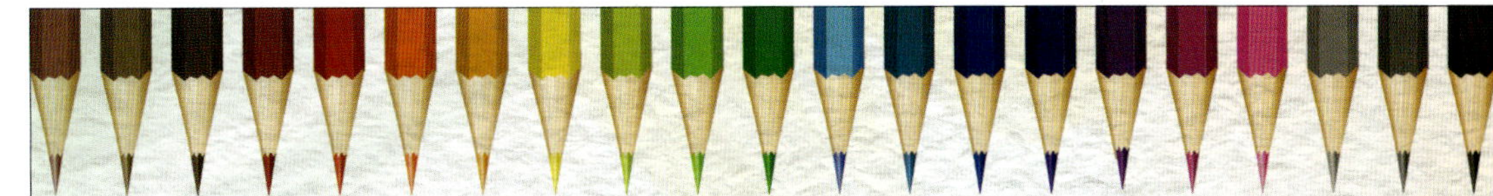

Image composites would be considered a separate category of subjects in colored pencil art. Note that it's hard to create an illusion of reality using composite pictures, meaning that you take several photo references to combine them in a single drawing. This is because light, color, and shadows should match in all pictures involved. While combining images is quite possible with still life or landscapes, it's a much harder task with fantasy art, mainly because you try to create a world that has no clear visual reference. Professional artists would use staged photography to facilitate the process. They dress and stage models in settings that become a prototype for realistic fantasy art. If you aim to create "fantasy" drawings in realist tradition (you would like to combine objects from different pictures), make sure that the light direction and color temperature match in all references.

Action Step: What makes a great picture is often taking a common subject and placing it in an unusual environment, or finding a totally unexpected angle or point of view. Browse for ideas and inspiration online, and then go out with your camera and have fun with it! The possibilities become infinite because it's the artist who makes the picture and not the other way around.

USING LIGHT AND SETUPS TO TAKE GOOD PICTURES

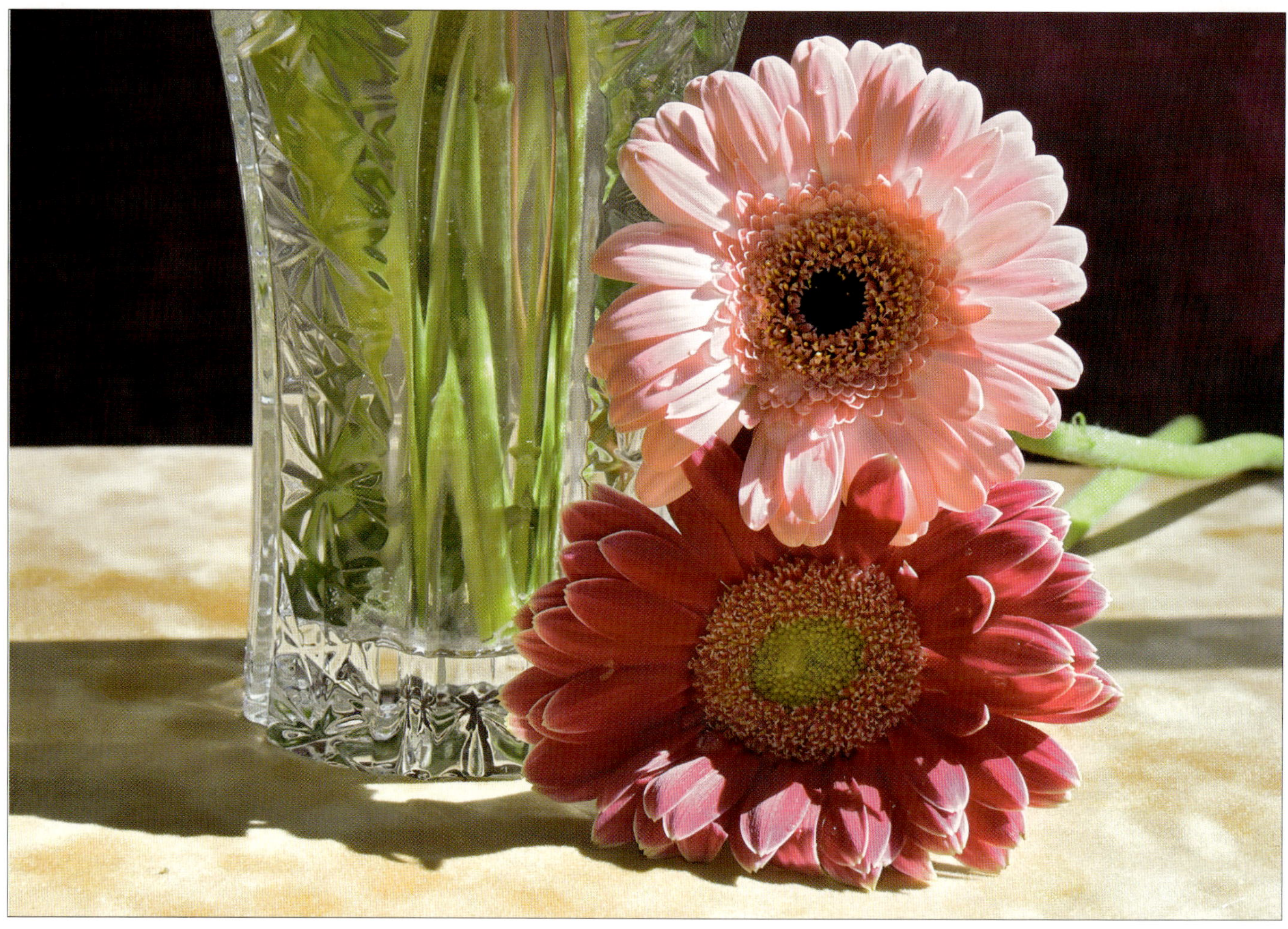

Finding the right light or understanding what it actually means is a daunting task for most beginners in art. Let's figure out why you need to pay attention to light, and look at several parameters that determine good lighting conditions for your photography.

Properties of light

Your goal of shooting in the "right lighting conditions" is to beautify your subject and to bring the best out in it. Ask yourself what attracts you to this object. It could be a specific texture, transparency, color, or an abstract pattern of light and shade that you see. You need to figure out what you love about your subject and how you can highlight its most attractive qualities in a specific light. If your subject looks boring in a picture, chances are that the lighting conditions were boring at the time it was shot.

Light temperature: The light can be either warm or cool. In the beginning it may be difficult to spot the difference, but if you ask yourself if it is yellowish or bluish, it makes more sense. Fluorescent lights tend to be cooler, while the tungsten lights are warmer. In nature, you see a beautiful golden light twenty minutes before the sunset. The light temperature affects how you see the colors and how they unify everything in the image. You also use the light temperature to understand the color on your subject: if the light is cool, it gives cool lights and warm shadows. If the light is warm, it gives you warm lights and cooler shadows.

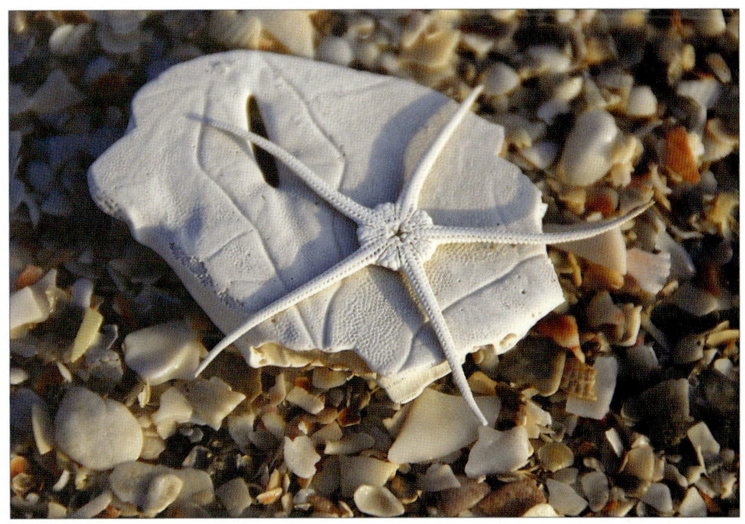

In this picture the evening light is warm (yellow) and the shadows are cool (blue).

Quality of light: Natural light is the most beautiful light we have as artists. While the soft, diffused light may give the artist beautiful, soft skin tones in portrait photography or a dream-like mist in a landscape, this light is difficult to master for a beginner who is shooting pictures of glass, fruit, or flowers. The glass loses its sparkle and reflections, the fruit doesn't have the volume or shadows, and flowers appear quite bleak. That's because the diffused light gives you very soft, almost unnoticeable shadows and highlights, which, in turn, are difficult to reproduce in art for a student. Whatever the light temperature is, the goal is to avoid getting monotonous images that often happen in diffused light situations when you have an overcast sky.

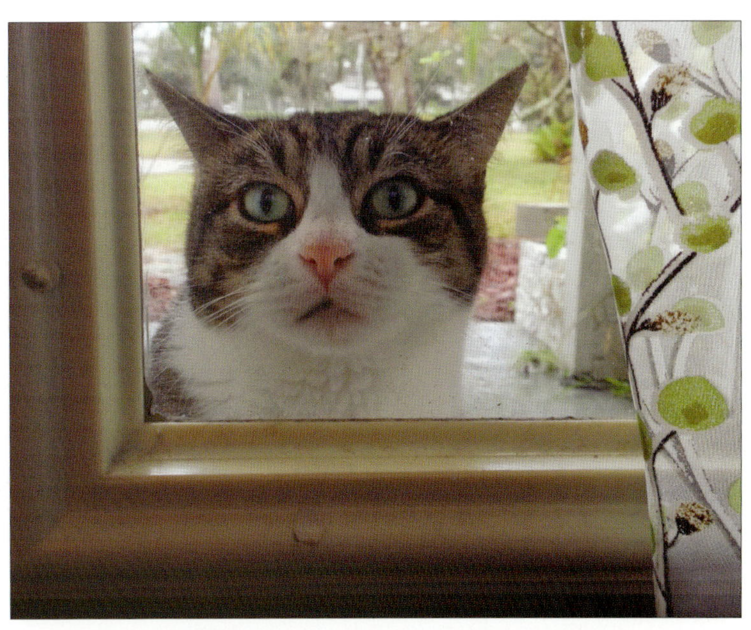

This picture has a soft, diffused light throughout. While the picture looks like fun to draw, it would be much harder for a beginning artist to create volume and to turn the form using this kind of lighting.

Action Step: Shoot pictures in natural light one to two hours before the sunset or in the morning on a clear day to capture the most gorgeous colors and contrasts on your subject.

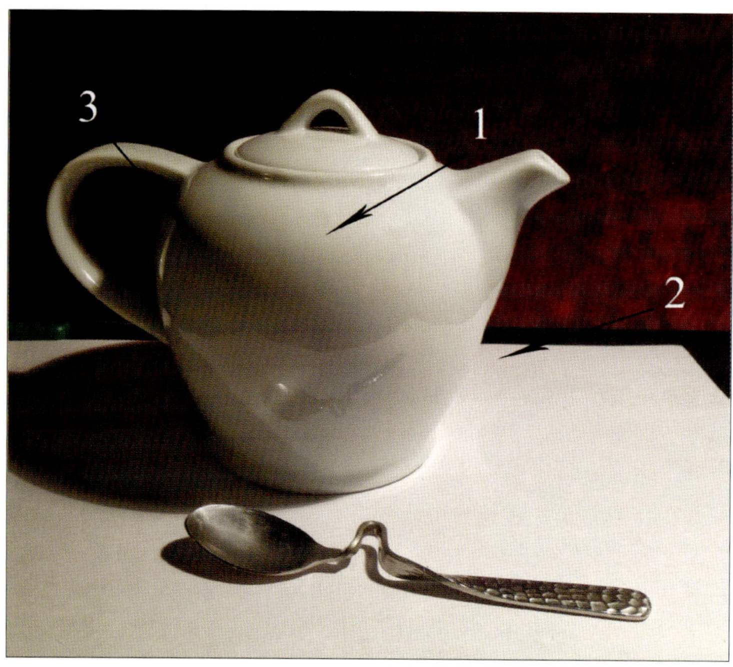

This teapot has one directional light set up on the right at night. Such light gives strong highlights and shadows that are easier to re-create in a drawing.

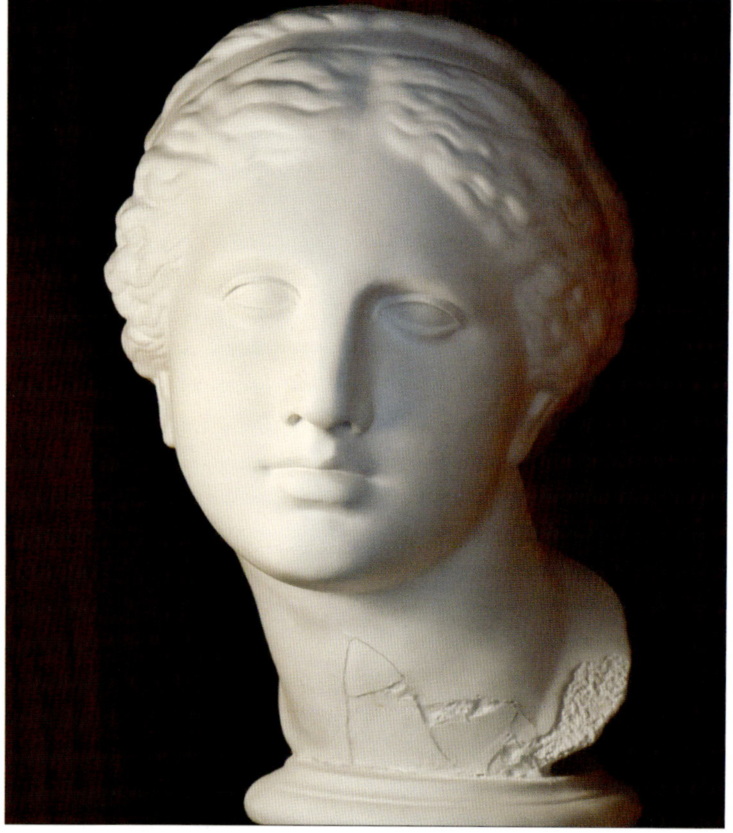
The head of Aphrodite features Rembrandt lighting that clearly shows half the face in the light with the rest falling in the shadow.

If you are just starting out, look for dramatic light conditions or high contrast situations (called "chiaroscuro" and perfected by the Italian master Caravaggio). Study Caravaggio's paintings to see how patterns of light and shade form abstract designs in his images.

Light direction and shadows: The most effective way to study the light on a form is to have a singular, strong directional light source set up at 45 degrees, which is often called Rembrandt lighting. This light direction creates beautiful highlights and shadows that will add dimension to your objects. If you go to an atelier school of classical painting, you'll see students draw from plaster casts and still lifes set under a single directional light that doesn't change direction for the entire drawing process. Such setups are vital to an artist's understanding of how to turn the form. So when you take pictures inside, find and focus on one primary light source, like a table lamp, and consider its strength. Look at your subject and find definite highlights and shadows on and under it because it will give you this 3-D quality you want to re-create in your drawing. (Also see Chapters 3 and 4).

Other guidelines for photography

Depth of field: Shallow depth of field allows you to capture your object in a sharp focus, blurring the rest of the image. A soft background supports the focal point rather than competing with it. When you have a high depth of field set at f16 on your camera, everything is in focus, and oftentimes the image will look too busy and indistinguishable from other elements in the background where everything competes with each other. Always think what you'd like to focus on, then make it your priority by zooming in or fixing the depth of field.

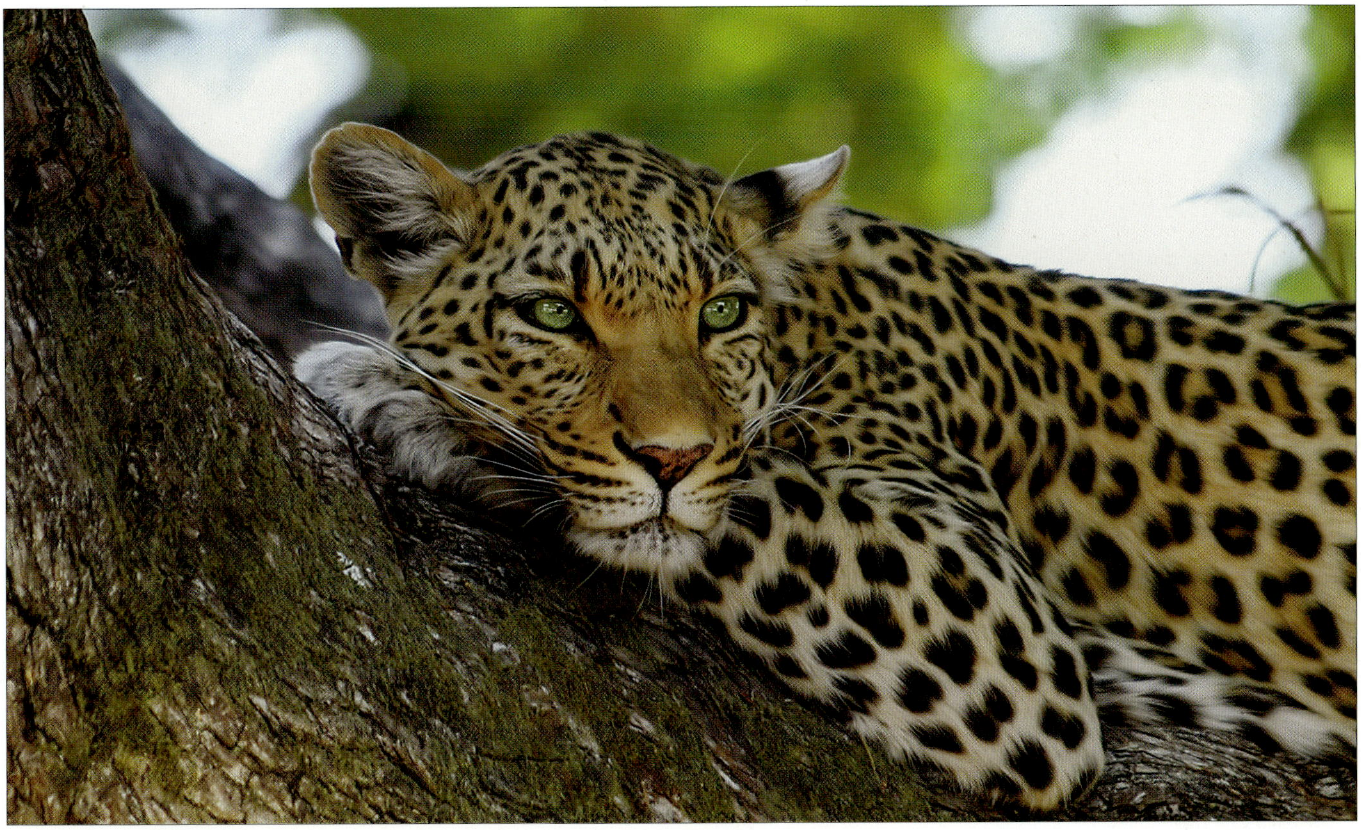

Shallow depth of field, which is the background here, brings this gorgeous animal forward, letting us see its soulful eyes.

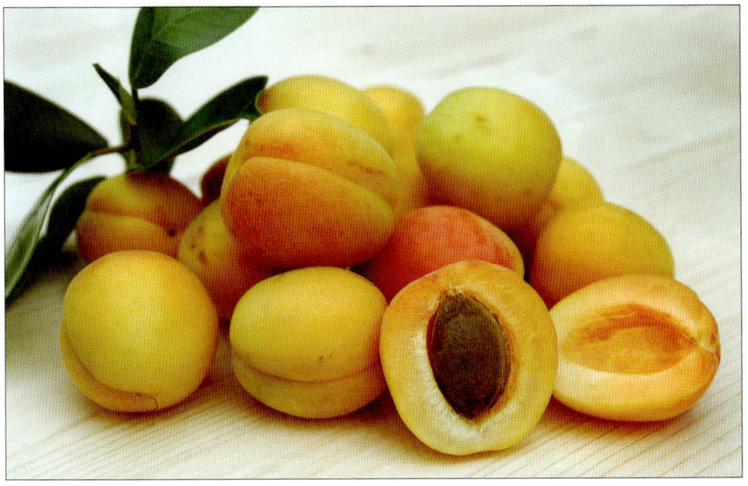

Keep it simple: Less is more, so remove busy, distracting shapes and elements that don't support your center of interest. Compose where you lead with your camera to your center of interest.

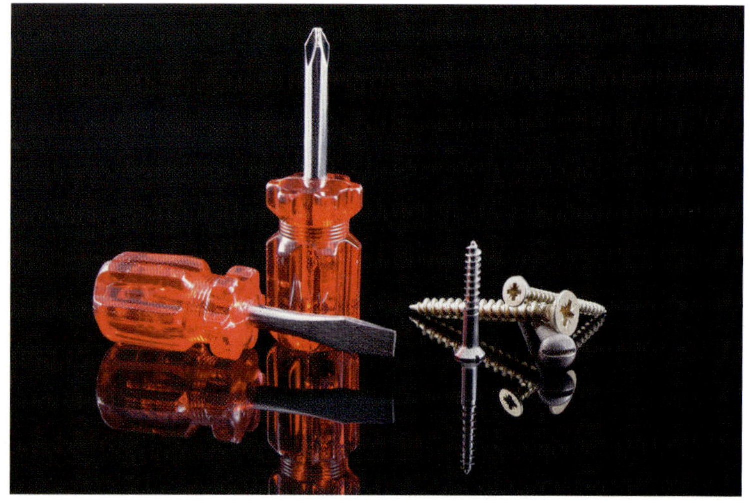

Use negative space as a design element: Background affects the edges and creates abstract shapes. As a beginner, stick to plain backgrounds to isolate your subject and to show contrast. After a while you can start playing with the color and complexity of your negative space as well.

Use backgrounds and boxes for staged photography: If you don't want to buy a light box, you can make a very simple setup next to your window. Use colorful but plain matboards, fabric, or paper as your choices. The result is a single image with a beautiful, natural directional light, a shadow, and a white or color background all around it.

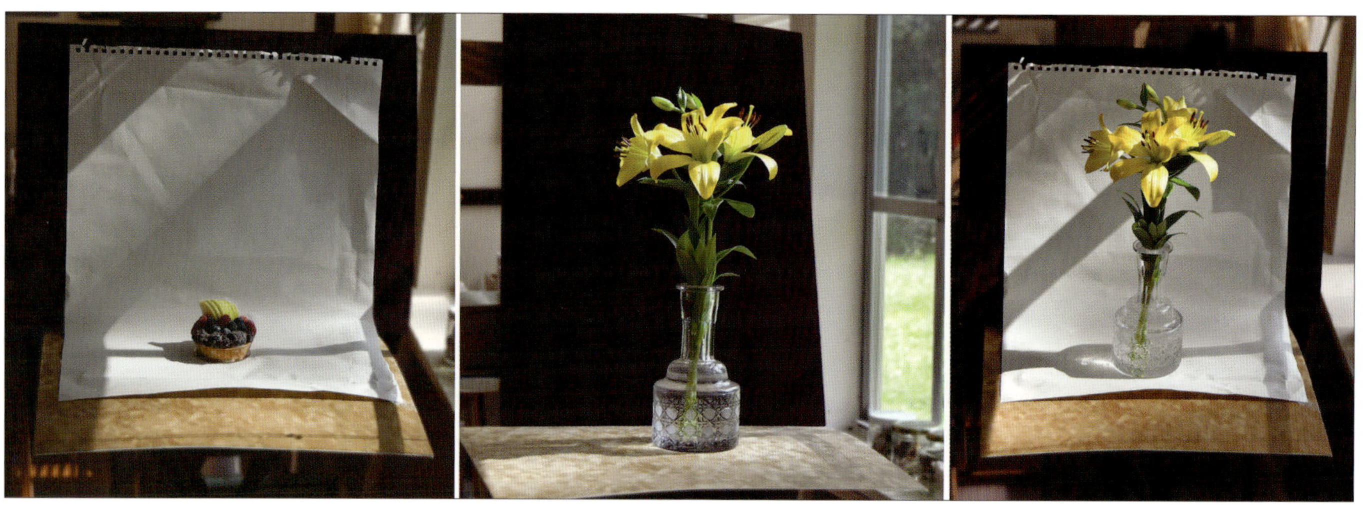

Boxed still life

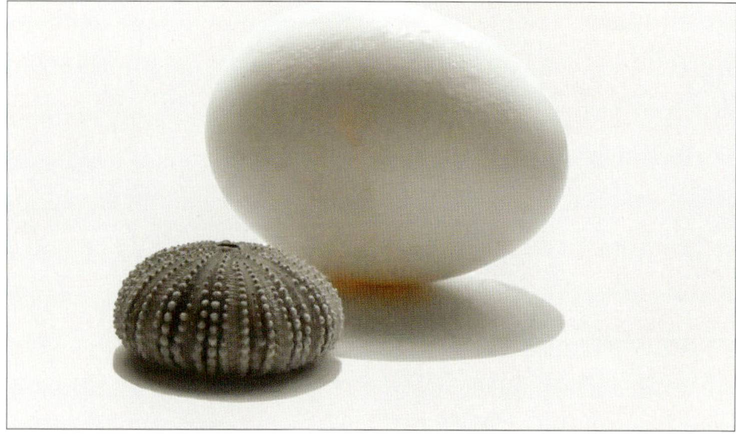

Final result

Crop it: Crop your still life when you shoot. Crop it even more when you edit your pictures.

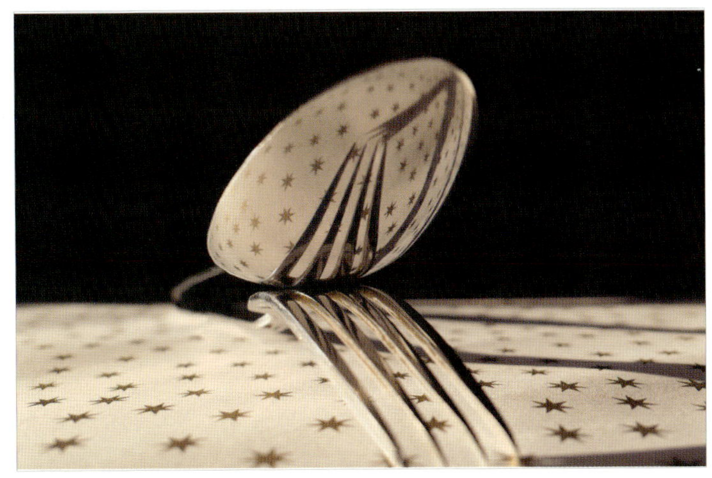

Avoid flash photography: Flash destroys the natural flow of light and its shadows. It flattens out the object and gives you strange, unnatural colors. Professional photographers know how to rotate their flash unit to get the right position of the flash, but most of us don't!

Beware of lens distortion: Don't transfer the outlines from your pictures aimlessly. Adjust the lines and shapes, fixing lens distortion that is especially noticeable in cityscapes, geometric shapes, and even faces (in situations where the lens is set too close to a person while taking pictures).

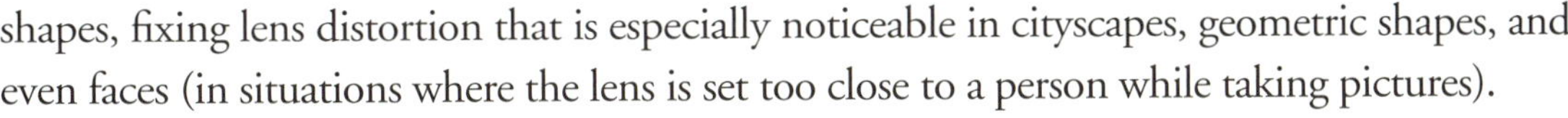

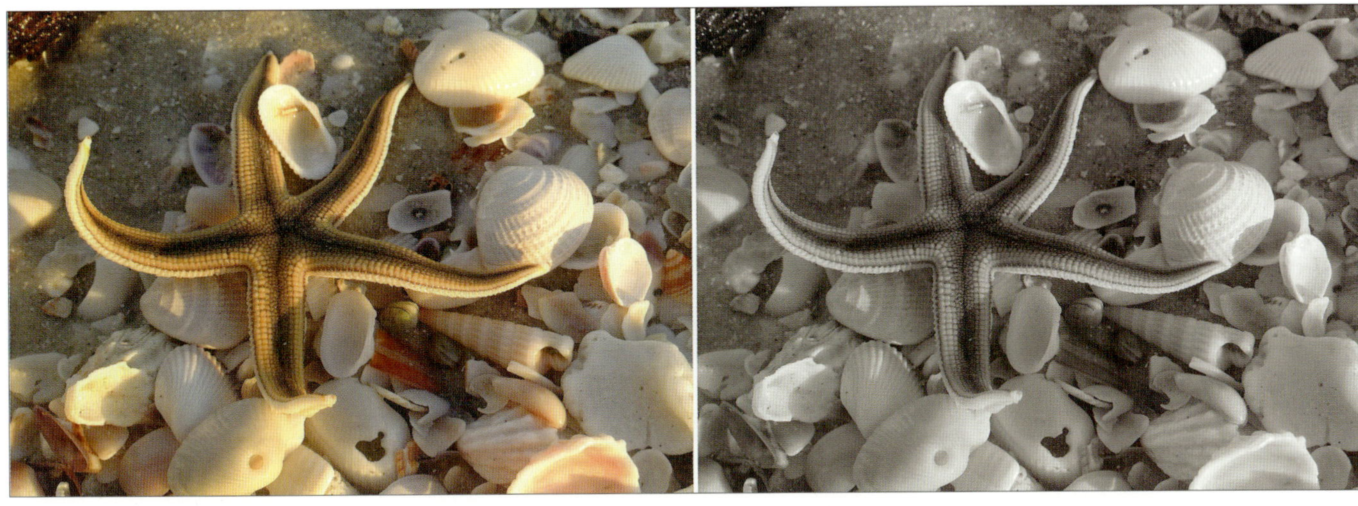

Prioritize values over color: Use printed reference in both color and grey scale in all your projects. The black-and-white picture gives you information in values, not colors, which is more important to master. When a student is learning, it is difficult to translate hues to tones. Such printouts help you to see the subject in correct values and thus contrast. Most students don't push their values dark enough or their lights bright enough and end up with middle-toned drawings.

Action Step: Pick one object that you are excited about to draw and take pictures of it at different vantage points and times of the day. Then look at images on your computer to see which light and composition works best.

Chapter 2

Composition and the Focal Point

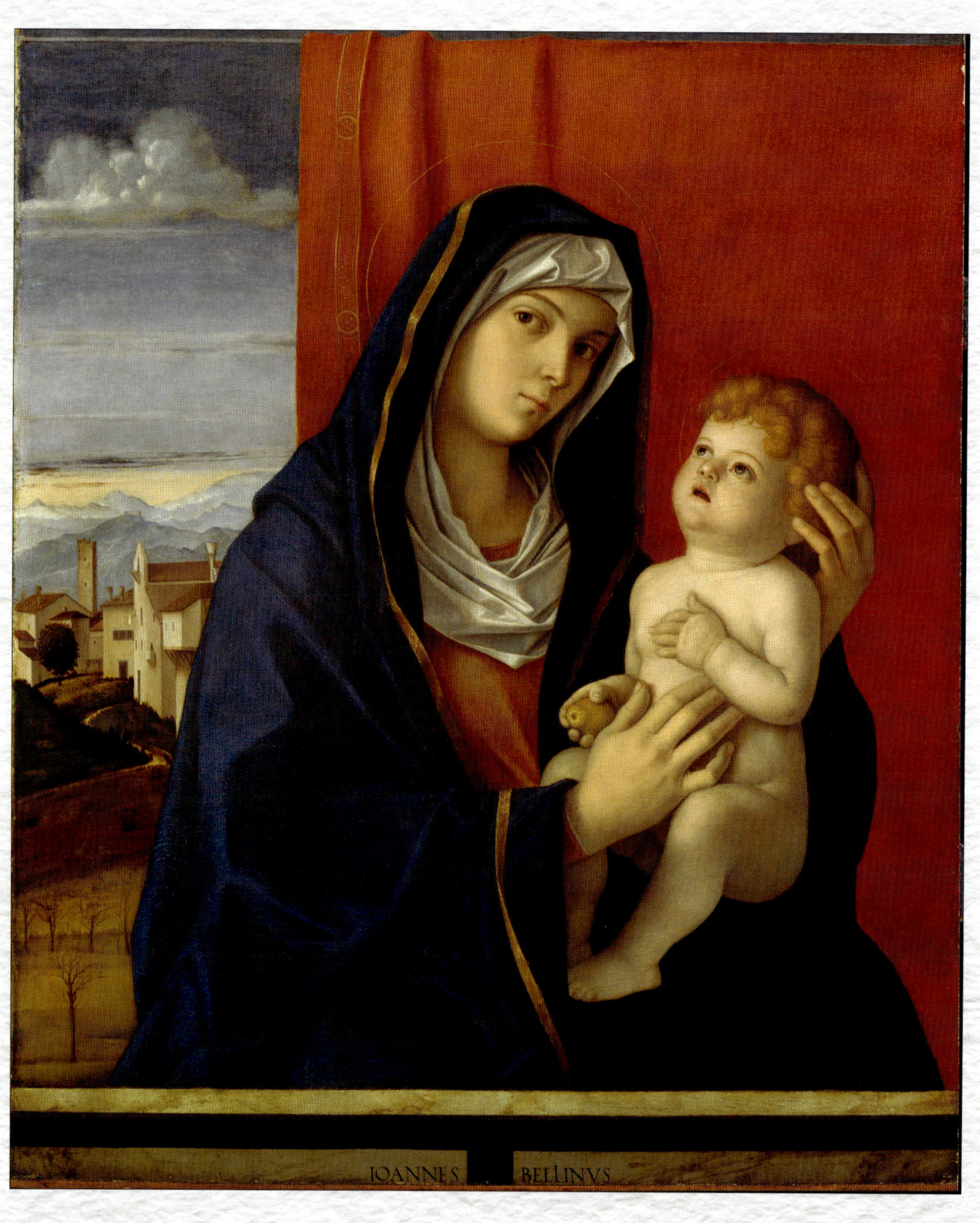

COMPOSITION

Composition is the most vital element to a picture's success. Thoughtful compositions feature strong designs that pull everything together seamlessly. The viewer's eye travels from one element to the next to arrive at the center of interest. The artist's job is to keep the viewer's attention on the picture as long as possible. Creative compositions facilitate this process. To understand the techniques, serious artists should study and learn from the old masters as well as from professional contemporary artists.

While looking at masterpieces, pay attention to how artists place their subjects at different angles or off-center to create movement. They play with various sizes and geometric shapes to break monotony. If artists crop the image, there is enough space left between the edge and the subject. We look at pictures from left to right, so artists often use a "stopper" on the right to keep you in the loop so you don't leave the artwork. Most artwork isn't symmetrical. Use symmetry to make a statement. For example, draw a butterfly's wings with perfect symmetry or a mirrored water reflection perfectly symmetrical to a landscape above it. Now let's look at proven compositions that work in greater detail!

Circular with a star pentagon (pentagram)

A **pentagram** is a circular design with a five-pointed star placed inside it. Every element in the painting "fits" within the star. Most Renaissance masters followed these designs when they used a linear perspective, correct size, and placement of figures.

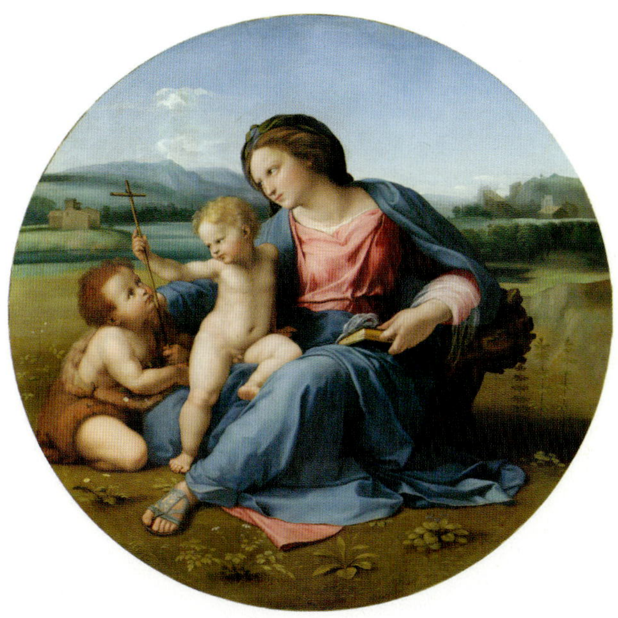

Raphael, *The Alba Madonna*, oil on panel, 1510, National Gallery of Art

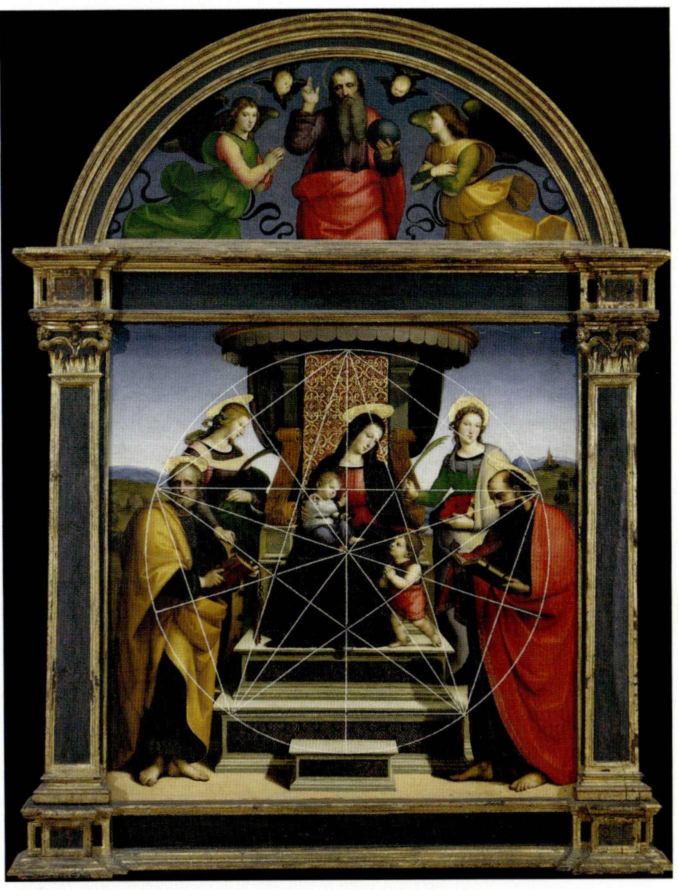

Raphael, *Madonna and Child Enthroned with Saints*, oil and gold on wood, 1504

Symmetrical vs asymmetrical

Symmetrical compositions feature artworks that have perfect balance with equal shapes placed symmetrically. In the painting by Desportes we see slight deviations on both sides of the canvas with the main composition rooted in symmetry.

Asymmetrical compositions reach perfect balance with different objects placed on both sides of the painting. Vermeer often places his main subject (a woman) in the center of the picture but carefully balances out both sides of the image with the interior surroundings; therefore, this image looks dynamic as we study each quarter of the painting. Asymmetry is prevalent in still-life drawing and painting. Artists place fruit or flowers with deliberate asymmetry trying to find the perfect balance of shapes in various sizes and textures. In this painting we see one subject—flowers placed at a diagonal, but the bouquet has a great variation in texture, color, rotation, and size of the flowers with no repetition.

Alexandre François Desportes (1661–1743), *Still Life with Silver*, oil on canvas, Metropolitan Museum of Art

Johannes Vermeer, *Young Woman*, oil on canvas, 1662, Metropolitan Museum of Art

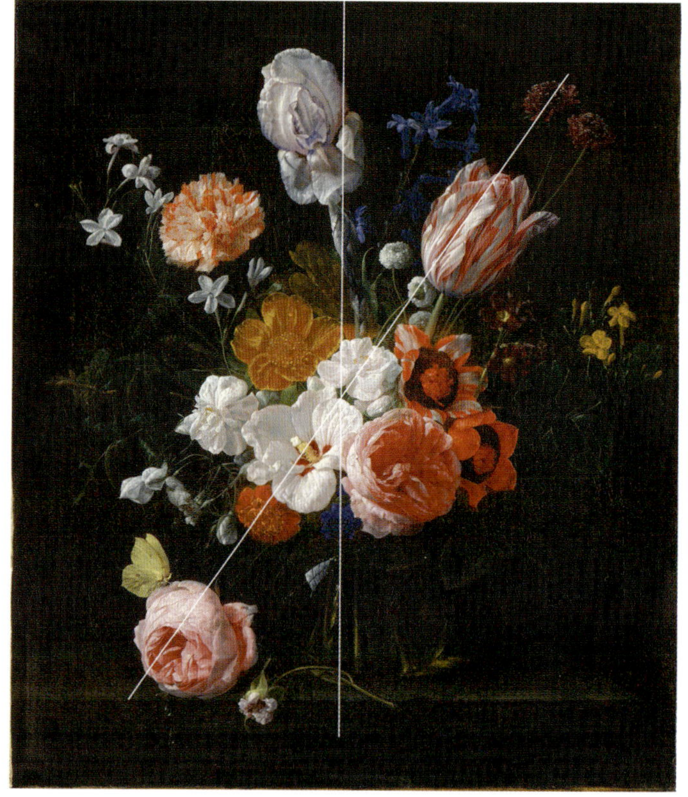

Nicolaes van Veerendael, *A Bouquet in a Crystal Vase*, oil on canvas, 1662, Metropolitan Museum of Art

Equal balance of various shapes

The artist strikes an equal balance of shapes around the middle of the painting where we see Christ's feet.

Here we can see how the artist balances various objects with equal distances and lines that create unity.

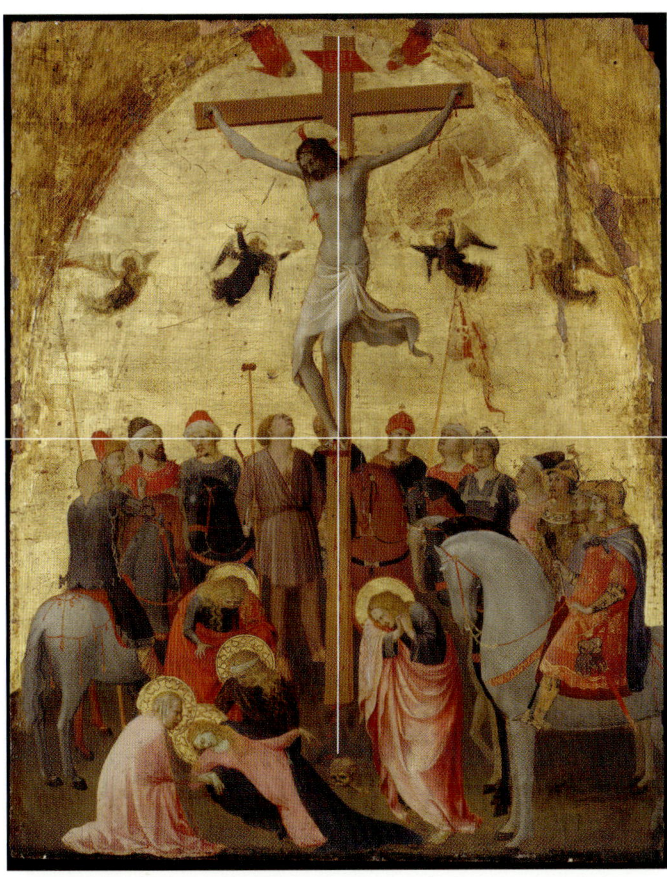

Fra Angelico, *The Crucifixion*, tempera on wood, 1420–23, Metropolitan Museum of Art

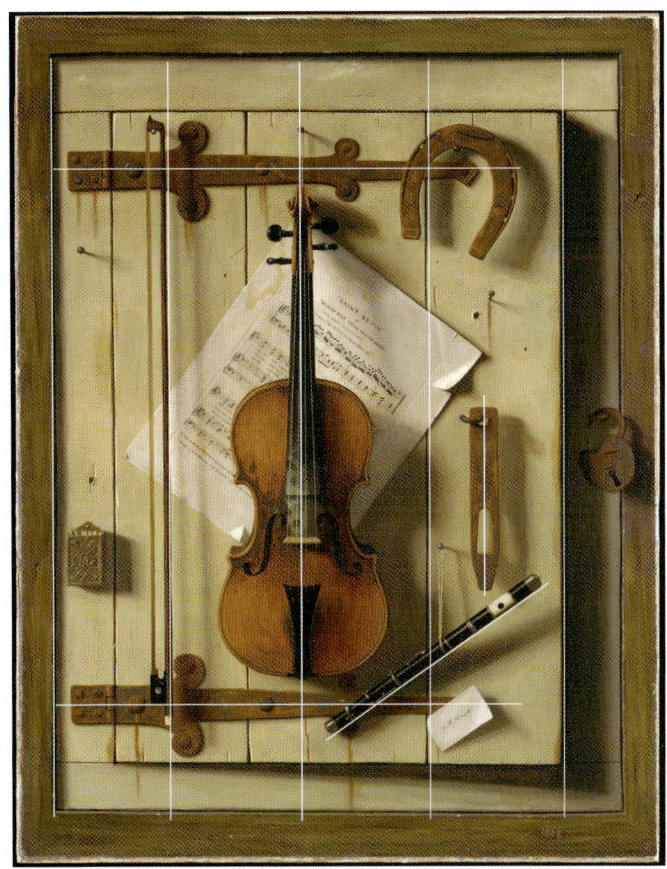

William Michael Harnett, *Still life—Violin and Music*, oil on canvas, 1888, Metropolitan Museum of Art

Diagonals and triangles

For centuries, the use of diagonals and triangles has been the most prevalent tool in painting. Most religious paintings were created using the triangular composition where the Virgin Mary or Christ is at the top of the triangle with secondary figures placed at their side. The triangle forms balance with a line falling from the apex of the pyramid, which divides the picture in half. In many paintings you'll find multiple triangles with a large, encompassing triangle that forms a pyramid. Diagonals often contribute to the compositional balance. Shapes placed at a diagonal can be found in almost any representational painting. Diagonals create movement and remove stiffness from figures and boredom from still lifes. The use of diagonals is so vital to representational painting that you cannot avoid studying this concept so you can understand and apply it to your drawings.

In the painting below by Italian artist Bellini we see a triangular composition with the Virgin Mary's indigo blue clothing forming the pyramid. Also notice the rotation of her head and her hand placed at a similar diagonal on purpose.

In the painting by Harnett we can see a whole stack of diagonals. They bring dynamism to the picture and make these ordinary objects look extraordinary.

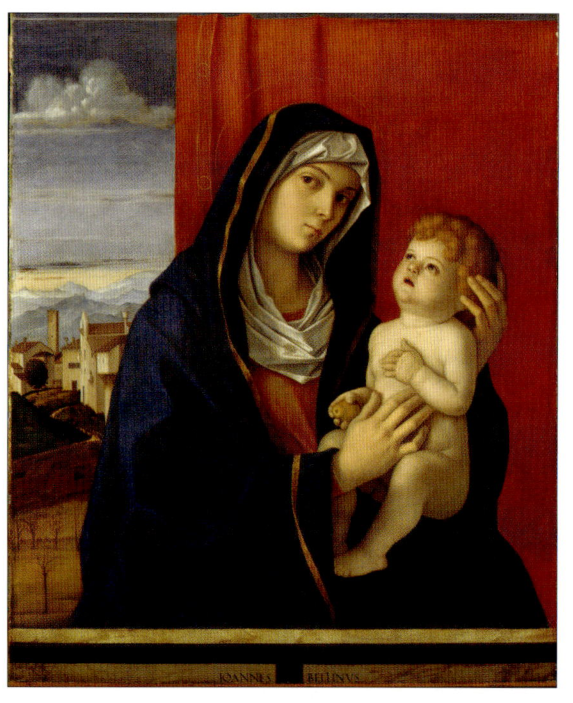

Giovanni Bellini, *Madonna and Child*, oil on wood, 1480s, Metropolitan Museum of Art

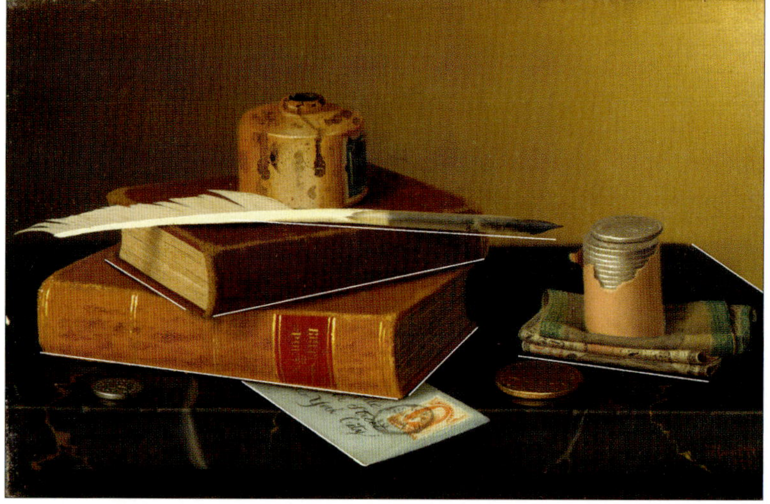

William Michael Harnett, *The Bankers Table*, oil on canvas, 1877, Metropolitan Museum of Art

Golden section

Golden section or the rule of two thirds is the most used and perhaps even overused design principle. The idyllic proportion comes from nature. Known to the Greeks and applied in their architecture, this mathematical division of space was forgotten during the medieval period and revived in Renaissance Italy. Wildly applied in art and photography today, the concept is easy to grasp. Divide your space into three parts and place your center of interest on one third of the image. By shifting your focal point to the side, you break away from possible monotony, keeping the viewer's eye moving around the picture.

This balanced proportion is often used in landscape art, figurative painting, and even still life.

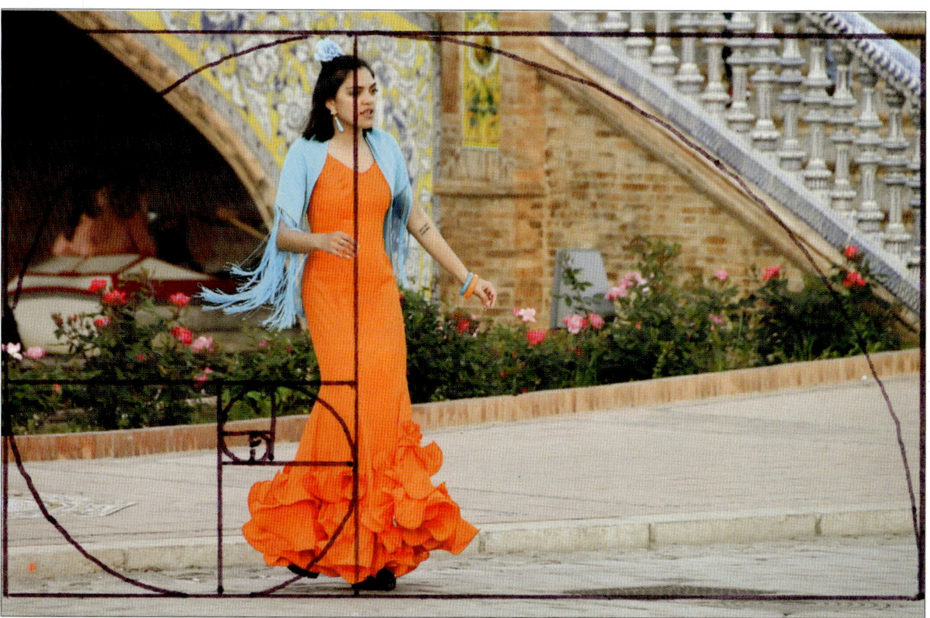

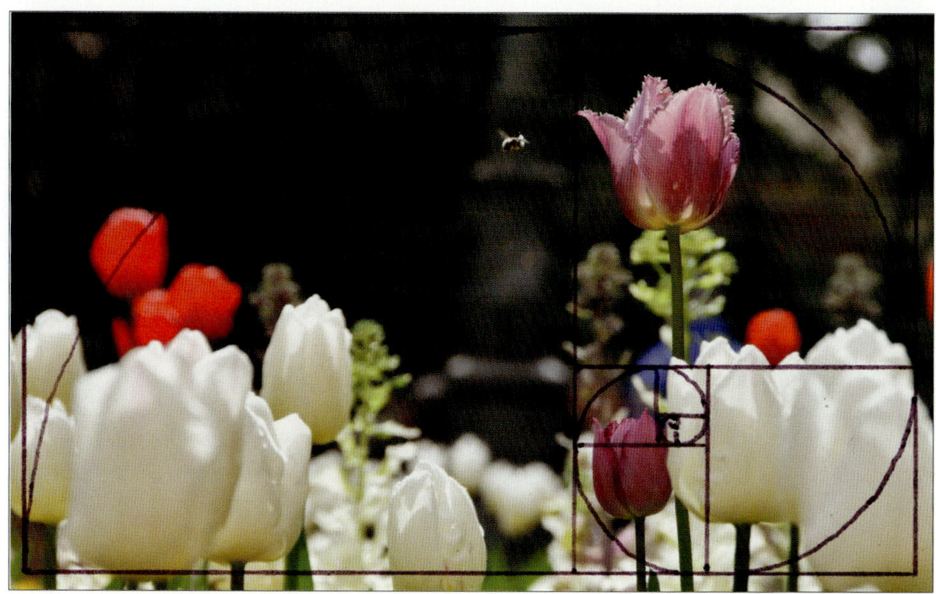

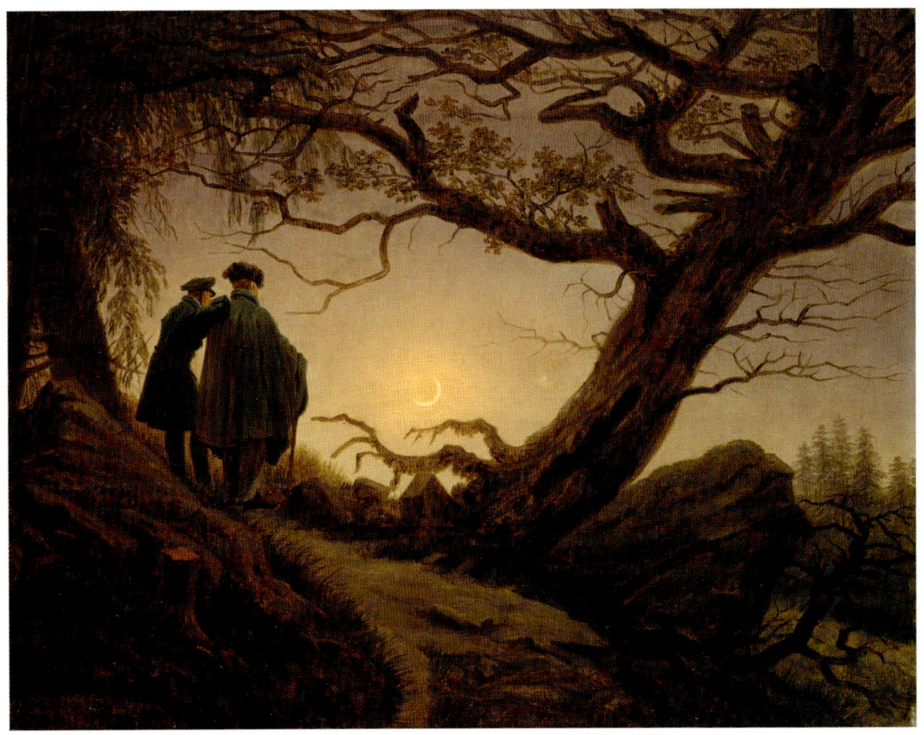

Placed off-center, these two figures lead us to contemplate the moon. The tree, which is painted at the diagonal, rotates left in the sky to keep viewers in the loop visually.

Caspar David Friedrich, *Two Men Contemplating the Moon*, oil on canvas, 1825–30, Metropolitan Museum of Art

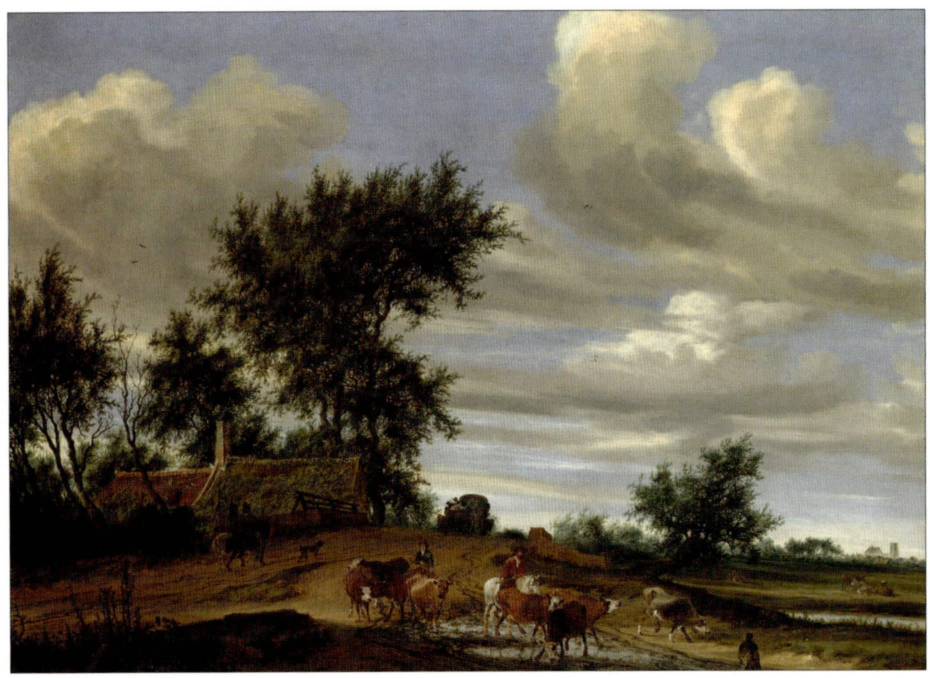

In this picture we can see a clear division of space: one third is the land and two thirds is taken up by the sky. The tall tree "connects" the sky with the ground.

Salomon van Ruysdael, *A Country Road*, oil on canvas, 1648, Metropolitan Museum of Art

Background/negative space

The background, its color, value, and texture should support your center of interest, not interfere with it. Artists carefully consider what to place in the background to help tell a story, but those elements receive much less light, texture, and detail compared to the subject itself.

In the painting below (left), we see that an artist plays a harp, but all our attention is on her face, hand, and shimmering fabric. The music sheets transition the figure into the negative space—the background with a dark wall and a column that describes the space but doesn't take our attention away from the woman. In the painting at right, the figure is placed at a diagonal where her red dress grabs our attention immediately. The same hue finds repetition in a rose and a carpet, but the color is less intense in those subjects. The negative space is very dark to create contrast. It brings the woman's light skin tone to focus.

You can see another example of a dark background painted in a floral composition by a rare female artist—Anne Vallayer-Coster in *Vase of Flowers and Conch Shell*, oil on canvas, 1780, available online in the free database of the Metropolitan Museum of Art at https://www.metmuseum.org/art/collection/search/437864.

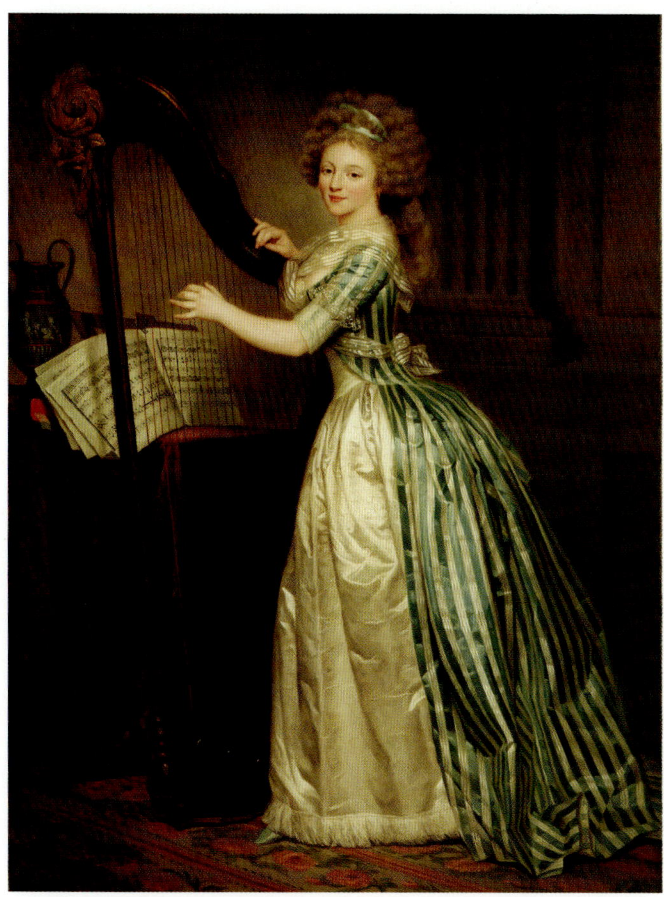

Rose Adélaïde Ducreux, *Self-Portrait with a Harp*, oil on canvas, 1791, Metropolitan Museum of Art

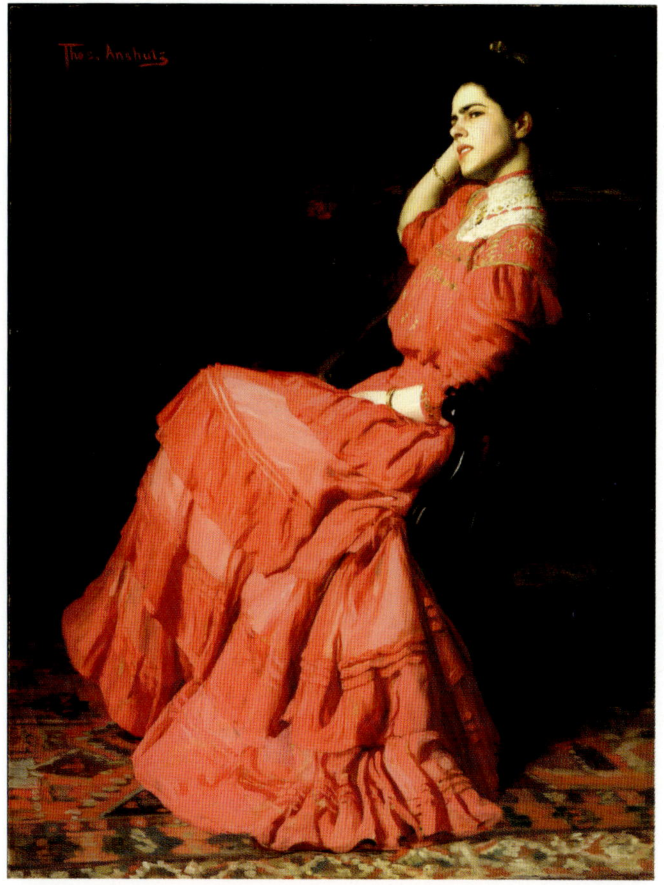

Thomas Anshutz, *A Rose*, oil on canvas, 1907, Metropolitan Museum of Art

Focal Point

Effective composition results in a deliberate movement around the picture where the viewer's attention is drawn to a focal point or center of interest. The focal point usually has the highest level of texture, color, detail, and value to create selective focus. You will prioritize what to draw with more detail and color intensity, and what to leave out.

Besides using the highest detail in the center of interest, you can also control value (or tone), which helps to move our eye around the picture. For example, when the entire picture has subdued hues or falls dark and the focal point is in a bright light, we as spectators are drawn right into it.

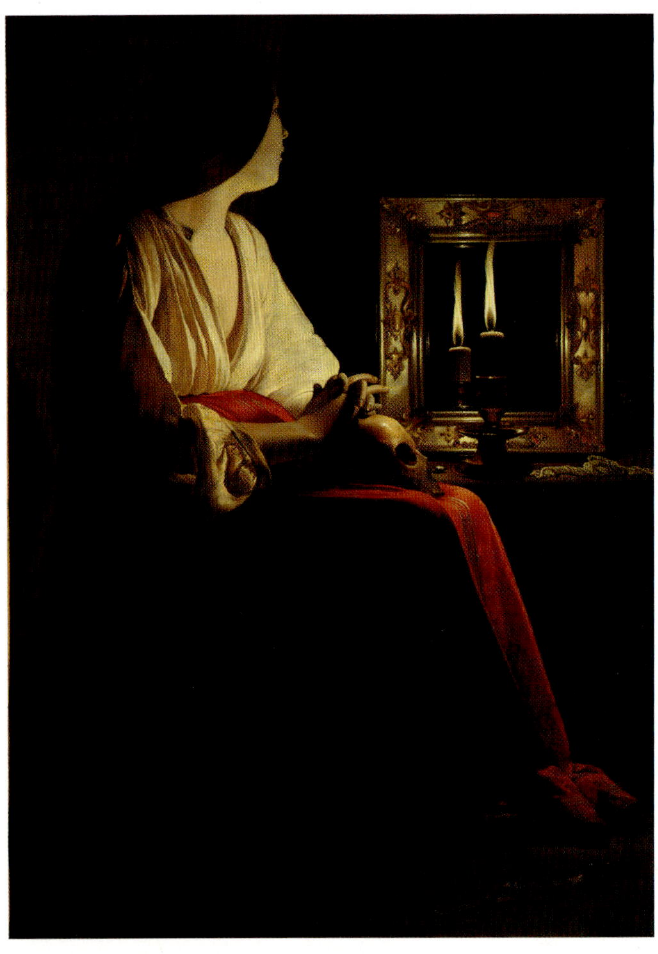

George de la Tour, *The Penitent Magdalene*, oil on canvas, 1640, Metropolitan Museum of Art

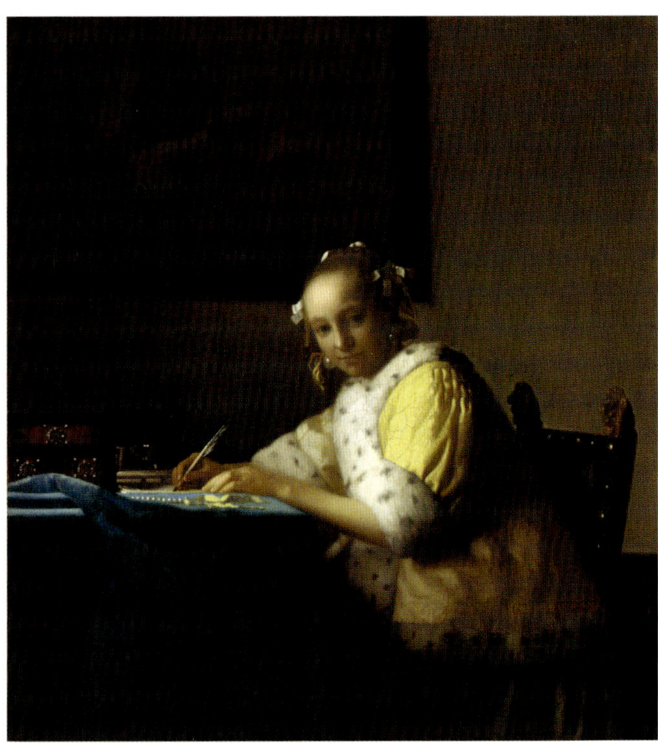

Johannes Vermeer, *A Lady Writing*, oil on canvas, 1665, National Gallery of Art

S-shape

One of the most famous paintings that has the S-shape design is Michelangelo's *The Creation of Adam* in the Sistine Chapel at the Vatican. The picture is divided in half by a curve that resembles the rotated S-shape. The S can rotate in different directions, but the objects are equally grouped on both sides of the painting.

In this painting we see two groups: the man on the chair is balanced by two women, and we are able to draw an imaginary S-curve between them.

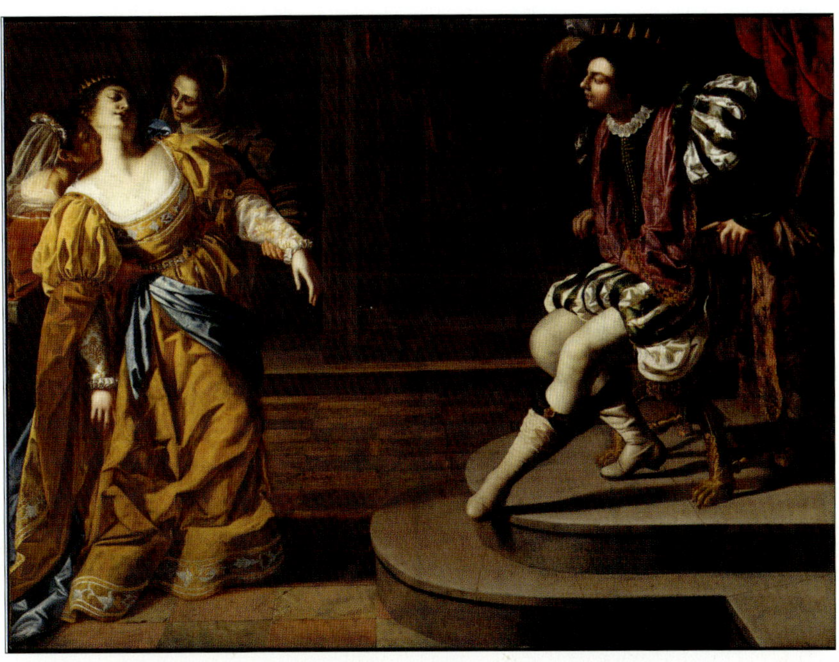

Artemisia Gentileschi, *Esther before Ahasuerus*, oil on canvas, c. 1628–1630, Metropolitan Museum of Art

Look at this similar composition by Caravaggio in the photo at right.

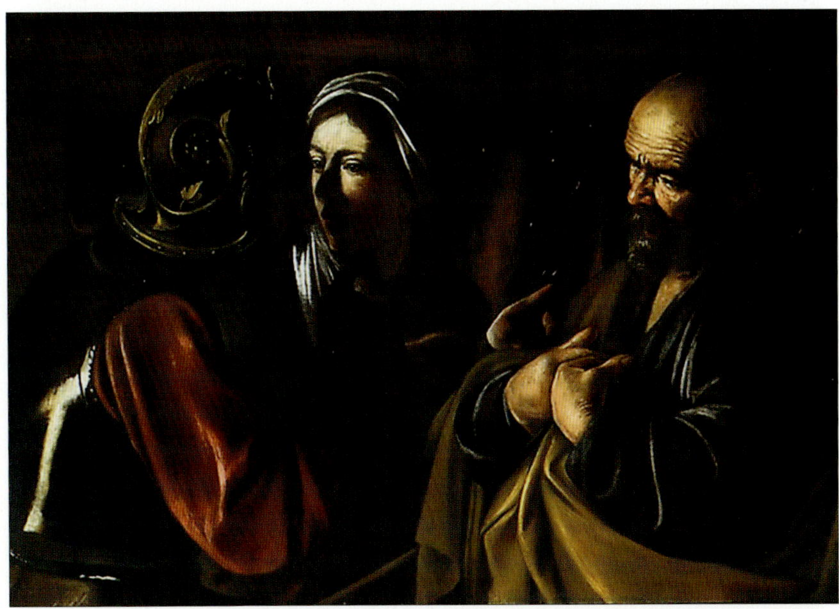

Caravaggio, *The Denial of St. Peter*, oil on canvas, 1610, Metropolitan Museum of Art

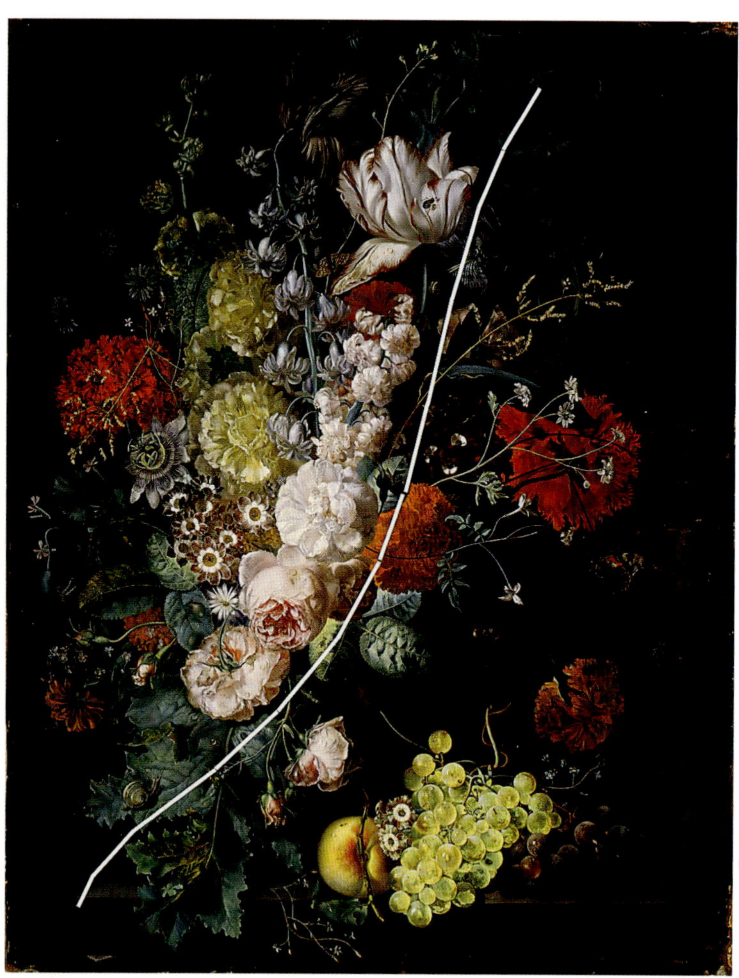

Margareta Haverman, *A Vase of Flowers*, oil on wood, 1716, Metropolitan Museum of Art

Look at this composition here to see a soft S-curve that could also be read as a diagonal. A streak of white flowers runs through the middle of the luscious bouquet forming a soft curve.

Note: Find more masterpieces online in the free database of the Metropolitan Museum of Art at https://www.metmuseum.org/art/collection.

Action Step: What is your favorite painting? Pick a few paintings to study their compositions. What's the focal point? How do artists use space, color, texture, and value to create a beautiful work of art?

Chapter 3

How to Turn the Form

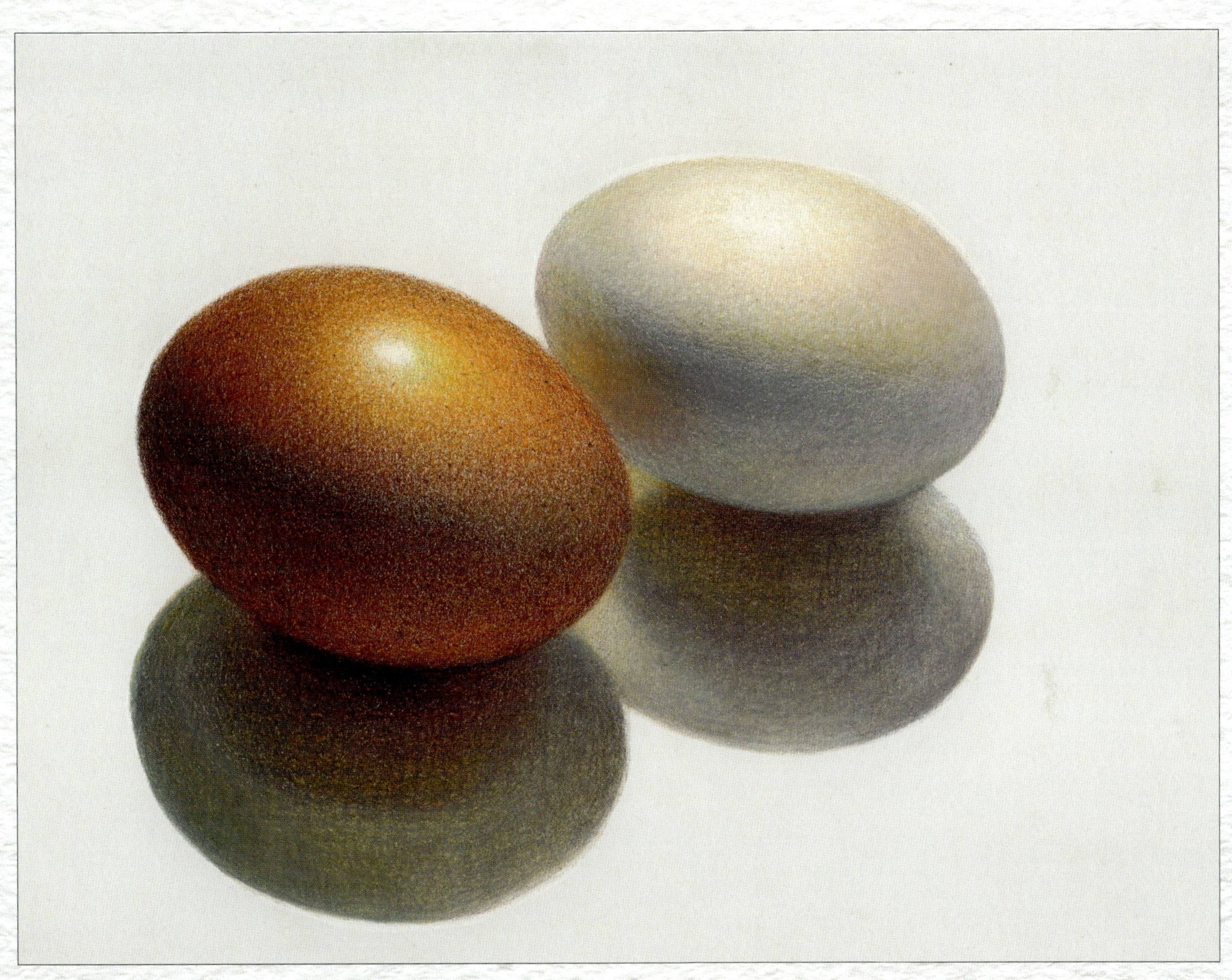

DISTRIBUTION OF LIGHT

Knowing the "formula" for turning the form (drawing solid objects in 3-D) is paramount to realistic drawing success. Beginning artists study the structure of light on solid, opaque, and simple objects lit by a strong directional light. Most shapes follow the same pattern of light and shade, including portraiture and human anatomy; however, complex shapes consist of simpler shapes having identical light structure. Usually, glass and reflective surfaces follow a different "formula" of light distribution that we will explore later. Now let's look at this image of tangerines to review the basic definitions.

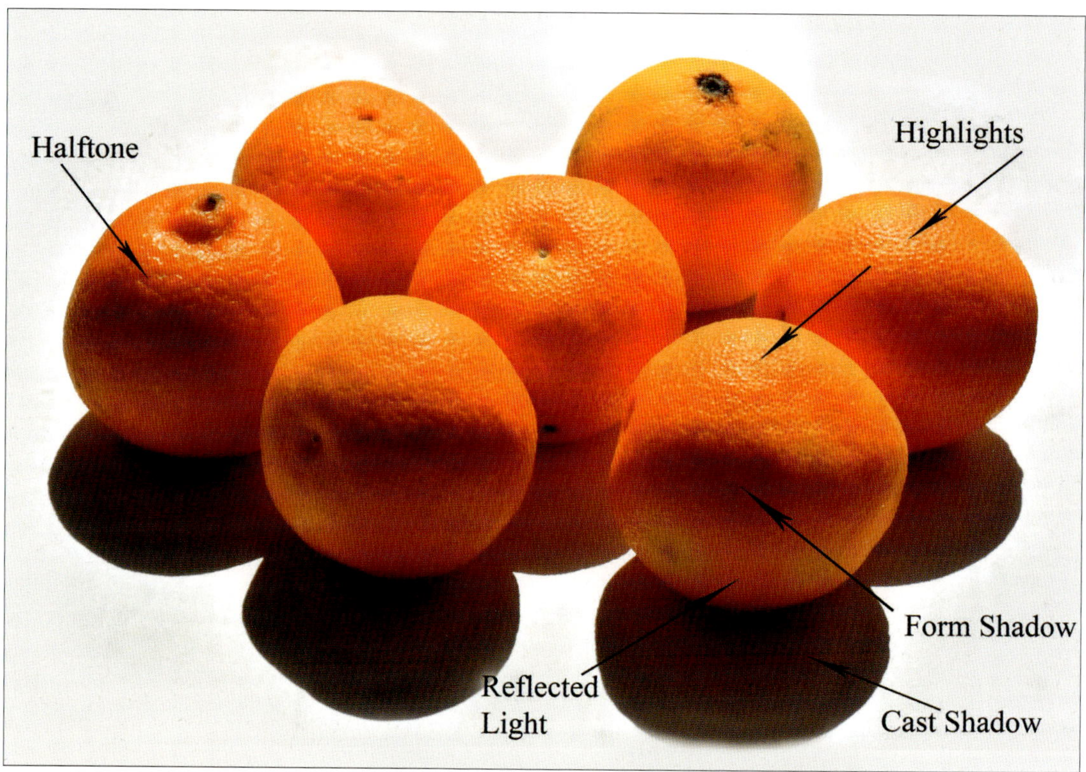

Highlight is the lightest area on your object, where light hits the surface the most. A highlight can be a tiny circle or a small line on a cup's rim, a bright white dot in an eye, the lightest spot on a pear, and on the tangerines as we see here.

Reflected light is slightly lighter than the form shadow and always sits on the object's edge.

Form shadow is the darkest area on your object that repeats its shape. Its placement is crucial in creation of the 3-D illusion.

Cast shadow sits under the object and attaches to it. Always make it a part of your composition because it gives physical presence to the object.

Here you see this formula work in a finished still-life drawing. You can also see a wide range of values used by the artist, ranging from light to dark.

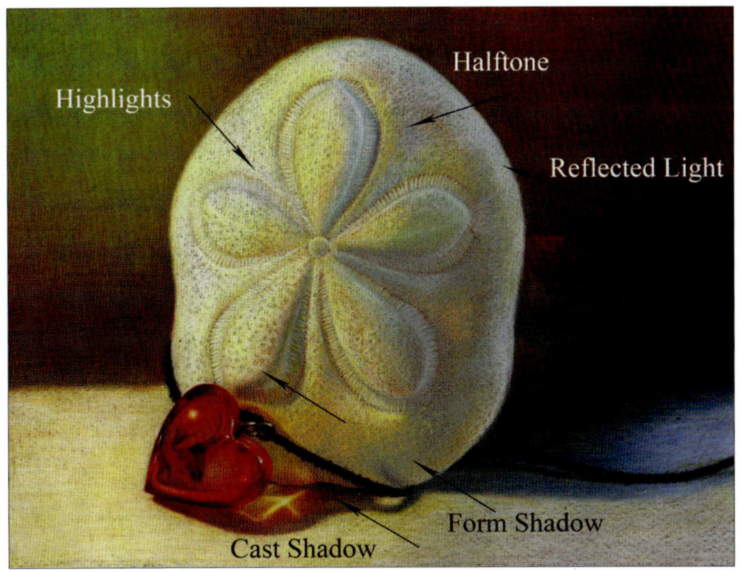

Value is the lightness or darkness of a color. Here you see the gradation of black ranging from 100% black to a pure white. It takes practice to see and control the gradations, which help artists describe the roundness of any form.

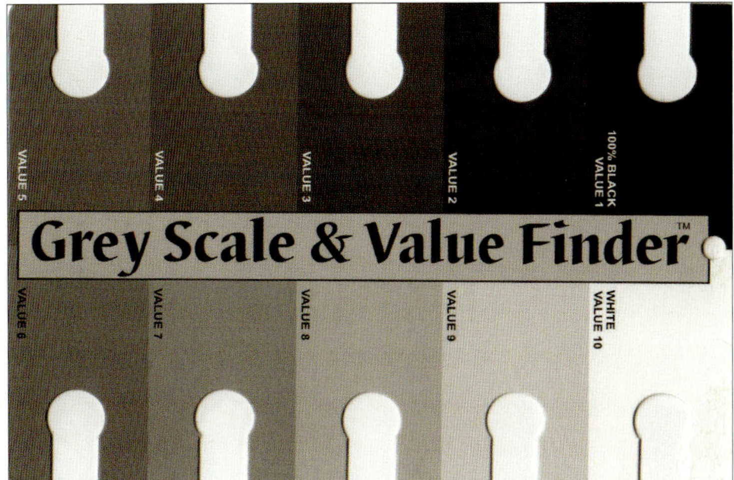

Not every color has the same value range. For example, much lighter colors such as yellow have a much shorter value range. Dark blue has a wide value range. Learning to see the value (or shades) of every color is a skill that takes time to learn through practice. To help yourself seeing tones and colors, make black-and-white printouts along with your color ones.

Hue is the color, such as red, yellow, or blue.

Chroma is the purity of a color, such as pure red or pure blue. The brightest color has the highest intensity.

We will discuss the properties of hue and chroma in Chapter 6.

STEP-BY-STEP INSTRUCTIONS

Turning the Form

Materials: Prismacolor Premier colored pencils (unless otherwise noted), kneaded eraser, Strathmore premium drawing paper

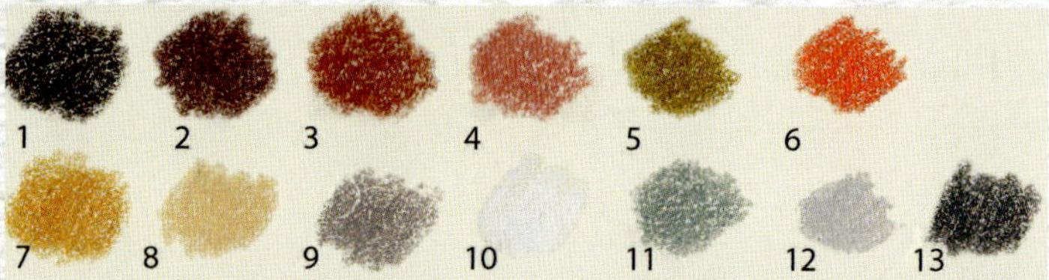

Color Chart: 1. Sepia or Dark Brown 2. Burnt Sienna (Pablo) 3. Burnt Ochre 4. Nectar 5. Artichoke 6. Mineral Orange (or other orange) 7. Yellow Ochre 8. Eggshell 9. 30% Warm Grey 10. White 11. Jade Green 12. 20% Cool Grey 13. 70% Cool Grey Small amounts of other colors may have been used as well.

Note: While the artist provides the names of the pencils, you should refer to the color chart to match colors in your box. Also, begin training yourself to see color temperature and value in every hue. It will set you free to make your own decisions in picking colors.

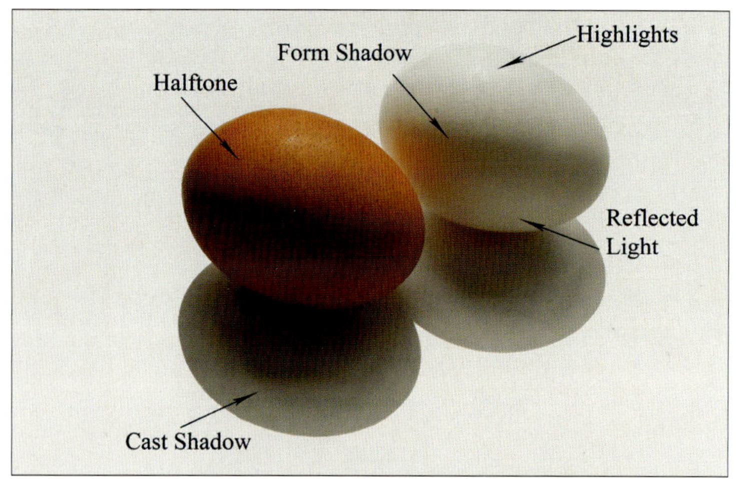

In this picture we see the distribution of light on the objects. Morning light comes from the window to illuminate the still life. Notice the highlights, form shadow, cast shadow, and reflected light.

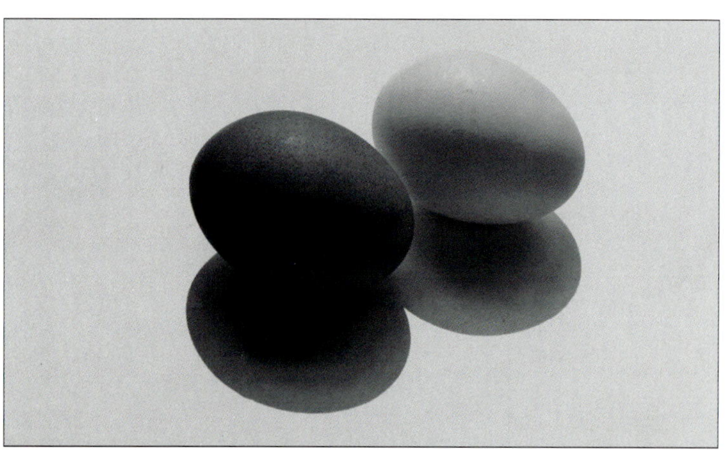

In this black-and-white printout you can see the tones, not the colors.

Whenever you begin working on a new drawing, follow this strategy:

- Ask yourself how light or dark you should shade your object.
- Find your highlights. Then determine your darkest values—a form shadow and a cast shadow—and start shading from there, working in a progression from dark to light.
- As you keep working on your still life, refer to both color and grey pictures to match the values in shading. Many times students tend not to have enough values in their drawings or keep their drawings too light in general.

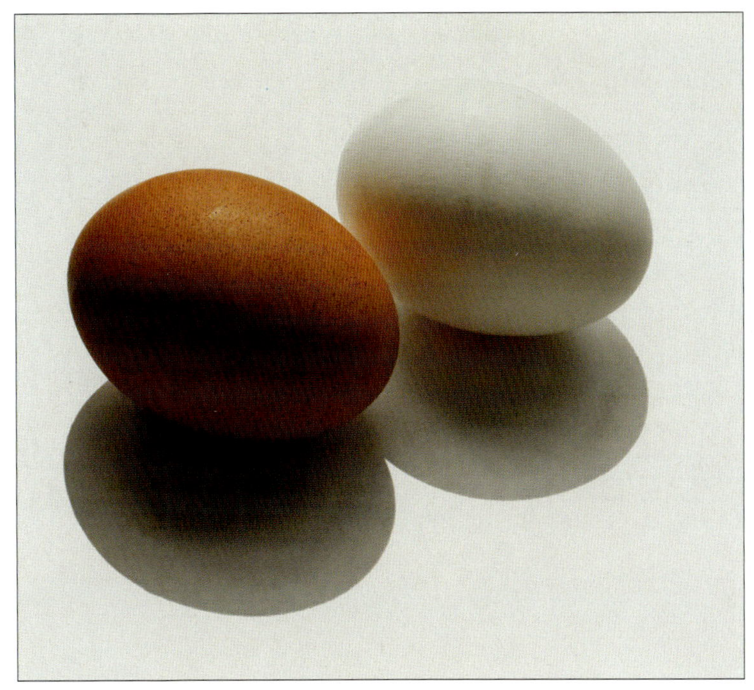

Tip: Before you begin coloring, make sure your pencils are sharp. Sharpen them constantly throughout your drawing process, as it greatly affects your ability to shade the picture evenly, minimizing texture.

Step 1

Transfer the outline using your favorite method: the light box, window, grid, or transfer paper methods using an HB (hard black pencil, considered to be equivalent to a #2 pencil) graphite pencil. If you prefer direct sketching, make sure your drawing is nice and clean. Colored pencil loves clean paper and hates messy, dark graphite lines that show through layering and flatten out space. Tap the lines with the kneaded eraser and use this eraser throughout your drawing process to clean up.

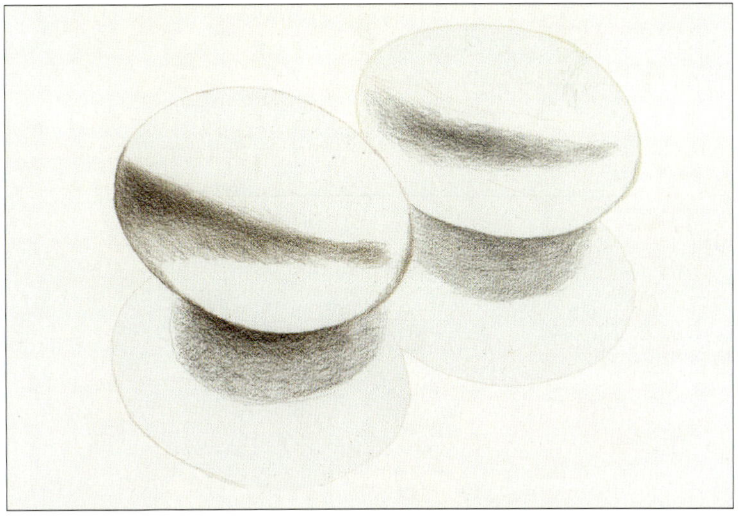

Begin defining a form shadow on both eggs with 70% cool grey. Drop the cast shadow as well. You will also see a bit of an outline done in yellow ochre for the brown egg.

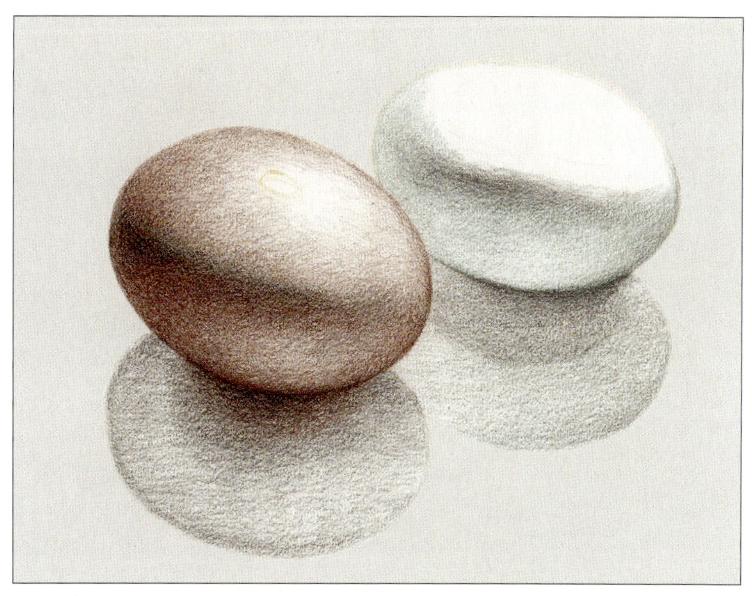

Step 2

For the brown egg, focus on the shadow area of the egg. Using light to medium light pencil pressure, begin filling in the egg with Pablo burnt sienna. Throw the same color into the cast shadow underneath the egg.

For the white egg, repeat the process using jade green.

Don't forget to shade over the initial grey hue on the eggs when applying these colors.

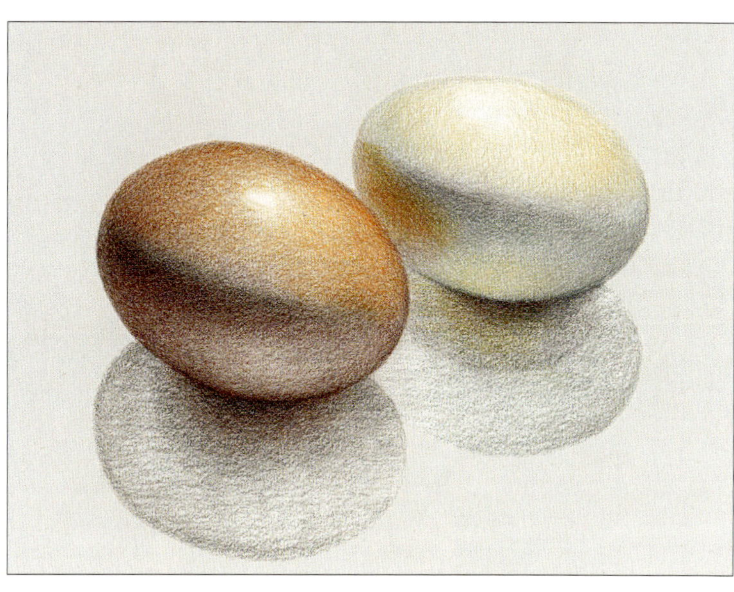

Step 3

Start thinking of your objects as having volume in space: rotate your paper to make the strokes following the form. Avoid just coloring up and down or sideways, which flattens out the space.

A form shadow and a cast shadow are your darkest areas. Therefore the rest of the values in the eggs should be lighter, transitioning softly from dark to light.

For the brown egg, take mineral orange or a similar orange and fill in the light values on the top of the egg. Control your pencil pressure to create tonal variations going from medium light to light. Overlap this color over the brown. Leave the highlight uncolored and use eggshell to color around it only.

For the white egg, use the same color, mineral orange or similar orange, to put the orange reflected light into the white egg. Use eggshell to fill in the light part of the egg. Leave the highlight uncolored at all times! Apply eggshell in the cast shadow too—it makes plain grey shadow look colorful since objects reflect their colors into the shadows.

Tip: Try transferring your outlines with a very light colored pencil instead of a graphite one; this will minimize possible smudges and dirt on the page.

Step 4

In this step you will continue layering the colors, building the hierarchy of values going from dark to light. Subsequent layering using the same colors intensifies them.

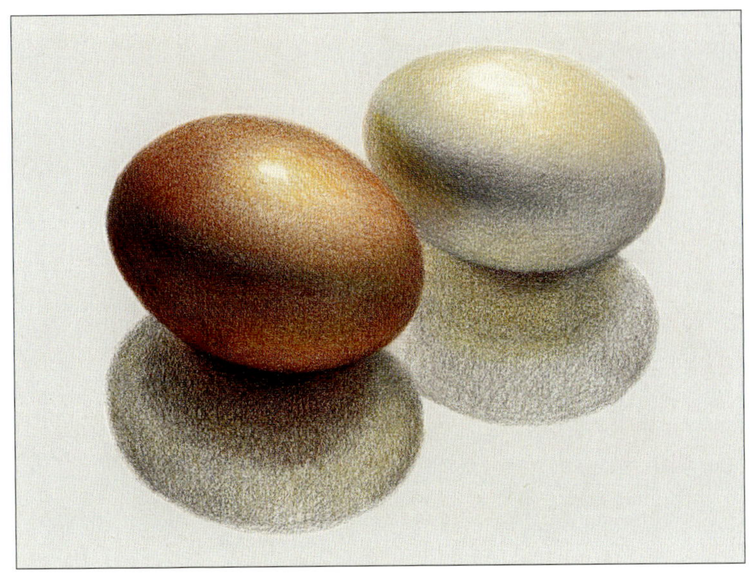

Always overlap your colors one over the other. While layering, students often tend to place colors next to each other instead, which leaves gaps or streaks of disjointed colors.

For the brown egg, use a sharp point of burnt ochre to deepen the browns on the left side and bottom side of the egg under the form shadow. Notice how grey blends with these colors. Overlay some artichoke and the orange in the reflected light at the bottom of the egg as well.

For the white egg, work on the shadow side of the egg with 30% warm grey. Shade over the form shadow as you move down the egg to the reflected light.

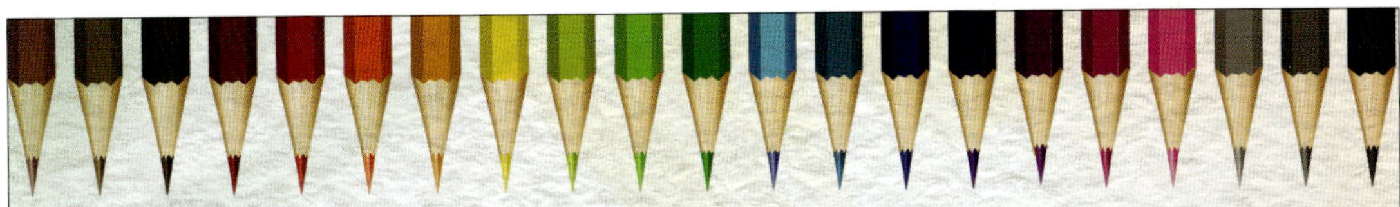

One of the main secrets to making the object appear round on paper is the correct placement of highlights. To make the brightest highlight on white paper, you simply reserve the white space (the color of your paper) on your page and shade around it. Usually, you don't see any white pencil used to create the highlight, and you normally shade with light or white colored pencils around it to create a subtle transition of tone. If you were to use a white colored pencil on white paper, you would make the highlight look dull, losing luminosity. White pencil is useful to create soft, blurred light tones that become blended.

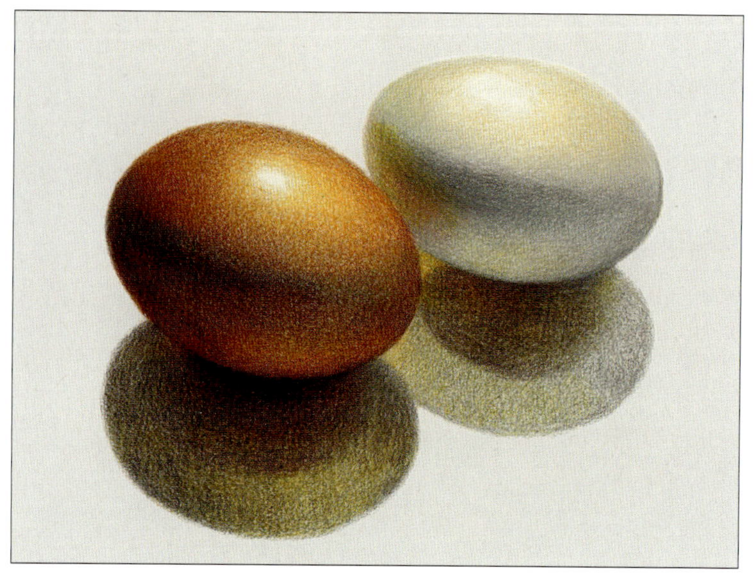

Step 5

Blend everything, including the cast shadow, using the pencil blender, and not a solvent. Pay attention to pencil direction as you blend! Think of the object's volume and repeat its shape by rotating the page while blending. (Forgetting about the stroke direction, students tend to blend horizontally, which flattens out the form). Use a very sharp point to blend and to fill in the texture.

Blend the cast shadow differently. Blend it only up and down or horizontally from left to right to create the illusion of a surface that the eggs sit on. This deliberate change in stroke direction creates a difference between the surfaces—the objects and the cast shadows.

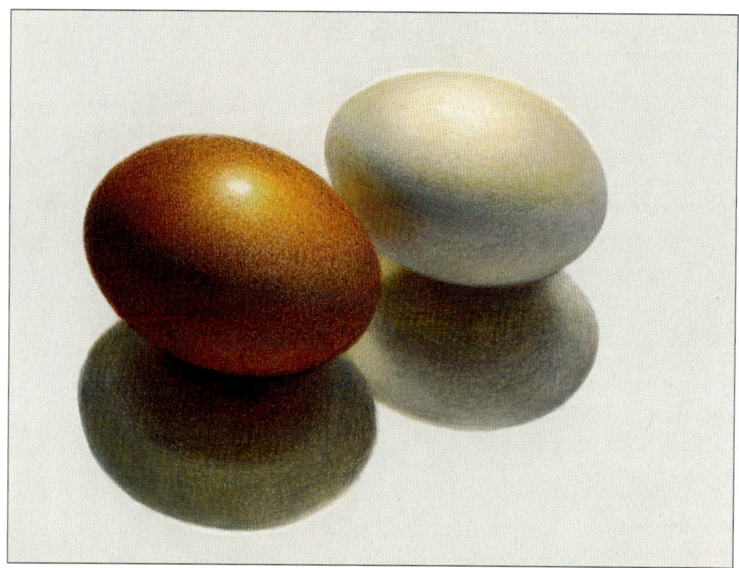

Step 6

In the last step you will focus on details and texture as well as on the final adjustment of tones. Often the same colors are used in additional layering to achieve this goal. Prioritize values over colors: step back to see if the bottom part of the eggs is dark enough in comparison to the top of the eggs, and if the shading of the cast shadow looks different from the eggs. Also, does the shadow have color besides grey? This is important because colors from objects always reflect into the cast shadows.

Brown egg:

- Use sepia or dark brown to darken the form shadow if necessary.
- Use nectar to add a colorful transition between the light tones on the egg.
- Use needle-sharp point of dark brown (any warm brown) to make tiny dots on the brown egg. Make sure the dots look small, are different, and don't repeat themselves in a pattern.
- Use yellow ochre and eggshell to blend the area around the highlight.

White egg:

- Use white over eggshell to blend the edge around the highlight on the egg.
- Use 20% cool grey to fuse the colors between the form shadow and middle tone (bottom part of the egg).
- Use eggshell and white pencils to blend the light areas of the cast shadow.

Use the kneaded eraser to clean up around the eggs so the paper stays pure white.

Apply two coats of final fixative in a well-ventilated area to protect the drawing against humidity and UV light. The artist uses Grumbacher final fixative, matte for pastel, charcoal, and pencil, which gives an even coat of resin to even out the surface and makes the colors appear bright and uniform.

Note: When working in color, avoid the mentality where you try to learn the technique "painting by numbers" with the given colors only. In general, many colors have very similar counterparts and the only true difference is pencil pressure or how you apply the colors. Follow these steps to make your own decisions about the colors:

1. Always establish the value (light/dark) relationships first.
2. Next focus on color, picking it based on tonality and color temperature (see Chapter 6).
3. Lastly, work on textures and details.

It's not enough to blend colors once. As you build layers of color and value, you blend several times to achieve your goals.

STEP-BY-STEP INSTRUCTIONS

Color Gradation & Rubbings

Materials: Prismacolor Premier colored pencils (unless otherwise noted), kneaded eraser, Strathmore premium white drawing paper, magic tape, Sakura Pen-touch marker

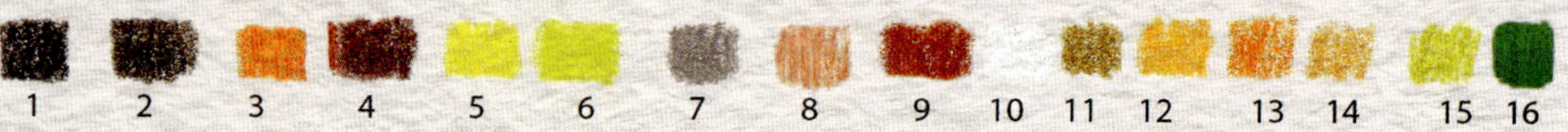

Color Chart: 1. 90% Warm Grey 2. Sepia 3. Mineral Orange 4. English Red Light 5. Canary Yellow 6. Yellow Chartreuse 7. 30% Warm Grey 8. Burnt Sienna (Pablo) 9. Burnt Ochre 10. White 11. Artichoke 12. Spanish Orange 13. Yellowed Orange 14. Yellow Ochre 15. Light Olive (Pablo) 16. Grass Green (Pablo)

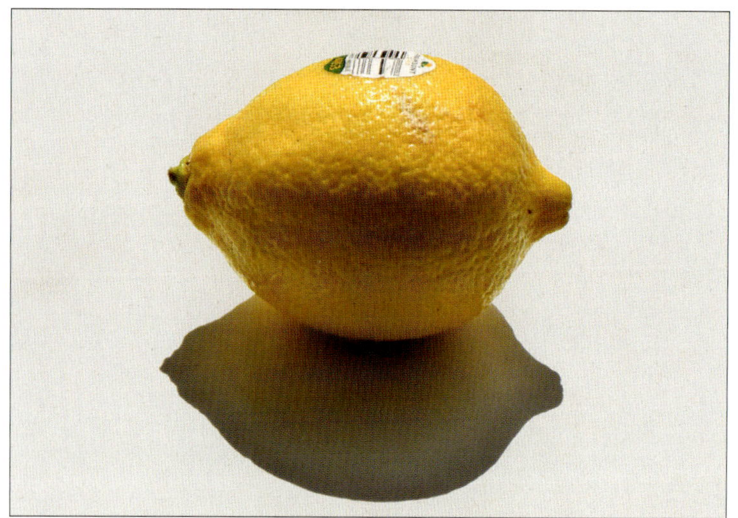

This photo was taken in a box setup placed next to a window. Beautiful morning light gives strong, crisp shadows to reveal the bright color and texture of the lemon.

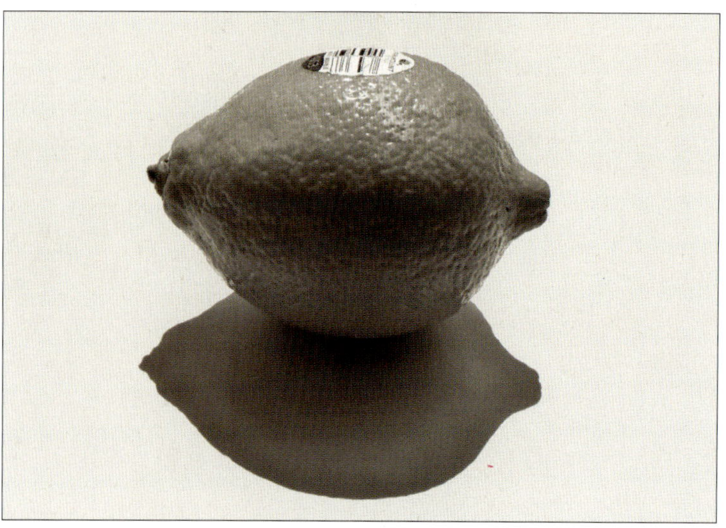

In this greyscale image you can see the values, not the colors.

Step 1

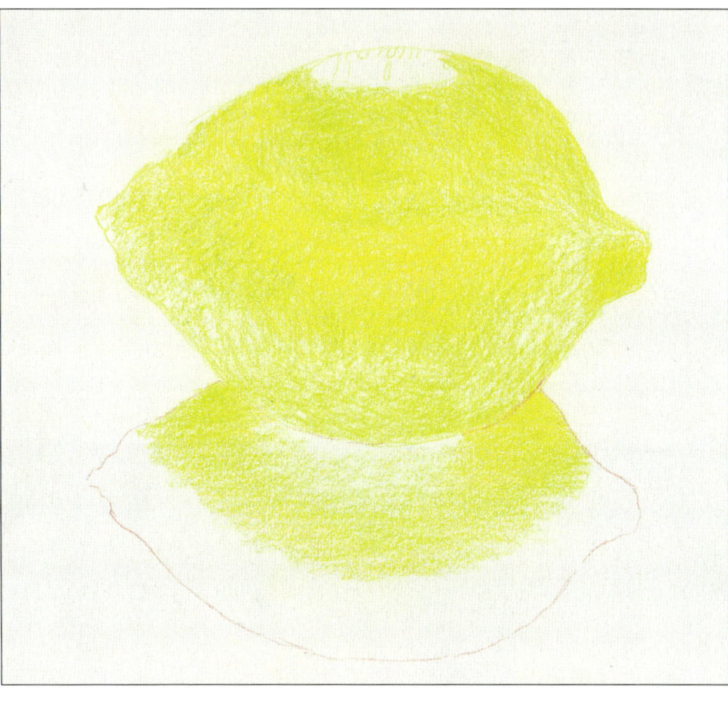

Transfer the outline using your favorite method: the light box, window, grid, or transfer paper methods using HB graphite pencil. Because this lemon is such a light object, the artist uses canary yellow for the lemon's outline and yellow ochre for the cast shadow's outline instead of using pencil. It eliminates the possibility of color contamination with graphite in subsequent shading.

You can either take a clean spoon and rub it over the lemon area only (avoid getting into the shadow or the background), or you can start shading over the lemon with colored pencils directly by placing the pumice stone underneath the paper.

Leave the pumice stone under your paper as you begin shading with a sharp point of yellow chartreuse. Next, increase your pencil pressure in the form shadow to make denser coloring with canary yellow, and place the same two colors in the cast shadow (not using the stone). You'll see that the pencil skips over the uneven texture of the pumice stone, creating texture in the lemon.

Step 2

Begin building layers, working in one color at a time. To begin layering the cast shadow, use sepia to outline the lemon at the very bottom. Shade with it softly to turn a line into a soft shadow. Change your color to mineral orange and English red light to fill in the warm brown color you see here.

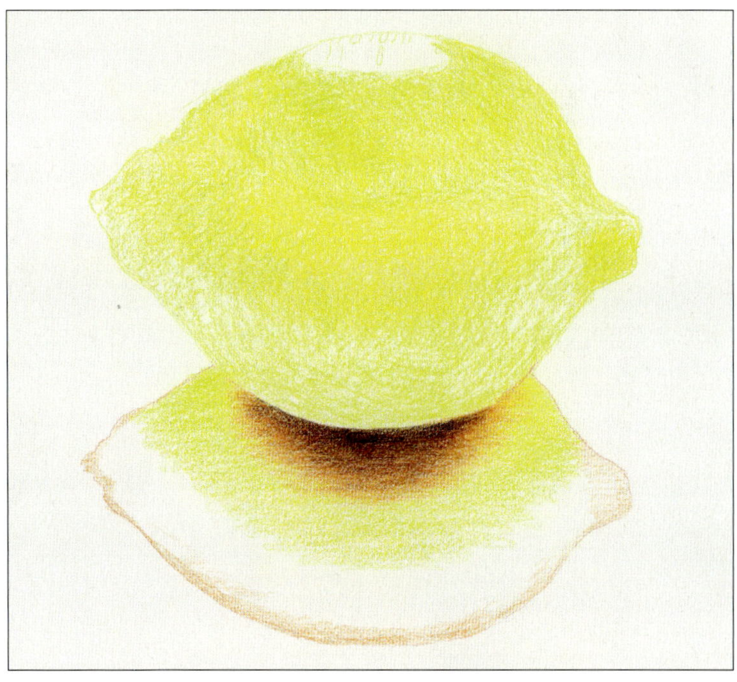

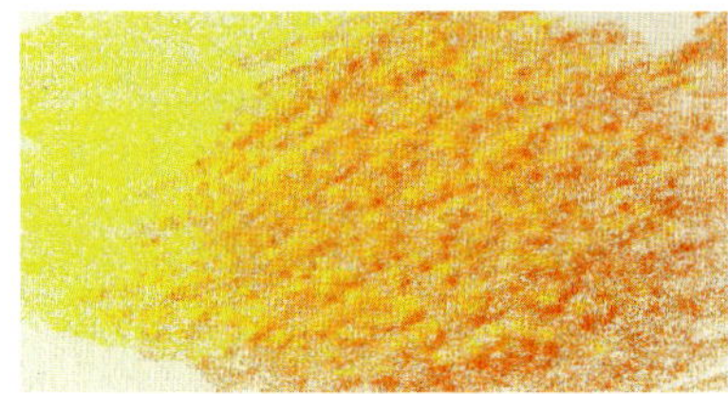

This image shows the initial rubbing of the surface with a pumice stone. Depending on the texture of your stone, pencil hardness, and pencil pressure, you'll be getting various results in texture. Therefore it is important to try this technique out on a scrap piece of paper first before committing to your drawing.

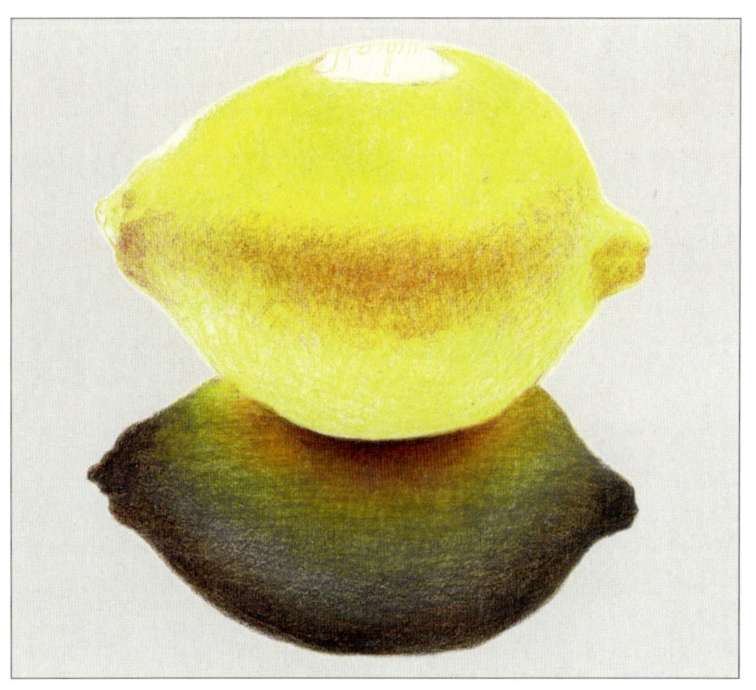

Step 3

Continue layering colors in the cast shadow. Use 90% warm grey with a very light pencil pressure to fill in the entire shadow, crossing over previously applied colors. Switch to Pablo burnt sienna to shade the rim of the cast shadow. Add more canary yellow, mineral orange, and 30% warm grey to deepen values and to intensify the color.

Take a small brush, dip it into a solvent and blend the entire lemon and the shadow. Use less solvent rather than too much. Let it dry completely before continuing your work! The shadow should look a lot darker and smoother after blending.

Add burnt ochre in light and soft circular strokes to create the form shadow on the lemon—this spot will be your darkest area on the fruit and you'll be judging the values based on this marker. Everything else should be lighter around it.

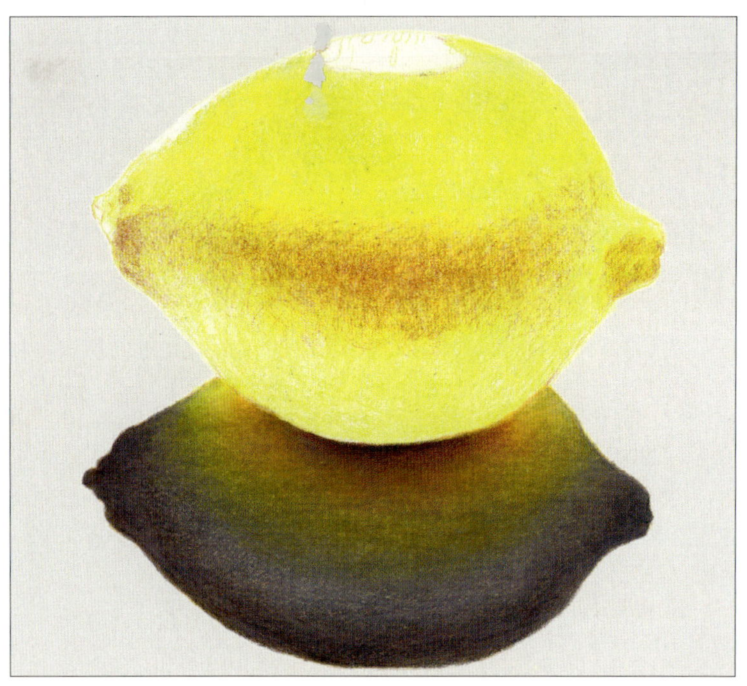

Step 4

The goal is to unify the colors in the cast shadow. You will layer the same colors but change the pencil pressure from light to fairly hard to burnish the surface and fuse colors. Here the artist works with canary yellow, Spanish orange, 30% warm grey, and white to blend the shadow completely. Notice that the colors layer easier after the blending with a solvent, and this grey unifies all the hues in the shadow, leaving it colorful.

Tip: The secret to creating artistic images is to layer colors softly. **Color gradation** means applying your tones from light to dark in a gradual manner with subtle transitions of values. This technique is necessary to describe the roundness of the form. When you draw, think of every object as a round shape, including stems, tiny flowers, eyes, and the lemon here!

Step 5

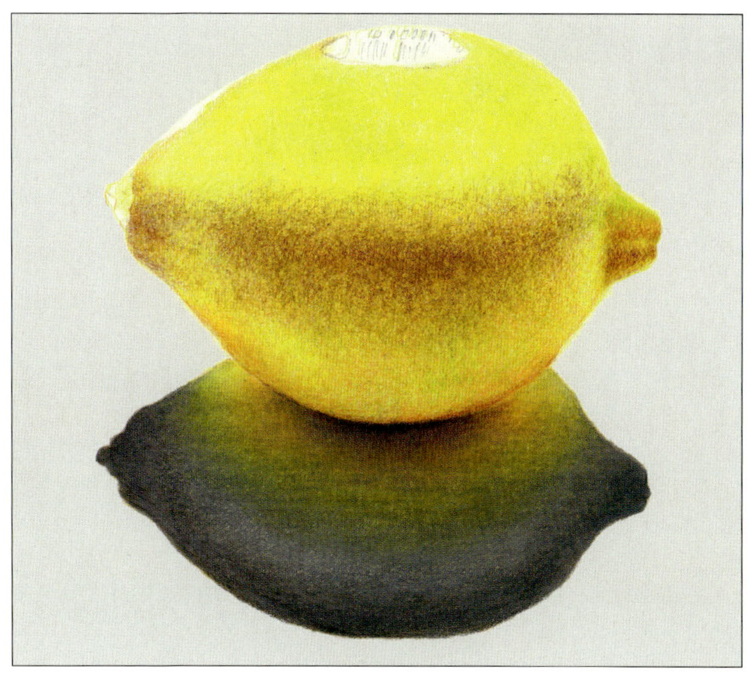

Now the goal is to focus on the lemon itself and develop the middle tones and reflected light at the bottom half of the lemon. For that you will need mineral orange or Spanish orange, canary yellow, burnt ochre, artichoke, yellowed orange, yellow ochre, and light olive (Pablo). Notice that there is some green in the lemon. Use a medium tone, natural warm green hue like artichoke to shade a large area below the form shadow. Overlap it over the previously applied brown. To add more texture, put the pumice stone under the paper again and shade over it with artichoke in circular strokes. This color transitions nicely into the reflected light.

Add some light olive (a lighter, warm green) at the bottom and on both sides of the lemon. It's a very light color that gives a slightly green tone to the previously applied yellow. You can also shade with this color in the reflected light (at the bottom of the lemon). Use a light touch of Spanish orange to define the lemon's bottom edge and then shade along the edge with it, controlling your pencil pressure from light to medium. Use light, circular strokes that are not linear and don't cut through the shape.

Step 6

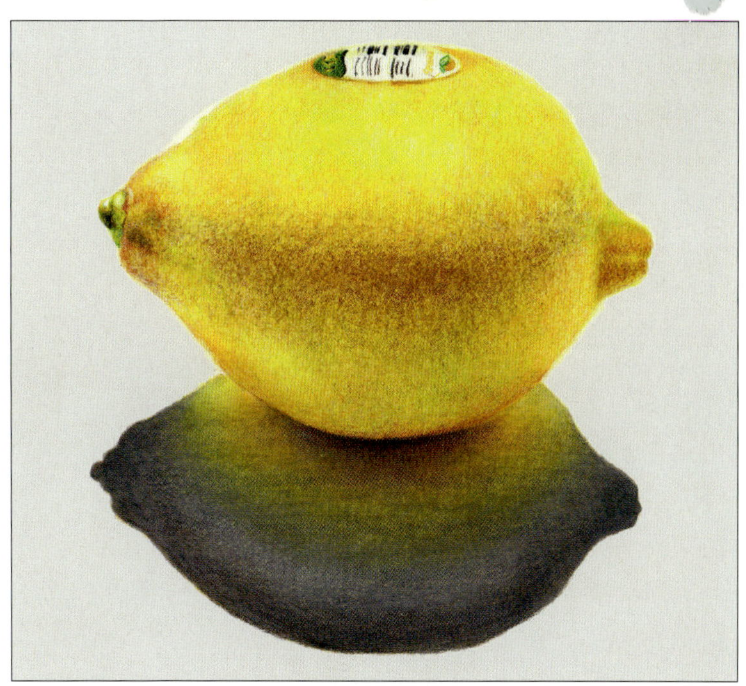

Once general values are established, you can dive into the details. At this time you should see the general texture of pumice stone in the lemon. The rubbing technique requires quite a lot of experimentation. It's best to try it out on a scrap piece of paper first before jumping into a full drawing. Also, different textures of pumice stone, the paper's thickness, and pencil pressure will affect the outcome. You will see that the adjustment of any of these variants will give you new results.

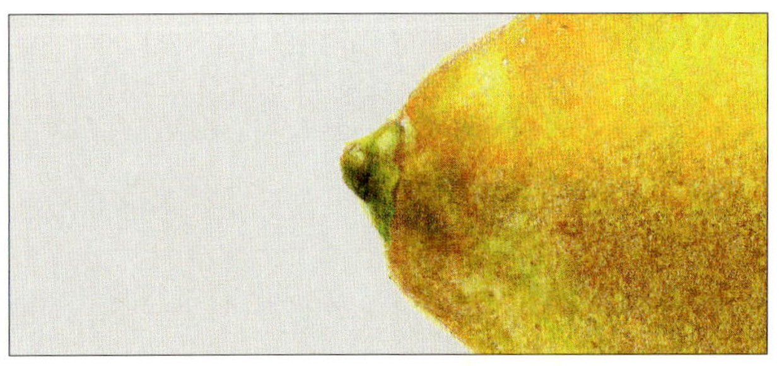

Once the basic values are established, you can begin working on details in texture. A combination of grass green and artichoke establishes the darker values. An addition of burnt ochre or English red light in those colors adds sophistication and deeper value found in the greens.

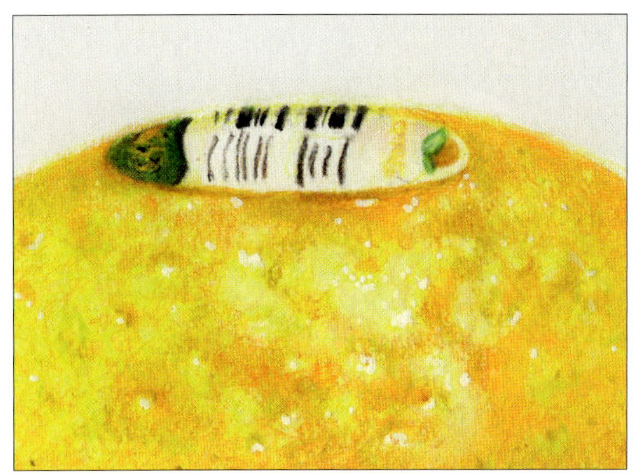

Draw the sticker with grass green, light olive, and Spanish orange. Fill in the tiny lines with some black. The top part of the sticker has yellow chartreuse over it to blend the edge. The bottom part that is closer to us has the sharper edge and no color is added in the white. To create texture in the light parts, burnish the uneven, light areas with white. With a light touch of burnt ochre and mineral orange create slightly darker, uneven passages around the white. The artist applies these two colors in tiny circular strokes around the revealed texture of pumice stone. The idea is to create light and shadow areas to reinforce the texture.

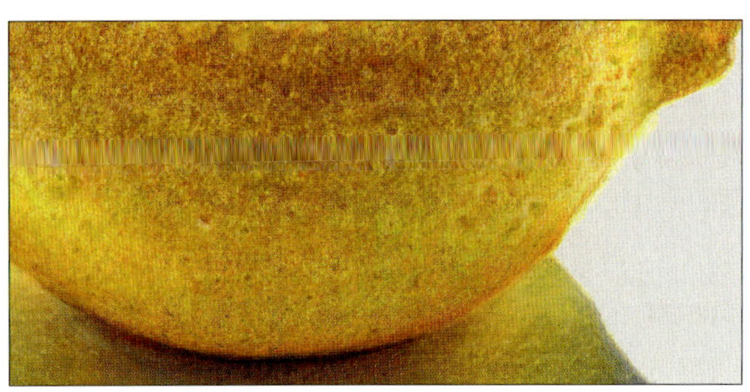

This close-up image shows the texture of the pumice stone and the complexity of layering one color over the next to create the subtle transitions of tones.

To create the brightest highlights as tiny dots, use the Sakura Pen-touch. Don't overdo the highlights by placing them all over the lemon. These should remain in the lightest light only—at the top part of the fruit.

To create volume in tiny dots, use burnt ochre and mineral orange to place very soft, uneven dots over the shaded lemon. Shade one, darker side of each dot with the pencil. The other side should stay lighter with some yellow peeking through. If it's not the case, take yellow chartreuse or white to shade the light side around the dot (you can see this texture on the right side of the lemon). The result is the uneven, textured dot.

Another way of doing this is to use magic tape. Place a piece of tape over the area where you want to create more texture. Take a ballpoint pen and make a few uneven strokes with it drawing right on the tape. Lift it. Some pigment will lift off, revealing lighter, yellow areas—this is the texture you can use to enhance by drawing around these uneven areas.

Action Step: Practice seeing form shadow and highlights on every object that surrounds you during the day. Place your favorite object under a lamp and manipulate the light to see changes in shadows.

Step 7

The final step is to evaluate the values, colors, and edges from the distance. The lemon should look three-dimensional and appear separate from the cast shadow in texture, strokes, and tone.

Step back to check your values from the distance. Are shadows dark enough? Are highlights bright? Do you have a smooth transition between the tones? The artist notices that the cast shadow is too dark in comparison to the greyscale picture and therefore uses a white colored pencil, shading over the entire cast shadow to lighten it up quite a bit.

Apply two coats of final fixative in a well-ventilated area to protect the drawing against humidity and UV light. Frame.

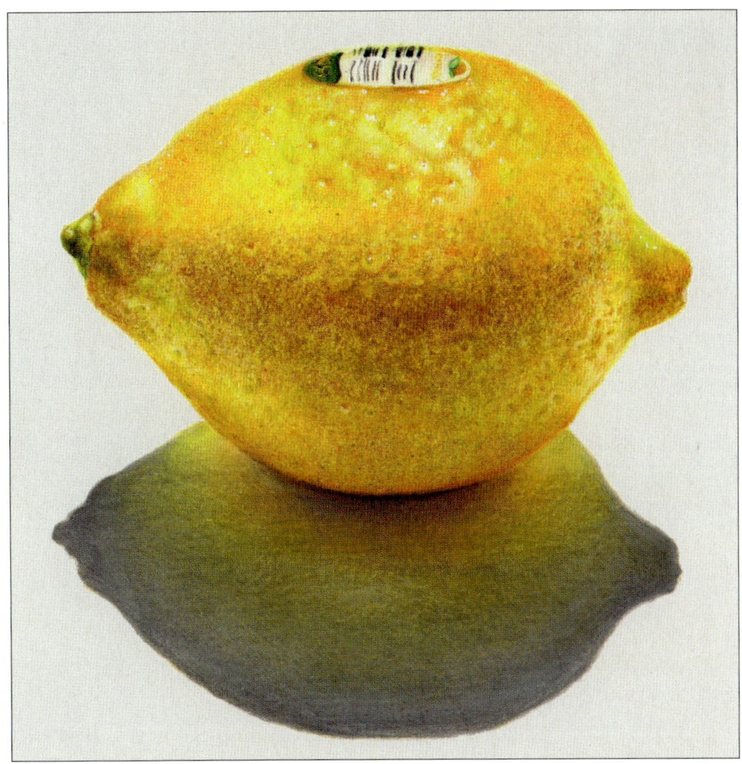

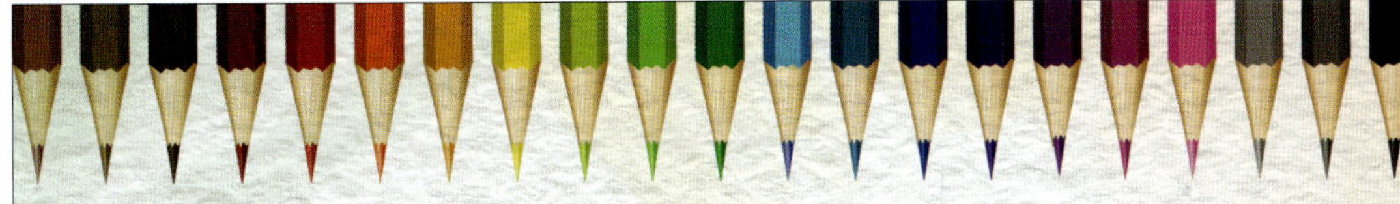

Common Mistakes

Most common shading mistakes and fixes:

- Not shading right to the edge of the contour line
- Uneven, sporadic layering
- Dirt and smudges left on the page, and strong graphite lines showing through the light color

Always remember!

- ✓ Clean up after your session
- ✓ Protect drawing between sessions at all times with a paper cover
- ✓ Erase graphite lines as much as possible when you work in light values

Chapter 4

How to Create Volume

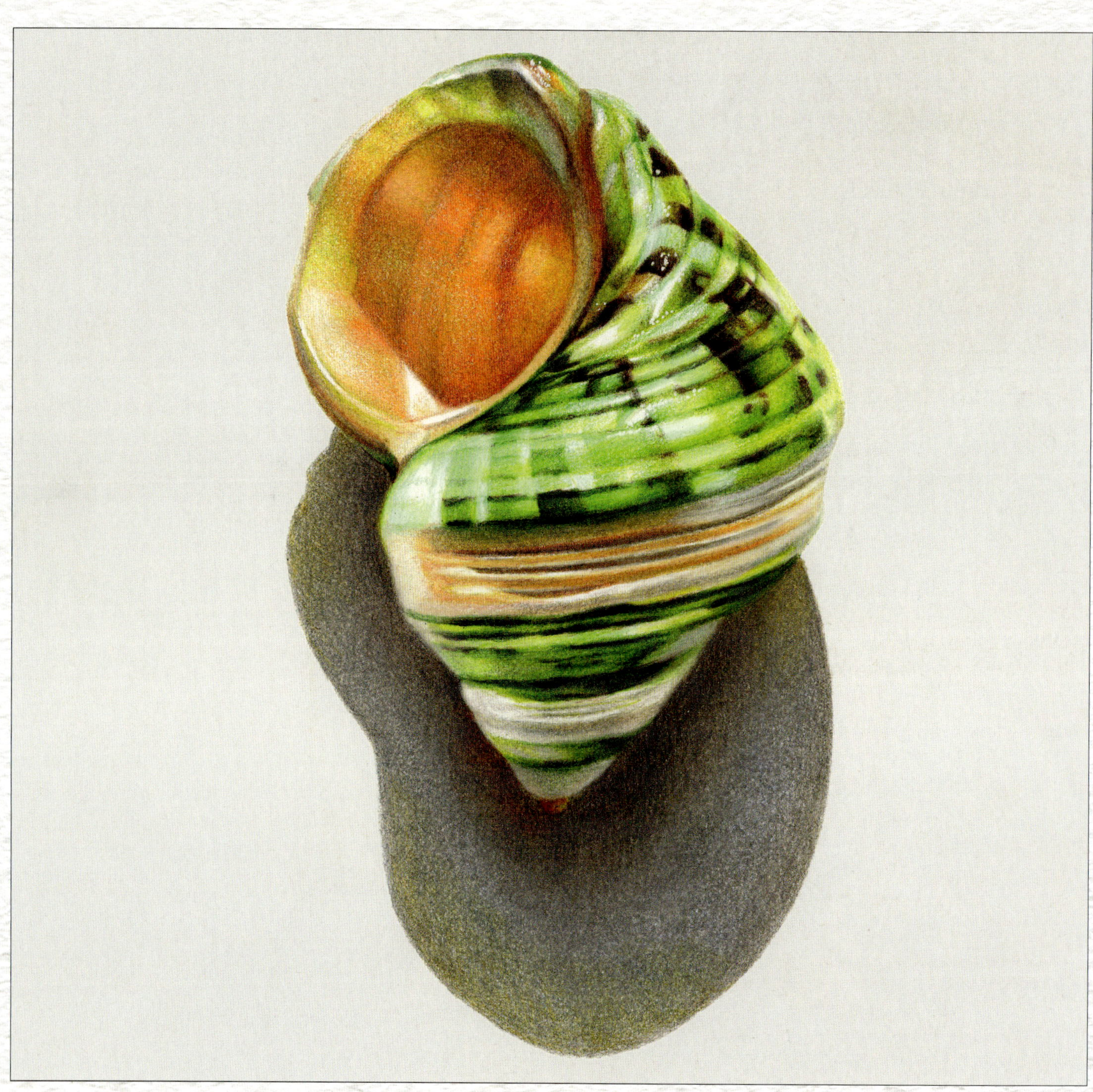

HOW PENCIL DIRECTION DEFINES VOLUME

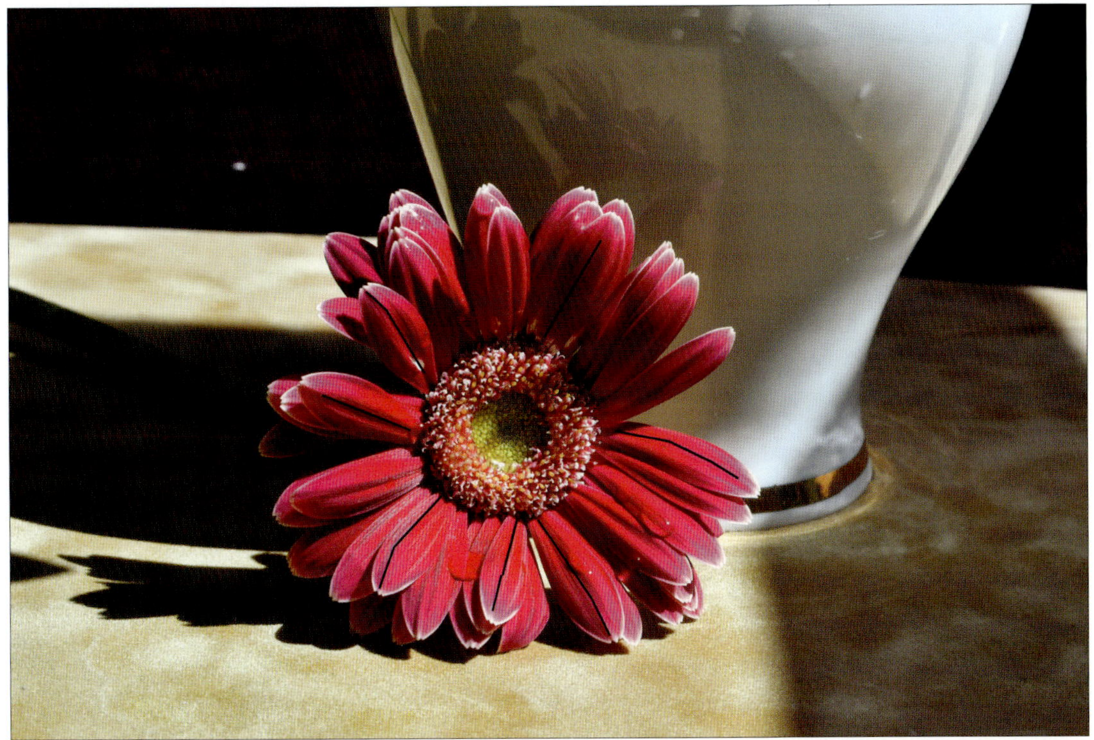

Besides understanding the formula for the distribution of light, you also create an illusion of volume in an object with a directional stroke that either follows the form or goes against it. Without it, your subject will stay flat. You've already done it in your first drawings, and here we'll practice this essential technique with more purpose. Let's look at some images to observe the curvature of objects and how you can apply this information to describe any form in directional strokes.

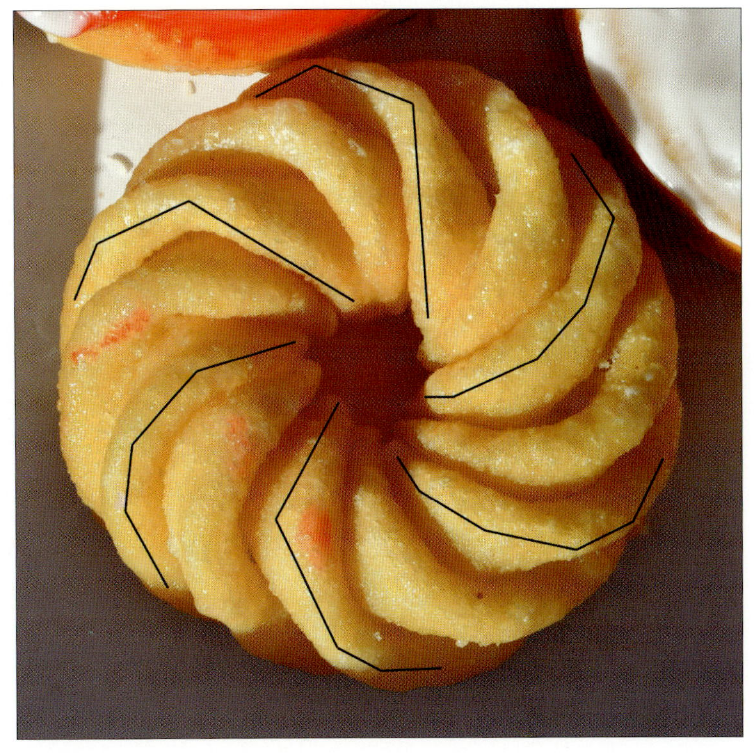

In the above image the flower consists of a large circle with two more small circles inside it. When you sketch out objects like this one, you draw these circles first and then place directional lines for every petal inside it. It's much easier to draw out the petals one by one, following the directional line of every petal. When you begin shading, you also follow the form to shade in the direction or curvature of every petal.

The donut is also a circle with curving subsections that form a unique pattern. Here you see black directional lines that illustrate a possible direction for shading every section of the donut. When you begin shading, you use short strokes in one direction, then change pencil direction in accordance with the change in a pattern. The idea is not to shade in long, aimless strokes that flatten out the form, but to focus on seeing these directional changes in every object you draw.

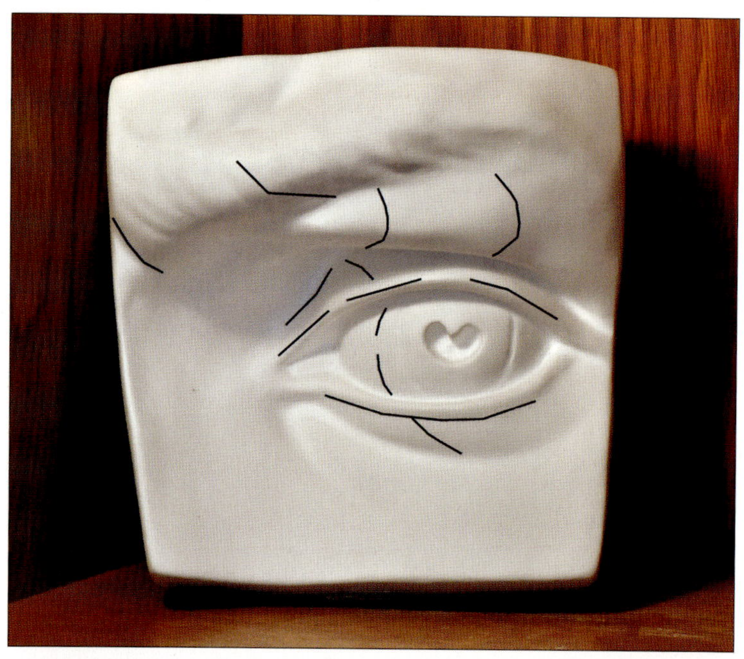

David's eye is a complex form with its own curvature pattern. Here you see a few major lines that describe general rotation and curvature found in the anatomy. These curves give you an idea of how many changes in pencil direction you encounter shading such a structure.

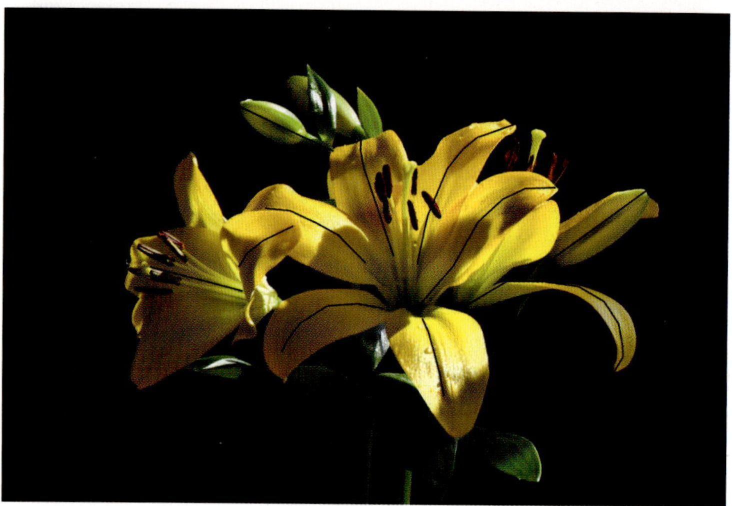

In this picture we can clearly see the unique, directional lines applied to every petal. Your pencil rotation and shading must follow this curvature to create volume in petals.

STEP-BY-STEP INSTRUCTIONS

Direction and Directional Strokes

Materials: Koh-I-Noor Polycolor colored pencils and Prismacolor Premier colored pencils; Koh-I-Noor Colored Pencil paper, 9 x 12, 114 lb.; kneaded eraser; Sakura Pen-touch marker

Note: Koh-I-Noor Polycolor pencil colors are named with numbers, and the actual pencils used for the artist's sample are given throughout this lesson. You don't need to buy the same pencils; simply use the color chart as a reference to match these colors. Begin thinking how you can achieve similar results using the colored pencils available in your box. The colors listed are the main colors used; other hues may have been used for minor details.

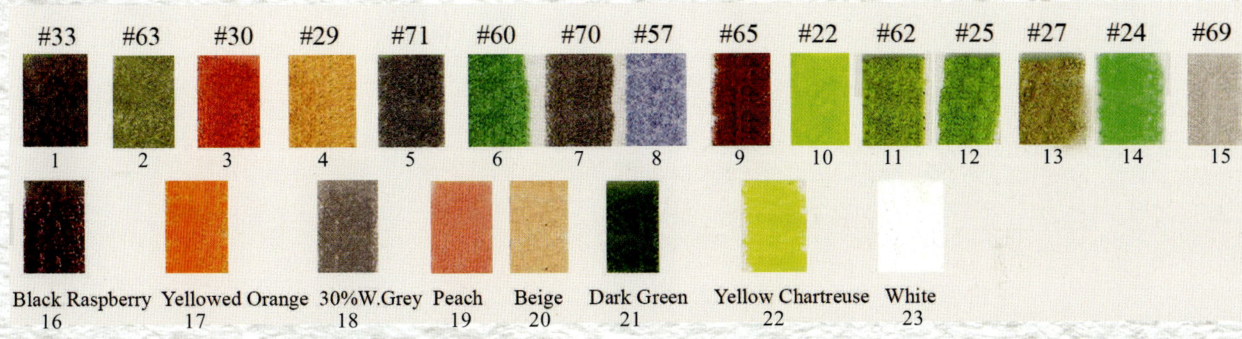

Color Chart:

1. #33
2. #63
3. #30
4. #29
5. #71
6. #60
7. #70
8. #57 (for steps 1–3, 5–6)
9. #65
10. #22
11. #62
12. #25
13. #27
14. #24
15. #69
16. Black Raspberry
17. Yellowed Orange
18. 30% Warm Grey
19. Peach
20. Beige (for step 4)
21. Dark Green
22. Yellow Chartreuse
23. White (for step 7)

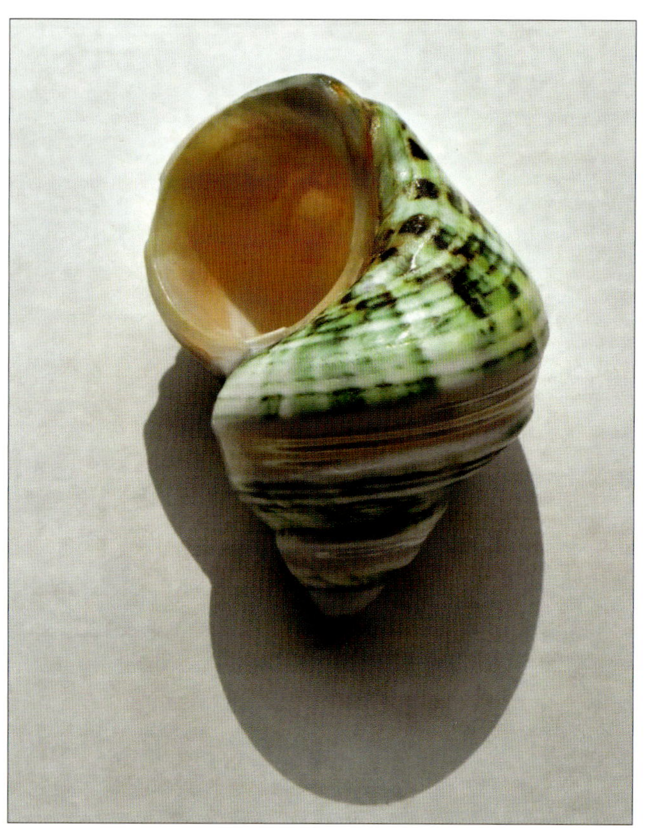

In this reference photo we can see that the light divides the shell into two parts. The top part of the shell receives lots of light with a few scattered tiny highlights seen on its surface. The bottom part of the shell is in the shadow, which is important to observe once you begin picking colors and shading it. It needs to be darker and greyer consistently despite the noticeable white stripes present throughout.

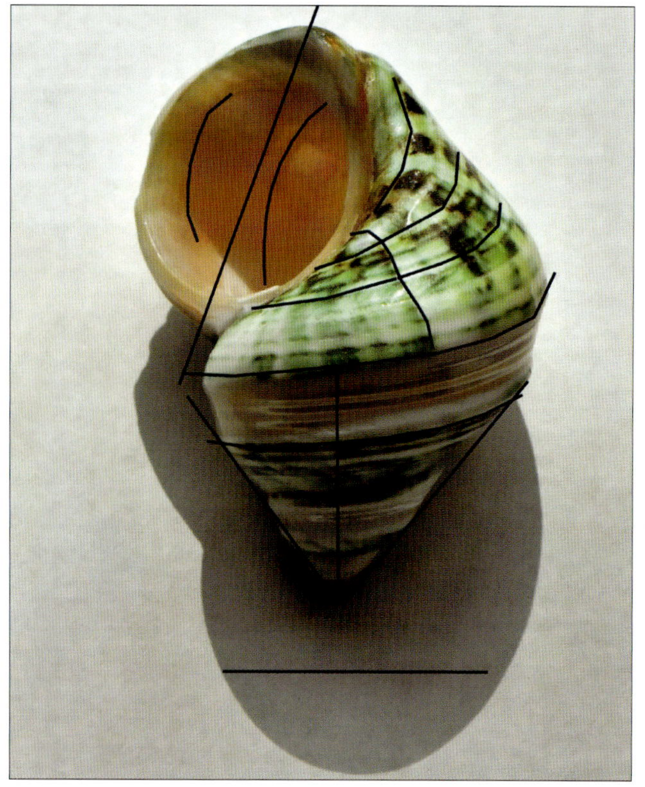

In this picture we can look at the structure of the shell to sketch it out correctly. The shell is broken down into three major planes: the oval at the top, the triangle at the bottom, and a connecting shape in the middle. Each plane has its own directional line that determines the curvature and shading pattern. Why is it important? When you layer and blend colors, you follow the contours and textures of the shell—you follow the form. By varying pencil direction and stroke length, you learn to draw subjects in three dimensions.

The cast shadow under the shell can be shaded in many ways; however, smooth, horizontal, directional strokes always work well to separate it from the subject itself.

You can simplify the pattern on the shell by either cutting the number of curves making them a bit wider than in the reference or by mapping out fewer green spires.

Step 1

Transfer the outlines. The artist uses a very light green for outlines instead of a graphite pencil to minimize grease. You can use Prismacolor yellow chartreuse, which is a very light color and blends in well with subsequent greens.

Block in a single warm green; the artist uses Koh-I-Noor 27. Simplify the object by focusing on major patterns you see in the shell. Instead of copying every dot, focus on the general breakdown and curvature of the shell as discussed with the previous picture. This curvature determines the direction of your shading. Place major curves with a very light green pencil.

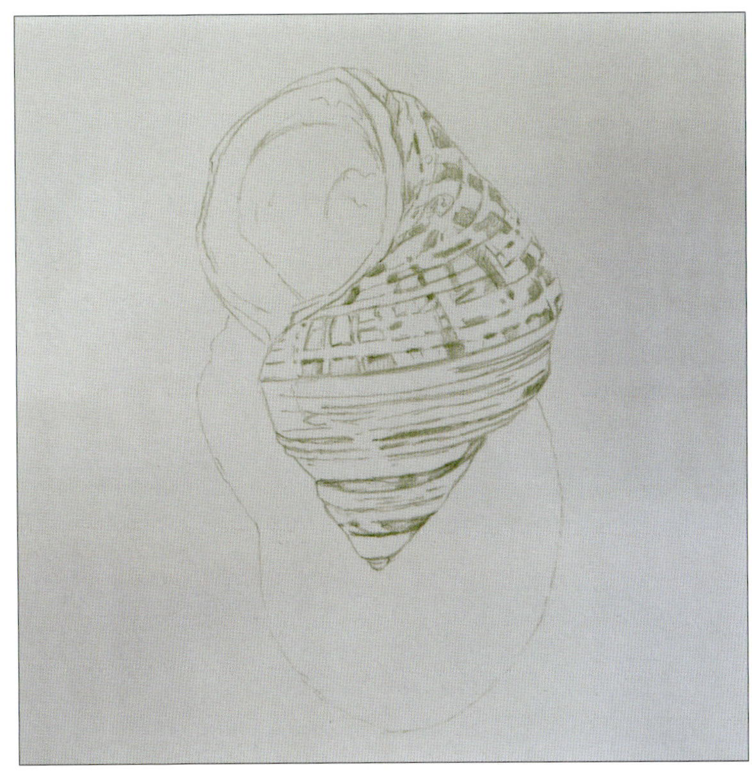

Step 2

Add dark brown into the darkest spots with Koh-I-Noor 33 and Prismacolor black raspberry. Shade a wide stripe in the middle of the shell with Koh-I-Noor 29. Make sure to curve it around the shell. Map out the green lines. Shade with Koh-I-Noor 60 and 22.

Shade the shell's interior inside the oval using one color only, altering your pencil pressure to record shifts in tone. The artist uses Koh-I-Noor 30. Don't shade up and down or straight across. Observe its concave shape and copy it with your strokes, rotating your pencil as you move across the interior of the shell.

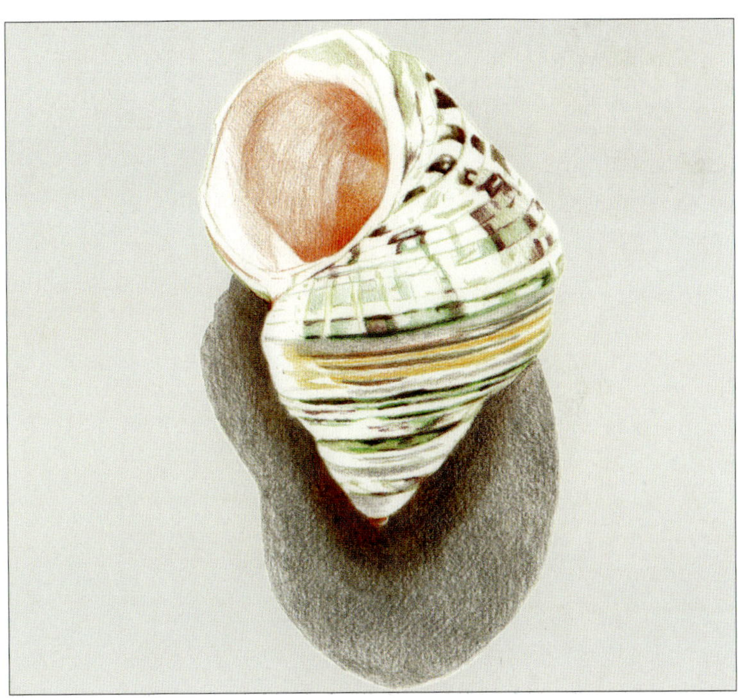

Cast shadow gives physical presence to any object. Always incorporate it into your still life to anchor your object to the space around it. The artist shades with Koh-I-Noor 70, 71, 30, 33, and 65 [medium greys and dark, warm browns]. Use medium pencil pressure shading the cast shadow, allowing some paper to show through. We are going to make this shadow more colorful in subsequent steps.

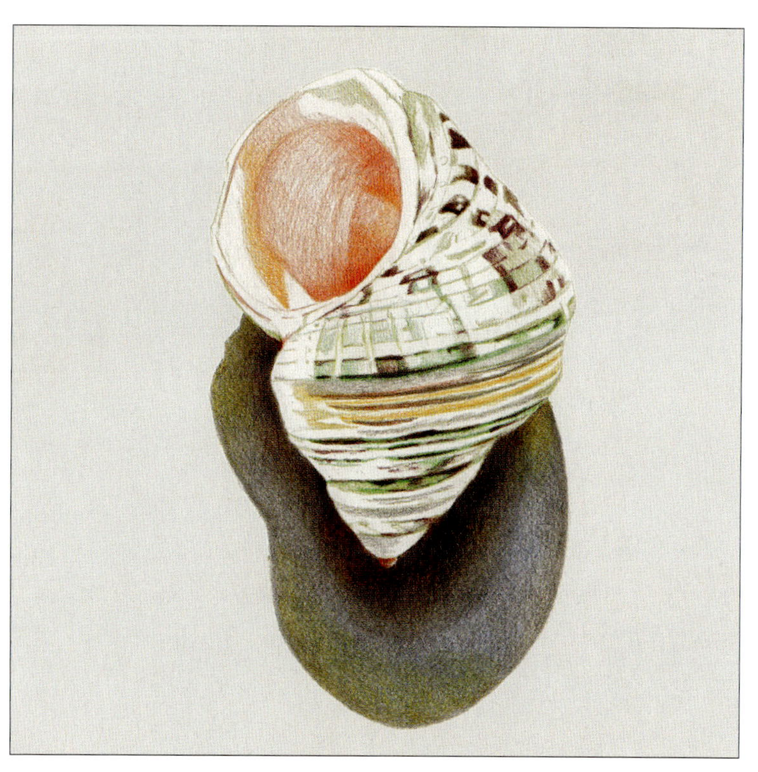

Step 3

Work on the color of the cast shadow. While it's not final, you can bring it to a high degree of finishing in this step. Use Koh-I-Noor 57 and 29. The sharper your pencils, the smoother your shading will be working on this paper.

Step back to check the shape of the shell and its rotation, and if the cast shadow is dark enough in comparison to the shell. The shell should pop in contrast to the cast shadow.

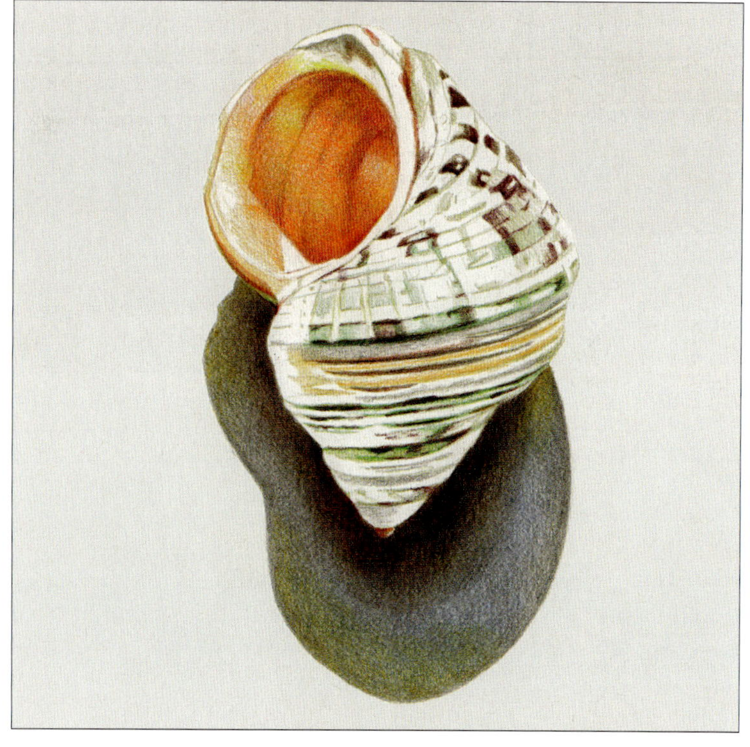

Step 4

Work on the interior of the shell again layering more color this time. Shade with Prismacolor yellowed orange, Koh-I-Noor 29, and a touch of Prismacolor yellow chartreuse (or Koh-I-Noor 62) in the lightest spots seen in the orange to enhance the light inside the shell.

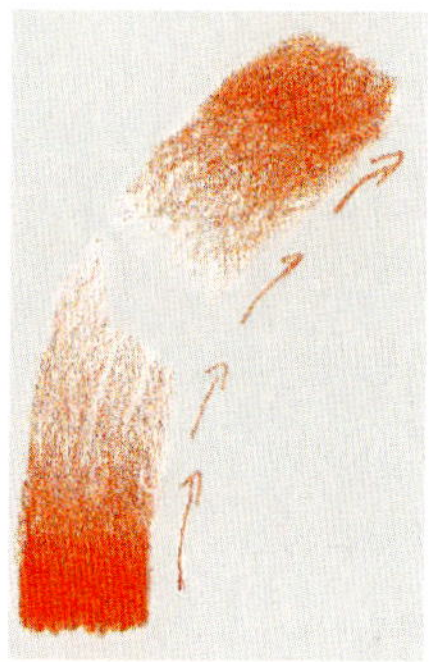

This image helps you to understand how you can adjust pencil pressure to rotate and curve your strokes in accordance with the object's form. The strokes must be descriptive of your object's form.

Step 5

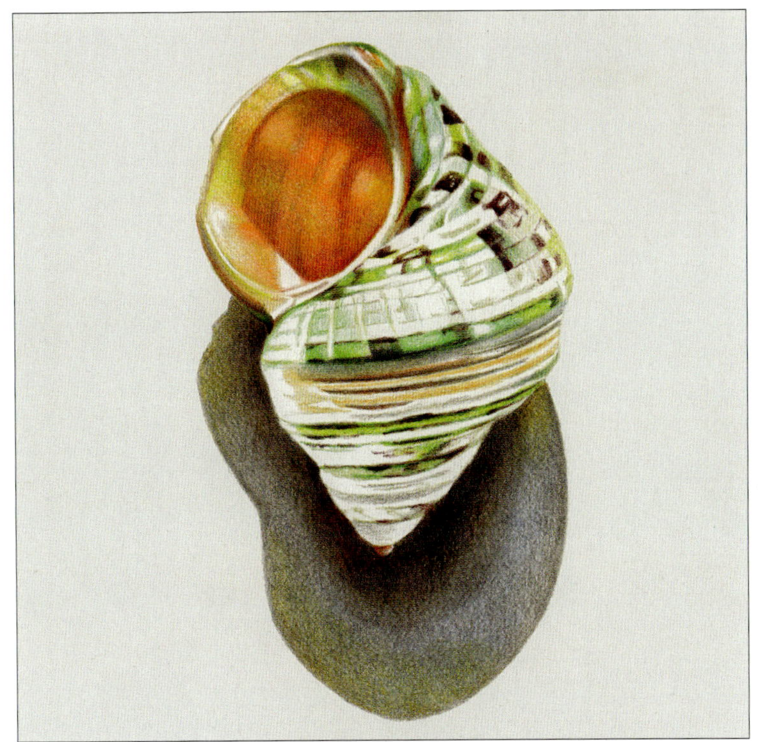

Finish up working on the shell's interior by drawing around the rim. Make sure you leave some paper white where you see the highlights along the left edge. You can use Prismacolor peach and beige for the lightest tones present near the rim.

To enhance the top edge of the rim, the artist uses Prismacolor 30% warm grey, Koh-I-Noor 65, 22, and 62. Begin developing the green stripes in the middle of the shell and watch for shifts in color temperature between the warm and the cool greens. Begin developing the green stripes in the middle of the shell and watch for shifts in color temperature between warm and cool greens.

Step 6

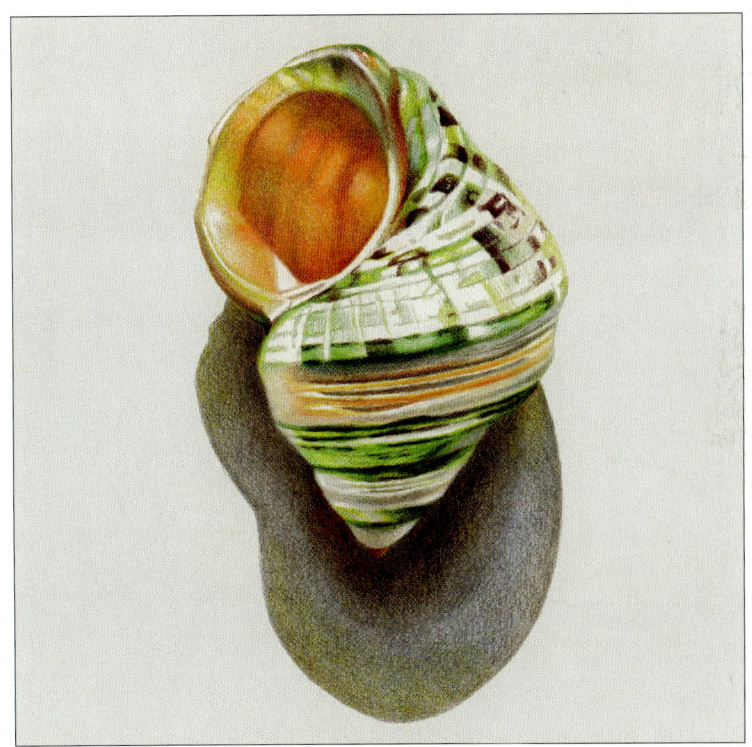

The shell has a major division of light and shade right in the middle. Let's focus on the bottom part of the shell in this step, which is darker than the top. Use this information to pick the colors in accordance with values, not color alone. If you prefer, you can apply the same colors you want to use in the light but shade with heavier pencil pressure to darken the values at the bottom.

The artist uses Koh-I-Noor 62, 63, 25, 27, 60, 33, and 57, which are also applied in the next step, but with a lighter pressure. To shade a large yellow stripe in the middle of the shell, use Koh-I-Noor 29, yellowed orange, and beige next to some light grey. Use Prismacolor white (the softest white) for blending the colors in the stripe on both sides of the shell. When you shade with these colors, make sure you follow the form or its curvature and don't make the lines too straight. The idea is to create volume with soft shading that curves around the shell. Because of the combination of colored pencil paper and harder pencils used in this project, extra blending is not necessary. Harder colored pencils such as the Koh-I-Noor brand tend to blend on their own when used on Koh-I-Noor colored pencil paper. If you use different supplies and see the texture building up at the moment, make sure you also blend your strokes with the colorless blender at this step.

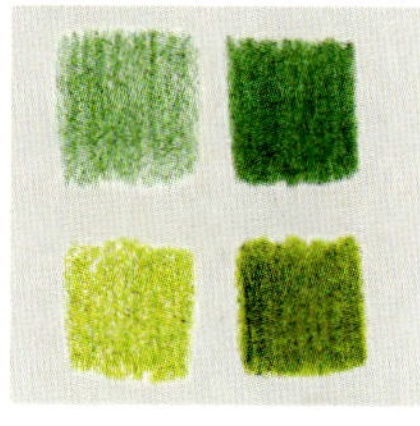

In this image you see cool green (Koh-I-Noor 60) at the top and a warm green (Koh-I-Noor 62) at the bottom. Notice how different they seem to be, depending on the pencil pressure applied. It means that you don't have to use a lot of pencils to describe the form. You can shade with a light touch of cool green at the top of the shell, and with a heavy pencil pressure at the bottom. The same is true for this warm green. Shaded lightly it almost looks yellow, but if you apply heavy pencil pressure, it darkens considerably. This change in values should inform you in making decisions coloring the shell and any other form as well.

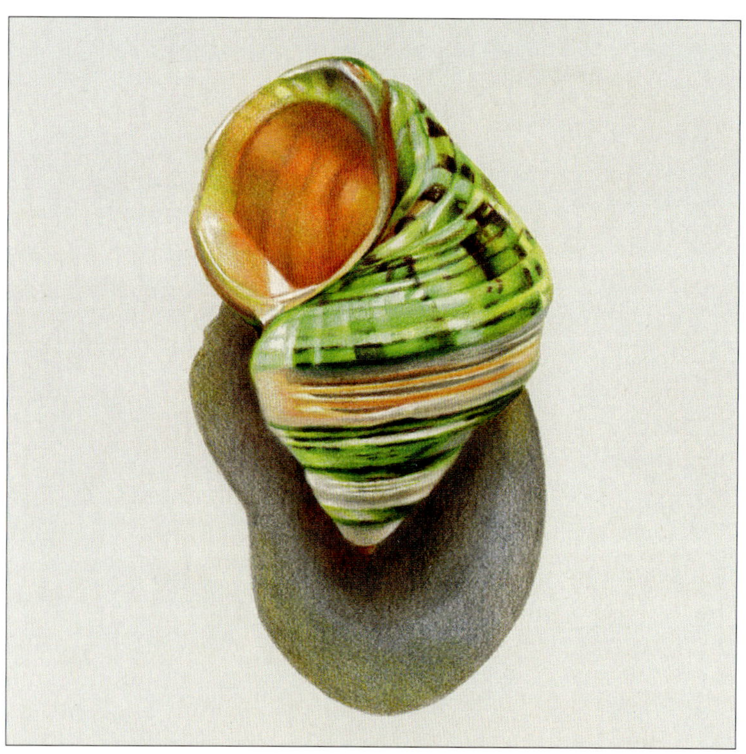

Step 7

Now work on the top part of the shell, shading with the same colored pencils but lighter pressure. Rotate your paper to apply soft strokes, following the curves of the form. Identify the patterns of color between the curves and fill them in. Make sure the edges stay rather soft between these patterns of color. Don't outline them. Overlap the colors to create seamless transitions between the hues. Blend with the colorless blender, if necessary.

Notice, the left side of the shell is cooler, while the right side is warmer. The artist shades with yellow chartreuse on the right edge and side of the shell. Use a variety of greens from the color chart to shade the top part of the shell and to darken the bottom part of the shell. The artist shades with Koh-I-Noor 24, 25, 27, 29, 33 (or black raspberry), 57, 62, and 63.

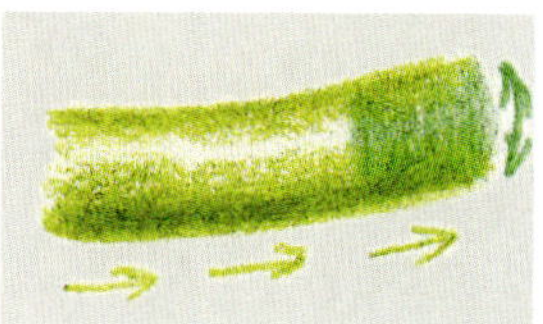

Here you can see a simplified model of shading the shell following the form and going against it. Depending on the pencil direction, the shape will either look three-dimensional or flat.

Step 8

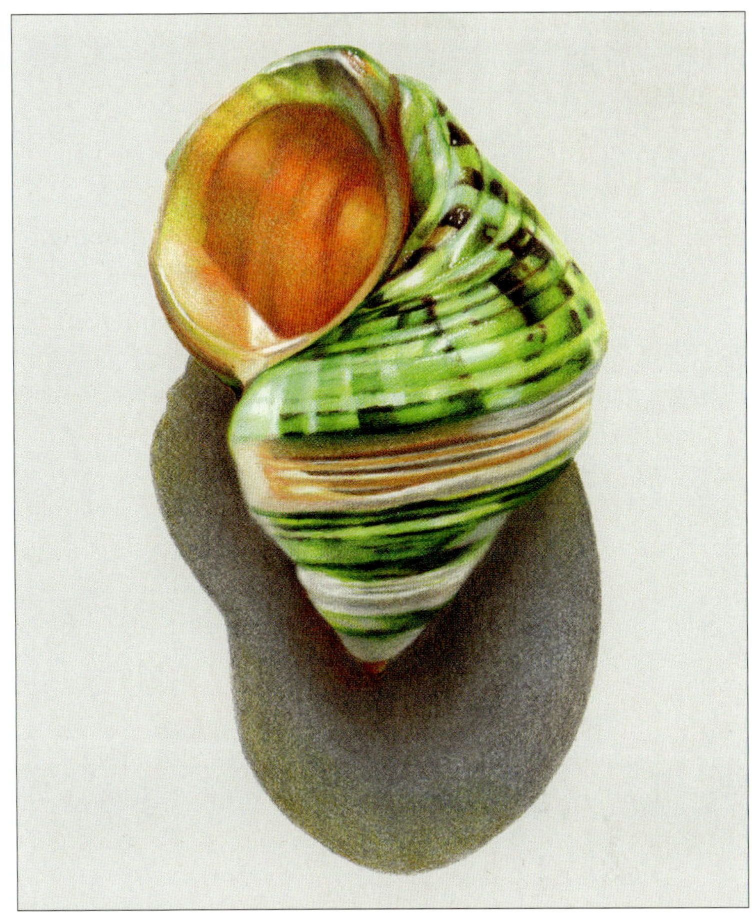

Often the surface becomes too waxy after considerable layering and blending, and as a result doesn't accept any more pigment. To overcome this challenge, spray your drawing outside with a workable fixative such as Grumbacher workable spray, matte. Let it dry completely. Now the surface is ready to accept a bit more pigment. If you don't have a workable fixative, the final one works well too, but make sure that it's a fairly thin coat.

When you get close to the finish line, step back to evaluate the contrast (values) and edges. The shell should have shifts in tone to rotate in space, but more importantly imitate the curvature pattern we see in it. The edges should be much sharper around the rim and much softer in the contour line of the shell and the cast shadow. With heavy pressure, use Prismacolor white to soften and lighten up the edges between the light green stripes on the upper shell, if needed. Use a combination of Prismacolor dark green and black raspberry to enhance the darkest stripes on the shell.

If the cast shadow doesn't look even, apply Prismacolor 30% warm grey across the entire shadow to "connect" and blend all the colors. The shadow should remain colorful but grey. Be careful about the outer edge of the shadow: make sure the line is not sharp or heavily outlined. You can apply the same Prismacolor 30% warm grey to grey down the shell in the shadow area too (the bottom half).

With heavy pencil pressure, apply Prismacolor dark green and yellow chartreuse to intensify the colors if needed. Shade with a very heavy pencil pressure in Prismacolor white to blend the lightest green tones in the light (top part of the shell), if necessary. (See Chapter 5 for how to blend art with light colored pencils.)

Use the Sakura Pen-touch to make tiny highlights. Clean up the smudges around the shell with a kneaded eraser and apply a final fixative, such as Grumbacher final fixative, matte. Make sure to spray it outdoors or in a well-ventilated space.

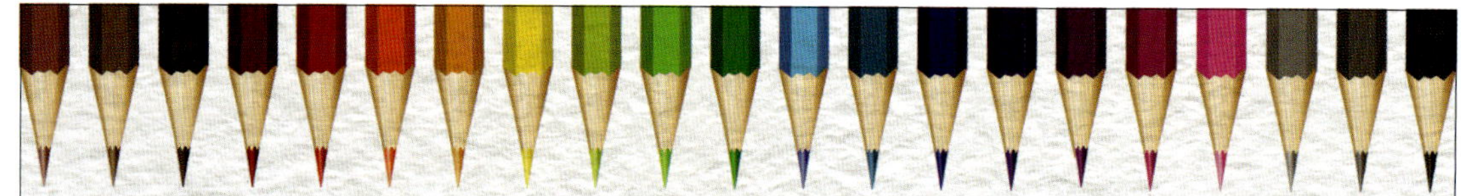

Common Mistakes

1. Uneven shading with gaps
2. Absence of highlights
3. Heavy-handed graphite lines that cause massive erasing and therefore weaken paper's tooth and ability to layer colors nicely. Messy sketching is the ultimate killer of realist drawing.

Always remember!

✓ Create volume with different pencil pressure

✓ Create volume with color gradation and overlapping

✓ Create volume with different strokes (crosshatching, uneven, circular, short and long strokes)

✓ Create volume by always shading on a hard surface. Place your paper on a hard surface to make layering easier.

Chapter 5

How to Blend Colored Pencils

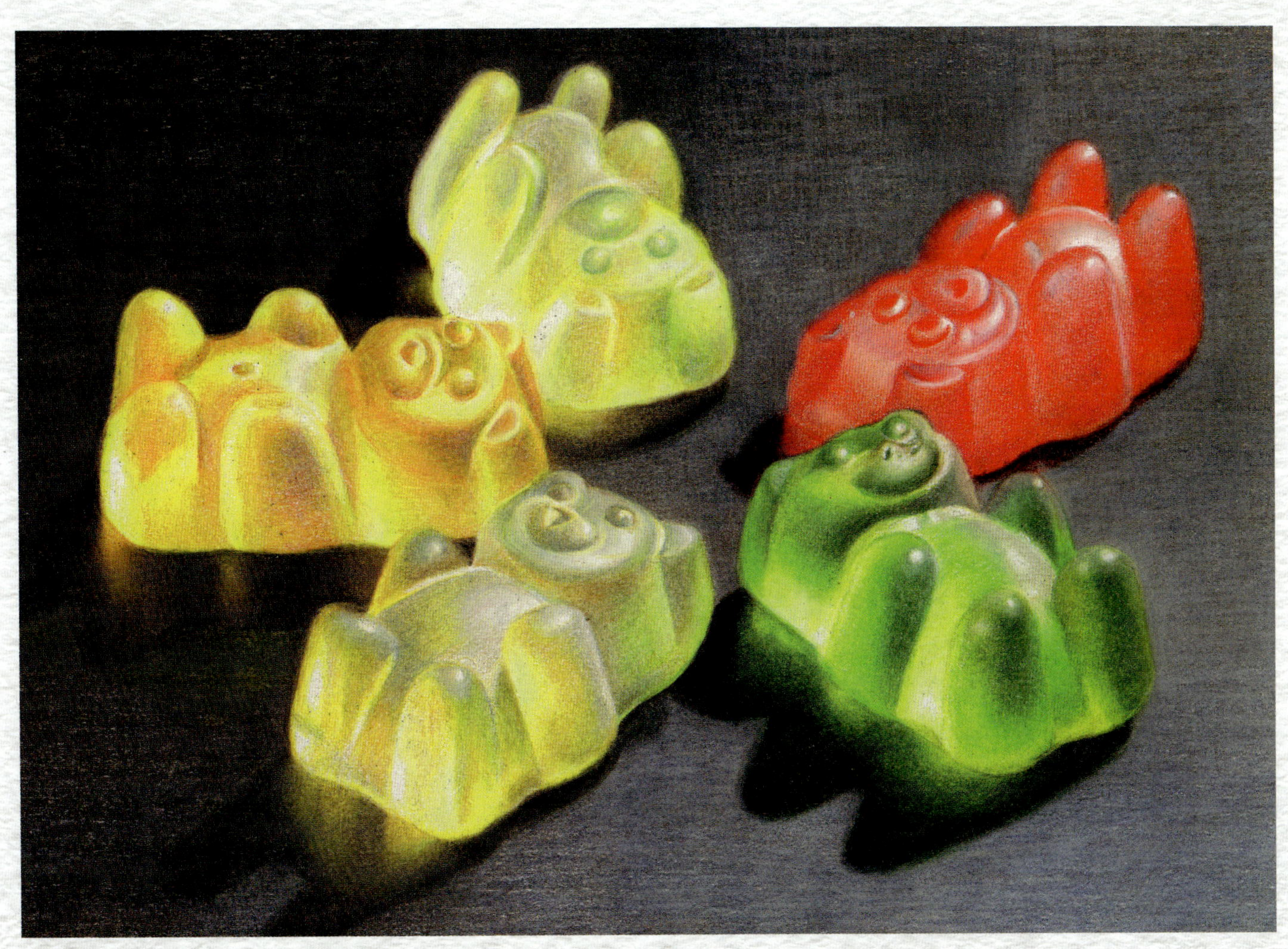

BLENDING TECHNIQUES

When you draw on smooth paper that is designed for colored pencil work, your colored pencils tend to blend on their own during shading. But what do you do once you work on a different kind of surface that may be very colorful but has a texture that subtracts from the drawing? Or how do you achieve glass-like appearance on some surfaces such as water or crystal? Blending becomes key.

There are several blending techniques that can work in conjunction with each other or separately. It really depends on the subject, paper, and your handling of the medium. While many artists like what the OMS (odorless mineral spirits or solvents) can produce, often they are too harsh or aggressive on the drawing and may "kill" its freshness. Also, it's not quite clear what happens to the diluted pigment in the long run. Does it stay 100 percent intact or fade away? The safer choice is blending with a colorless blender, but it is a slow process when blending large backgrounds. They can be very difficult and time-consuming, and the achieved saturation is just not the same as with the OMS blending. Another technique would be to blend with light or white colored pencils by using the heaviest pencil pressure to lighten up and blend a specific area. The best solution is to practice all of these techniques so you can understand their potential, and then arrive at the method that works best for you!

Burnishing is a blending technique of layering colored pencils with very heavy pressure. It saturates colors while smoothing out the surface completely.

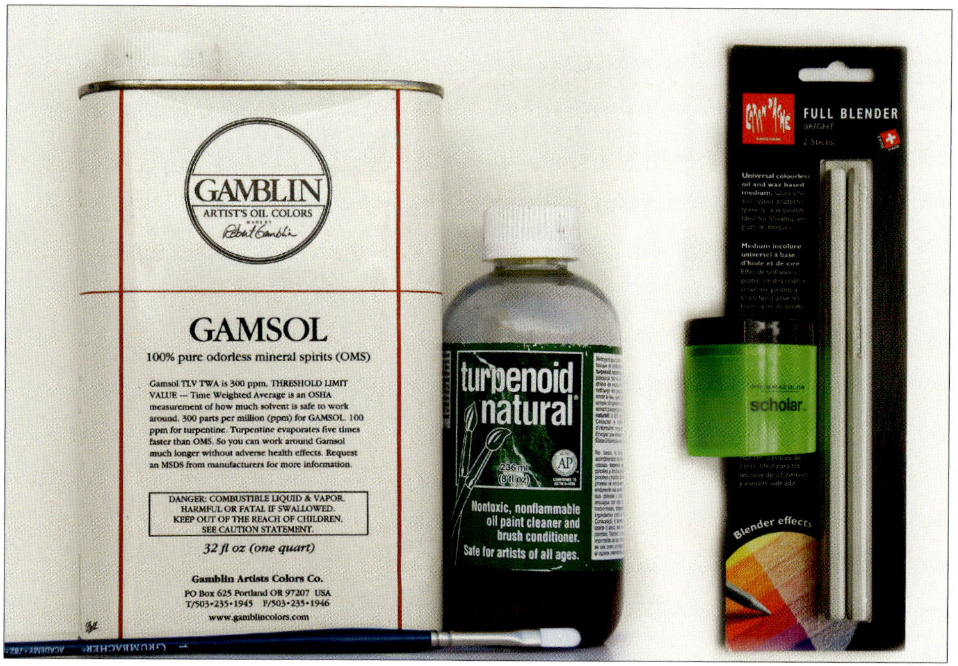

Odorless mineral spirits and Caran d'Ache full blender

OMS blending

Solvents like Gamsol, Zest-it, rubbing alcohol, or Turpenoid Natural melt the pencil pigment, producing a saturated, even surface that eliminates pencil strokes. Always handle solvents with care and store a small amount of a solvent in a glass jar with a lid for easy access. Try not to inhale it or let it come into contact with your skin. To move the solvent around your drawing, you need to have either a brush or a cotton-tipped swab. Buy an inexpensive synthetic brush that can keep a fine point and reserve it for colored pencil blending only. The alternative to a brush is a cotton-tipped swab, but the fine point of the brush makes it much easier to work around the edges with care. Solvent-based Finesse blender pen for colored pencils is the closest alternative to OMS as it melts the pigments the same way but has a limited lasting period.

Some things to keep in mind about OMS Blending:

- Painting with a solvent works on most colors but it works particularly well on dark to medium dark colors. It's not noticeable on light hues. Solvents work, so if you start blending and don't see the results, it means you either don't have enough pigment on your paper yet or your colored pencils don't have much wax in them.
- This blending works best with very soft, waxy pencils such as Luminance, Prismacolor Premier or Colorsoft.
- Always blend your colors from light to dark to avoid contaminating light colors with dark smudges.
- It's time to blend the colors when you see that everything is colored except for the highlights. Burnish carefully in the light and around the highlights.
- When you use solvents to blend, wait for the page to dry completely before reapplying the colors!

In this image, you can see the unblended version, the blending process with a solvent, and the final image with additional shading done over the solvent.

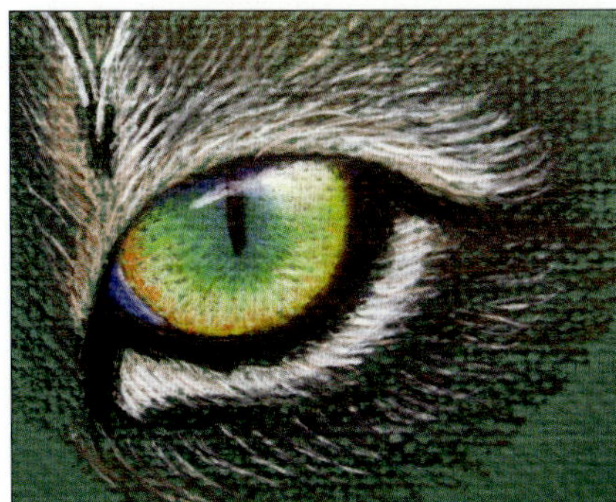

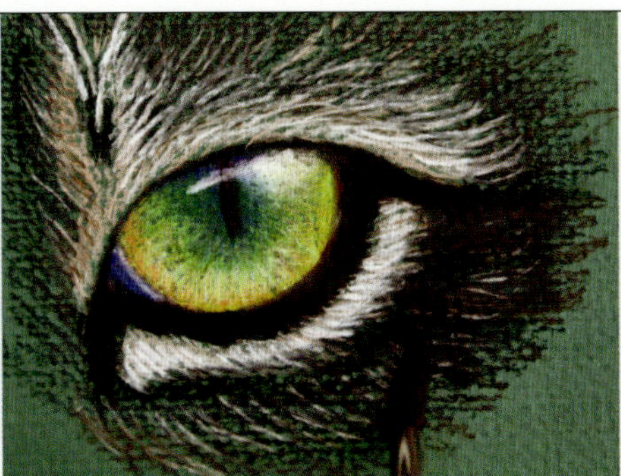

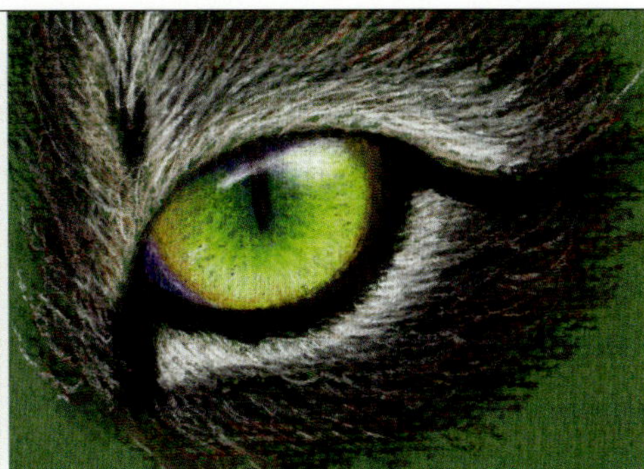

Colorless pencil blender

The colorless pencil blender has no pigment in it, but it moves the pigment in the drawing to get rid of texture. The surface becomes smooth and bright and the result is not as harsh as OMS blending. The pencil makes the surface waxy quickly and limits additional layering. Use this blender closer to the end of your drawing, unless you spray the artwork between layers. The main advantage to blending with the colorless blender is its nontoxic quality, greater control, and handling ease. The major disadvantage is the difficulty of working with it: you must apply a very heavy pencil pressure to achieve the desired effect, especially on textured paper, which is time-consuming and exhausting when working in large areas. While it is easy to give up and shade in crosshatching to move faster, such strokes may flatten out the form.

These pencils are necessary to smooth out the edges softly, especially in the light and around the highlights. The author's favorite pencil blender is Caran d'Ache full blender because it's 100% colorless, blends exceptionally well, and creates a barrier against UV light like a final spray. Other colorless blenders tend to have a slightly grey tone and offer no protection against the light.

Some things to keep in mind about colorless pencil blending:

- To blend colors effectively, you must use medium to heavy pencil pressure. If the blender hasn't made much difference in your drawing, it means that you either have not applied enough pigment to blend it well, or that you haven't applied enough pressure to the blender to produce results.
- It's impossible to blend colored pencils with paper stumps used for graphite and charcoal drawing. Never blend the colors with your fingers either!

Blending with white and off-white colored pencils

Very soft and light colored pencils such as Prismacolor premier light cream, sky blue, light peach, beige, and white can lighten up the surface considerably while burnishing it. This technique works best with the off-white colored pencils for blending edges around the highlights as well as lightening up an entire area. When working with very soft colored pencils, shading usually requires medium to very heavy pressure for it to work well. You won't be able to achieve the same results with harder colored pencils.

Effects of blending with light-colored pencils:

- Much lighter and more unified color
- Reduced chroma or color intensity
- Blended surface, especially around the highlights
- Subtle, dreamy effect

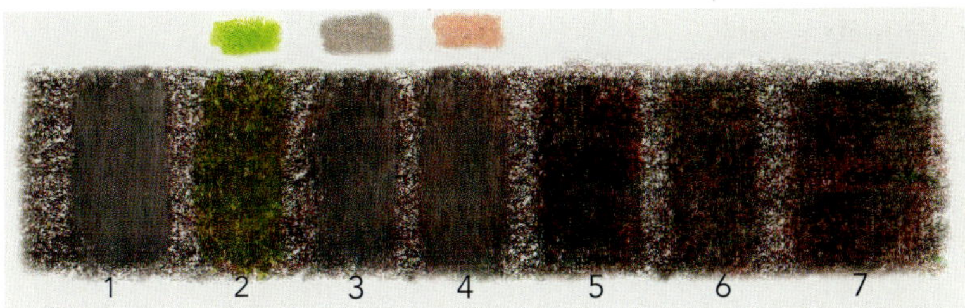

Here you see a summary of all these blending techniques used. The initial mix of black, dark red, and dark green is blended with 1. Prismacolor white, 2. Prismacolor chartreuse, 3. Prismacolor 20% cool grey, 4. Prismacolor light peach, 5. Caran d'Ache full blender, 6. Prismacolor colorless blender, and 7. Gamsol (solvent). Notice how similar the effect of Gamsol and Caran d-Ache full blender is. The same is true with off-white colored pencils.

Icarus Board blending

Artist-inventor Ester Roi does colored pencil blending with her invention—the Icarus Drawing Board, which is an electrically heated drawing board that helps blend the wax-based pigments while you draw. While it speeds up the entire drawing process, softens the edges, and burnishes the drawing, it doesn't work with every colored pencil. You can watch instructional videos to understand if it will work for you at www.icarusart.net.

Blending with a solvent to achieve rich darks

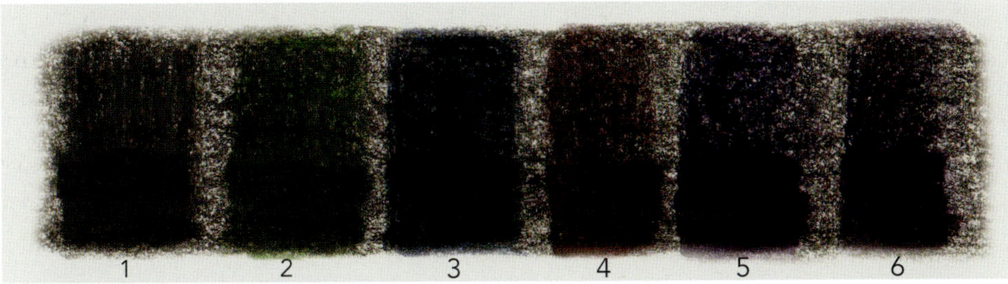

This image illustrates how you can make your backgrounds rich and colorful by using dark colored pencils over the initial black layer. Why do you need to have more color rather than just black? Black by itself doesn't exist. It's the absence of light. Even in high-contrast situations, light bounces off other objects to produce color in the dark. Pictures are often Photoshopped heavily and as a beginner you may not pay attention to subtle colors present in the black. In colored pencil drawing, pure black backgrounds look lifeless; as an artist you should avoid creating such drawings.

Here you see various color combinations produced when just one hue is applied over black and blended with a solvent. 1. Prismacolor Premier 90% warm grey, 2. Prismacolor dark green, 3. Prismacolor indigo blue, 4. Prismacolor black raspberry, 5. Prismacolor dioxazine purple hue, and 6. Prismacolor dioxazine purple hue mixed with dark brown over black. You can mix several colored pencils over black to get rich, colorful dark backgrounds. Experiment.

What is wax bloom?

Wax bloom happens naturally as an oxidation process of wax-based colored pencils. It often happens in warm and humid climates as well as in drawings with lots of burnished black colored pencil. If you have very soft, wax-based colored pencils, chances are you'll encounter wax bloom in your art once in a while when you start blending and burnishing the surface. Wax bloom looks like a white fog over your drawing, especially if you use lots of black, and may arise a few days later after the drawing is done.

To get rid of wax bloom:

- Wipe the drawing off with a clean, soft dry cloth, or even with your finger.
- Spray the drawing with a final fixative. Sometimes two to three light coats of professional spray are necessary. Always use professional-grade final fixative for dry media such as Grumbacher Final Fixative, Matte, for pastel, charcoal, and pencil.

To prevent wax bloom from appearing:

- Avoid the use of too much black (rather underpaint the area with dark markers or use a combination of dark colored pencils instead of black).
- Spray your drawing with a workable fixative between the layers.

STEP-BY-STEP INSTRUCTIONS

Blending with White, Off-White, Solvents and Colorless Blender

Materials: Koh-I-Noor Polycolor colored pencils and Prismacolor Premier colored pencils; Koh-I-Noor colored pencil paper, 114 lb.; kneaded eraser; Caran d'Ache full blender; Grumbacher fixatives, Sakura Pen-touch marker

Note: The names of the pencils used in the artist's work are given throughout this lesson. The Koh-I-Noor Polycolor pencil colors are named by numbers; all of the Koh-I-Noor pencils listed provide a Prismacolor substitution in parentheses. Please refer to the color chart to make your pencil color choices.

For this technique to work well, you must use very soft colored pencils in the background to blend them with a solvent. Harder colored pencils like Pablo or Koh-I-Noor Polycolor won't produce the results. You must use a very soft white colored pencil like Prismacolor Premier to blend in the light. The artist uses soft colored pencils in the background and mixes them with the harder ones when drawing the gummy bears.

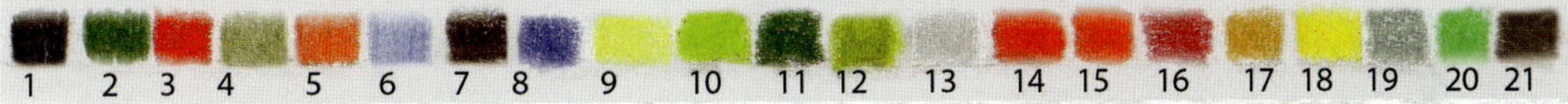

Color Chart: 1. Prismacolor Black 2. Koh-I-Noor 26 (or Prismacolor Grass Green) 3. Prismacolor Crimson Red 4. Koh-I-Noor 63 (or Prismacolor Kelp Green) 5. Koh-I-Noor 5 (or Prismacolor Orange) 6. Koh-I-Noor 57 (or Prismacolor Cloud Blue) 7. Koh-I-Noor 33 (or Prismacolor Dark Umber) 8. Koh-I-Noor 54 (or Prismacolor Ultramarine) 9. Prismacolor Yellow Chartreuse 10. Prismacolor Chartreuse 11. Koh-I-Noor 26 (or Prismacolor Dark Green) 12. Koh-I-Noor 62 (or Prismacolor Apple Green) 13. Prismacolor 20% Cool Grey 14. Koh-I-Noor 47 (or Prismacolor Crimson Red) 15. Koh-I-Noor 48 (or Prismacolor Poppy Red) 16. Koh-I-Noor 8 (or Prismacolor Pomegranate) 17. Prismacolor Yellow Ochre 18. Prismacolor Canary Yellow 19. Prismacolor Jade Green 20. Prismacolor True Green 21. Prismacolor 70% French Grey
Small amounts of other colors may have been used as well.

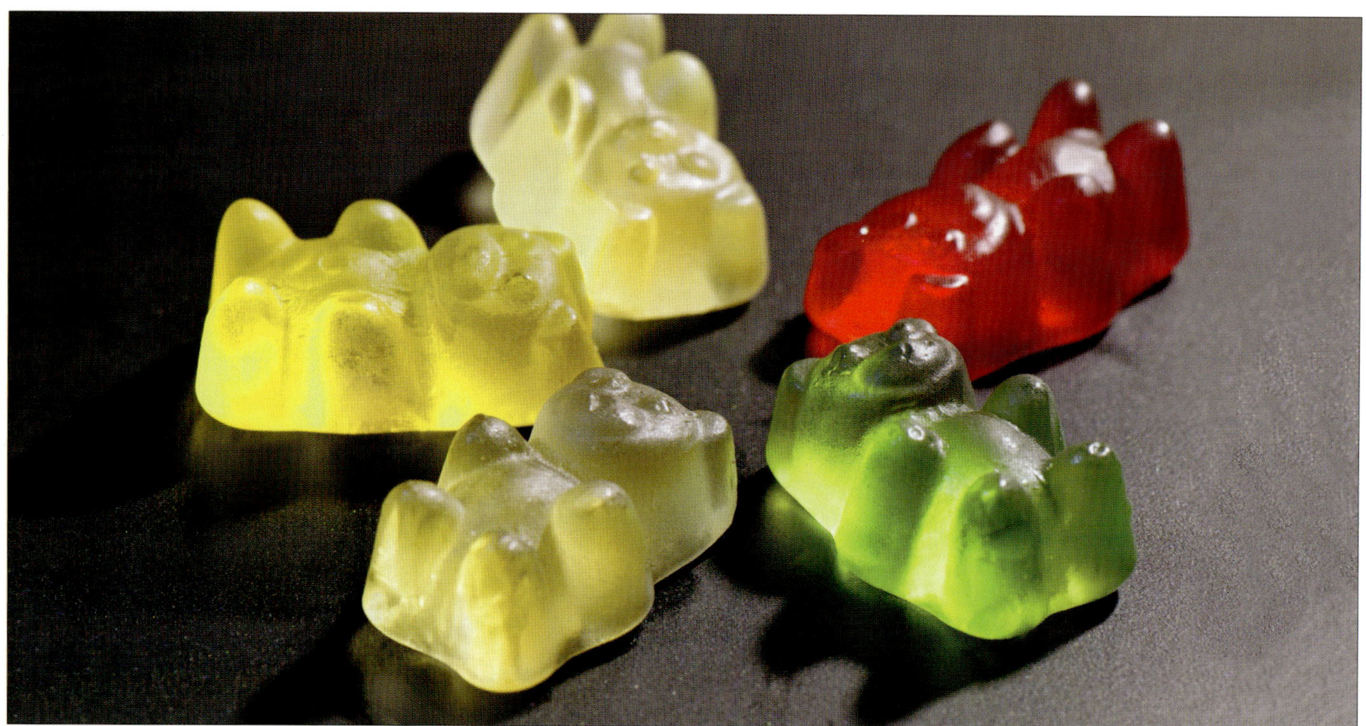

Before you begin coloring, let's analyze the light direction and the directional lines for each gummy bear that you should keep in mind while drawing. The light comes from the right and travels across the candy, producing long, dark shadows with fractions of colors reflected from the candy. To imitate the light direction you'll shade the background with varied tones instead of simply filling it in black.

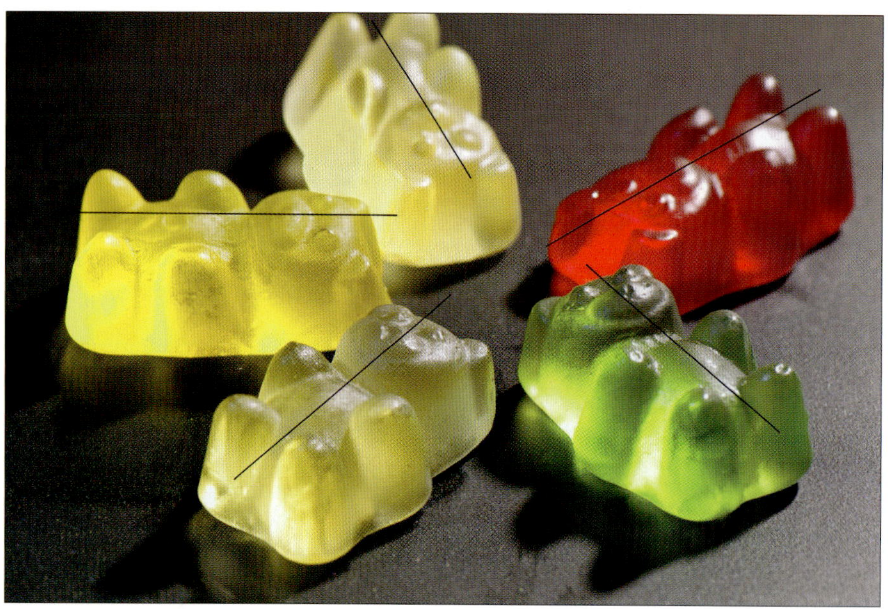

To simplify the image and to cut down on time in drawing it, you can draw one gummy bear instead of all five. Just pick your favorite! If you draw all the gummy bears, place a directional line for each one to rotate it in space correctly. Once you determine the direction, you can sketch out the outline for each bear keeping the lines parallel to that single directional line. It's similar to placing the bear in a box where legs, top, and bottom all line up in accordance with the directional line.

Step 1

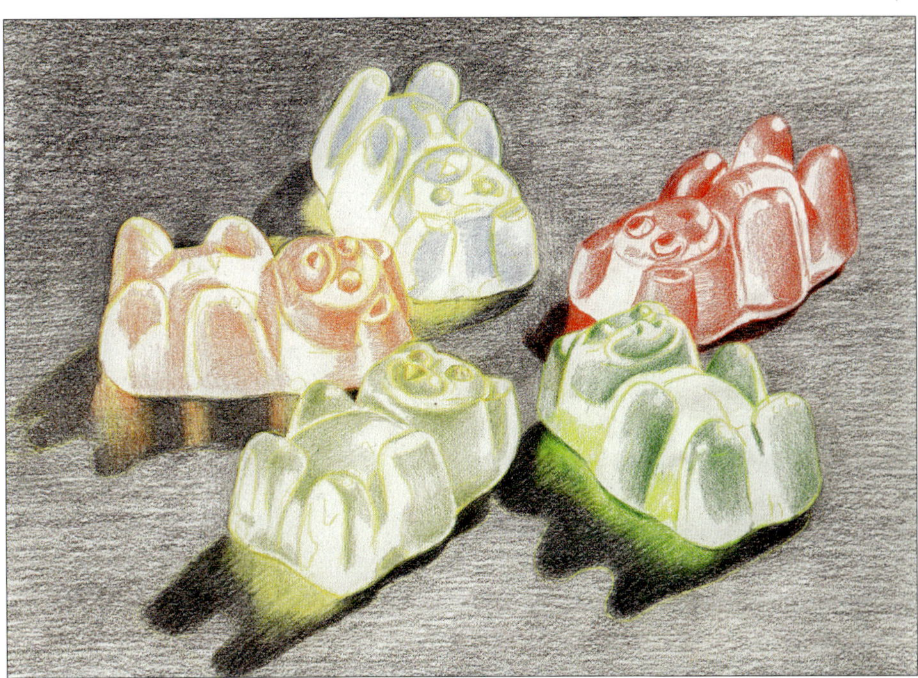

Because the bears are light in color, it's best to avoid sketching in graphite pencil on your drawing paper. Instead use a soft and light colored pencil to transfer the outlines onto drawing paper. Shade with a soft black pencil horizontally to fill in the background. Layer more color in the top left corner as well as in the cast shadows under the gummy bears, observing the specific shapes.

Where do you begin coloring the gummy bears? Focus on the deepest shadows of each bear. Shade the red bear with Prismacolor crimson red and the green bear with Prismacolor grass green or dark green, reflecting these colors into the cast shadow seen underneath each gummy.

Because the next three bears are quite similar in color, the artist decides to separate them by using three different light colored pencils on each candy: Koh-I-Noor 63 (or Prismacolor kelp green), Koh-I-Noor 5 (or Prismacolor orange), and Koh-I-Noor 57 (or Prismacolor cloud blue). You can pick your own base color and see how it affects further coloring.

Step 2

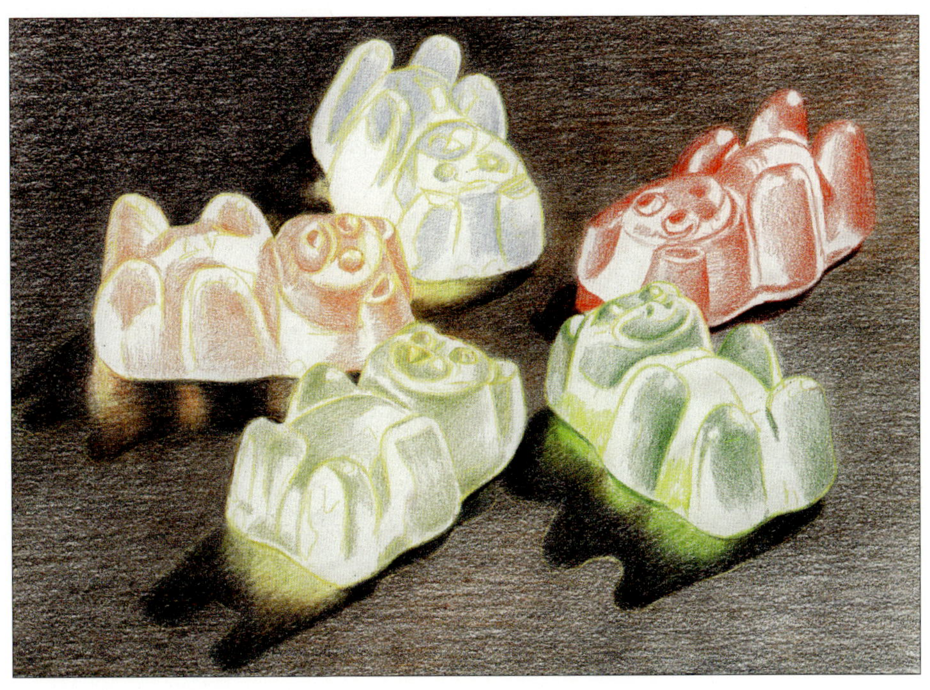

Add warm brown to the background. There is no need to pick the exact color the artist uses, rather train yourself to see the basic hue and color temperature in the black. The artist shades with a mix of Koh-I-Noor 33 (or Prismacolor dark umber), and Prismacolor orange. Make sure to shade all the colors right to the edge of the gummy bears to keep their form. Also overlap these colors over the edge in cast shadows for softness.

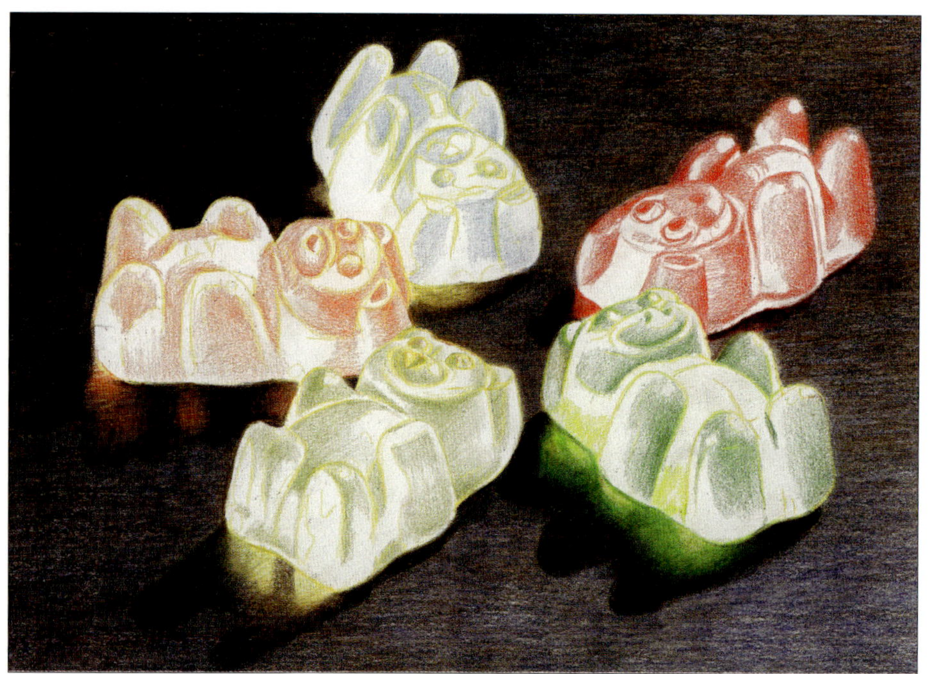

Step 3

For this project to work, you will need a solvent and a small clean synthetic brush. Do not use this brush for watercolor or other painting methods. Keep it for colored pencil blending only. You also must use professional-grade soft, wax-based colored pencils for this technique to work well. Dip the brush into the solvent, tap it against a paper towel, and start painting with it over your image. Start somewhere in the corner to warm up and get a feel for the technique. Immediately, you will see how the pencils darken and blend. It takes some practice to learn how much solvent to use on a drawing. Use a little rather than a lot. Be conservative in your application because it can dissolve the pigment completely or dilute the colors to a great extent, making them muddy. Solvents work best on dark to medium colors, meaning that the blending of light colors doesn't show as much, although it is okay to apply the solvent on them as well.

Don't paint with a solvent over the bears because they haven't been colored yet. Do paint over the cast shadows to blend them with the background. Do not touch the paper with your hands while it's still wet; allow it to dry completely once finished blending! Once the image is dry, you are ready to shade with even more color. It is much easier to apply the pigment this time, since the subsequent shading becomes smooth and effortless after the solvent's application, especially if you work on textured paper.

With a light pencil pressure, apply blue (Prismacolor ultramarine) on the bottom right side of the background to make it cooler. Re-apply the same colors (black, dark umber, orange) if you see that the background is not as dark as you need it to be after the blending.

Tip: Colored pencils are semitransparent when shaded one over another, which allows for the creation of sophisticated hues. Professional artists always use at least two colors in any given area to create beautiful color. **Transparency** is the ability of any given color to show through if applied with a light or medium pencil pressure. To vary the transparency of the color, vary your pencil pressure.

Step 4

Apply Prismacolor yellow ochre to all three bears. Overlap over the base color you already have and extend it over to fill in the middle tones of each bear.

Don't forget to rotate your pencils and shade in varied directions to create volume in every part of the body such as the stomach and arms.

Reserve more white paper than you think you need for the highlights. You can always come back and shade over the white, but you can't restore the white 100 percent by erasing.

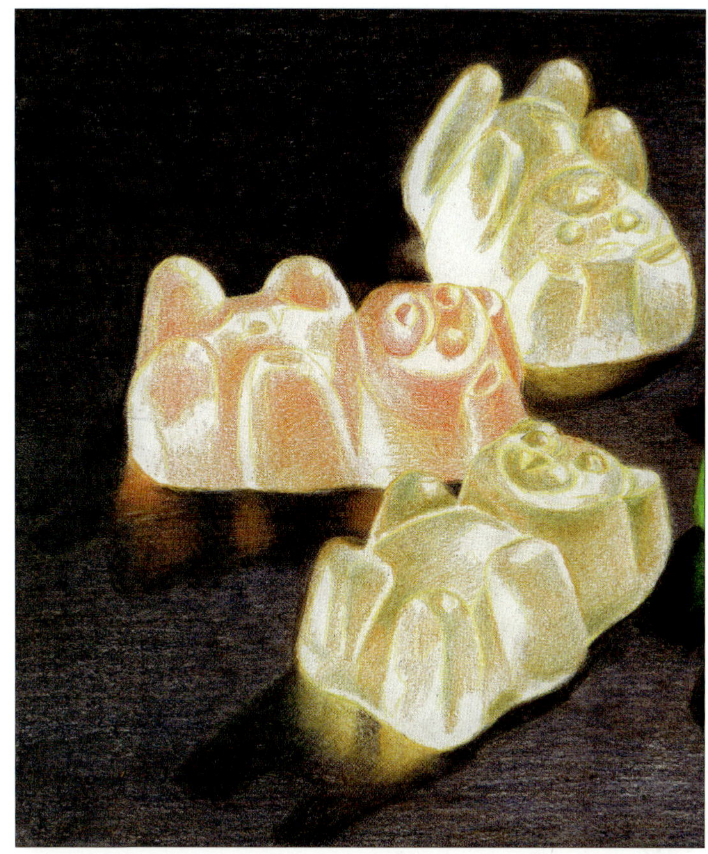

Step 5

Shade with canary yellow in the three bears, shading around the highlights. Canary yellow will give you warmer yellow while yellow chartreuse will give you cooler yellow (light, greenish yellow).

Come back to the light green gummy bear and shade with Prismacolor chartreuse and jade green. Jade green gives a cooler hue that blends well with 20% cool grey—these are the colors that you see around the cool highlights in this gummy bear. Apply Prismacolor white with a very heavy pressure around these cool highlights to blend the edges even more.

Use Prismacolor true green on the right side of the head and ear to create a reflected light cast from the green bear next to it. Blend everything with the colorless blender, if needed.

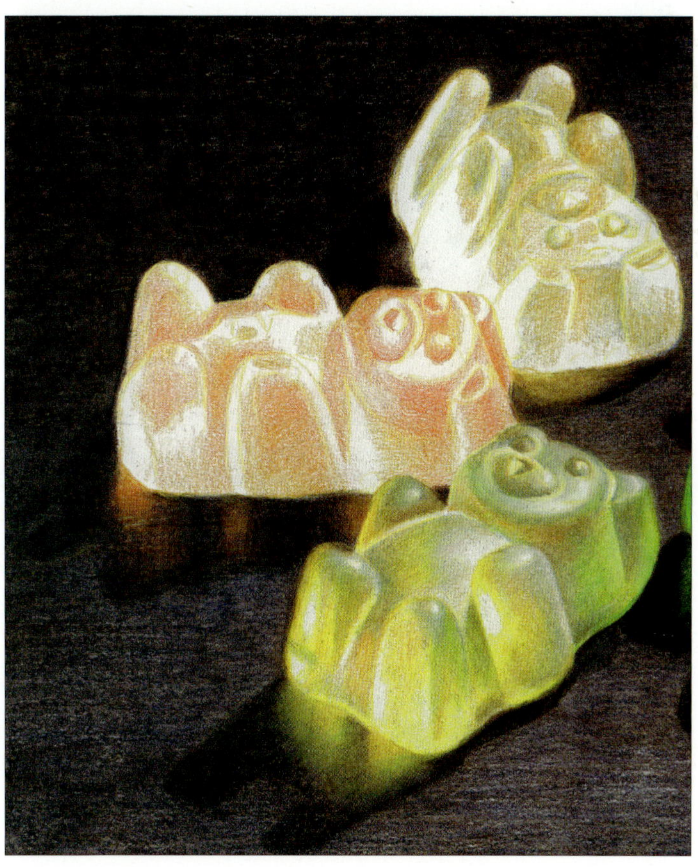

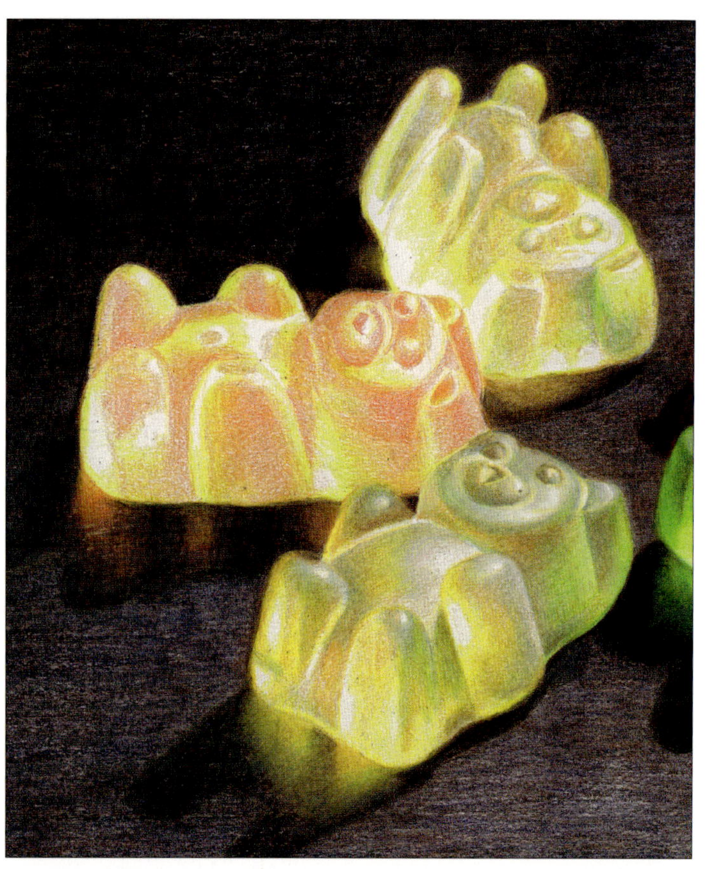

Step 6

You can color the top two bears simultaneously with Prismacolor canary yellow and a touch of Prismacolor yellow chartreuse and orange. Blend the colors with the colorless blender, following the form (going in the direction that shows the roundness of the head and arms). Shade with white around the highlights.

The top bear remains much softer with no visible details or hard edges. All three bears have the same colors in essence but because the initial base hue differs, they vary in color quite a bit.

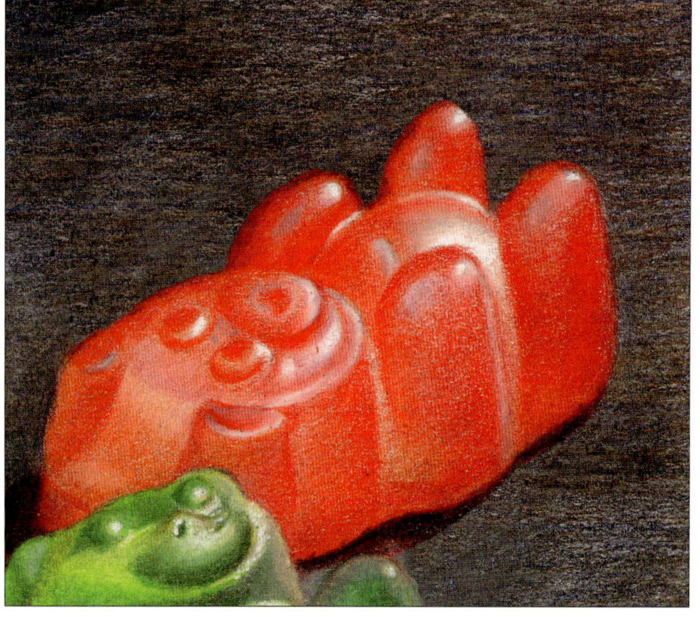

Step 7

Here you work the same way from dark to light applying more color over the first layer. In the first layer you established the shadows, and now you create transitions between these darks and highlights. Avoid coloring the highlights.

Colors used here are Koh-I-Noor 47 (or Prismacolor crimson red), Koh-I-Noor 48 (or Prismacolor poppy red), Koh-I-Noor 8 (or Prismacolor pomegranate), and fractions of orange.

Blend with white around the highlights and use the colorless blender to blend other hues in this gummy bear. Gummy bears need to have soft edges and blended colors to appear candy-like.

Step 8

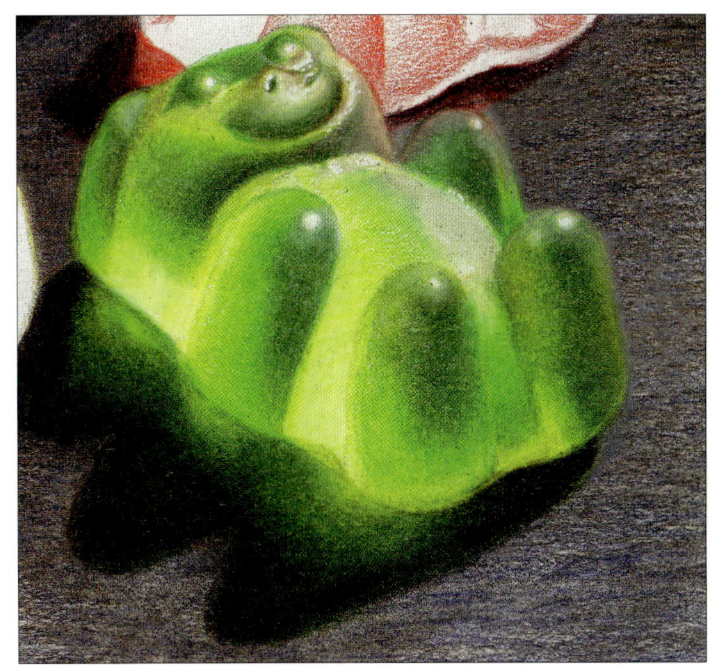

Start to work on the green bear. In the first layer you established the darkest shadows. Now you will create subtle transitions between these shadows and the highlights. So you don't color the highlights by accident, outline them with a light color like yellow chartreuse and shade around them first. Colors used are Prismacolor chartreuse, dark green, apple green (or Koh-I-Noor 62), grass green (or Koh-I-Noor 26), and yellow chartreuse. Prismacolor poppy red is used to deepen the darkest areas on the green bear. To shade the edges around the highlights, use Prismacolor 20% cool grey, cloud blue, and white. This combination of colors blends and softens the spaces around the lights. Use the Sakura pen to place a few tiny highlights on the face of the green gummy bear.

Step 9

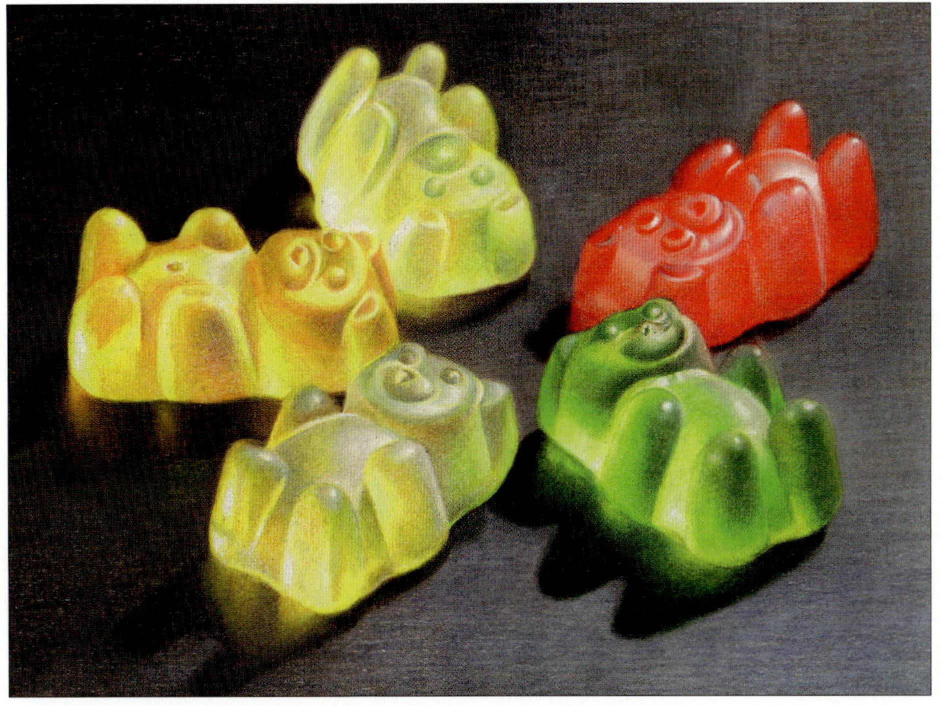

Spray the image lightly, let it dry, and work on the background one more time to unify the colors. With heavy pencil pressure, apply Prismacolor 20% cool grey in the light (right side) and 70% French grey in the dark (left side). Adjust pencil pressure to create soft transitions between the tones. You'll see how light grey blends and lightens up the colors, while French grey unifies the darks. This way you've created a very colorful background that's also grey and doesn't compete in brightness with the subject itself. Spray with a final fixative outdoors. Done!

As you can see, we've applied all the blending techniques in this one picture of the gummy bears: Gamsol in the background, colorless blender, and white and off-white colored pencils.

Chapter 6

Color Theory in Practice: Color Harmony

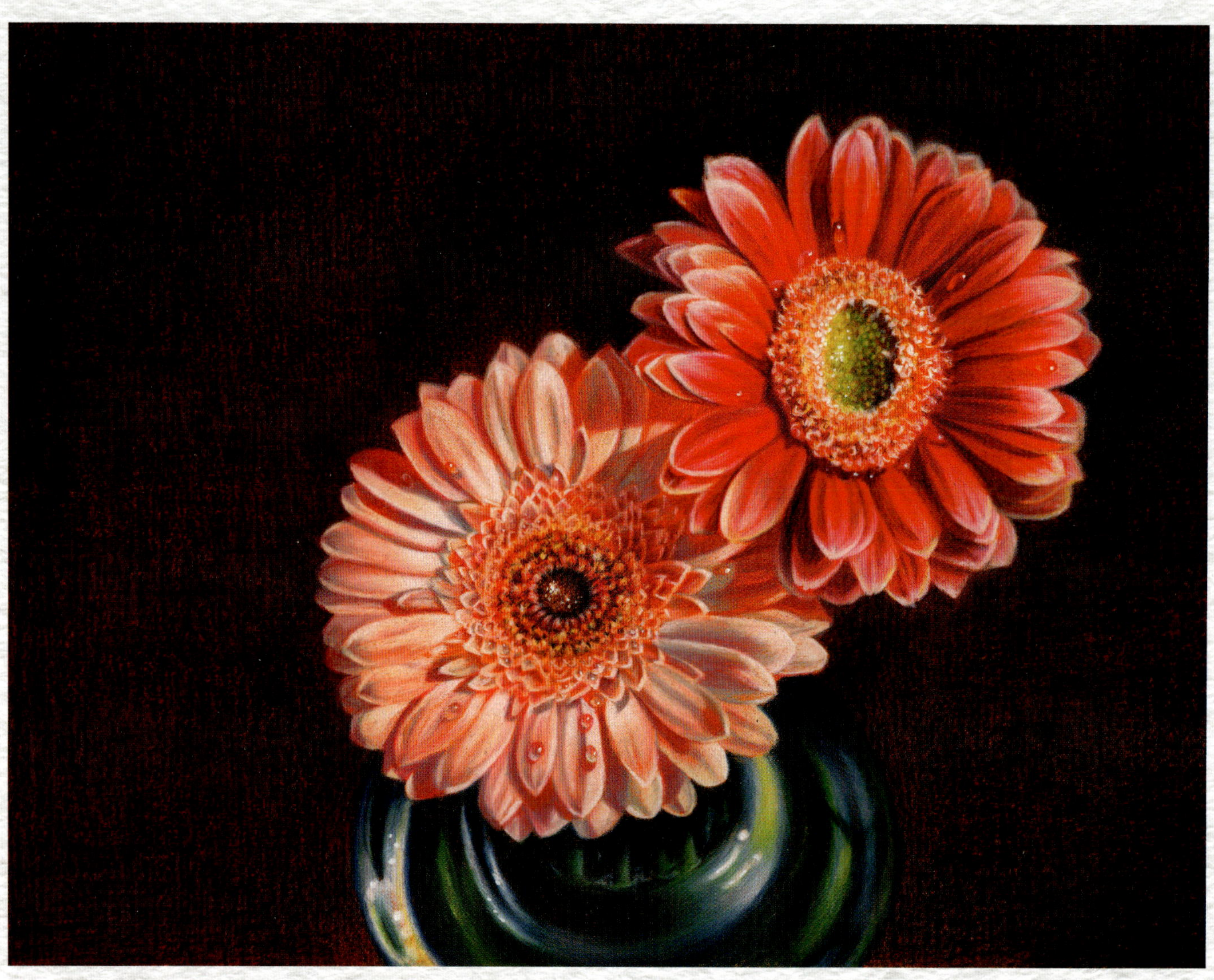

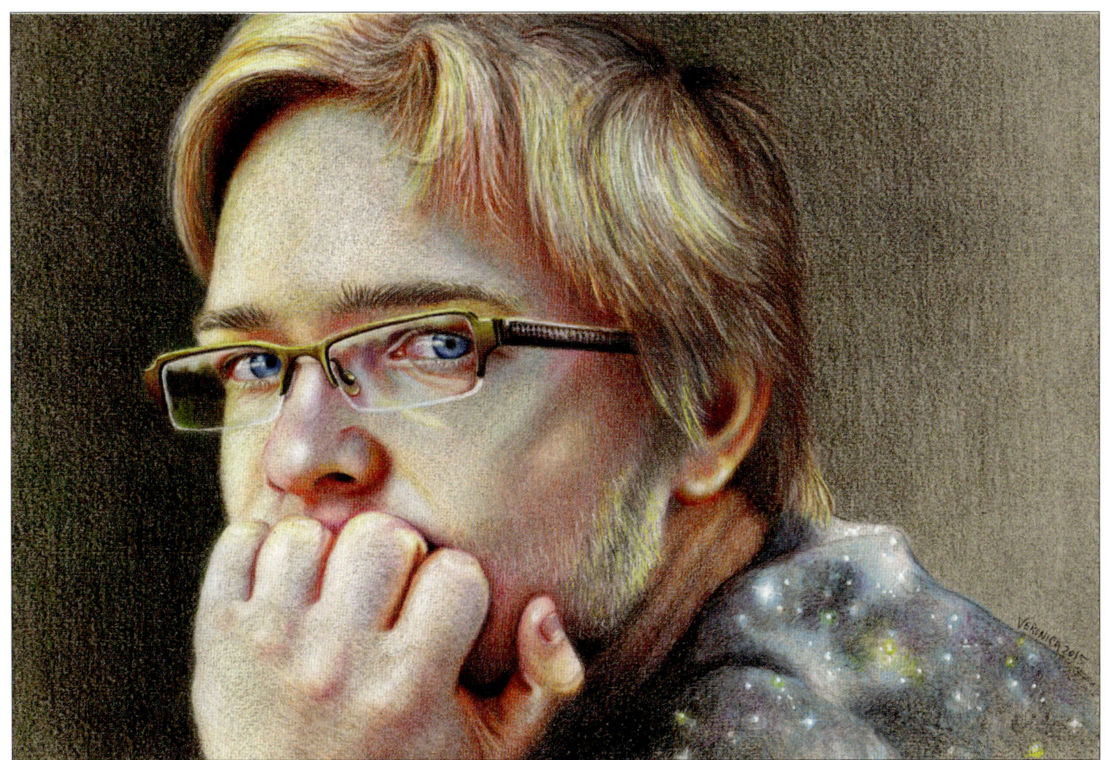

Are you having a problem seeing color in black, white, or grey? Are you confused by all the colors in your colored pencil box and don't know how to pick the right ones for the job? Is color mixing a nightmare for you? In this chapter you'll see a different approach to coloring that goes beyond general information and triads of colors. In this chapter you'll discover how to use a few colored pencils efficiently, getting great results. You'll also get introduced to a different color system—the Munsell Color System, which will help you think of color three-dimensionally, using three terms all artists keep in mind while drawing: hue, chroma, and value. These three parameters are always at play as artists keep layering color to define form, alternating between so many hues we see in time-lapse videos that fascinate us. Normally it looks like an unexplained process that goes on inside the artist's head, but we're going to demystify it by studying these fundamentals here.

To begin, buy the Artist's Color Wheel at an art supply store and become aware of basic definitions and triads of colors and harmonies. This information is widely available online, but the color wheel helps you study theory visually, which is so important to us as artists!

Hue is the color, such as red, yellow, or blue.

Chroma is the purity of a color, such as pure red or pure blue.

Local color is the natural color of an object as it appears in normal light (red of the tomato or green of the grass). Beginners often see only local colors in objects rather than the color combinations that happen due to various lighting conditions.

Value is the lightness or darkness of a color. Every color has its own value range, going from the darkest dark to the lightest light. Darker colors have a wider value range as opposed to lighter ones.

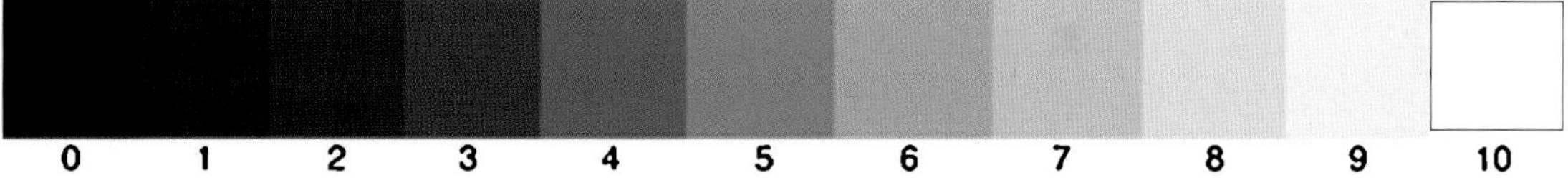

Color intensity is the saturation and purity of a color.

Neutralized color is the color with less intensity that is either greyed down or mixed with its complement.

Primary colors are red, blue, and yellow. They cannot be re-created by mixing with other colors. All other colors are derived from these three colors. These are the brightest colors.

Secondary colors are orange, violet, and green. The colors in this triad are created by mixing two primary colors. They are evenly spaced out around the color wheel and create a very vibrant drawing. In practice, it's best to have a single dominant color and use the other two to a lesser degree to create a visual harmony in art. These are less bright than the primary colors.

Complements are the colors that are across from each other on the color wheel, such as yellow and violet, green and red, blue and orange.

Split complements are tertiary colors that are paired up with one primary color, for instance red, blue-green, yellow-green *or* yellow, blue-violet, red-violet.

PRIMARY	COMPLEMENT
Red	Green (yellow + blue)
Yellow	Violet (red + blue)
Blue	Orange (red + yellow)
SECONDARY	**COMPLEMENT**
Yellow-Green	Red-Violet (both have blue)
Blue-Green	Red-Orange (both have yellow)
Blue-Violet	Yellow Orange (both have red)

Tertiary colors are created by mixing primary and secondary colors. These are even less intense than primaries and complements.

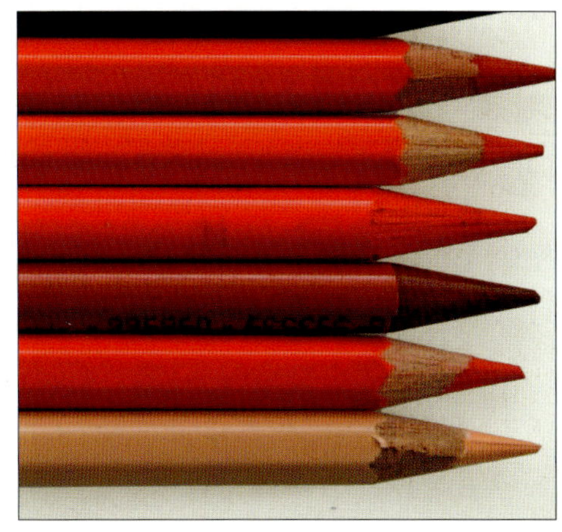
Monochromatic reds

Monochromatic harmonies are colors composed of variations of the same hue but different in value and intensity. For example, red is a hue, and its monochromatic harmonies are reds, pinks, and maroons.

Complementary harmonies are colors that are opposite each other on the color wheel. Complements intensify each other.

Analogous Colors are the colors that are adjacent to each other on the color wheel. They harmonize well.

Tint is the addition of white to a pure hue to create lighter variations of color. Because colored pencils are premixed, you simply find a lighter version of the pure color in your box. A series of tints of the pure color vary in intensity from full strength to palest tint.

Shade is the addition of black to a pure hue to create darker variations of color. Unlike paint, colored pencils are premixed, so you find darker versions of a color, or bring the color down to darkness by layering black or the complement.

Key color is the dominant color in a color scheme.

Color transparency is the ability of any given color to show through if applied with a light or medium pencil pressure.

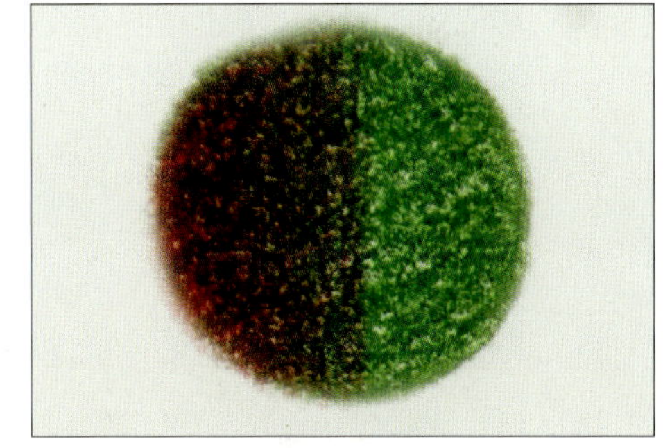
Example of color transparency

Because colors are semitransparent, you are able to lighten or darken the colors in progression building the correct value and color intensity.

All of this information is easy to understand visually by moving the slider on the Artist's Color Wheel and learning about the color harmonies. You don't have to remember the entire theory at once. You can also plan out your color schemes using the color wheel or observe the colors you see in your reference picture and see if you can enhance the color harmony already present in your reference. For example, take a single triad of colors, make one key color the strongest and the other two less color intense. When you plan your color schemes in terms of shading, it doesn't mean that you shade with just three colored pencils matching three colors of the triad. Every colored pencil has variations in value and color temperature from one pure color.

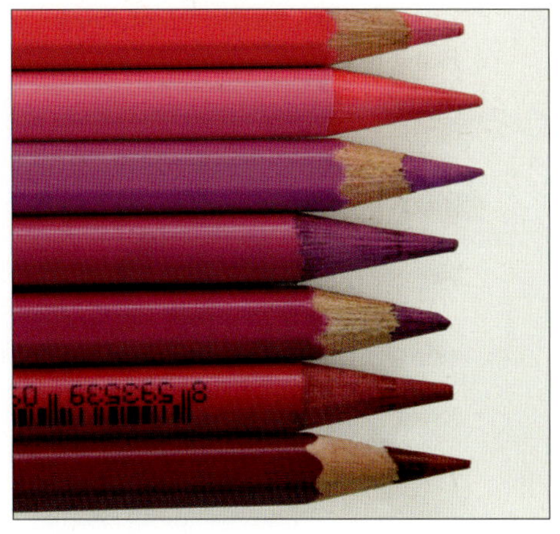
Monochromatic pinks

The colored pencils on the right are all variations of cool red. They differ in value and chroma.

THE MUNSELL COLOR SYSTEM

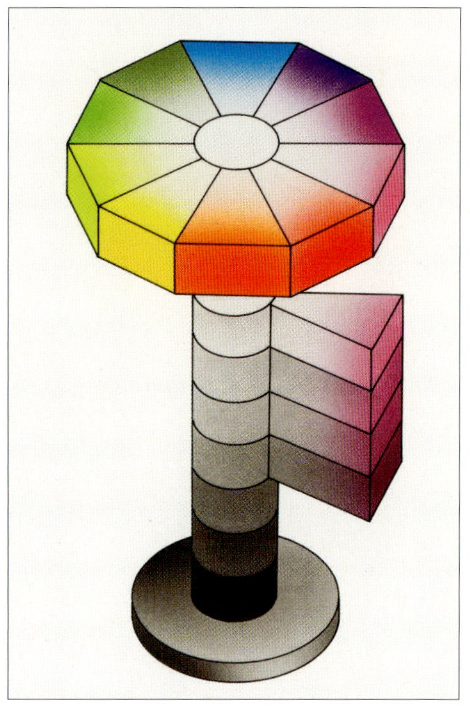

Getty image

Created by Albert H. Munsell, the Munsell Color System helps you visualize color relationships in three dimensions, which leads to a much better understanding of color because all artists think of color in three dimensions, which include hue (color itself), chroma (color purity) and value (relative lightness/darkness). These three parameters affect the artist's color choices and layering at all times. If you research the system further in the *Munsell Book of Color*, you don't need to dwell on its complex numbers, rather understand the basic concept that connects all three elements in one chart. This information is also important to artists who plan on becoming representational painters because color mixing with few pigments becomes key in painting.

Put the value scale (lightness/darkness) column in the center. It ranges from pure black (value 0) at the bottom to pure white (value 10). Five principal colors sit in the circle around the Value column: Red, Yellow, Green, Blue and Purple. The five intermediate hues are: Yellow-Red, Red-Purple, Purple-Blue, Blue-Green, and Green-Yellow.

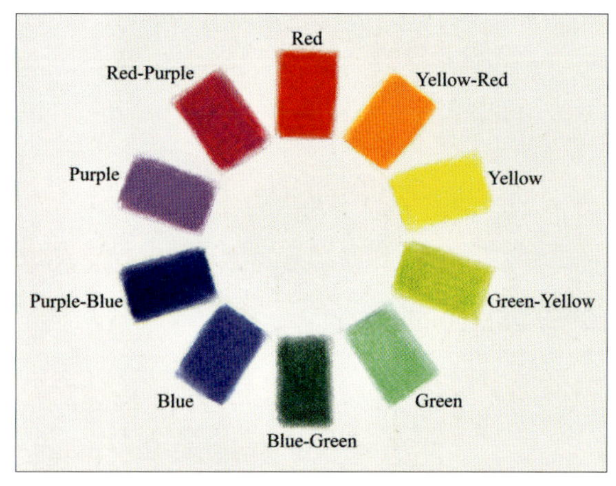

Color Circle

Chroma or the color "purity" scale for each principal hue goes outward on the value scale radially, and becomes stronger located further away from the value column and greyer when close to it. The closer a color to the value column the lower the chroma is, getting greyed down incrementally until it reaches neutral grey in the value scale. The strongest or the purest colors sit on the outer edge of each color, being farthest away from the value column. Different colors have different maximal chroma. For example, deep reds would have a much wider chroma range as opposed to light purples. That's why you see varied lengths of the color strings.

Unlike in oil painting, your colored pencils come premixed. The more colored pencils you've got in your box, the more variations or (strings) of the same hue you have. The Munsell Color System gives you an understanding of how to pick your colored pencils based on chroma (purity), value (lightness/darkness), and hue.

These are examples of Munsell color swatches where you can see how colors relate to each other in terms of value and chroma. The left column shows the greyed down colors, while the farthest on the right has the strongest colors. If you have large boxes of colored pencils, you have a wide variety of colored pencils that differ in value, chroma, and hue. But if you have limited resources, you can achieve similar results by mixing and layering colors.

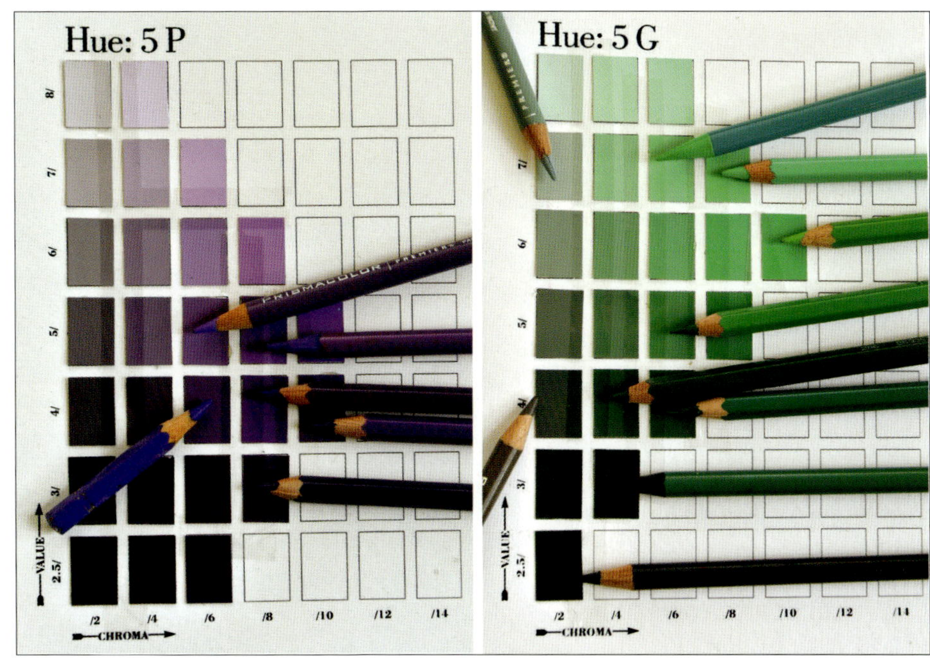

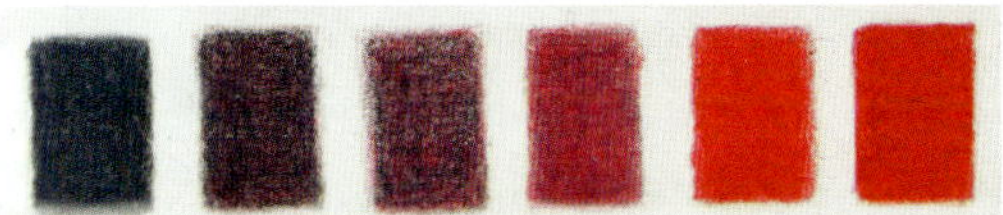

This is a string of greyed down red. The artist uses single red to shade all color chips and then greys every chip down with a grey colored pencil, adjusting pencil pressure gradually. You can see how different red looks going from grey on the left to the highest chroma red on the right.

Be aware that colored pencils don't mix to grey, therefore companies have developed their strings of greys that are often sold as open stock and are not included in boxes. It means that you grey down the colors with either greys or the complements (see next chapter for more information on grey colored pencils).

How to analyze color and pick colored pencils

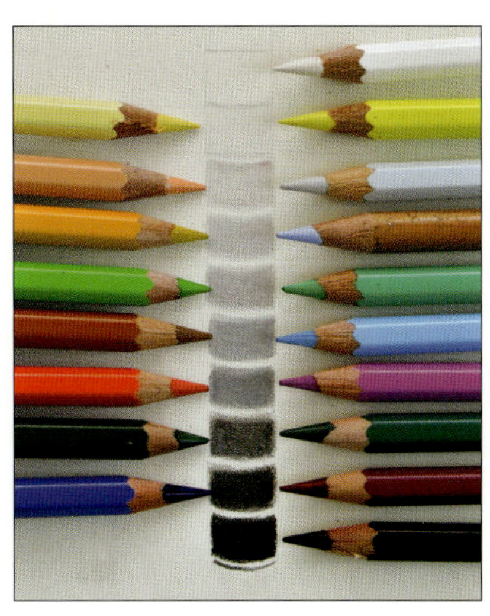

First, learn to see the colors in terms of value. In the reference image you can see how colored pencils vary in lightness and darkness. Now let's imagine you were to draw red poppies. Begin your color analysis by determining the basic hue, which is red. Then you determine how light or dark that red is (value) and look at your colored pencils to see that specific value in color. Determine how bright or dull it is (chroma). The last step is to take a note of color temperature (warm or cool), bringing you to very few choices left in picking reds.

Colored pencil is a very forgiving medium because you can develop both value and chroma in subsequent layers, unlike in paint where you mix color matching for all three parameters at once to make a single stroke. Just like all the other demonstrations shown in this book, you can start developing your first layer in a single color seen in the deepest shadow (or a form shadow) that you see on the object. You shade with this single color with varied pencil pressure throughout the drawing. By layering one color at a time throughout your picture you learn to control hue, value, and chroma gradually, as opposed to layering all the colors from start to finish in a given area. The second approach would create "isolated" finished areas that lack unity or consistency in the drawing.

Tools to help you read color and value in your pictures

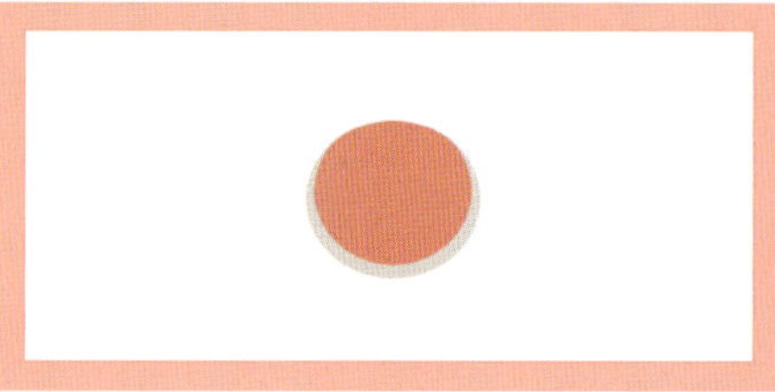

- If you find it difficult to read color in any given area of your picture, this simple tool might help you see the color and value by isolating the color from its "surroundings." Take a white, 1 x 1-inch card and punch a hole in the middle. Now place this card against the image and look at a color seen through the dot.

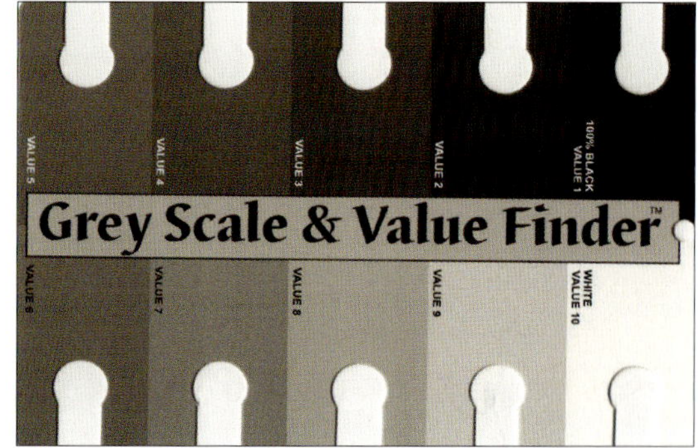

- The value scale helps you read the values in your image. Just place it against the area in your reference and/or next to colored pencils to determine the correct value.
- To read the values, you can also convert your drawing to black and white in Photoshop and compare it to the greyscale photo to see the difference. Usually, beginners don't push the shadows dark enough to create volume, or they color the highlights while they must stay white (if you draw on white paper).
- Squint, looking at your art from a distance. This method forces you to focus on value rather than color, so you will be able to see the big shapes working rather than focus on details.

Color temperature

Color temperature greatly contributes to color harmony in your art. In general, yellows and reds are associated with the sun and thus are warm colors, while blues and greens are associated with water and are cool hues. The earth tones—browns and greys—are considered to be neutral. Each hue, however, has a warm and a cool counterpart.

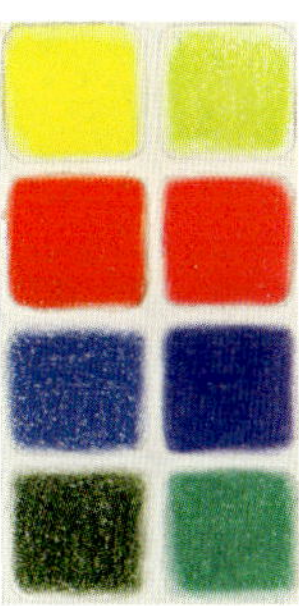

This image gives you an example of warm and cool hues present in every basic category of colors. The left column consists of hues that lean toward the yellow and thus are warm colors, and the right column has cool colors that lean toward the blue. It takes some time to "see" the shifts in color temperature, but the more you practice the easier it gets.

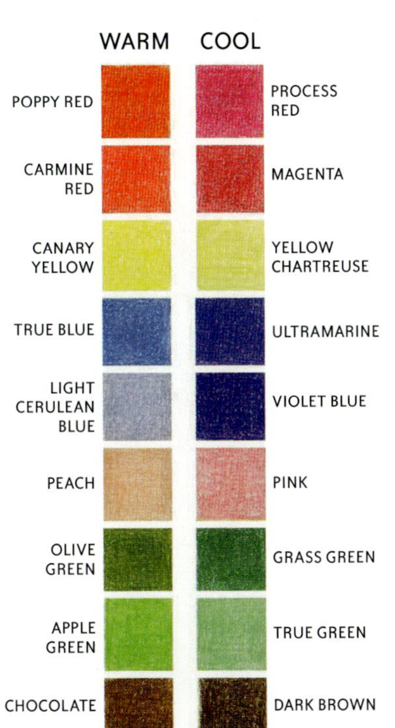

In this image you can see some warm and cool colors in the Prismacolor premier line. Although browns are considered neutral, chocolate leans toward yellow and dark brown may appear slightly cooler next to other colors.

Action Step: Take your colored pencils out and begin grouping them by either color temperature, or value, or hue.

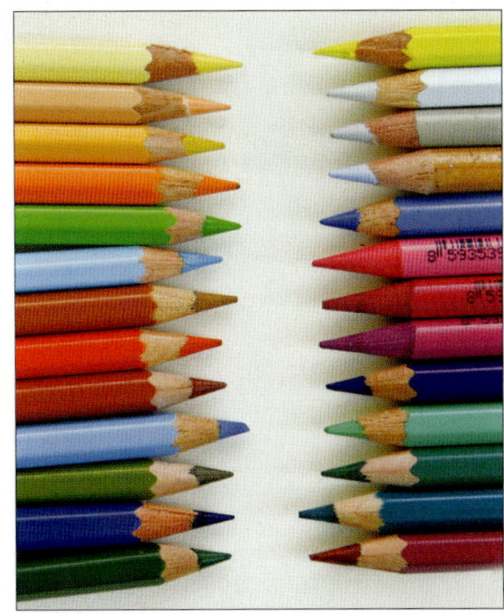

Advancing and receding colors

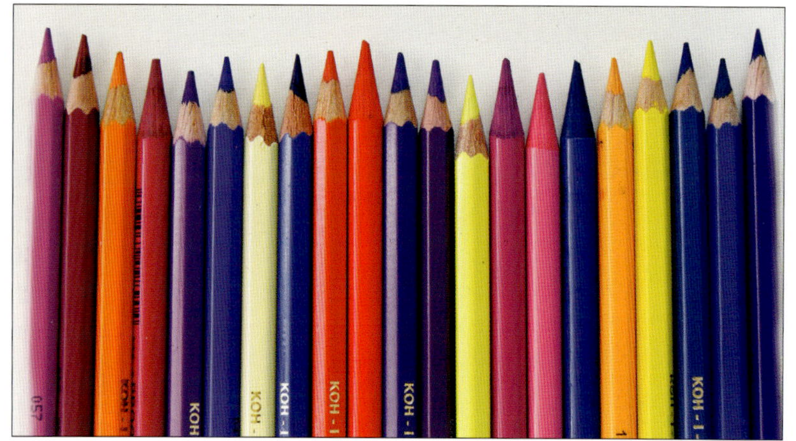

You can also analyze color in your reference based on light and time of the day. If it's a sunny day you'll see warmer colors in the light; if it's a grey day you'll see cooler, greyer, and more neutral colors.

Why do you need to know this? Cooler colors recede in space; for instance, mountains have pale, bluish-purplish tones. Warmer colors—yellows, reds, and warm browns—advance into the foreground. Picking the right colored pencil helps you to create a believable atmosphere and to control the color of your focal point, which should be the maximum chroma. Take a look at the reference image to see what colors advance and recede. Squint to see the difference in color intensity between the hues.

Color in black and white

Pure black and white don't exist in nature, they represent the color's value with no actual color in it. There are lots of colors in areas or objects that look either black or white. It happens because every surface absorbs and reflects the surrounding colors. You don't see subtle shifts in color in heavily Photoshopped images, while images that are more true to nature always have "hints" of color that you as an artist must learn to see in reflected light and shadows to bring into your drawing. If you don't have enough color in the shadows, black and white, your pictures will look lifeless.

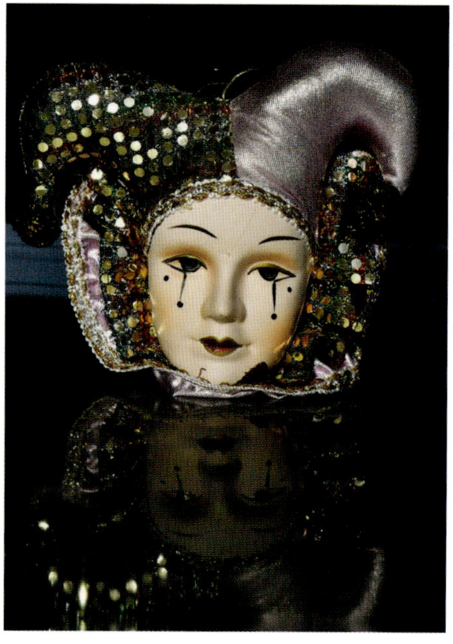

In this picture the background appears black. However, if you look closely, you notice a lot of blue in the black. The reflection at the bottom also has lots of colors that reflect the colors from the object but are of much lower chroma.

This reference photo shows colors registering in the white.

The David's eye has no direct light source and the colors look washed out. However, you can still see shifts in value and color temperature even in such lighting conditions. Remember that colors absorb and reflect the neighboring hues, so you find these colors in your object as low chroma hues. This plaster cast takes a lot of color from the surrounding wooden box.

1. Neutral grey with a hint of blue. 2. Reddish white 3. Cool blue white 4. Warm, yellowish white

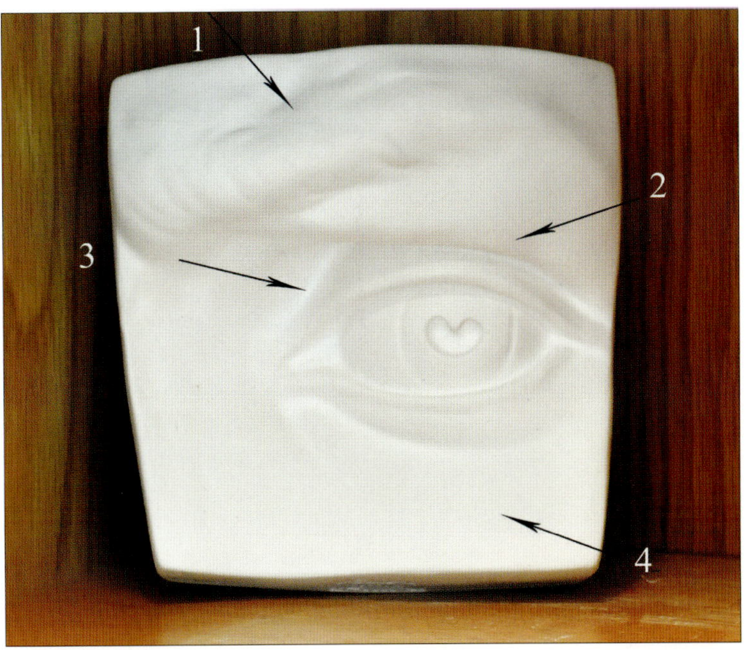

In this picture we observe a still life under a direct, electric light source, which means that the lights are much warmer and the shadows are either neutral or cool. We can see deep red in the background, which varies in value from the darkest on the left to the medium dark on the right.

1. Warm, yellowish white 2. Light, low chroma red reflecting into the white paper 3. Neutral grey from shadow and a cool, bluish white in reflected light next to it.

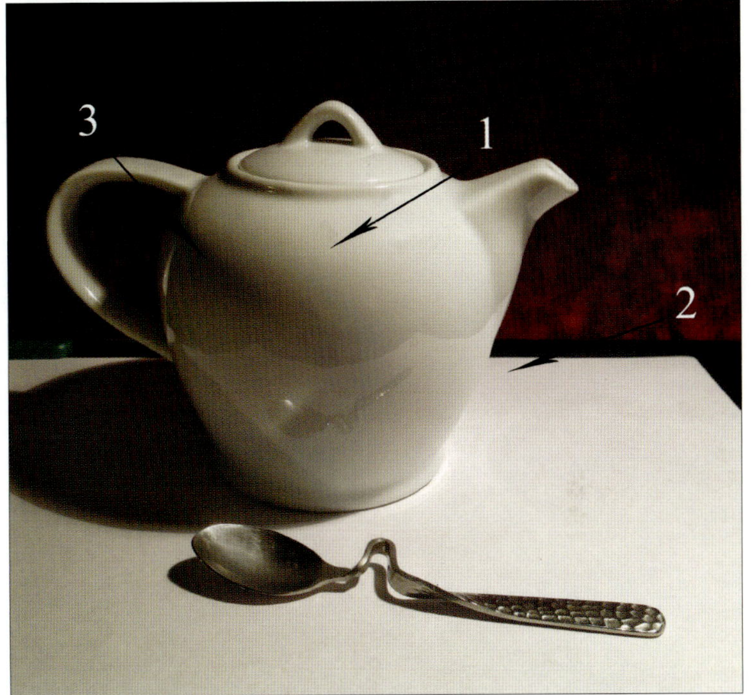

COLOR HARMONY

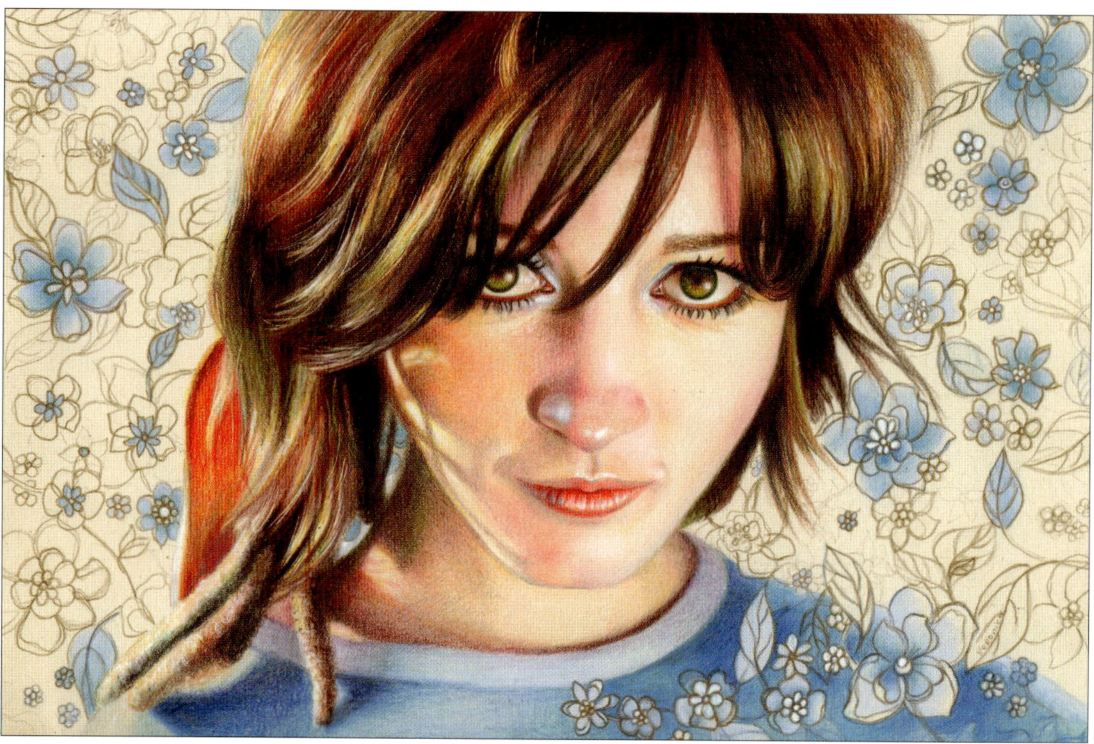

In this drawing the key color is light blue. You can see this color throughout the image in the flowers, shirt, eyelids, upper lip, nose, and even in the hair.

How to achieve color harmony

- Most beautiful paintings have a reserved color palette as opposed to a wide range of colors. By overlapping the same colors in different ways, you can make your drawing look very colorful without using a high number of colored pencils.
- Avoid drawing with primary colors in the background as they are the strongest colors and will jump forward, competing with your center of interest—unless it's your plan to break the rules!
- Avoid drawing with bright color in the shadows; focus your color intensity on the light. Remember that the color in the shadows can't be stronger than the color in the light.
- Prioritize value over color. Determine value and find color of that value.
- Have a single dominant color of a triad and use the other two to a lesser degree to create a visual harmony in your art.

- You can use just a few colored pencils efficiently, getting great results by varying pencil pressure as well as by applying one color at a time throughout your artwork. Instead of jumping between all the colors, trying to finish one section, you should pick one color and apply it throughout your artwork, varying the pencil pressure. This method gives you color unity on autopilot.

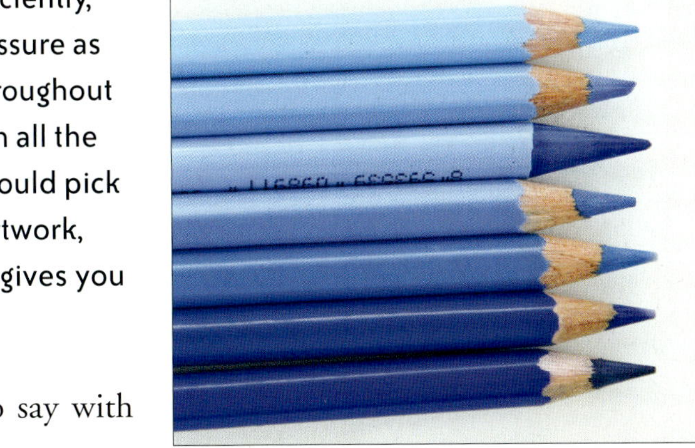

Color is emotion. Decide what you want to say with your artwork.

Action Step: Practice your understanding of hue, value, and chroma. The image above shows monochromatic colors of blue. Create a monochromatic drawing utilizing most of your colored pencils based on your favorite hue.

Try to harmonize your colors. This image shows the analogous colors in the Munsell color wheel, for example, yellow-red—yellow—green-yellow, etc.

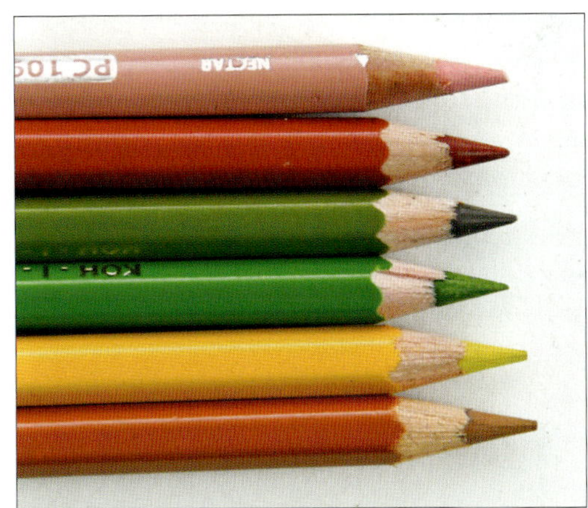

Find your dark, low-chroma colors that you can use in your dark backgrounds later on.

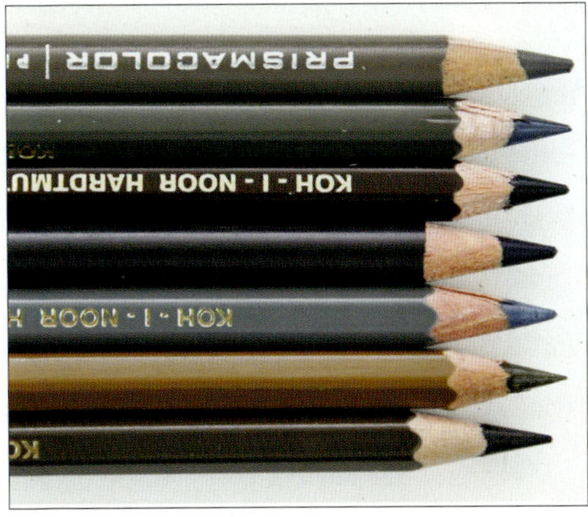

Color relativity

A color is relative to the light itself. The same blue object will look warm and light during a sunny day and very dark or even black in the evening. It will look less color intense in the shadow and more intense in the light. The artificial light creates a totally different perception of color.

A color is also relative to the surroundings and varies in relationship to its neighbor. Colors usually read much brighter if they are placed next to a neutral hue or grey.

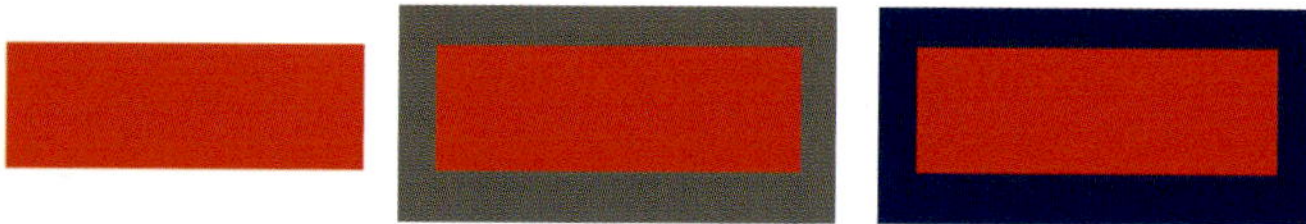

In this example we see high chroma red set against white, grey, and deep blue. You can see that the same color reads differently set against three backgrounds.

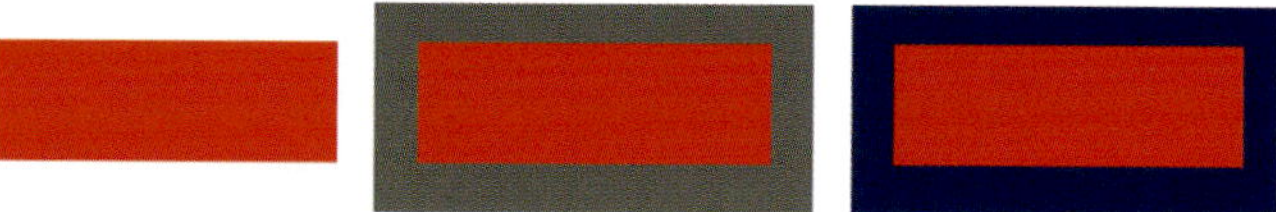

This much lower chroma pink is set against the same white, grey, and deep blue backgrounds.

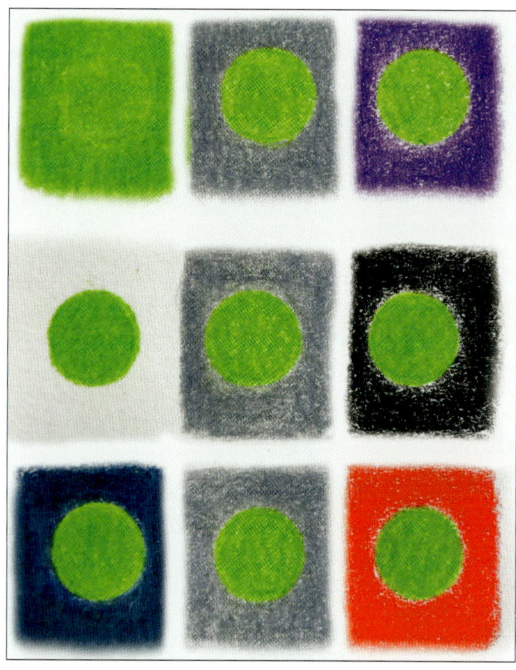

These color chips show how a single color of warm, light green plays with our visual perception and shifts in chroma, value, and hue in green although the same colored pencil is used in all chips. The middle vertical column shows green set against a neutral background. Cover the surrounding chips with your hand to see the difference.

In the top row green appears much stronger set against purple and looks washed out on the left side. In the second row we can observe shifts in value. Colors appear lighter set against the black and darker set against the light background. In the bottom row we may experience change in the purity of green, depending on the surrounding color. (This information is based on *The New Munsell® Student Color Set*, Second Edition.)

Colors appear brighter in warm light and duller or "bluer" in a cool light. Diffused light makes the colors look less intense and greys them down.

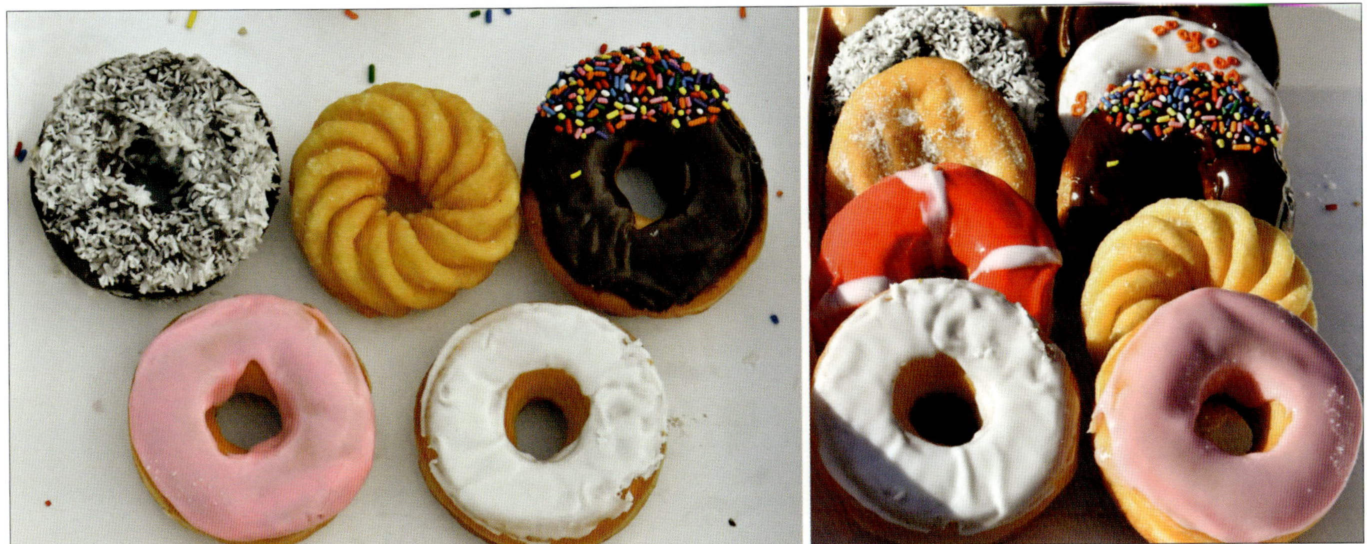

We can see this in the images of the donuts. The picture on the left shows the diffused light situation, while the picture on the right shows the donuts under a bright sunlight. Notice how deep, colorful, and cool the shadows are on the right. All donuts shift toward yellow in the light. So despite having various local colors, all of them have fractions of warm yellow. They are also brighter than the donuts on the left and appear to have more volume.

All colors reflect themselves into lesser light and the shadows receive reflected colors. In the image of donuts on the right, you can see how colors reflect one into another on the sides of the donuts.

What it all means for you is that you look for fractions of other colors in the local color you normally see, including black and white subjects. You also begin to analyze general lighting conditions, and whether your subjects are under warm or cool light.

In nature you can rarely find the purest, strongest color. It means that you can reserve your strongest colors for sharp edges and accents in a focal point.

Avoid placing all your pure colors next to each other. They will lose their color intensity and compete with each other.

STEP-BY-STEP INSTRUCTIONS

Creating Color Harmony on Colored Paper

Materials: Prismacolor Premier colored pencils, unless noted in color chart; large sheet of Canson Colorline paper in clementine, 92 lb.; kneaded eraser; Caran d'Ache full blender; Gamsol with a small brush; Grumbacher fixatives; Sakura Pen-touch marker, extra fine point

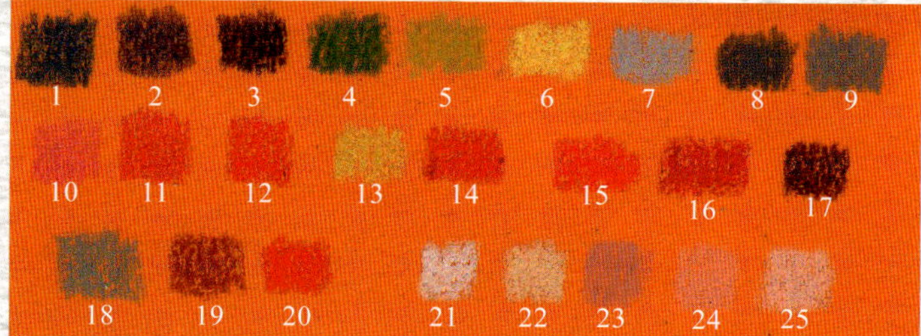

Color Chart: Please pick your colors based on the reference color chart. Most brands have similar colors, only their names differ.

1. Polychromos Bluish Turquoise 2. Caran d'Ache Pablo Ultramarine 3. Dark Umber 4. Grass Green 5. Luminance Olive Yellow (or Prismacolor Apple Green or Lime Peel) 6. Yellow Chartreuse 7. Luminance Light Blue (or Prismacolor Cloud Blue) 8. 70% Cool Grey 9. 30% Warm Grey 10. Pablo Purple 11. Pablo Carmine 12. Permanent Red 13. Canary Yellow 14. Crimson Red 15. Carmine Red 16. Pomegranate 17. Black Raspberry 18. Jade Green 19. Henna 20. Permanent Red 21. White 22. Light Peach 23. Nectar 24. Peach 25. Eggshell
Small amounts of other colors may have been used as well.

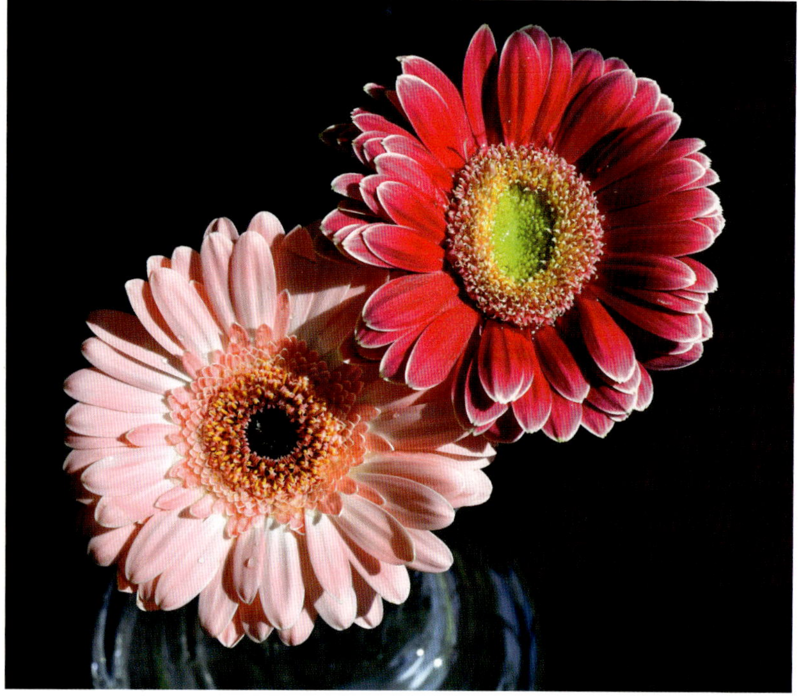

In the reference picture the background looks pitch black, which wasn't the case in reality. It was low-chroma, value 3 red. Therefore, you'll see the artist coloring the background in accordance with her actual reference. You can certainly go with much deeper reds to increase contrast, but don't use a single black for that.

This image was designed to harmonize well in color Red–Red-Purple (Munsell color).

To simplify this rather complex, time-consuming demonstration, feel free to draw a single flower instead of the two flowers.

How to pick colored paper based on your image

Often beginning students choose the local color of the background as their paper's color. The result is dull because they wind up shading with the same color as their paper. The approach to color must be different. Try to pick colored paper that is fairly close to the middle tone (value 5), has natural vibrancy, and complements your basic local color that you see throughout your reference image. Colored pencils "react" to vibrant colored papers and even if you burnish the surface, you still see the difference in color. Another advantage to drawing on colored paper is speed. Layering goes much faster when working on vibrant colored papers because you already have an initial color block in.

Be bold and discover how your colored pencils react to colored paper. Never begin working on a large piece without a preliminary test of your colors. Test colors on a scrap piece or on the other side of colored paper. As you practice, you'll see how some colored pencils look much stronger and appear to have higher chroma on toned paper, while others remain weak in chroma.

A word of caution about shading on colored paper because most colored papers have some texture in them. It takes some trial and error to find colored papers with vibrant hues and minimal texture. Strathmore Artagain toned drawing papers and Canson Colorline papers have fairly smooth surfaces with great color variety. You might also wish to explore other options in Facebook® groups dedicated to colored pencil drawing.

Step 1 **Step 2**

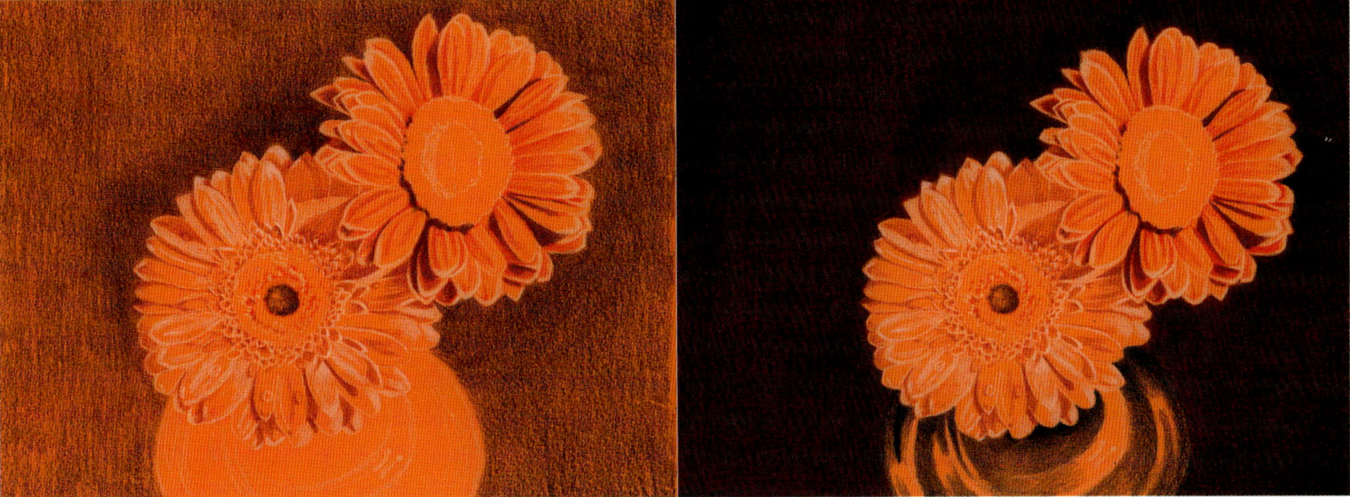

Step 1

Block in the background in dark umber, black raspberry, and a touch of black (because Prismacolor black gives a lot of wax bloom, the artist barely uses it here). Map out the petals by placing lights with either eggshell (warm white) or white (cool white), and marking the deepest reds with pomegranate in the red flower and henna in the pink flower. Add black raspberry into the deepest shadows in the red flower.

Step 2

Continue blocking in the background by shading with sharp pencils, filling in the grooves to create smooth layering. Increase your pencil pressure as you go. The artist shades the background with black raspberry and dark umber because the background was actually low-chroma, value 3 red, not black as you see in the reference picture. Feel free to experiment and add your choice of dark, low-chroma colors into the background. You can add 90% grey, dark green, or dark blue. Usually one area in the background looks darker than the other because the light passes through the still life. Therefore, don't shade everything uniformly: find variations in value and color.

The artist shades with Polychromos bluish turquoise and Caran d'Ache Pablo ultramarine to map out the darkest curving shapes in the vase (you can replace these colors with Prismacolor indigo blue). Make sure not to make these dark areas in the vase too linear. They must wrap around and rotate in a circle in space. Add some bluish turquoise to the background sparingly and see how it cools down the previously applied colors.

Step 3

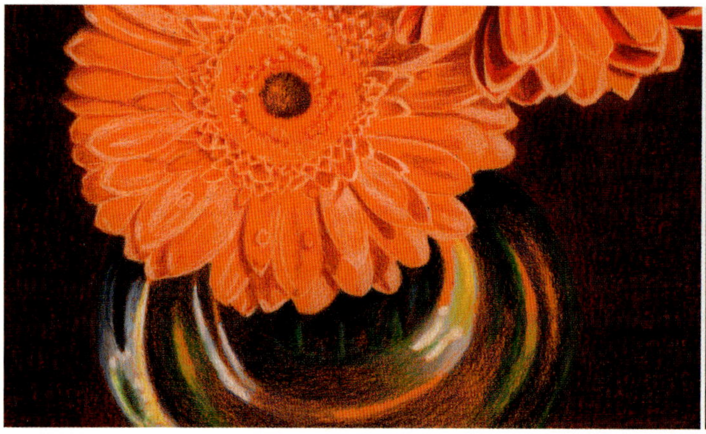

Step 4

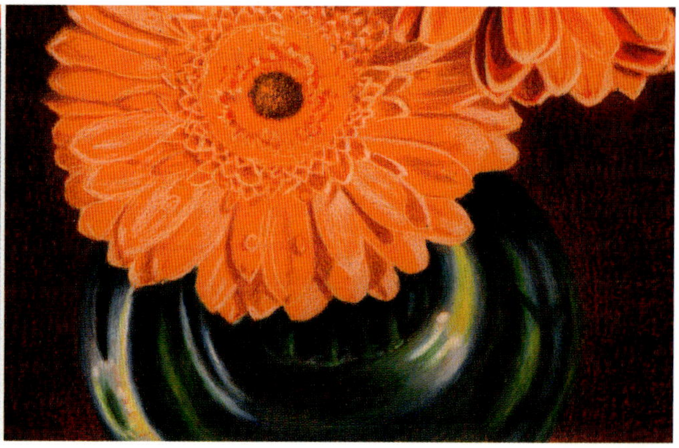

Step 3

Continue working on the vase. Mark the strongest highlights in white with heavy pressure. After that you begin to create transitions between this strongest white and the deepest shadows you made in Step 2. Add grass green to the curves and overlap it over the previously applied bluish turquoise. Grass green makes a nice transition between the deep shadow into lighter values (tones).

With heavy pressure, add Luminance olive yellow (or Prismacolor apple green) and Luminance light blue (or Prismacolor cloud blue) in the light around the white—it creates smooth transitions in the light. Overlap the colors. The paper's color still shows through.

Step 4

Here we are going to burnish all the colors in the vase by applying heavy pressure and then using Gamsol if needed. (If you work on a rather textured surface you blend with a solvent; but if the paper is smooth, blending happens via heavy pressure layering and blending with the full blender.)

In essence you go for a second round in layering with the same colors, but increase your pencil pressure and overlapping so much so that the colors begin to blend on their own. Don't apply Gamsol if you have little pigment and paper still shows through. Apply lots of color, so you have enough pigment to blend it well. Let it dry. The outer edges of the vase should blend into the background nicely. If your background looks different, you can blend it with a solvent too.

Once it is dry you can blend the edges around the highlights in the vase even more, using white or light blue colored pencil. (Any light color will blend the pencils with heavy pressure. Just pay attention to color temperature to see if it is warm or cool and pick the pencils accordingly.) You can also grey down slightly the light areas that appear blue. Light grey colored pencil appears as a low-chroma blue on this paper.

Step 5

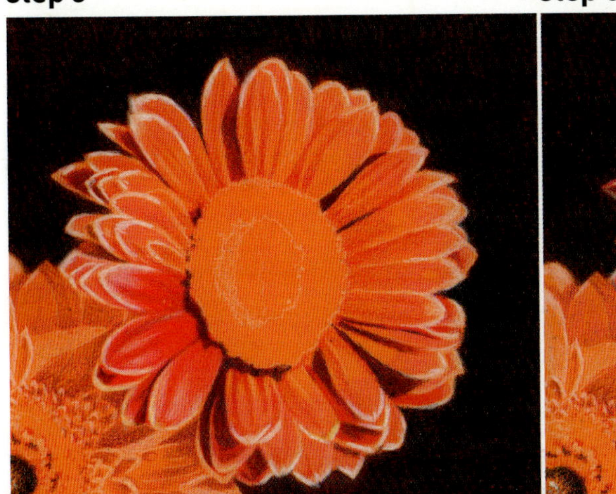

Step 6

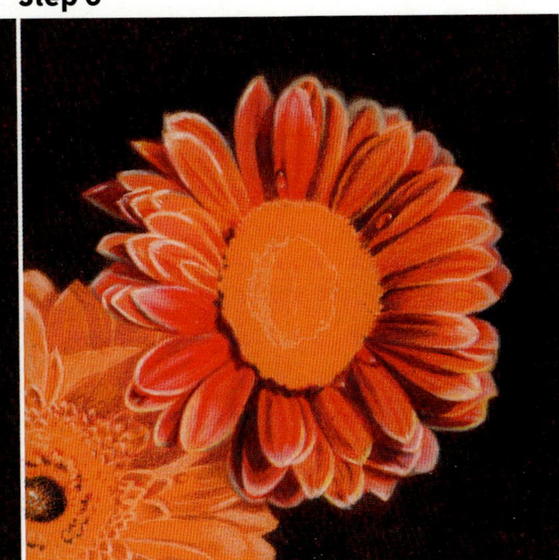

Step 5

In the following steps let's focus on the purple-red flower, which has cool red hues. Define the white edges with a sharp point of a soft, white colored pencil.

Work on middle tones in varied pressure, shading with Prismacolor carmine red and Pablo purple (a lighter value of Prismacolor carmine red). This marks a transition between the shadows and the whites you already have.

Step 6

In this step you enhance the curvature of each petal with subtle transitions between the values seen in cool reds. The artist shades with Prismacolor pomegranate and strengthens shadows with a mix of permanent red, crimson red, and black raspberry (the same black raspberry was used in the background).

White is a cool color. The artist ads a touch of yellow over white to make some white edges in the petals to appear a bit warmer.

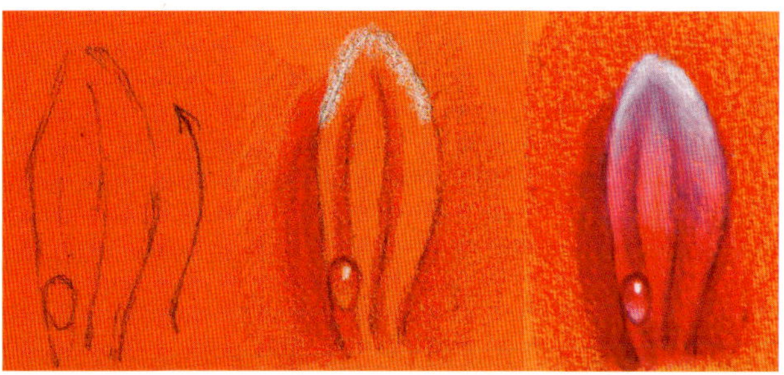

In this simplified diagram you see how you can approach drawing every petal. First, determine its curvature/direction. Next, mark the brightest lights and the darkest darks. Lastly, create transitions between these two notes.

Step 7 **Step 8**

Step 7

In this step you finalize the shading of petals, blending them with the full blender and Prismacolor white on the edges. White lightens up the tips of the red petals making them appear cooler and pinker when overlapped over the cool red.

The artist works on the center of the flower by shading lightly with Prismacolor black raspberry for the deepest shadow; with Luminance olive yellow (and shading in tiny circles with Prismacolor grass green in the shadow); and with Prismacolor eggshell (light, warm white) in the light. Apply these colors in tiny, soft circular strokes.

Step 8

Here you work on details in the oval center, developing stronger contrast. Unlike in the shading of petals with short and soft strokes, you change your strokes to definite, circular, and uneven curves in Prismacolor white and eggshell. It creates texture in the center.

Use grass green and black raspberry to draw tiny circles in the shadow side of the green center (right). Add yellow chartreuse on the left side to brighten up the light green more.

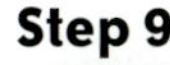

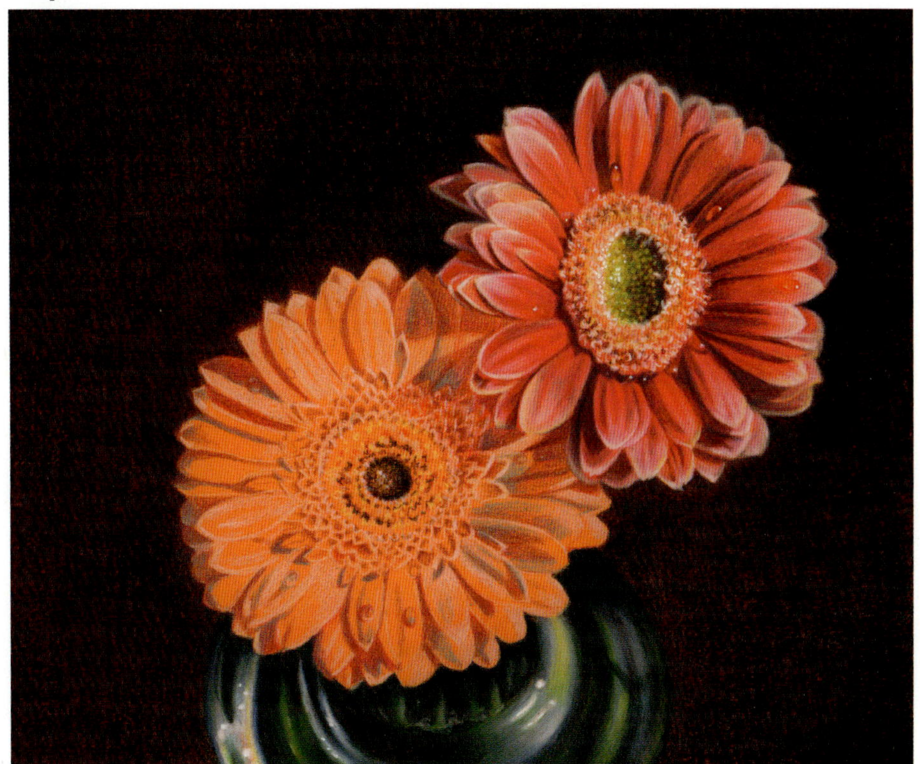

Step 9

Next you develop the texture in the light elliptical shape going around the red flower's center. You create texture with uneven, short strokes by shading around the little white curves with a mix of carmine red and canary yellow on the right side and with black raspberry on the left side. As you develop your drawing, constantly refer to the reference picture to pick up on details and colors you can add here. Notice that the artist repeats shading with the same colors in different parts of the drawing.

Add Prismacolor canary yellow or yellow chartreuse in the light side of the green center (on the left) and touch up the brightest lights with the Sakura pen. Don't make too many highlights with this pen because you want your lights to have a punch, limiting them to very few. You can also brighten up the highlights in the vase the same way, if needed. If the surface becomes too waxy and you can't make adjustments to the petals or center, spray the red flower with a fixative, covering the other flower with a piece of paper.

Now begin working on the light pink flower by following these steps:

1. For the center, fill in the circle with dark umber. Pay attention to a change in values: the outer rim is darker than the very center. Place a few white dots in the center with a Sakura pen.
2. For the tiny petals around the brown center, make very short strokes going out radially away from the center with dark umber, white, canary yellow, and light peach. For that, sharpen your pencils and map out the tiny petals: outline them with either light peach or eggshell. Fill in the deepest shadows of every tiny petal with Prismacolor henna.
3. Place the deepest shadows in the largest petals with a mix of henna and jade green (jade green is very similar to Prismacolor 30% warm grey in value, only a bit greener). Shade with permanent red lightly in the shadow area cast from the red flower (right side of the pink flower underneath the red flower).

Step 10

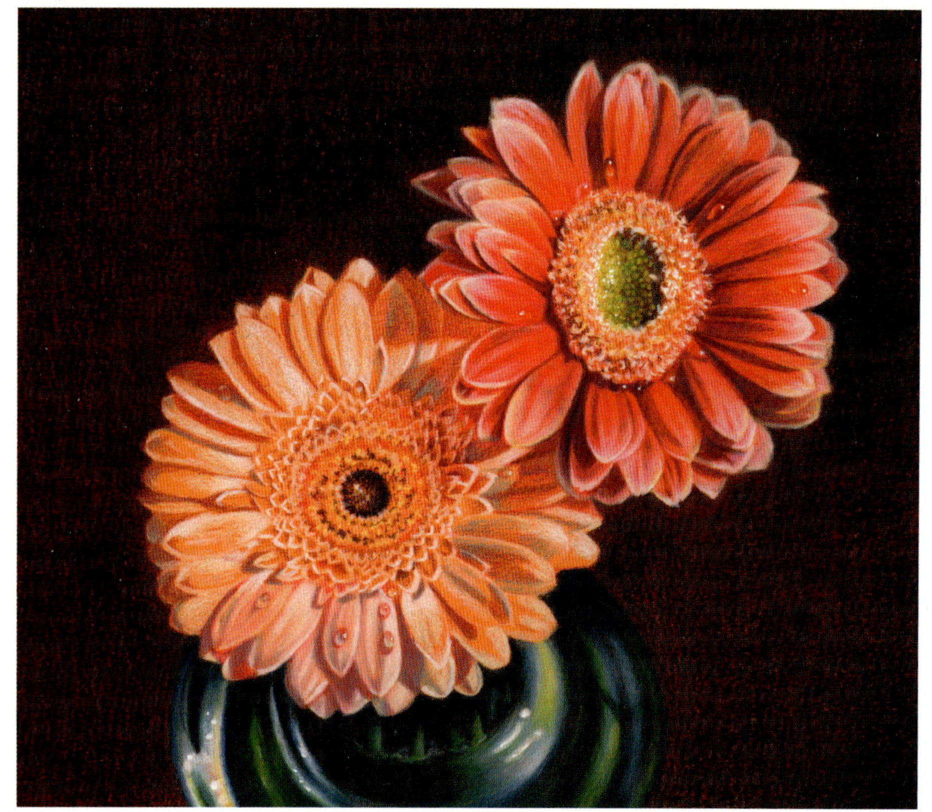

Step 10

The artist shades the pink petals with mostly peachy colors (Prismacolor peach, light peach, nectar, eggshell, and henna) rather than with light pinks due to pencil choice limitations (many pinks have a short life and fade quickly in the Prismacolor line). You can change these colors to light pinks.

After the placement of shadows, you work on the lights and their transitions. Therefore begin shading the brightest white areas in the petals. The artist shades with a combination of light peach underneath white and eggshell underneath white.

Keep checking the accuracy of the petals' rotation and length by looking at your drawing in the mirror. If you see weird shapes in the mirrored image, you need to fix them in your art.

In this simplified diagram you see how you can approach drawing every pink petal. First, determine its curvature/direction. Next, mark the brightest lights and the darkest darks. Lastly, create transitions between these two notes.

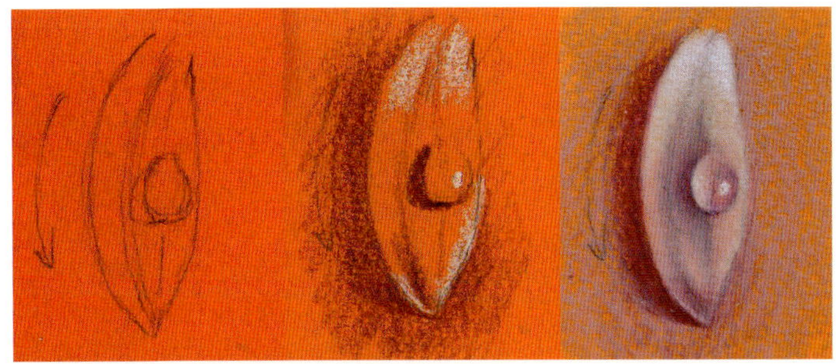

Step 11

Fill in all the petals with the colors mentioned in Step 10 (peach, light peach, nectar, eggshell, and henna). Once again you follow the same formula of shading every petal by drawing shadows, then highlights, then making transitions between the two.

Overlap all shadows in the pink petals with nectar and 30% warm grey, use peach to blend transitions between the shadows and the lights.

Blend the petals with a full blender and white, depending on your layering. If you want your petals to be lighter, use white; if the values look right, use the blender.

Step 11

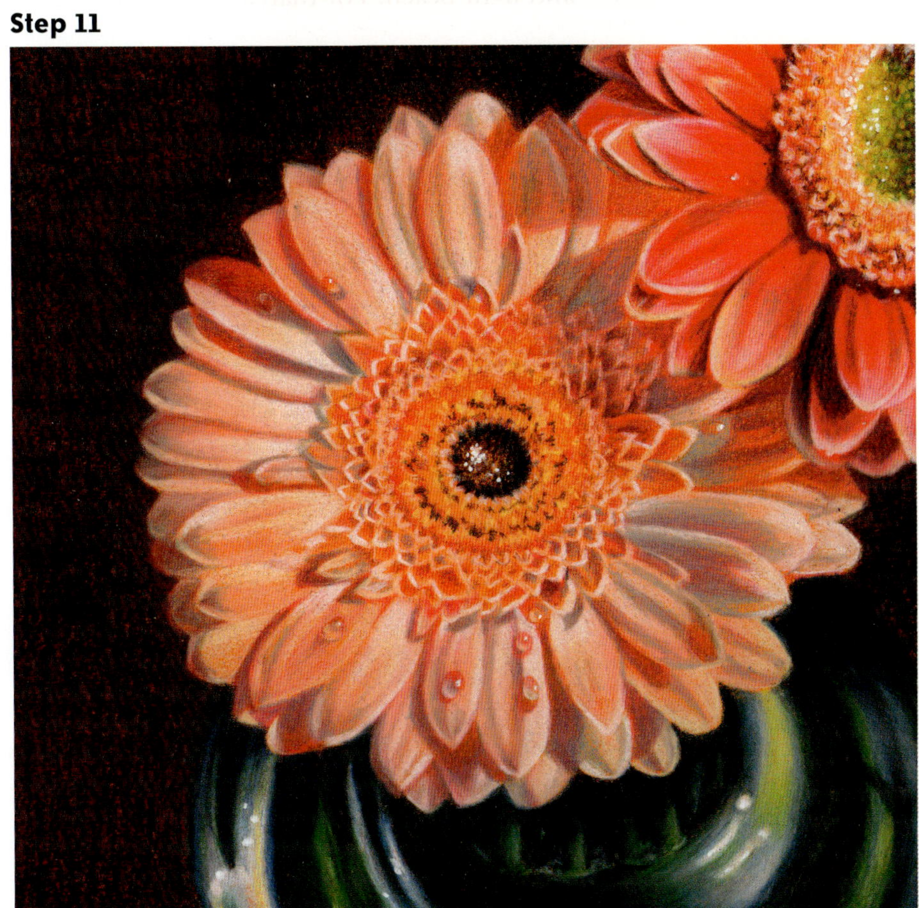

Shading with white will make the petals appear slightly cooler. Also notice how beautiful the color of the shadow is! There is no boring grey, is there?

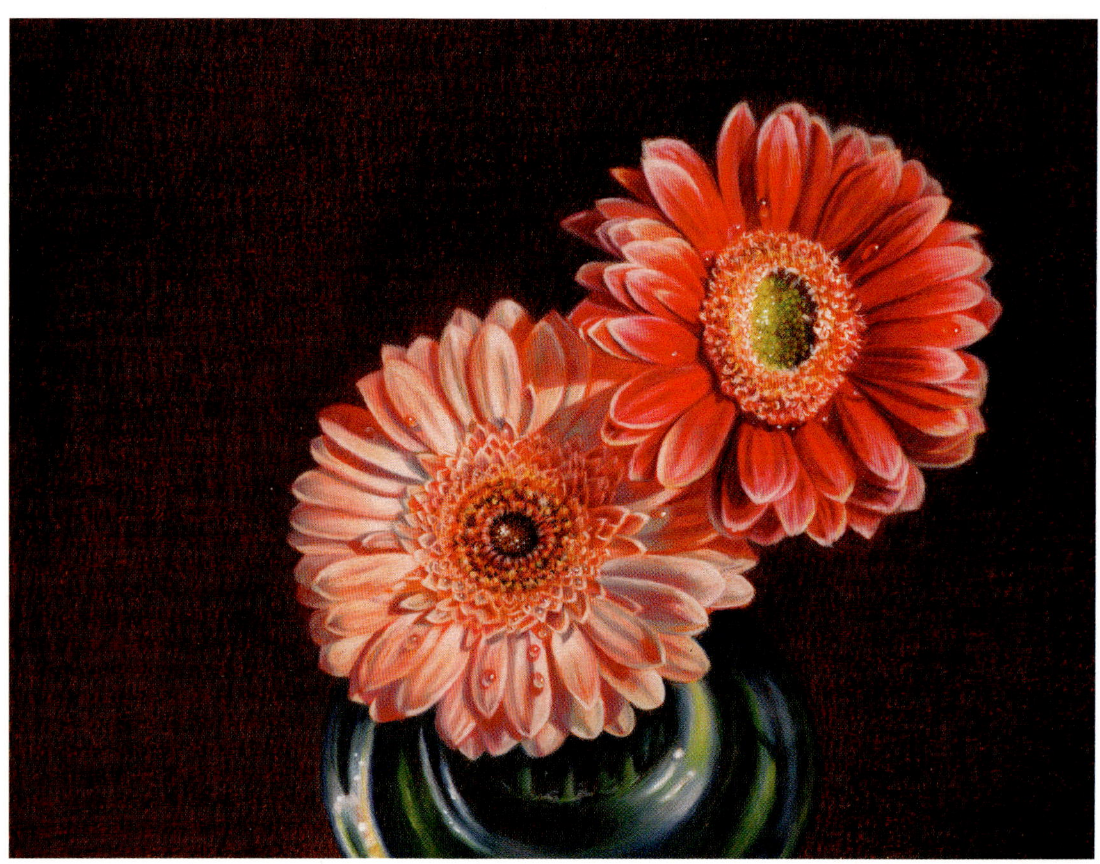

Step 12

Spray your artwork lightly with a fixative and step back to check the edges and values. The red flower should be darker than the pink one. Look at the edges of the vase to see if they blend into the background well enough. Look at the edges of the petals and make some of them much sharper than the outer ones. The flowers' centers should have definition and the petals should curve. Fix your mistakes and spray the drawing with a final fixative outdoors.

Chapter 7

How to Draw Fabric: The Use of Greys

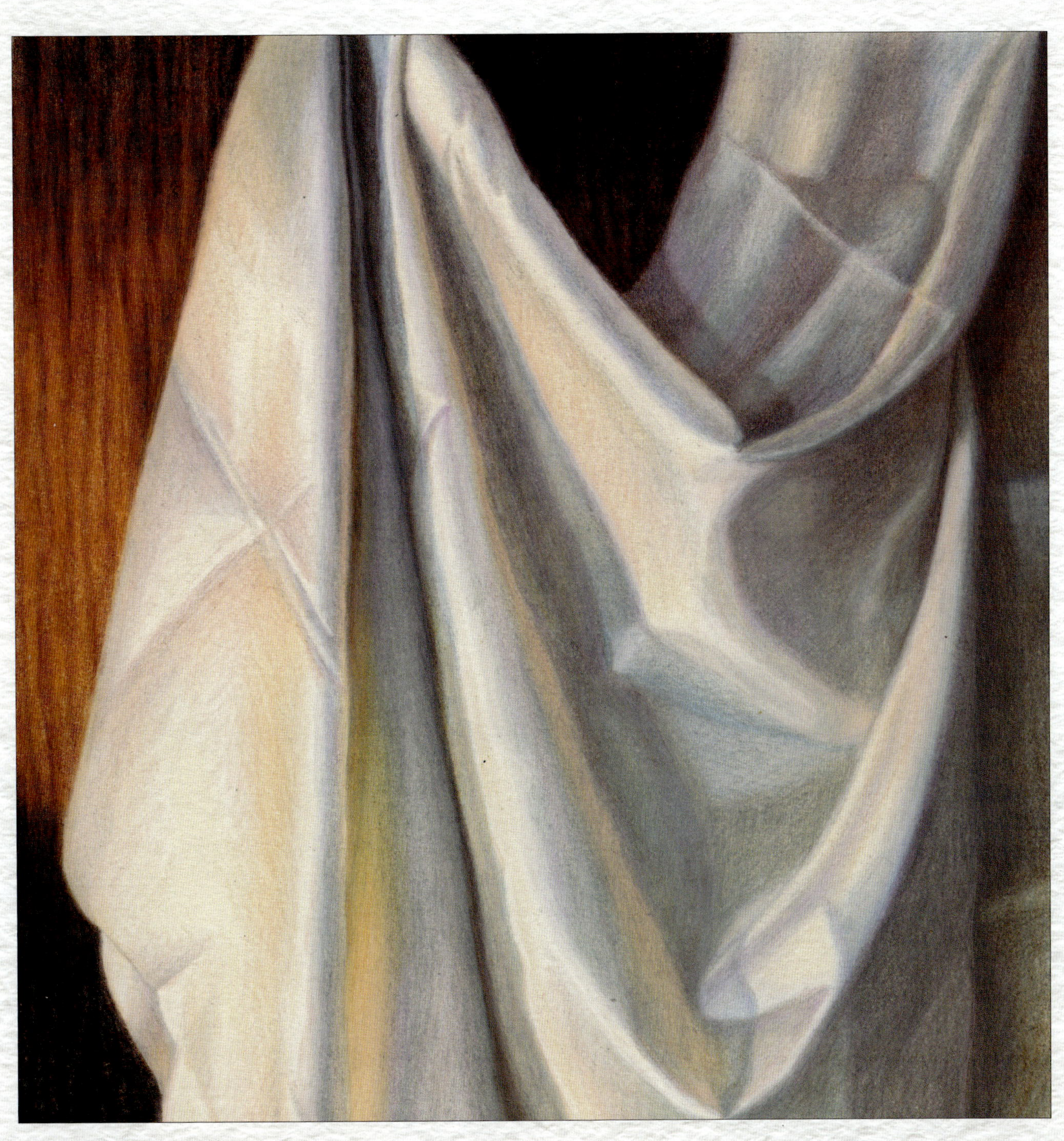

Here is a secret. Unlike paint, colored pencils do not mix to grey. Therefore, you can't really mess up in your color mixing, or get the wishy-washy greys that easily happen in watercolor painting. But if your goal is to neutralize and desaturate colors without shading with complements, companies do manufacture pencils in various greys to use for this purpose and you must know how to do it. While most people like the vibrancy of colored pencil art, the right use of greys shows a sophisticated color palette in your drawings.

Why do you need greys?

- Greys neutralize (desaturate) colors, creating subdued hues.
- Greys push the vibrant colors back, which is very useful in landscape drawing.
- Greys blend colors that are applied over the colored layer, especially the lighter greys.
- Greys bring sophistication to the color.

How do you use greys?

Greys appear boring shaded straight on white paper. It is best to establish the colorful base and then shade with a grey pencil over it. For instance if you see a grey shadow, try to spot some reflected colors in it. Shade with those colors first and then add the grey over it.

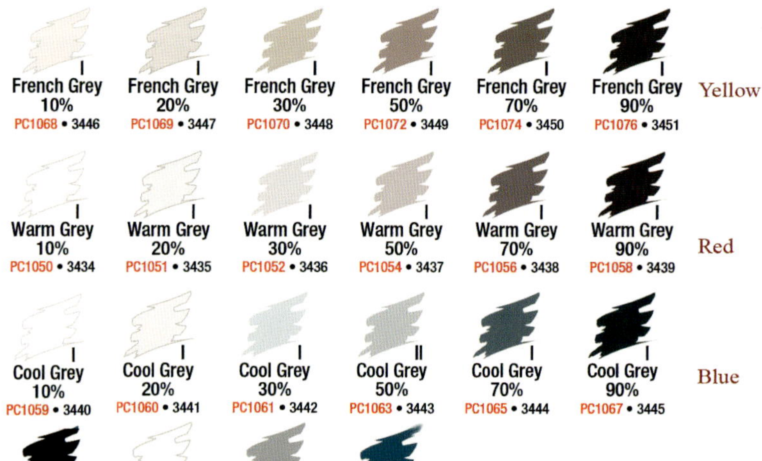

Here you see the swatches of Prismacolor Premier greys. Most of them have excellent lightfastness. Their percentages correspond with the grey scale. The value scale has ten shades from black to white, so that there are eight grey intervals with 12% each.

Cool greys lean toward the blue, while warm greys lean toward the red, with French greys leaning toward the yellow in the Prismacolor Premier line.

Action Step: To understand how greys work, test your colors on a separate piece of paper. Pick your color palette, make the color swatches, and then apply various greys over those color swatches to see how each of the greys affects your hues. Refer to the information about the Munsell Color System in the previous chapter to grey down the colors. Also, try these greys on colored paper. While greys may look boring on white paper, some of these greys look gorgeous on toned papers.

In the previous projects you have utilized the greys without even paying close attention to them, but here we'll continue exploring the possibilities.

How light shapes the form on fabric

Drapery and dynamic wrinkles take a big part in drawing clothing, still-life fabric, and curtains. While the complexity of folds discourages beginners from drawing fabric, this subject actually follows the same drawing formula discussed in Chapter 3. Therefore the same rules apply in analyzing light and its direction, and how it travels across the form. You need to become observant of highlights, form and cast shadows, and reflected light.

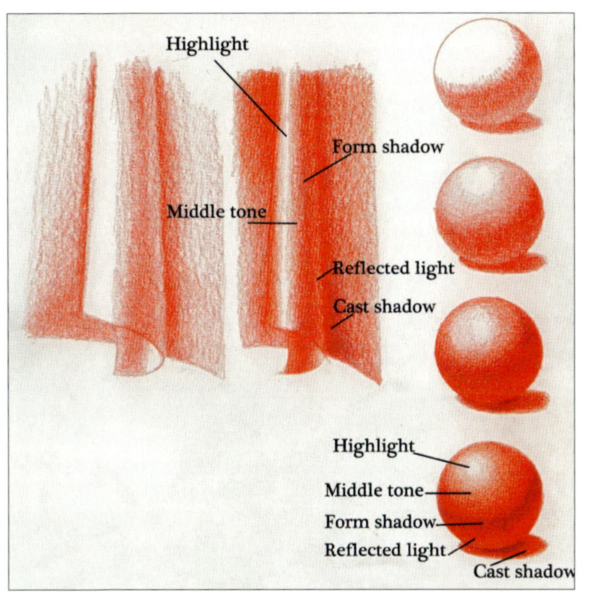

This drawing illustrates the formula for drawing fabric three-dimensionally. In the beginning of the book you drew a drawing of eggs that helped you understand how to make objects round on paper. This same concept is illustrated in the image of a ball and a fabric fold next to it. Always try to find the form shadow that makes nonreflective objects appear three-dimensional.

How shapes underneath fabric create folds

You should also visualize folds three-dimensionally (just like any other subject) and study how the fabric gets pulled, sculpted, or wrapped around the surface it sits on.

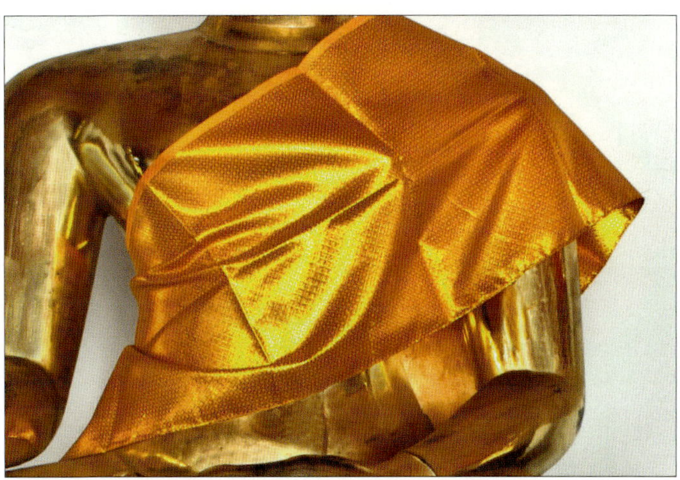

In this picture, the fabric wraps around the Buddha sculpture creating tension wrinkles and folds. Understanding how the shoulder pulls the fabric helps you to draw the folds, because most of the folds form in that area and travel across the body until they turn around the waistline.

Begin drawing fabric that has no pattern on it, so you can focus on the fabric's movement rather than on pattern detail. Once you understand basic form and begin to see changes in light in the fabric's movement, you can add patterns. You need fabric patterns to work to your advantage in describing the volume. Therefore pay close attention to how patterns repeat the curvature and the movement of the folds, curving and wrapping around each fold. If necessary, simplify images by drawing major folds and patterns only. Always study how patterns change shape and perspective in accordance with the folds' curvature: some may look stretched, others squished.

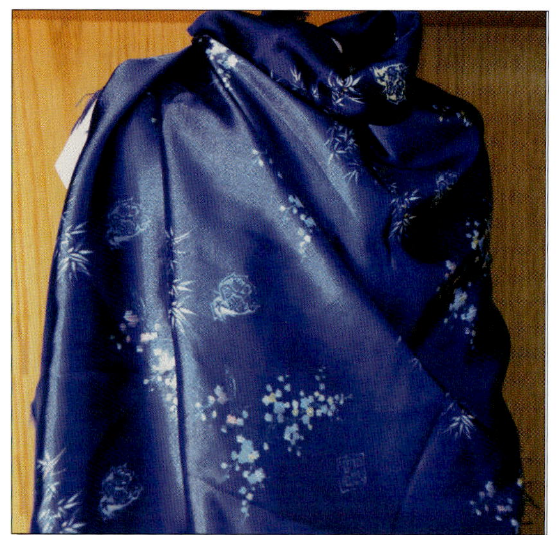

In this picture the deep blue fabric flows freely, wrapping around the neck. It creates loose folds that are easy to repeat in drawing. The fabric also has a quite simple floral pattern that can be established over the general pattern of folds. Notice how some flowers get cut by the wrinkles or curve around the fold and disappear on the other side. In other words, you draw the general curvature of folds and wrinkles and then add the pattern over it not to get confused with all of the information at once.

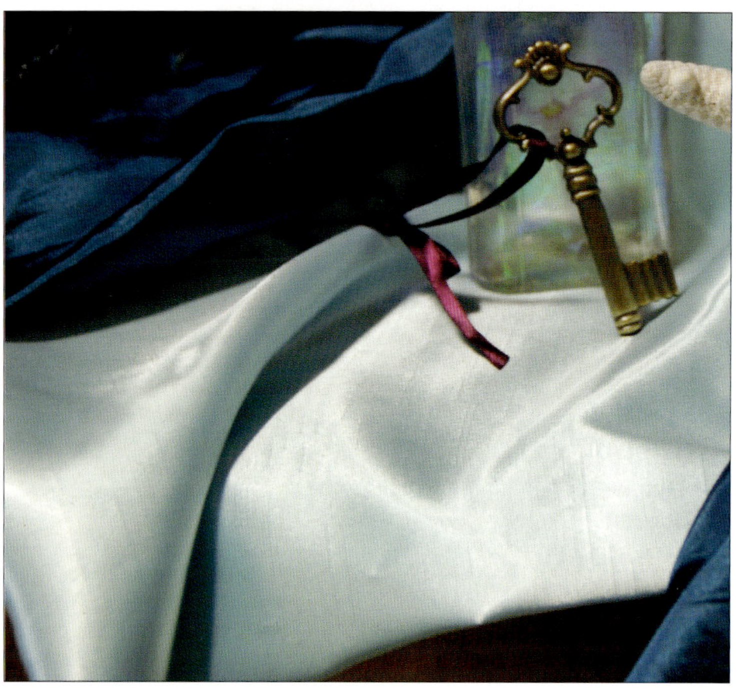

In this image you can see how both fabrics roll over the table, producing folds. Strong highlights define the fabric flow. The largest fold to the left in the light turquoise fabric has a strong highlight and a form shadow with the reflected light. The cast shadow is the darkest in value. Seeing these shadows and highlights and copying it into your art makes the fabric look 3-D on paper.

How to turn the form and find color in white fabric

In this reference photo you can see once again how light turns the form. You can also study the difference in warm and cool light. Because the single light source is an electric light, the light areas of the fabric are warm, while the shadows are cool.

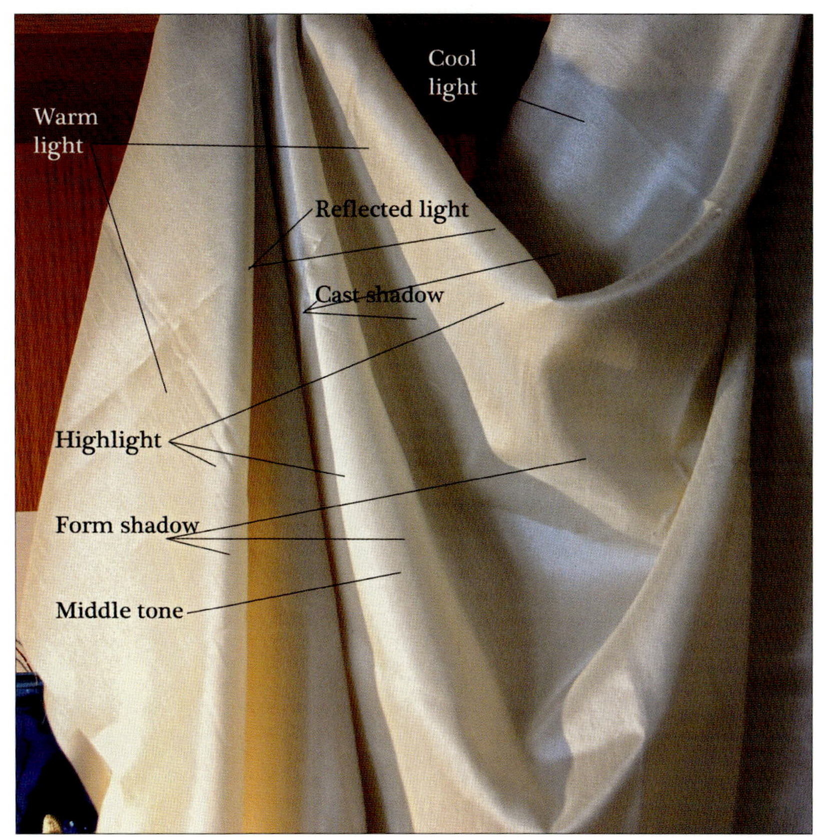

STEP-BY-STEP INSTRUCTIONS

How to See Color in White and the Use of Greys

Materials: Prismacolor Premier colored pencils, Stonehenge warm white drawing paper, 9 x 12, or Koh-I-Noor colored pencil drawing paper, 9 x 12; colorless blender; kneaded eraser; white transfer paper; sketch paper; soft white colored pencil for blending

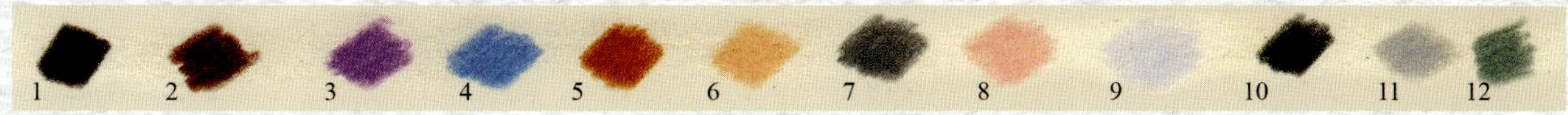

Color chart: 1. Dark Umber 2. Sienna Brown 3. Lilac 4. Light Cerulean Blue 5. Goldenrod 6. Beige 7. 50% Cool Grey 8. Light Peach 9. Cloud Blue 10. 70% Cool Grey 11. 20% Cool Grey 12. Jade Green

Small amounts of other colors may have been used as well.

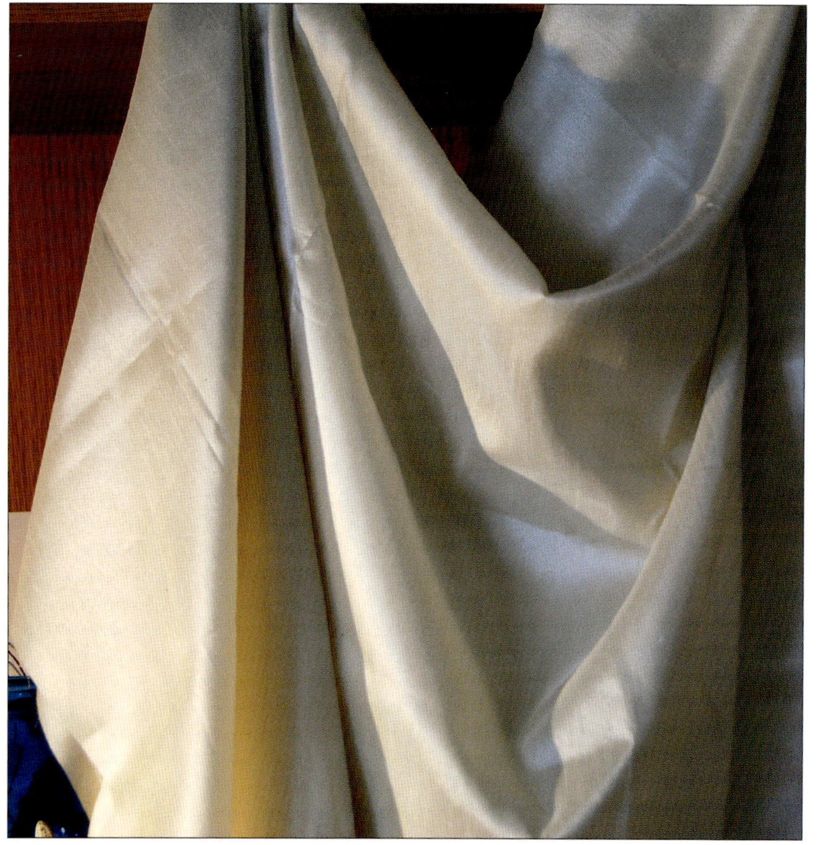

If you are a beginner, consider drawing part of an image, focusing on one fold only. Also draw on 8 x 10 or 9 x 12 paper. As you begin following the steps, constantly refer to the picture to study the light and the colors further.

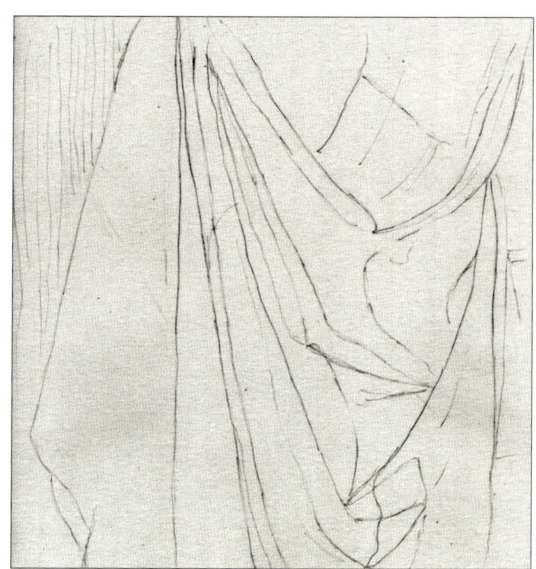

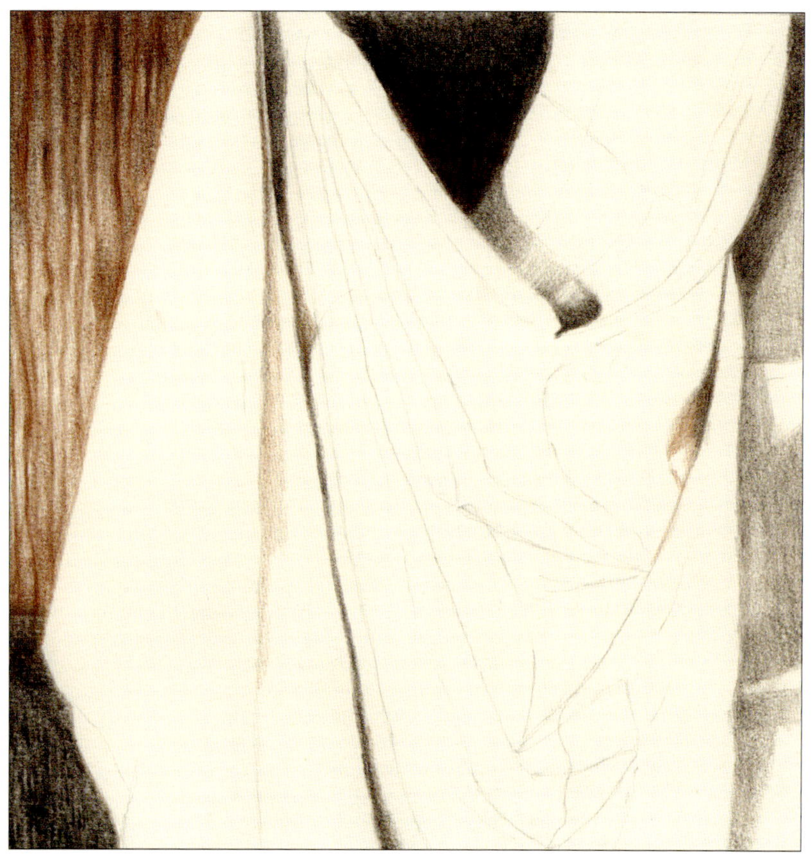

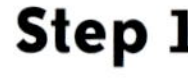

Step 1

Work on the outline on a separate piece of sketch paper that matches the size of your drawing paper. You can trace the image from the photo, but in doing so you're skipping a very important skill every good artist needs—understanding of forms, spatial relationships, linear perspective, and gesture.

Trace the outline using an HB graphite pencil and your favorite transfer method (window light, light box, or transfer paper). If you use a softer graphite pencil, it will leave unwanted residue and will interfere with light colors during shading. Tap the outlines with the kneaded eraser to lighten up the lines as much as possible.

Step 2

Using dark umber and a light pencil pressure, map out the darkest areas in the folds and the background. Keep your shading very light and soft on fabric with overlapping directional lines. Use medium to heavy pressure in shading the wood.

For the wood, create uneven but soft lines with sienna brown, imitating the texture of wood. Shade softly right next to these lines to make the base for the wood. Vary pencil pressure to achieve different varieties of darkness. Darken it with dark umber at the bottom for contrast.

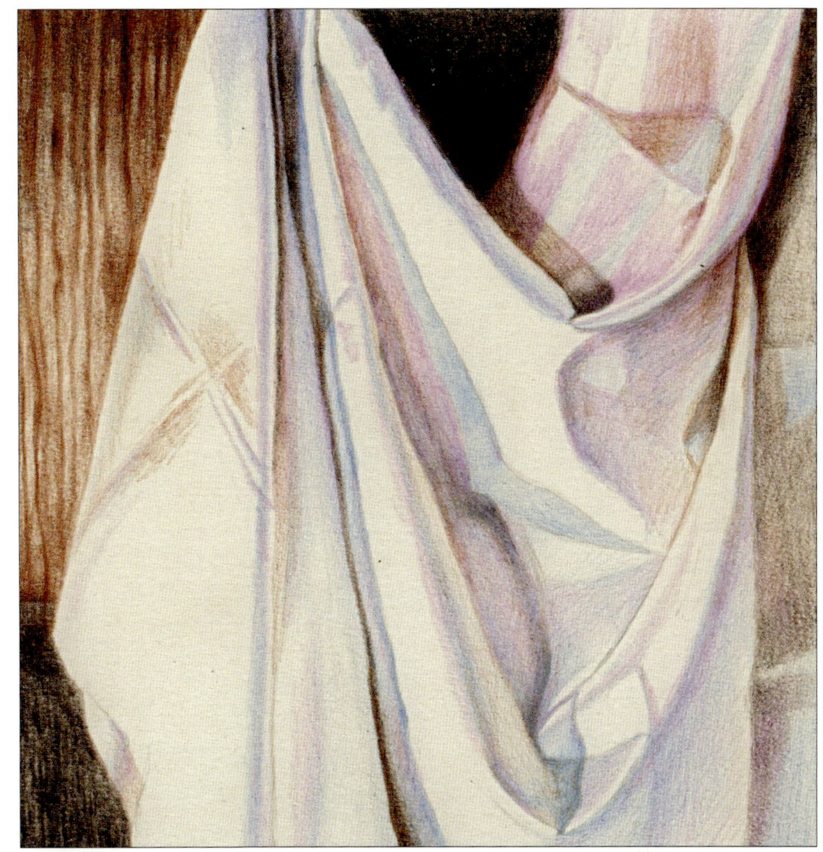

Step 3

To bring color into the white fabric, study the light and light temperature as shown in the reference image, and then put the observed colors underneath the local color (white of white fabric is the local color). Begin drawing fabric from shadows with light cerulean blue and lilac. Add sienna brown to the mix in warmer areas at the top. By placing these shadows you begin to create volume in the fabric and it becomes an underpainting, over which you can layer the greys later on.

Refrain from rushing to draw in full color. By adding colors one at a time throughout, you achieve volume in a controlled progression. Keep looking at values—the relative darkness/lightness of the area—to map out the shadows in the rest of this drawing.

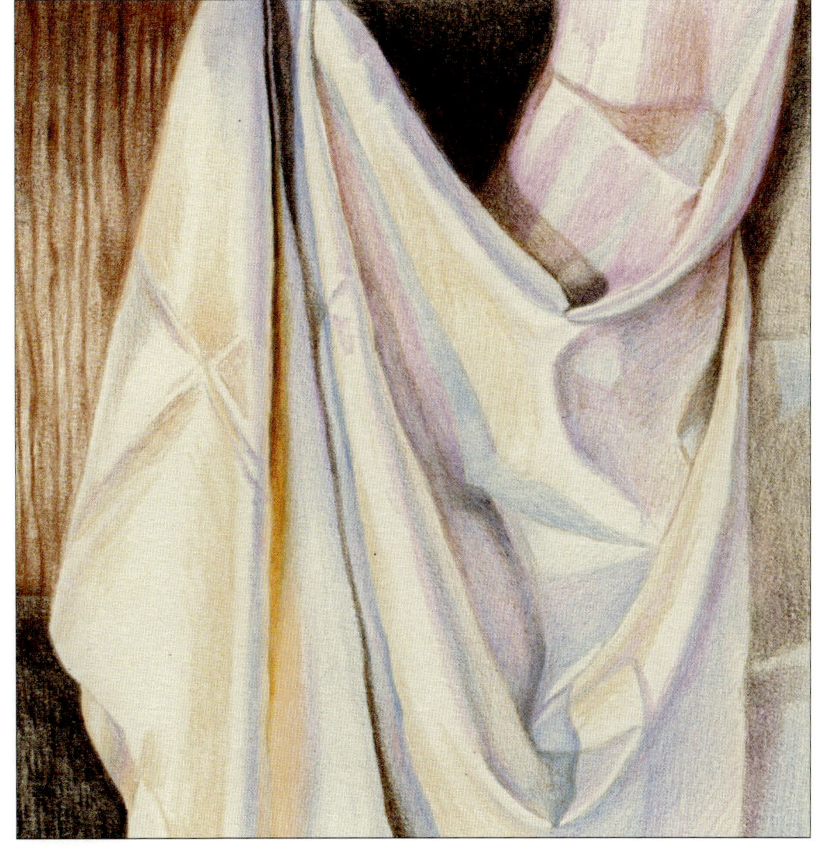

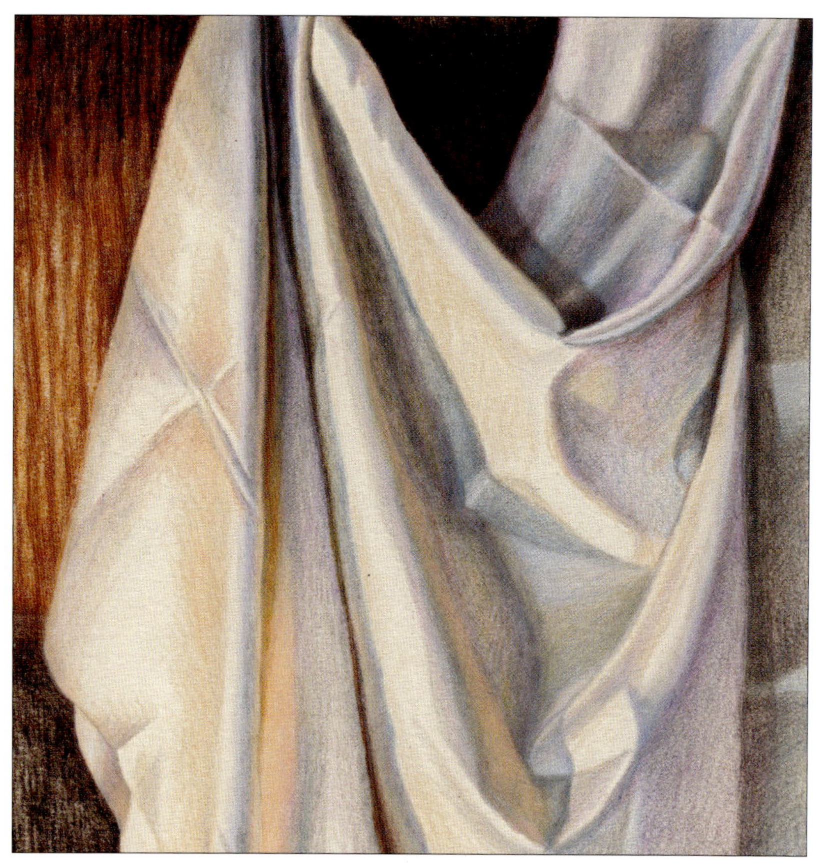

Step 4

As you continue coloring, keep thinking of the fabric three-dimensionally and how each fold hangs, pulls, and rotates differently in space. Don't forget about creating volume with short, directional strokes, observing the light direction and its strength.

You've underpainted the shadows, now you can draw the lights, and later create the transitions between the two. The fabric on the left receives the most light, thus it must remain the lightest area in the drawing. It is also a warm light, so a combination of goldenrod, beige, and some light peach works well to define light, warm values. Continue shading with the same colors in the subsequent folds in the light.

Because this paper is white, be mindful of reserving space for the highlights and leave them uncolored. It will give shine to the white fabric.

The light comes from the left, which means that the fabric is illuminated the strongest on the lefthand side, and then each fold receives less and less light as it moves to the right, changing its strength (color intensity) from very high to low and its color temperature from warm to cool.

To develop the shadows further at this step, shade with 50% cool grey over the form shadows. Keep a light touch and just keep layering to see how much darker you need to go. Your previous colors should show through because of colored pencil transparency.

Soften the edges between the form shadows and the light, making transitions with cloud blue or 20% cool grey. You can shade with medium pencil pressure to see how these colors soften and blend the colors beautifully.

Step 5

To grey down areas in deep shadows on the right side, shade with 70% cool grey. To grey down areas in lighter shadows, draw with 50% cool grey. Your previous coloring should show through a little. These greys create a unified appearance, darkening and cooling down the shadows.

Make sure to continue layering with the same soft, circular or short strokes to keep the fabric soft and fluid. If your strokes look harsh, you would have to rely on blending more, but here you can see that because of soft layering, blending is not required. If you notice that some lines become too dark, hard, or too linear by accident in your artwork, either use a kneaded eraser or the Tombow Mono eraser for gentle lift outs.

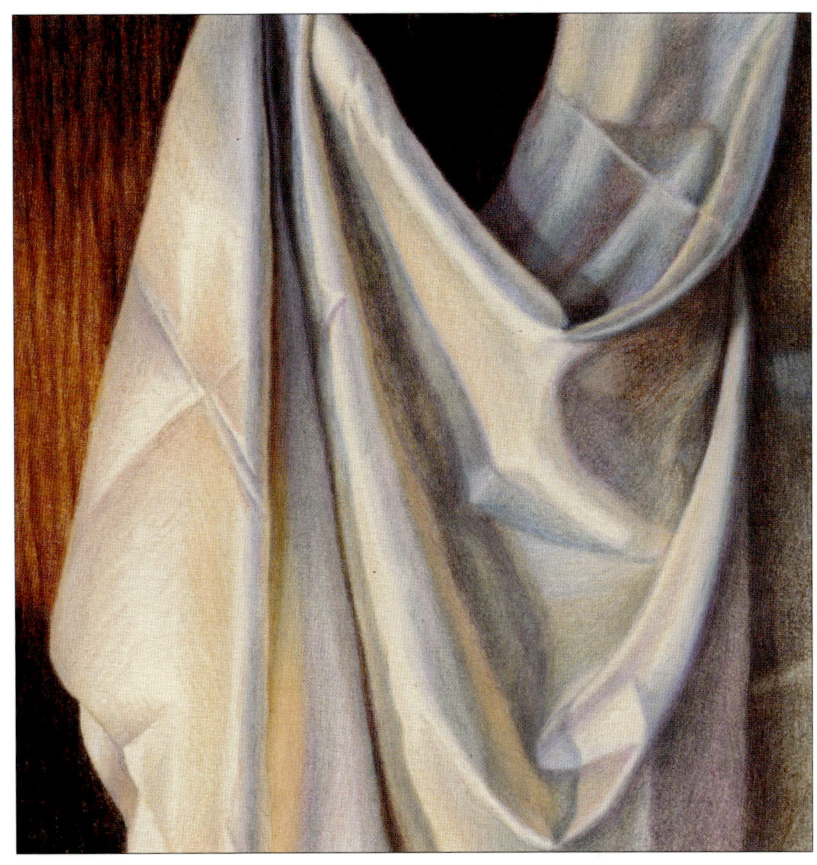

To shade the wood, which is warm in color temperature, layer goldenrod, sienna brown, and dark umber, observing the light's strength. Rely on values to create lighter areas in the middle, darker area at the top, and the darkest at the bottom.

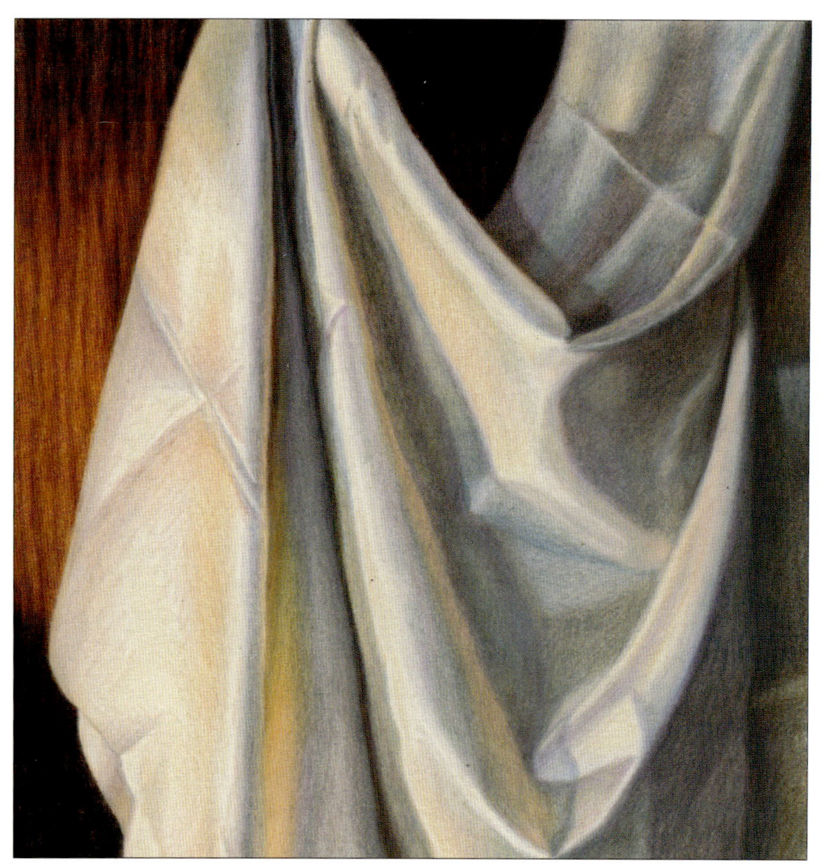

Step 6

As the light travels from left to right, step back to evaluate if the right side of your drawing is darker than the left. Darken the right side of the fabric by layering the same colors or greying it down more in the shadows with either 50% or 70% grey, depending on your previous progress. Even if some folds have highlights on the right, they are not as bright as on the left and must be slightly less bright (or color intense). The artist colors over the highlights with beige and light peach in the right corner to make sure it doesn't compete with the highlights on the left side of the fabric.

Use the same colors, 70% cool grey, sienna brown, light cerulean blue, lilac, and beige to deepen all colors and shadows. For color variety you can add jade green to shade over the blue areas and 20% grey can replace cloud blue.

Step back from your drawing again to see what needs to be worked on. Softening the edges? Adjusting the values? Darkening the shadows? Lifting out for highlights?

Blending happens naturally on Stonehenge paper when layering and overlapping colors. Apply lighter colors over the darker ones with heavier pressure to achieve the seamless blending of edges between the colors and edges in the light to medium values. If it's not enough, blend with Caran d'Ache full blender, adjusting pencil pressure in accordance with your needs.

Note: Gamsol or Zest-it would not be effective here because the values and colors are fairly light and also because the fabric must remain soft with gentle transitions between the tones; the solvents would create a much harsher contrast.

Apply sharp and soft white colored pencil with heavy pressure to blend the edges around the highlights on the left side of the fabric. Spray with a final fixative 2–3 times outdoors.

Chapter 8

How to Create Symmetrical Shapes

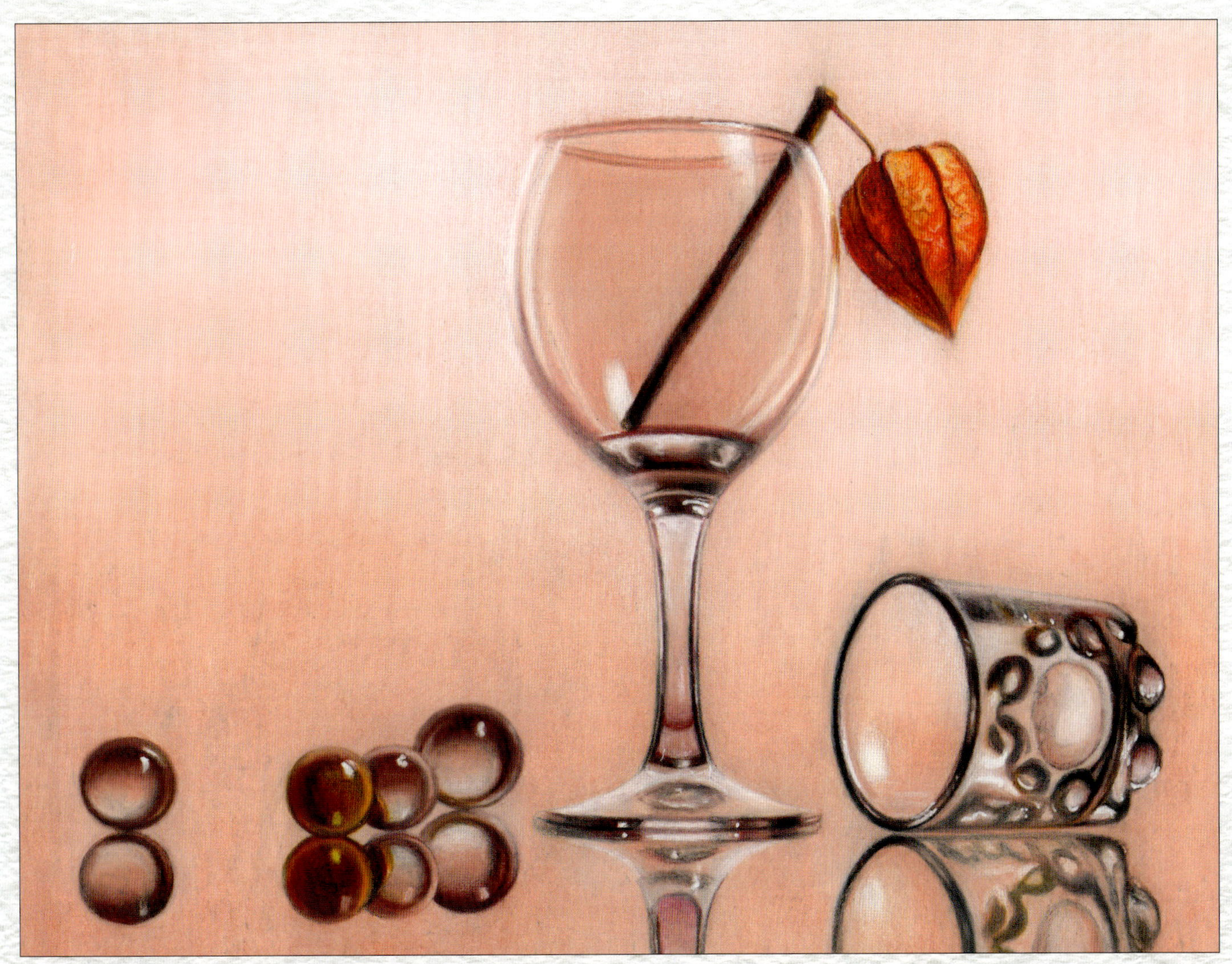

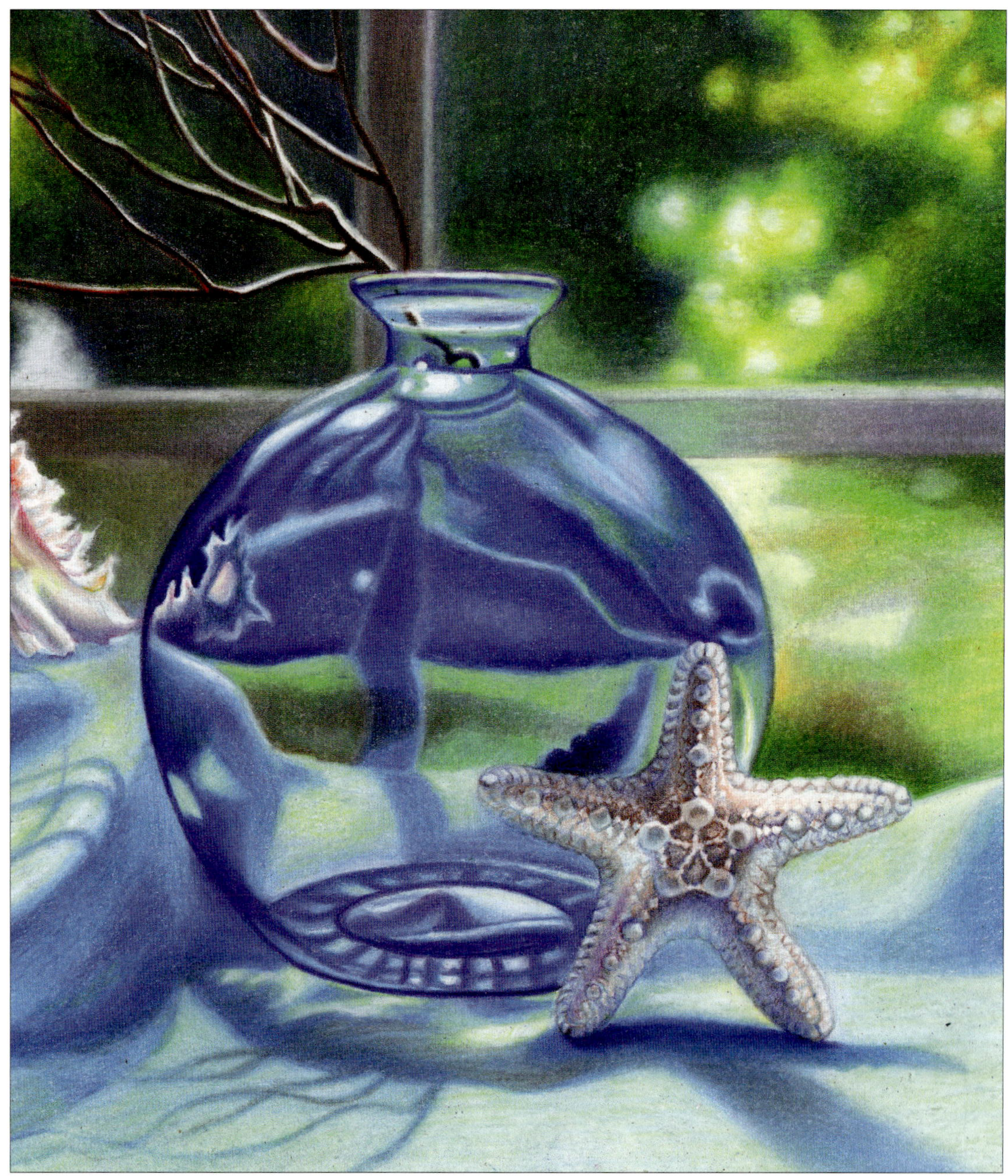

Realism requires the perfection of drawing. While it applies to any subject, drawing with perfect symmetry is necessary in still life, portraiture, and beyond. Here we are going to look at the basic principle of drafting vases, cups, and similar shapes that requires the understanding of symmetry and ellipses. We will study how ellipses rotate in space depending on your point of view, which determines the naturalism of your drawing. The artist has done a lot of sketching over the years so it is much easier to draw out the shapes freehand symmetrically. Eventually, you too will be able to speed up and perfect your technique, but in the beginning follow the general outline presented here to understand the process. You must draw on sketch paper or tracing paper to draft your images correctly and then simply transfer the outlines onto your drawing paper or matboard for coloring.

Drafting ellipses

An **ellipse** is a circle in space that rotates depending on your line of sight. A circle becomes a simple line when we look at a cup at eye level. However, when we move our line of sight up or down, meaning that we look at the vase from above or below it, this line becomes an ellipse of different width. In other words:

- The ellipse's width changes with our point of view.
- The more complex your vase or cup, the more ellipses you must draft inside one object.
- You must draw through the shapes, completing the ellipses even if you don't see them in full (the object could be opaque or obscured by another shape up in front). This will ensure the drafting accuracy of ellipses.

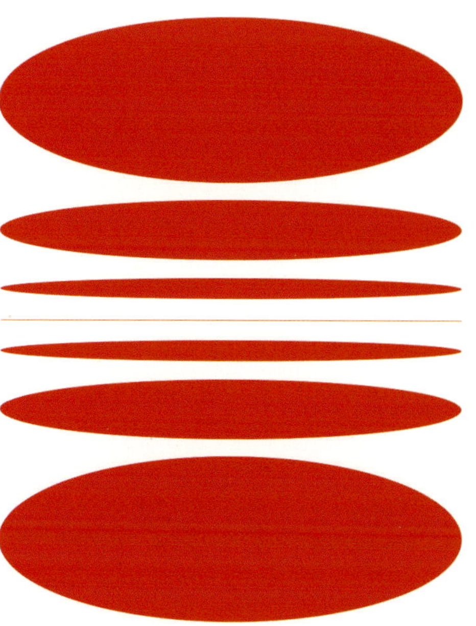

Images of ellipses rotating in space, depending on your point of view

This image illustrates how you can find ellipses in symmetrical objects. The width of each ellipse changes with your line of sight. Therefore a single object would not repeat the ellipse width throughout: the top ellipse would be different from the bottom one.

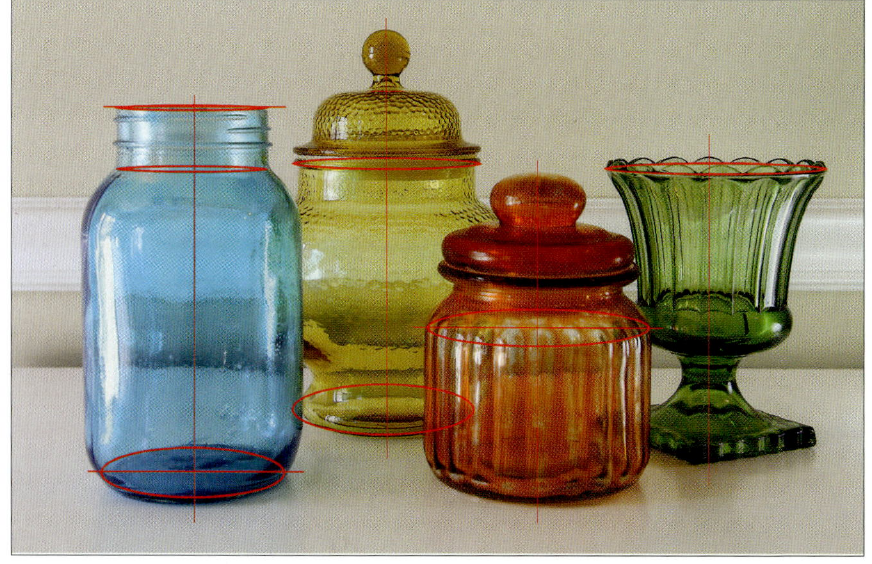

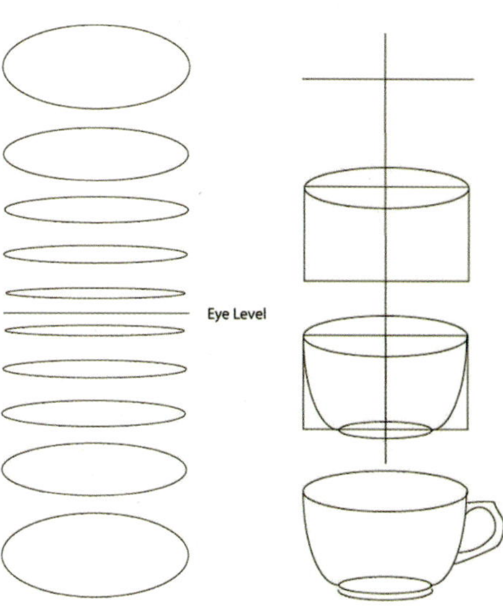

This schematic drawing shows you the rotation of ellipses and how you can draft out symmetrical cups and vases using a central line (that always remains parallel to the paper's edge) and measuring equal distances from it.

Folding method

Let's look at the folding method in steps. Be sure to practice this technique on tracing paper first before committing to a colored pencil drawing.

STEP-BY-STEP INSTRUCTIONS

Creating Symmetry As You Draw

Materials: tracing paper, 2B pencil, kneaded eraser, ruler, a symmetrical object to sketch

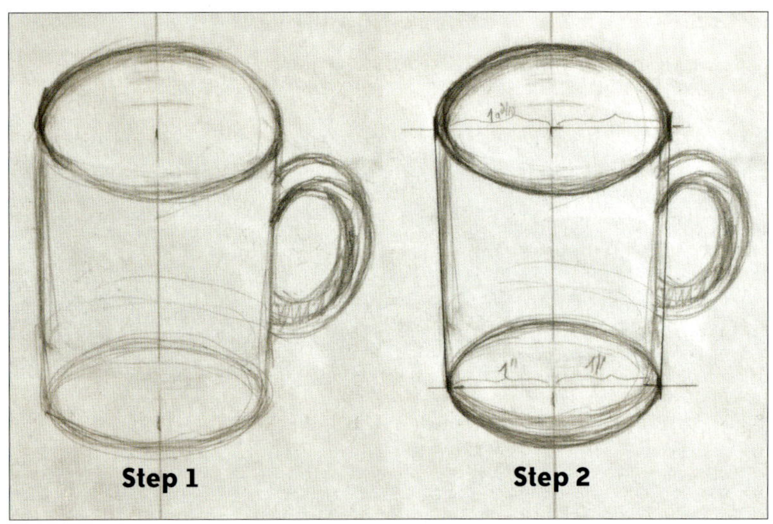

Step 1

To practice this technique, begin sketching your cup freehand on tracing paper. You don't need to be perfect at this stage, rather you should aim to capture the general size, proportion, and rotation of the cup in space. Observe how wide the ellipses are at the top and bottom of the cup.

To aid yourself in this process, make a straight line that marks the center of the cup and sketch out the cup freehand around this line. It gives you a general idea how to begin creating symmetry freehand by matching your dimensions visually on both sides of the line.

Step 2

Once your freehand drawing is complete and proportions look right, place parallel lines for each ellipse you see in the object. Here we see just two ellipses and thus make two lines. Use your ruler to make lines that are perfectly straight and parallel to each other and to the paper's edge. A freehand line is never straight or parallel enough unless you are an excellent draftsman.

Next, measure equal distances between the center line and the outer edge in the top ellipse, basing it on your freehand drawing in Step 1. Now you have two equally distanced points from the center that connect the top ellipse. Draft the ellipse again, going through these two points precisely (most students place the points but don't draw through them). You'll begin to see how a freehand ellipse differs from your measured one. Don't forget to observe the correct width of the ellipse too!

Repeat the process for the bottom ellipse. Usually, the width of the bottom ellipse is slightly different from the top because we observe it at a different line of sight. Make sure to draw through the cup even if it is opaque or obscured. It guarantees drafting accuracy.

Step 3

Now use the measured markings at the top and bottom ellipses to connect the sides of the cup. If the lines appear straight, use a ruler. If it's a curving line, do your best to connect the ellipses freehand. Depending on your drafting abilities and experience, the vase or cup can look quite perfect at this stage, especially if your object is simple. If the cup or vase has many ellipses, you might want to proceed to the next step.

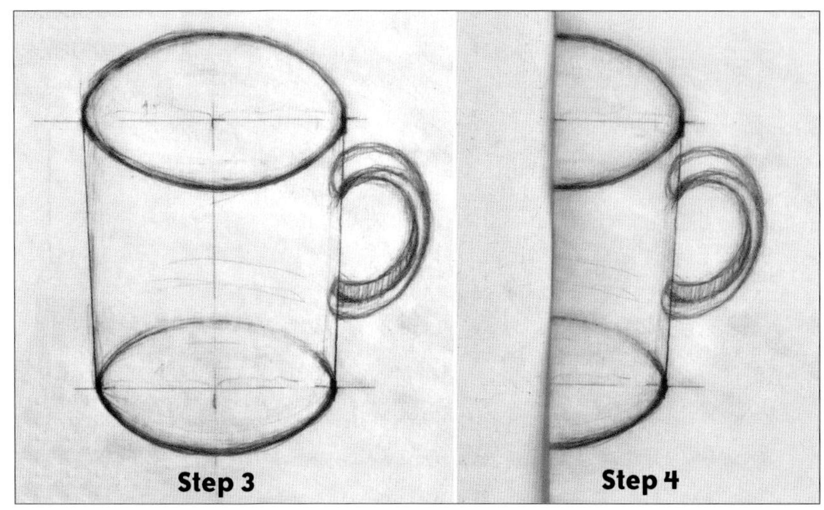

Step 4

Look at the two sides and decide which one appears the best or more perfect. Fold your tracing paper along the center line. Erase the "worst" side with a kneaded eraser. Because this paper is so transparent, you will see your best side's pencil markings through the erased one.

Step 5

If you work on sketch paper, take it to the window light and trace your chosen, correct side over the erased side. Unfold. The cup should look perfectly symmetrical with identical curves.

Step 6

Practice this technique several times before committing to an actual colored pencil drawing. At first your shapes might look a bit crooked or uneven, but if you follow these steps, you will improve quite quickly as you gain precision freehand.

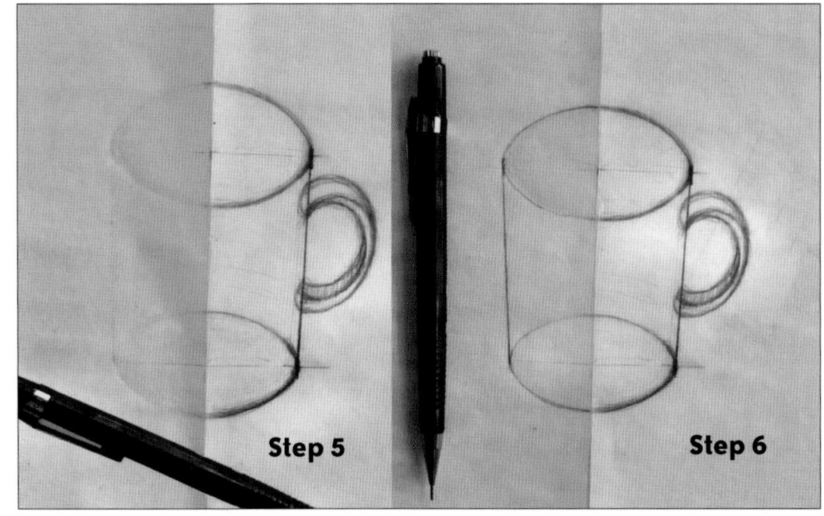

Examples of folding method:

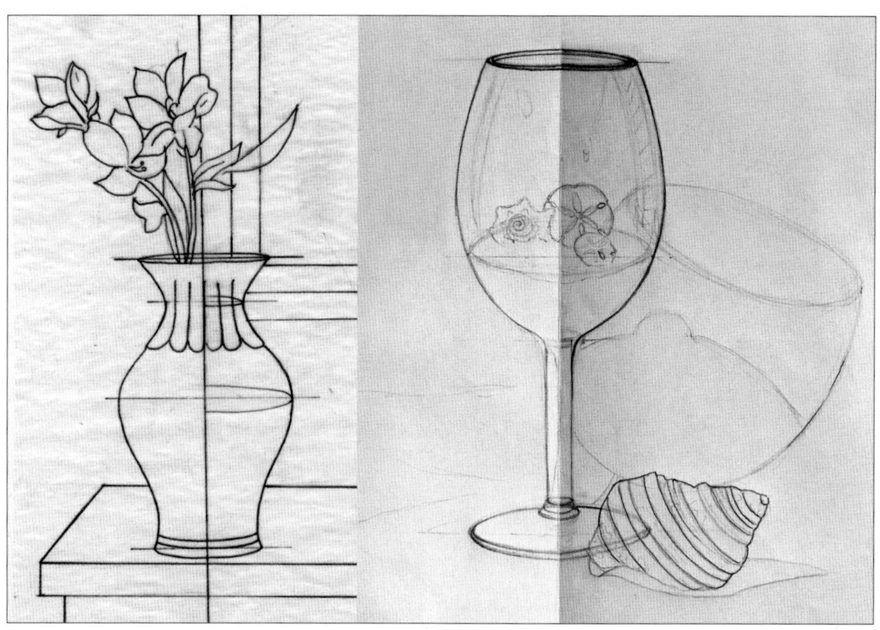

Examples of folding and drawing through on tracing paper:

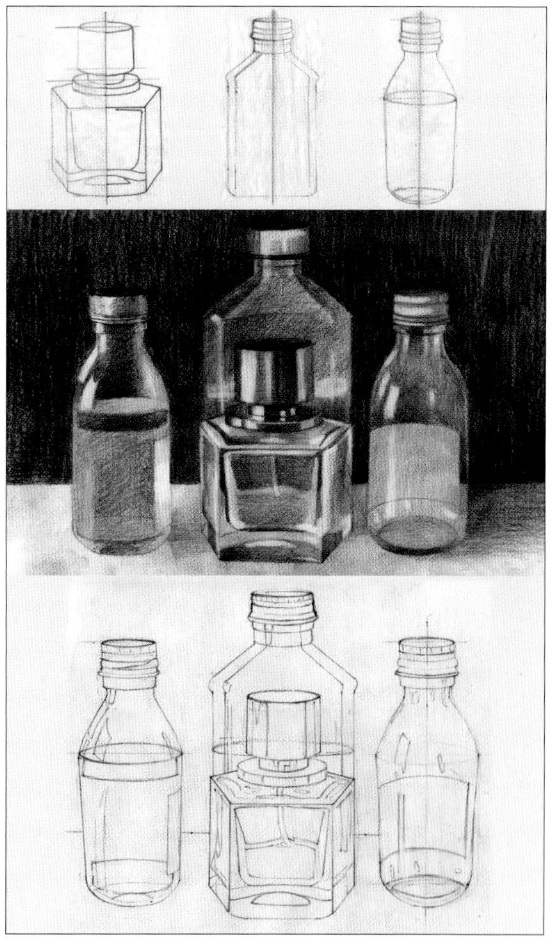

Why don't we just transfer the outlines right from a reference using a window light or a light table? Camera lenses distort reality and produce crooked forms. If you use a zoom lens, sometimes you can almost see a fish-eye effect that is very noticeable on linear subjects and architecture. Don't be a slave to your camera.

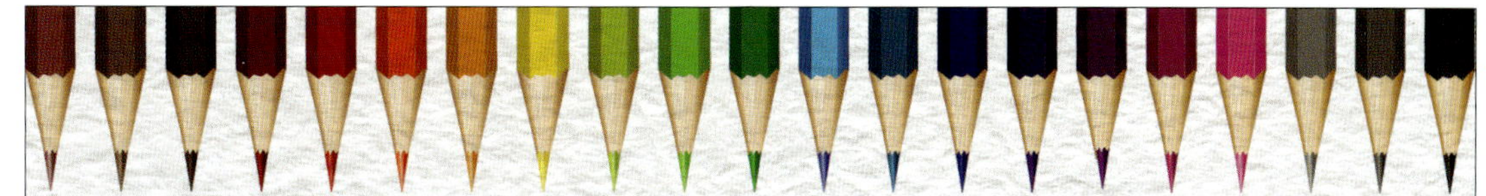

Common Mistakes

These are examples of cups taking the wrong turn. Ellipses don't have corners, they must be parallel to the paper's edge, and they rarely come to a straight line (they come to a straight line at eye level only).

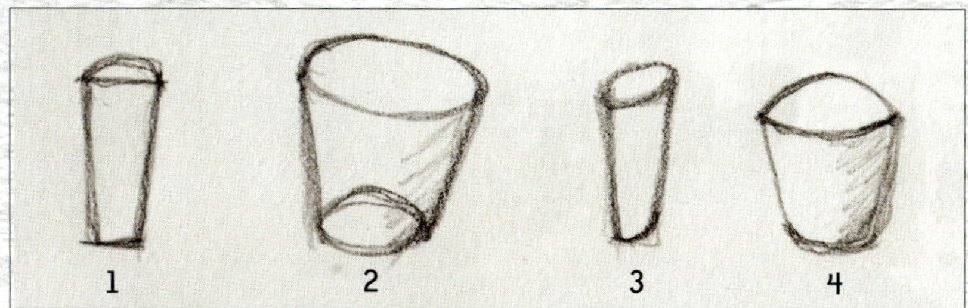

1. Drawing ellipse with a sharp angle. To fix, practice the rotation by drawing this area as a curve with minimal width.
2. Drawing crooked ellipses. To fix, follow the folding technique, making sure you draw straight and parallel lines first, around which you rotate the ellipse.
3. Objects don't look solid or connected. To fix, draw through the shapes even if you can't see them completely.
4. Tracing the photo, thus "copying" the camera's mistakes, which include a distorted perspective and distored ellipses.

STEP-BY-STEP INSTRUCTIONS

Drawing Glass (and Using Markers for Underpainting)

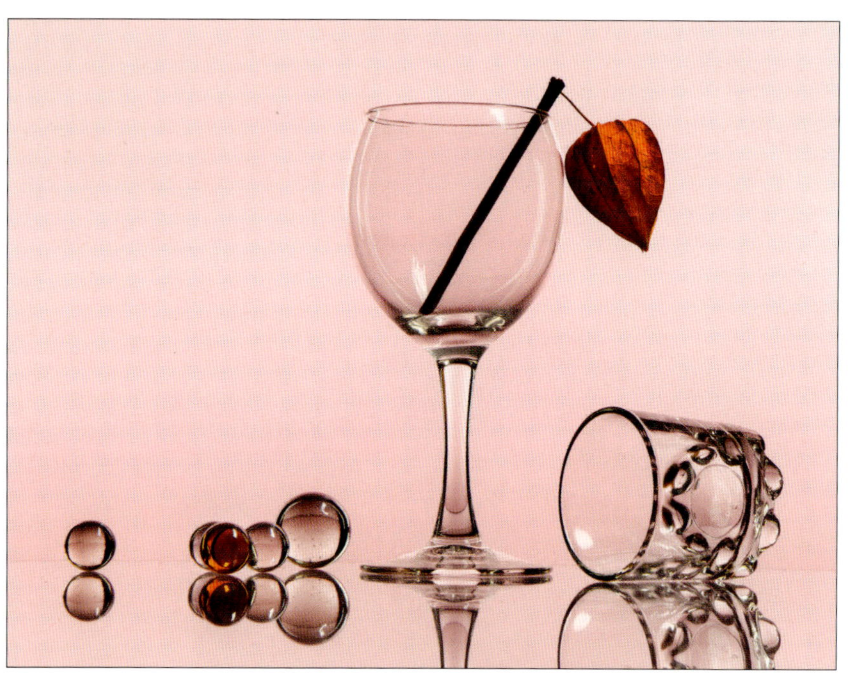

Materials: Prismacolor Premier pencils; Koh-i-Noor woodless pencils for minor touch-ups; Winsor & Newton pigment markers in portrait pink, white, magenta, lemon yellow, and scarlet (optional); Winsor & Newton pigment marker heavy weight paper; coins: penny (1 cent) and nickel (5 cents); ruler; kneaded eraser; Tombow Mono eraser; Sakura Pen-touch marker; tracing paper; sketch paper; white tracing paper (optional); Caran d'Ache full blender

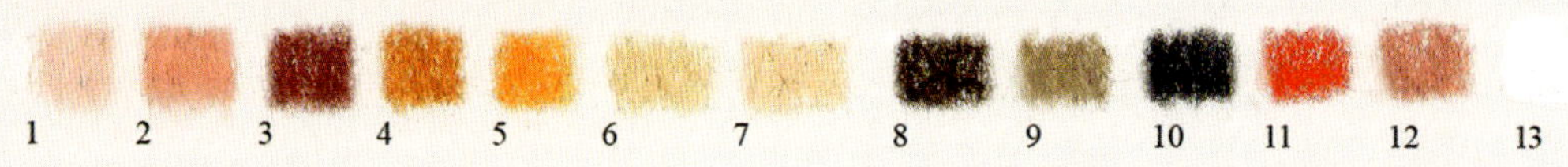

Color Chart: 1. Light Peach 2. Peach 3. Henna 4. Mineral Orange 5. Yellowed Orange 6. Eggshell 7. Beige 8. Dark Brown 9. Beige Sienna 10. 90% Warm Grey 11. Permanent Red 12. Nectar 13. White
Small amounts of other colors may have been used as well.

Note: The artist takes creative license in this lesson, using a warm version of pinks that deviates from the original reference where pinks are cool. This project was created with limited resources during Hurricane Irma and its aftermath.

To simplify, draw only one object, such as the wine glass, repeating all the steps.

Step 1

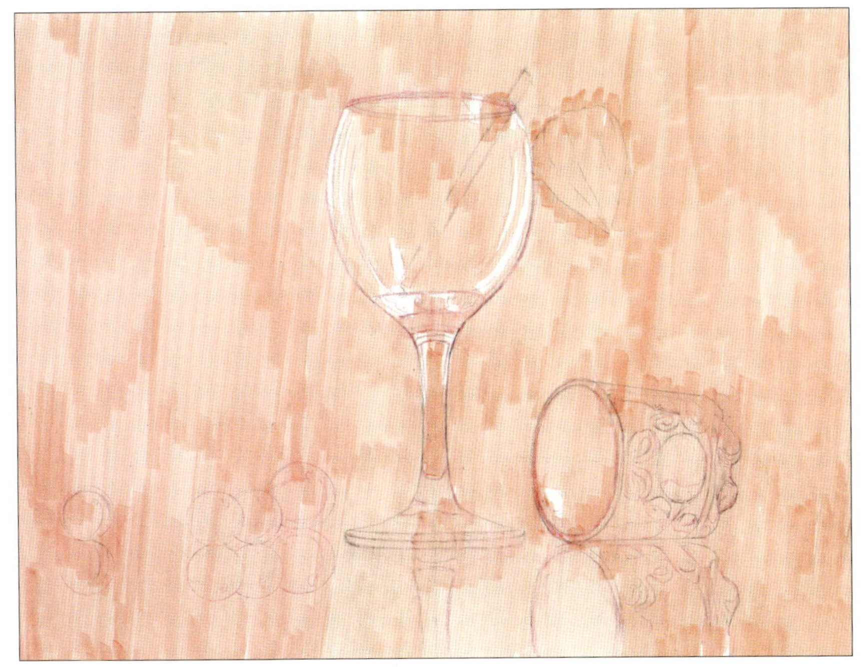

Develop your drawing on either sketch or tracing paper using the folding method. Transfer it. If a graphite outline shows, make sure to use a kneaded eraser to get rid of all the graphite lines. You won't be able to erase the intensified lines once you begin shading!

If you draw on white paper, transfer the outlines with Prismacolor light peach instead of using a graphite pencil. Once done, check your outline drawing in a mirror to check for mistakes or possible unevenness of the shapes. Fix the discrepancies—areas that look weird or not perfectly even in the mirrored image.

Shade the entire page with a pink marker of your choice. The artist paints with a chisel tip in Winsor & Newton portrait pink on Winsor & Newton pigment marker heavy weight paper that is smooth and doesn't bleed through as regular drawing papers do. Let it dry for a few minutes.

If you don't have the markers, don't worry! Repeat the same steps using your colored pencils! Markers speed up the process a bit and open you up to new possibilities to try out in the future. If you follow the warm color scheme chosen by the artist, use Prismacolor peach to fill in the background but leave all the highlights uncolored. Vary the pencil pressure to create lighter values at the top of the page and darker ones at the bottom.

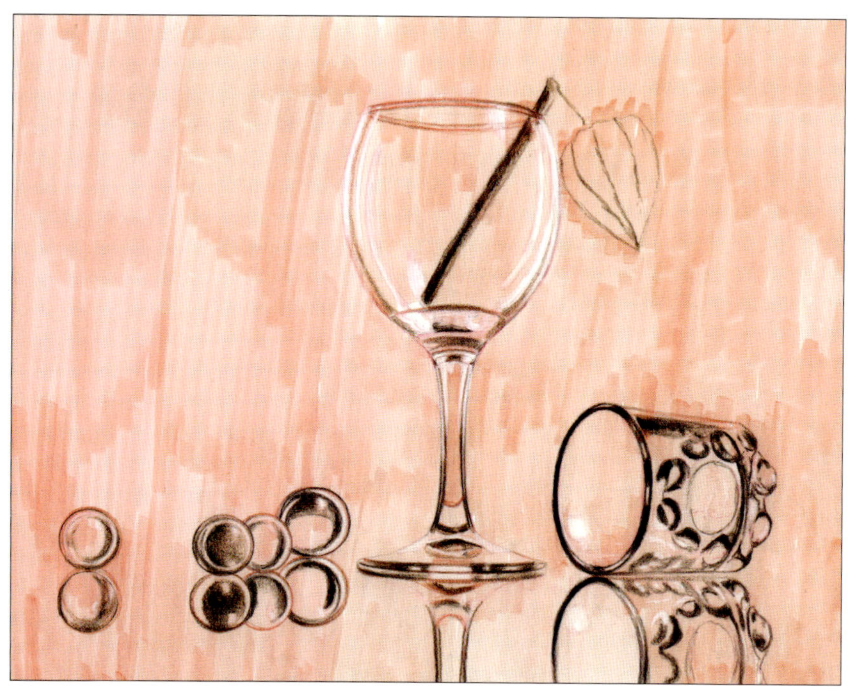

Step 2

Place large highlights with a white marker. Depending on your brand of markers, your whites may be different in strength. The Winsor & Newton white marker is very subtle and requires multiple applications. However, it leaves the edges soft, which is necessary for a realistic appearance. Don't worry if the lights are not too bright at this point. You will just want to establish points of contrast now, and you'll strengthen the brightest highlights in the end with the Sakura pen.

If you work using colored pencil only, just make sure to reserve the space for the highlights and don't color them! Your white paper is your highlight.

Use Prismacolor 90% warm grey plus dark brown to fill in the darkest abstract shapes you see within the wine glass, marbles, and glass. Use a very sharp point to define edges at the wine glass's foot and at the rim in the small glass. Make small, circular strokes to create soft shading in the marbles and the stick. Control your drawing, paying close attention to the accuracy of your outlines at all times as you keep shading. Shading must be soft inside each shape.

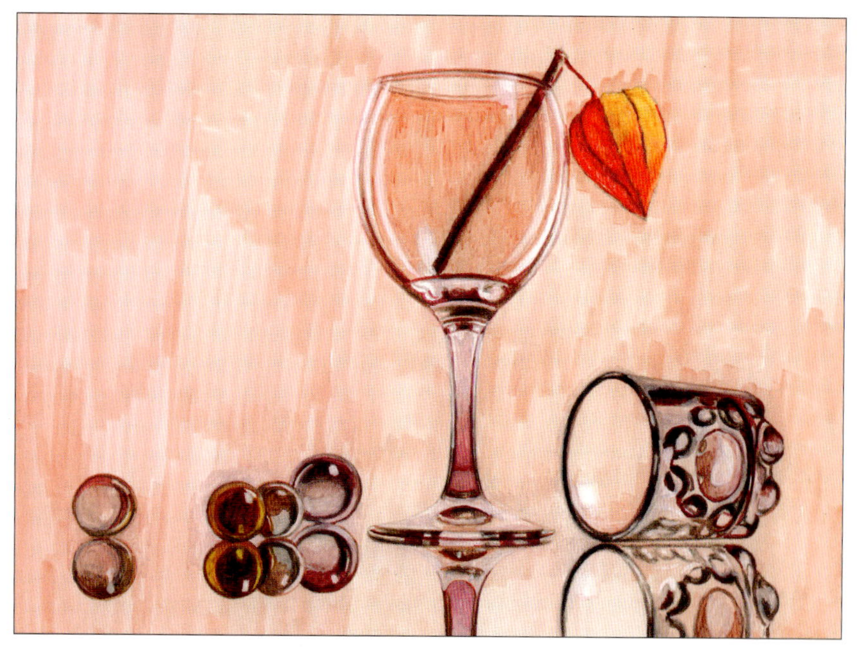

Step 3

Next, you underpaint the marbles and the floral. You have a choice to either continue working with markers (magenta, portrait pink, lemon yellow, white, scarlet) or replace these hues by working in colored pencil.

Shading with markers vs. shading with colored pencil

- If you underpaint in markers, shapes look flat and you will create volume with subsequent layering in colored pencil.
- If you work in colored pencil 100%, you begin layering thinking of volume from the start.

The artist paints with the portrait pink marker inside the wine glass, then adds magenta marker throughout the still life, finding this color in all shapes. In the image for this step, you can see magenta as a cool, dark pink. Lastly, the artist paints with scarlet and lemon yellow in a single marble and the floral. What could have been done better at this point would be the preservation of the circular shapes of the marbles. Therefore you constantly must check your drawing for accuracy by stepping back from it so the perfectly created outlines don't fall apart while shading.

Step 4

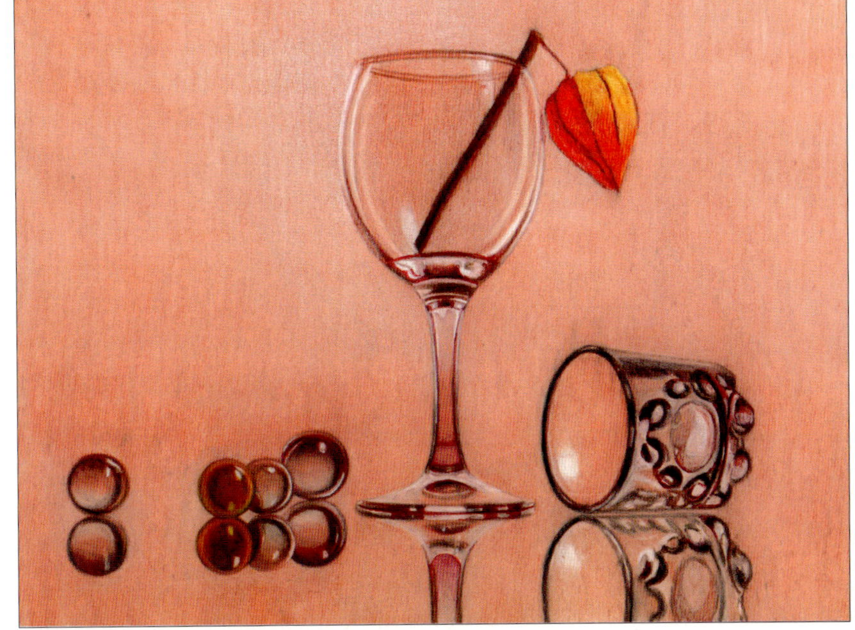

Here you develop the color and values further. Shade the background with Prismacolor peach and light peach, adding these colors into the glass and marbles simultaneously. By doing so, you fill in large areas with light tones present inside each transparent object. With heavy pressure add white at the top of the page (note that white is added over the peach to lighten up and blend the surface). Draw around the highlights, leaving soft edges.

If your dark edges and outlines get lost, re-establish them with 90% warm grey to define the form. Prismacolor henna is a beautiful low chroma pink that you can shade with to create soft transitions between the darks and middle tones in the marbles and in the short glass.

Tip: Sometimes layering and blending goes on easier when your wax-based colored pencils are warm. To warm up the Prismacolors, set them by a warm, sunny window for a few minutes to soften their cores even more.

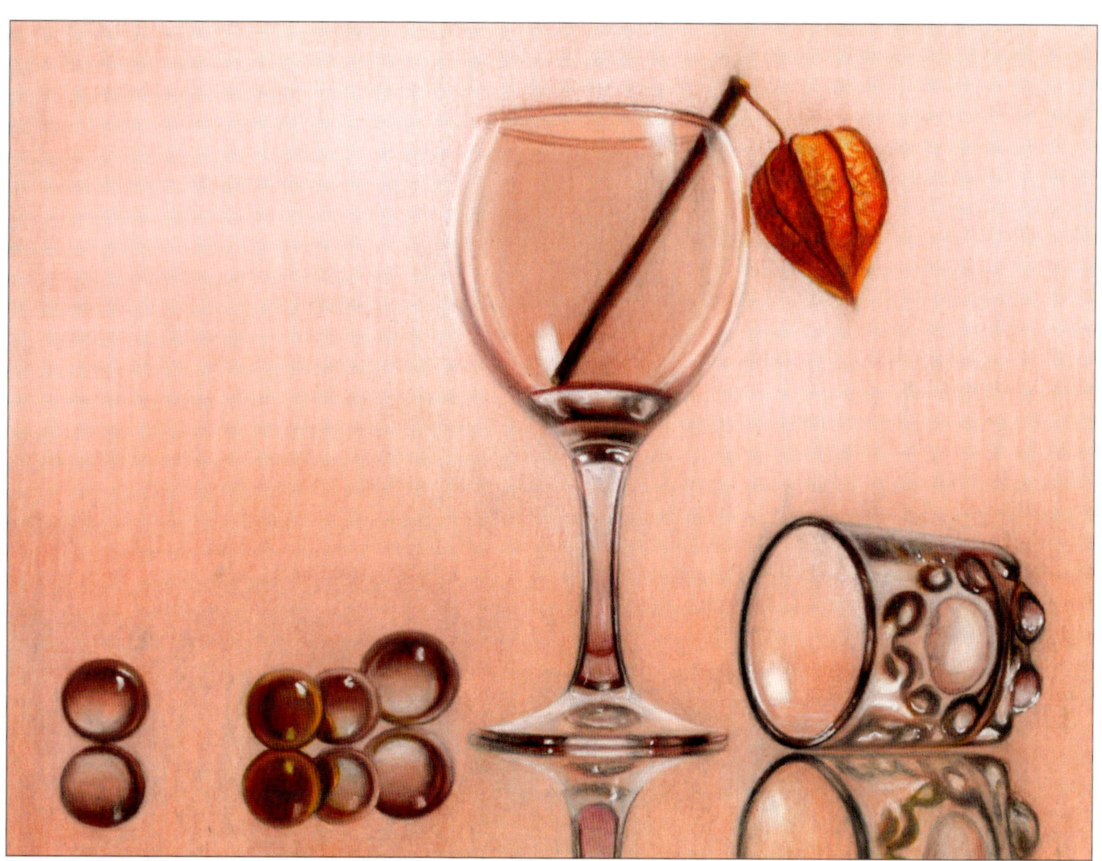

Step 5

In the last step you mull over the details, blending, and perfection of your drawing. To draw the floral, shade with permanent red on the left and darken the veins with henna and dark brown. Shade with mineral orange, permanent red, and yellowed orange in the light. You can create tiny veins with a sharp point of permanent red, then you can add a much lighter color (yellow) on the opposite side of it.

Increase pencil pressure, adding more color to the marbles and the short glass with beige sienna and nectar, and shade with eggshell and beige at the bottom of each marble. Soften the edges around large white areas in the glass with a white colored pencil. Glass must look smooth, so overlap and layer your hues to create smooth shading. Blend with a full blender, if necessary. Use the Sakura pen as your last mark, making tiny highlights in the short glass, wine glass, and marbles. Unlike the marker, the Sakura pen raises the surface with white paint, producing hard edges so apply it with caution.

Now for the finishing touches. Step back and look at your drawing from a distance. Intensify or adjust your shading. Is it smooth with nice transitions? Are shapes accurate? Are highlights strong? Often, the blending step is intermediate and additional layering is necessary to develop the artwork further. When the surface doesn't accept any more layering, it has become too waxy to accept pigment . . . spray it with a fixative to continue working.

Chapter 9

How to Draw Metal, Reflective Surfaces, and Crystal

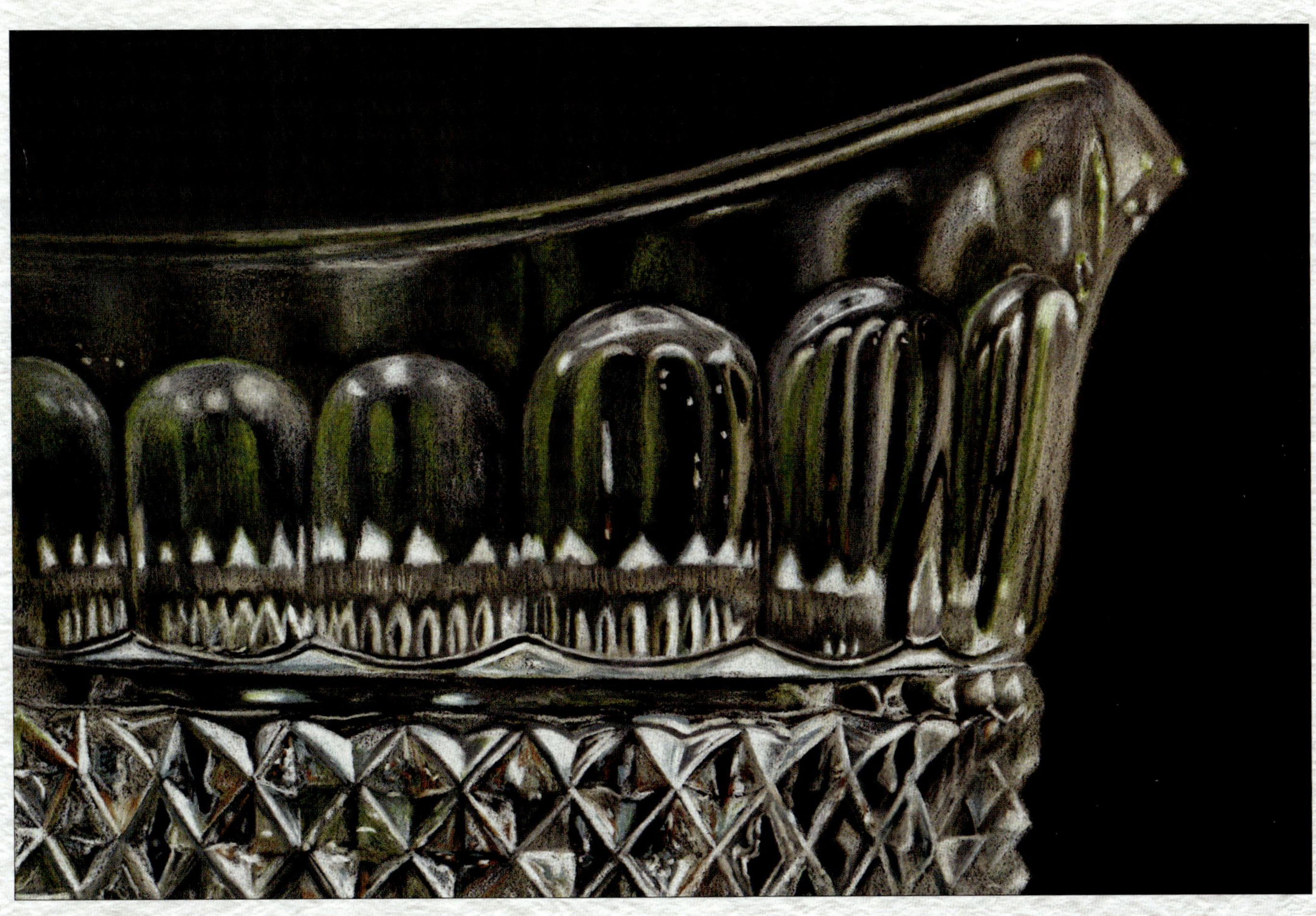

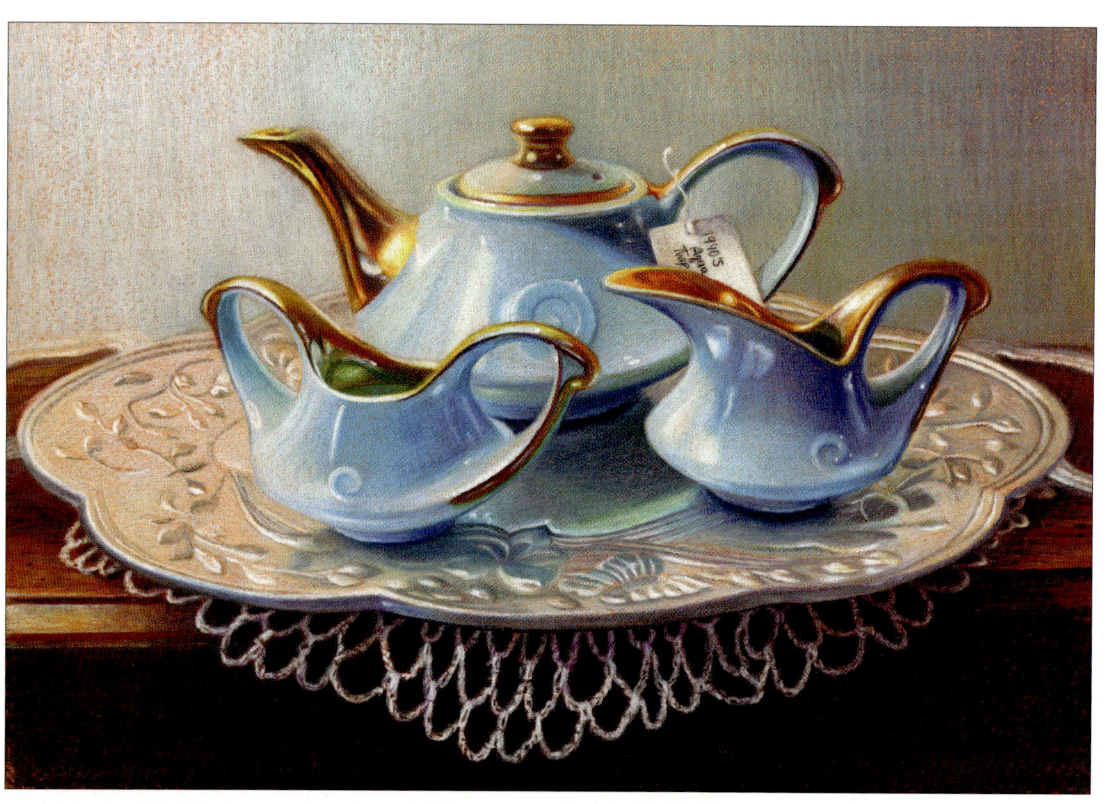

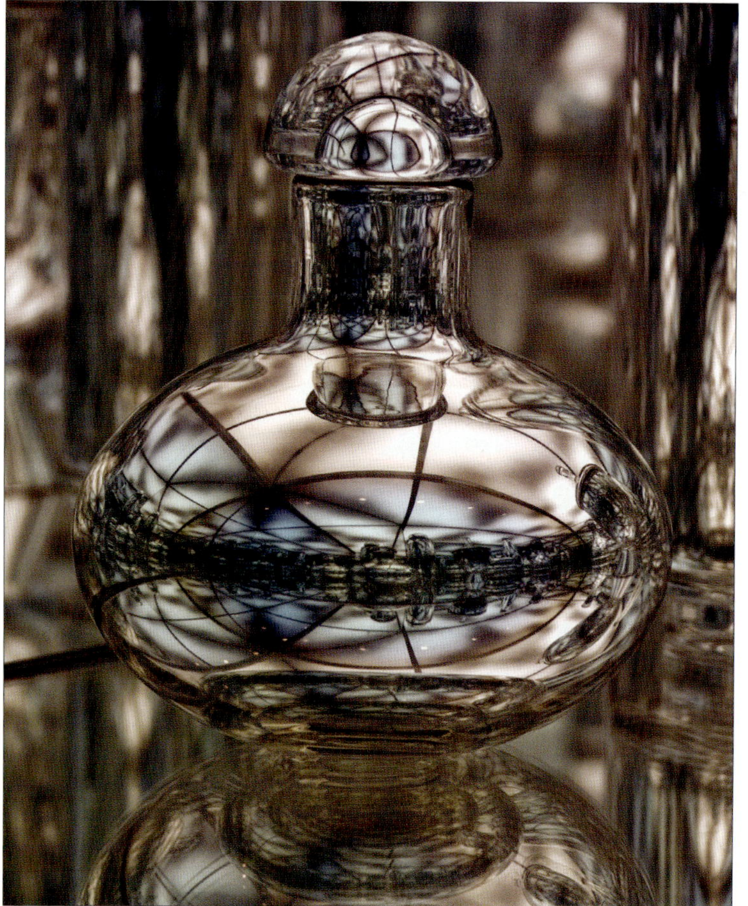

Drawing metal, reflective surfaces, and crystal is not as difficult as you may think once you understand the basic principle behind it. Observation is key!

The first thing that is relevant to drawing any surface or subject is the accuracy of the shapes. The better draftsman you become, the easier it will be for you to keep the shapes accurate, even, or symmetrical as you shade within the outlines. What this means is that when you draw a reflective cup, the shape of the cup itself must be accurate with symmetrical sides and perfect ellipses, regardless of the surface you create in it.

Second, in drawing metal and reflective surfaces, you observe moving abstract patterns and colors. Unlike matte objects with diffused reflections, shiny objects have specular reflections that change with your position. The reflections in metal are mirror-like and always move and change with your movement in relation to it. That is why it's good to have pictures where there is no movement so you can focus on studying the form and patterns of light on it.

Students tend to want to shade metal with metallic colored pencils, which doesn't solve the problem because metallics don't look shimmery on white paper; instead they appear quite dull on their own. The trick is to learn to see colors in the subject that get reflections from the environment it is in. The shape of the reflective object produces and reflects abstract lines, figures, and curves too.

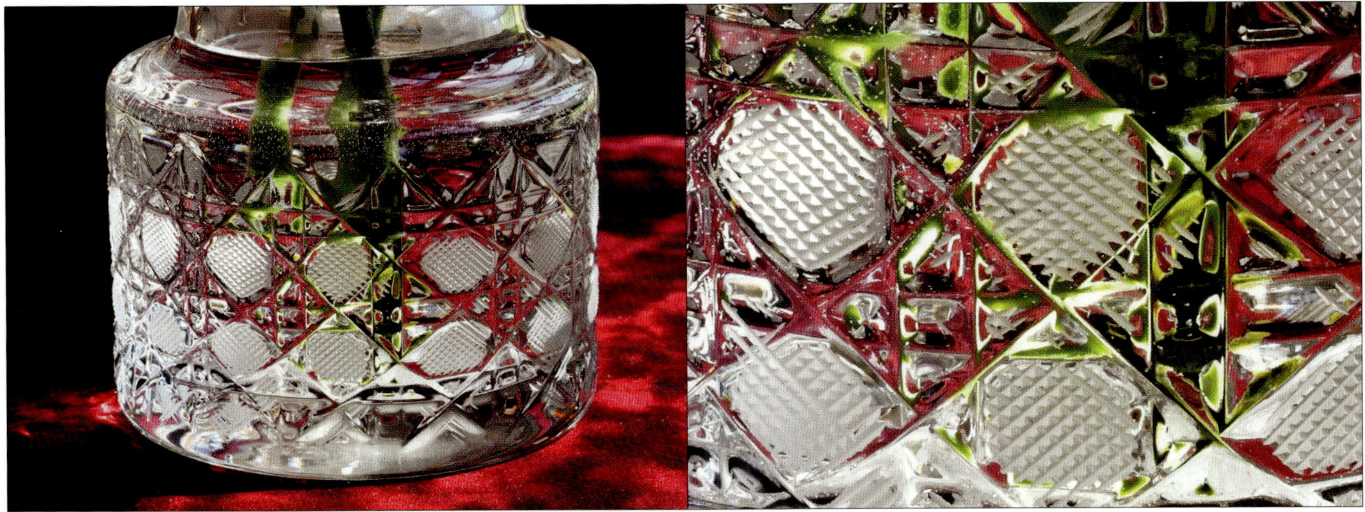

In drawing crystal you should aim to break it down to the general pattern first. See if the glass has patterns with rhombs, squares, ray cuts, etc. You want to be perfect at repeating this pattern as it curves around the form. Then you look at the abstract shapes and colors found within this pattern, and basically aim to copy the largest shapes found within the design. The more sophisticated the general pattern is, the more work you have ahead of you. Therefore, either draw big, so it will be easy to put all the abstract designs you see in your drawing, or pick a crystal vase with a very simple pattern.

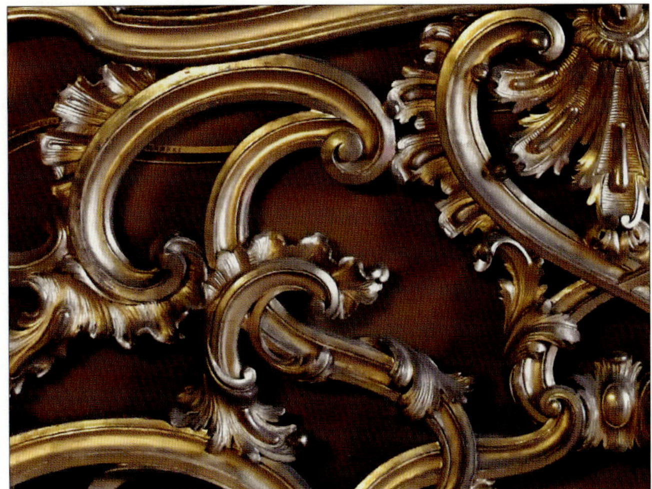

Usually silver and gold reflect the colors surrounding them, especially if the object is shiny. This is a gold-gilded wood with a matte surface that's not very shiny or reflective, but you can still see many different colors here besides the expected "gold." There are light pinks and peaches, greyed browns, warm dark browns, warm burnt ochres, yellow ochres, and some very light, warm yellow mixed with white. Greyed down shadows on the wood create contrast in color temperature with the shinier yellow ochres observed in the light.

STEP-BY-STEP INSTRUCTIONS

Reflective Objects on White Paper

Materials: Koh-I-Noor Polycolor colored pencils and Prismacolor Premier colored pencils; Koh-I-Noor Bristol vellum drawing paper; tracing paper; kneaded eraser; Grumbacher final fixative, matte; Caran d'Ache full blender

Note: Koh-I-Noor Polycolor pencil colors are named with numbers, and the actual pencils used for the artist's sample are given throughout this lesson. Please refer to the color chart to make your pencil color choices. The colors listed are the main colors used; other hues may have been used for minor details.

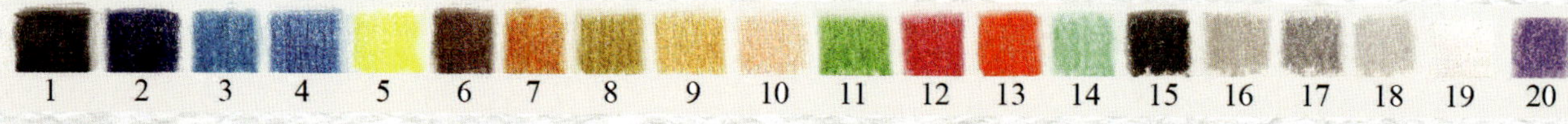

Color Chart:

1. #36
2. Indigo Blue
3. #52
4. #18
5. #2
6. #33
7. #64
8. #66
9. #29
10. #9
11. #61
12. #8
13. #47
14. #24
15. 90% French Grey
16. 20% French Grey
17. 30% Warm Grey
18. 10% Warm Grey
19. White
20. Parma Violet

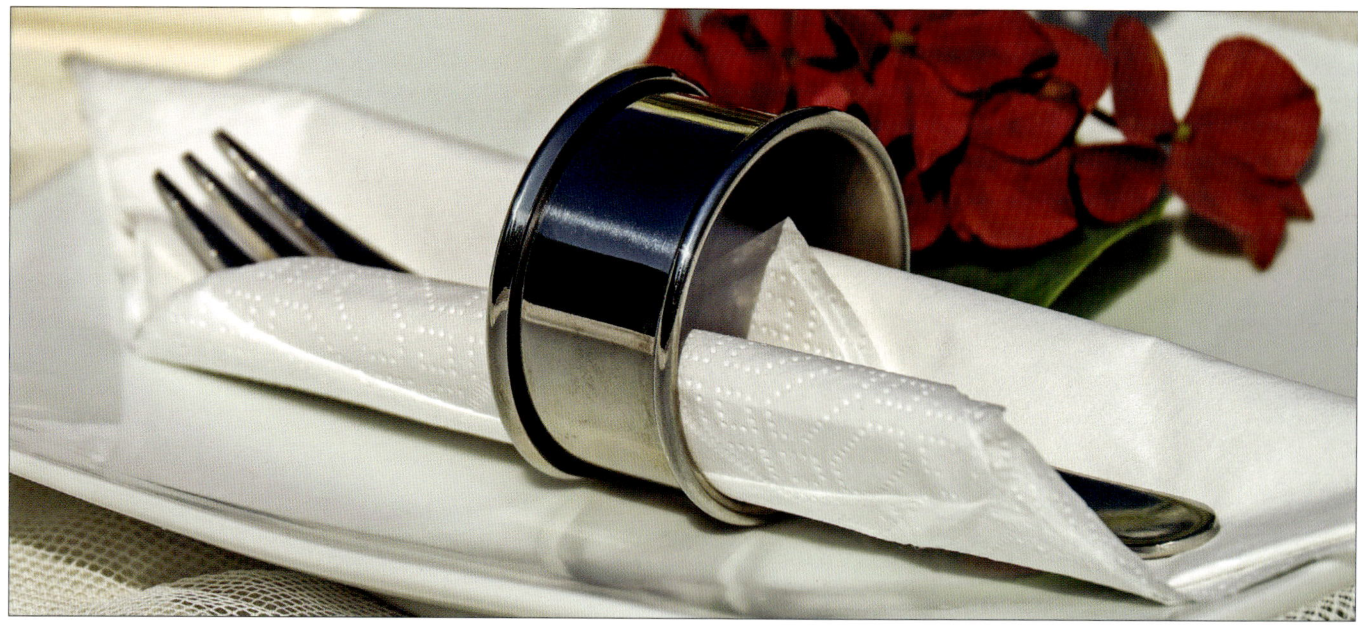

Pixabay image

Step 1

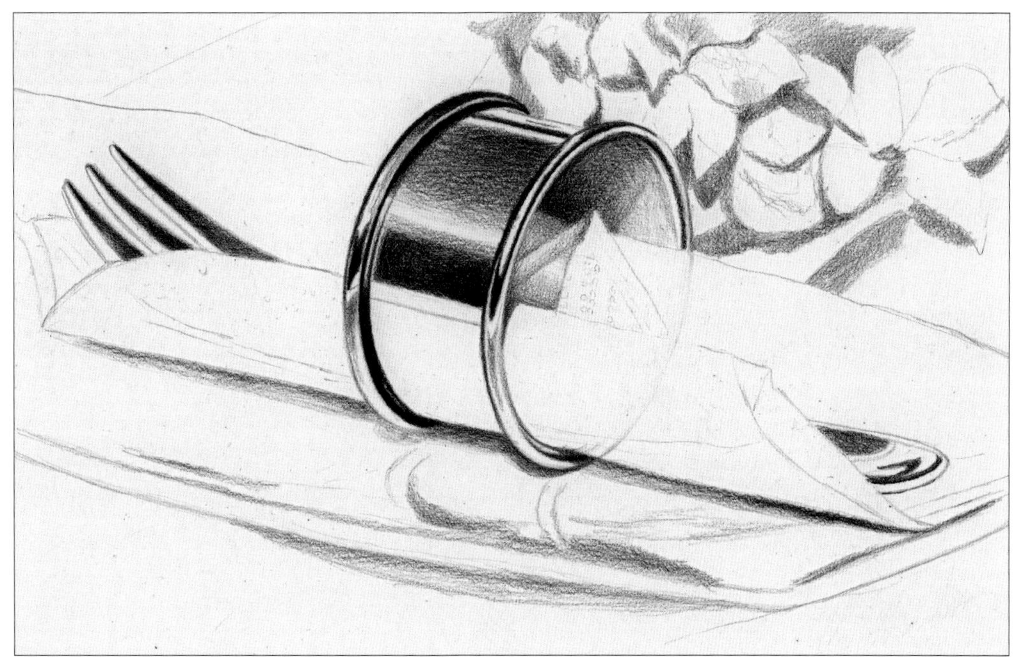

Work on the outline on sketch paper and then transfer it onto your drawing paper. Make sure that the ellipses for the napkin ring are as perfect as possible.

To simplify, don't develop the details in the flowers and the netting under the plate, which you'll see the artist do in the following steps.

Lighten the graphite lines to make them barely visible because most of the still life is white and the pencil marks would darken and enhance once they are shaded over in colored pencil.

Now look at the reference photo to analyze the colors seen in the napkin ring and the fork. Usually gold and silver reflect and produce abstract shapes in dark browns and yellow ochres. The napkin ring is also reflective: it reflects the paper napkin at the bottom and the blue sky at the top with fractions of other colors seen at the top side.

Don't jump between the colors and objects while coloring it. To begin, map out the darks in the ring and the fork only. The artist outlines the darkest shapes and fills them in with Koh-I-Noor black because it is less soft than Prismacolor and therefore keeps a sharp point longer, which is excellent for defining edges and working on details. Next, the artist shades over the black with Prismacolor indigo blue. Notice that the shadows of the flowers are also indigo blue.

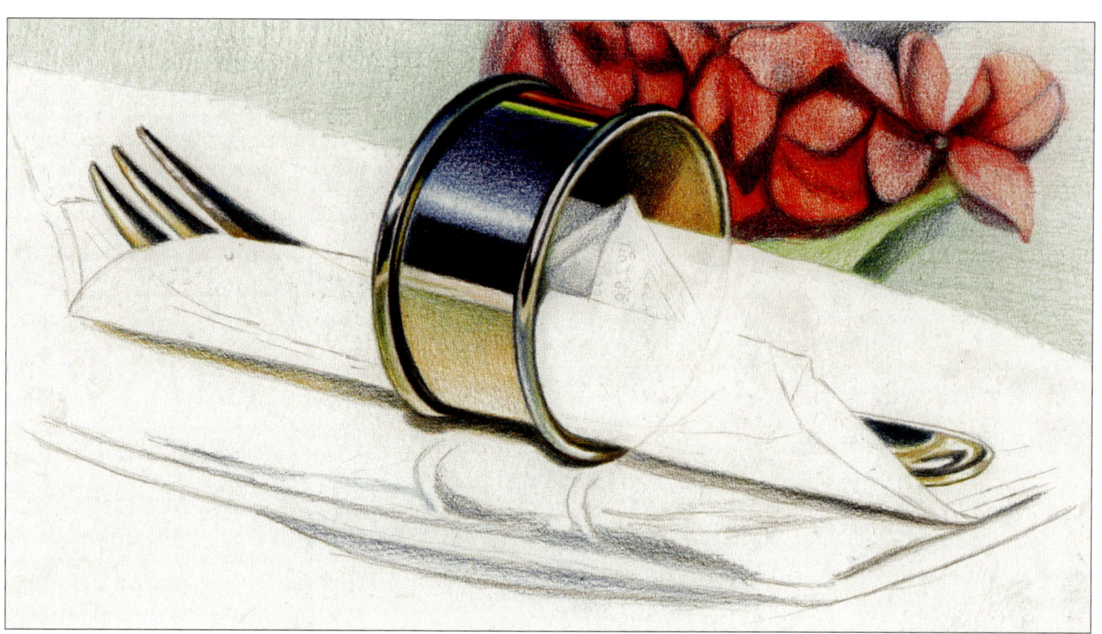

Step 2

Continue working on the napkin ring. Add lighter blues over the dark ones with Koh-I-Noor 52 and 18. Skip over the highlights. They must stay pure white (uncolored)! Shade over the indigo blue, so the blues "melt" into each other.

Once the blue section is complete, shade the light metal section at the bottom and inside the napkin ring. Use colors similar to Koh-I-Noor 64, 66, 29, and 9. Notice that shading is very soft and follows the direction/rotation of the object.

Darken the deepest shadow inside the napkin ring with Koh-I-Noor 33. To draw a single yellow stripe at the top of the ring, use Koh-I-Noor 2. While you shade, pay attention to the structure of the ring. If it falls apart, strengthen the edges with a sharp pencil.

Use a very light, cool green pencil to fill in the background very softly. The artist shades with Koh-I-Noor 24. The flowers should stay soft, nonintrusive, and just support the focal point, rather than compete with it. Red is a powerful color. Therefore try to keep the flowers simple with soft edges and no details. You'll grey them down more in the next step. Shade with Koh-I-Noor 8 and 47. The first color is a cool dark red that you apply over the indigo blue shadows. The second color is a warm red that you use in the light. Throw the same reds into the napkin ring's top reflection.

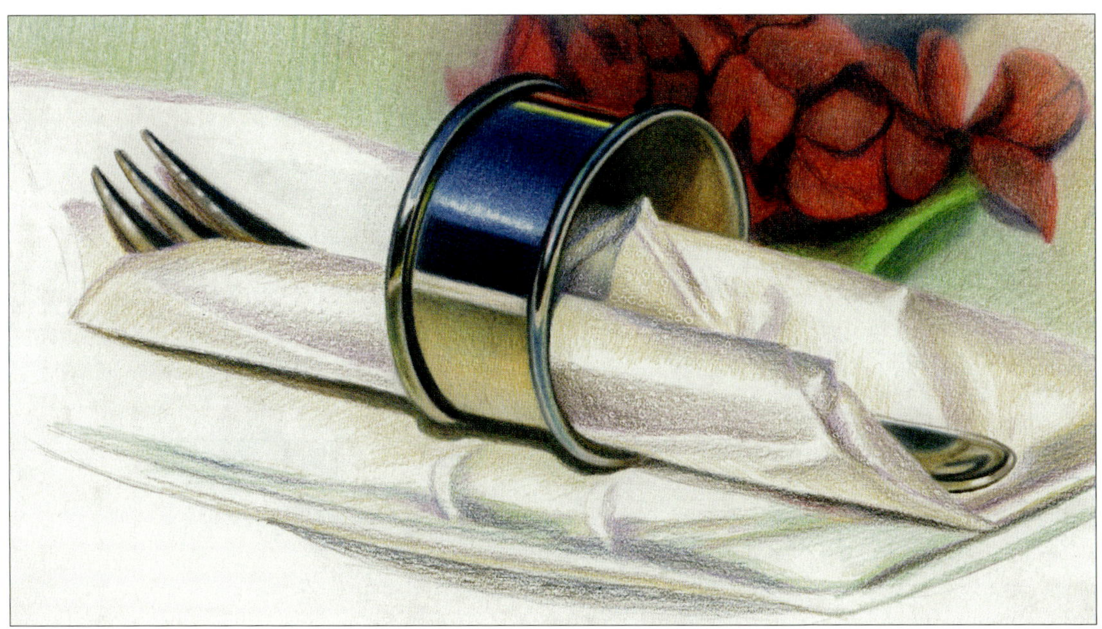

Step 3

Strengthen the colors in the background by reapplying the same colored pencils used before and blending everything. Also, blend the napkin ring and the fork with a pencil blender (Caran d'Ache full blender). Make sure the edges look crisp on the ring and somewhat soft on the fork. Blend the flowers and the background in circular strokes to make soft edges. Use the greys to blend the flowers, pushing them back into the background.

Start working on the paper napkin and the fabric napkin. Both are white, but the textures differ somewhat. The paper napkin is a bit rougher and has a pattern with dots, while the fabric napkin is softer with no design on it. To make the texture in the paper napkin you can either indent the paper or create small circles with a sharp pencil later, or you can even try a combination of both methods. If you decide to indent your paper with the tiny circles you see in the paper napkin, be aware that the design should wrap around the napkin. Next, place the colors for the shadows seen in both napkins with Prismacolor parma violet, Prismacolor 20% French grey, and Prismacolor 30% warm grey. Also think of the volume and rotation of the napkins in space: your strokes should describe the rotation by shading following the form.

To add the warm light in the napkins, don't use pure yellow, rather pick a color in the family of yellow ochres that is natural and shade the light areas with a very light touch. The artist uses Koh-I-Noor 29. Leave the brightest whites uncolored! Also add the same very light green into the fabric napkin's shadow.

With a sharp point place Prismacolor 90% French grey in the cast shadow under the napkin ring and napkin.

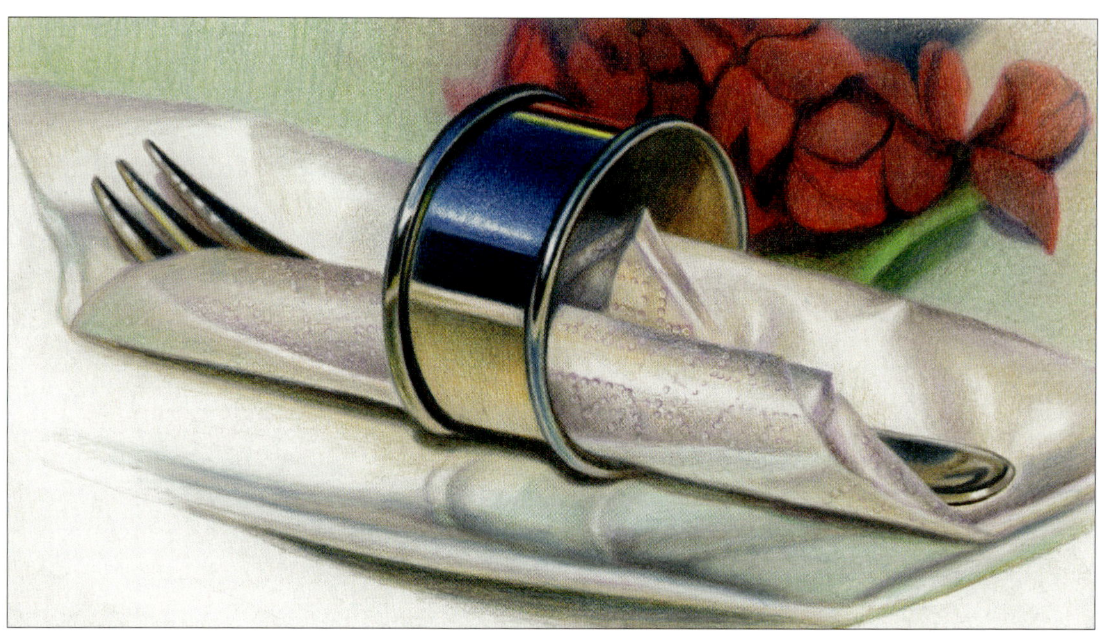

Step 4

In this step you work on softening the transitions in the white napkins and placing texture on the paper napkin in particular. You should already see paper indentations as you have shaded it. Now you can increase the appearance of texture by placing darker strokes around each circle with Prismacolor parma violet (or grey) and Prismacolor white on the other side. Maintain this pattern of placing dots that wrap around the paper napkin.

Use the greys shown in the chart, especially Prismacolor 10% warm grey to grey down the colors and to create light value transitions in both napkins. With heavy pressure, shade with Prismacolor white around the highlights in the fabric napkin to blend the edges and to unify the colors. Keep the napkin ring with crisp edges and soften the rest of the image around it.

Do's and don'ts of working on black paper

Draw on black paper when your image has a lot of black, black-brown, or blue-black in it. Some artists create striking black-and-white artwork using a single white pencil. If you love color, drawing on black paper can be fun but you need to understand its unique properties so you will use this paper to its fullest potential. Its color (or the absence of it) represents several challenges for the artist:

- Duller colors. Hues lose their color intensity on black. Many dark and medium dark colors "disappear" on black paper.
- Because shading is limited to lighter colors, it may be difficult to create an illusion of volume so see what images would work better than others.
- You can't sketch with graphite pencil on black paper as it doesn't show on it. Therefore image transferal is effective with white transfer paper only.

How to make it work:

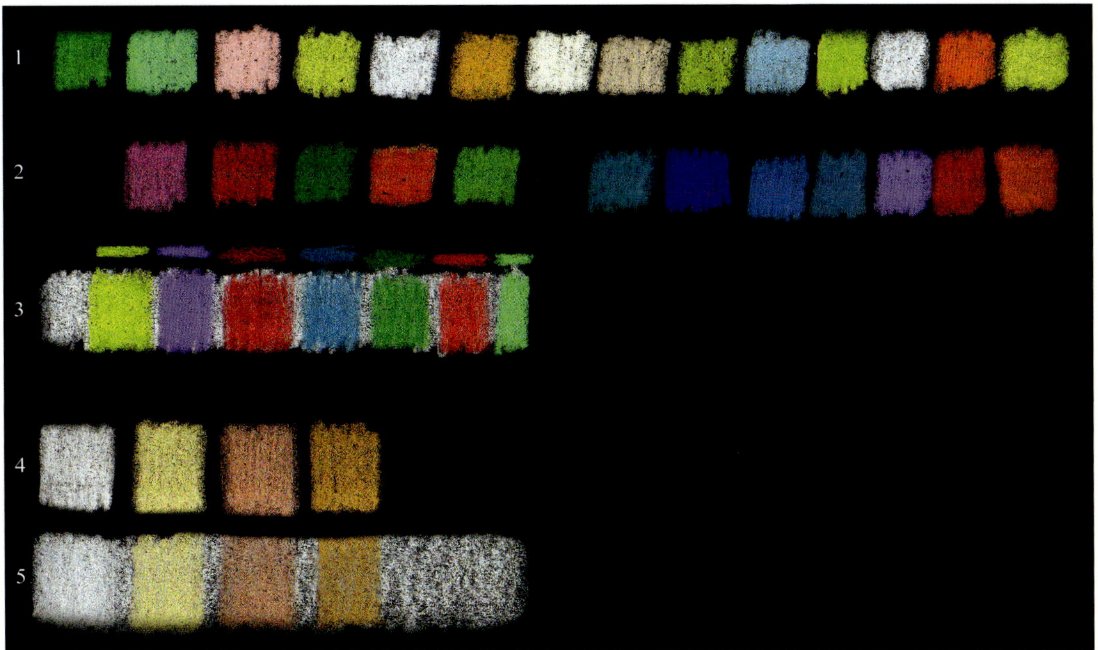

- First thing is to test all the colors you have on black paper, making color swatches. It will help you to see which hues stand out and which disappear on black. In Row 1 you see how light colors look super vibrant, while darker colors (Row 2) vary in color intensity significantly.
- One of the techniques used when colors become dull is to make a white underpainting using a white colored pencil first and then shading with colors over it (Row 3). In the example you can see how much brighter the colors become when shaded over the white, especially the darker hues. With this method the challenge for beginners will be to think in advance about how you can create values in a form, shading in white and then in color.
- A more efficient way of making the colors pop on black paper is to use a spray fixative. Spray the paper once the outline is on it and then spray it in between the layers while you shade. Depending on paper and fixative brand, workable fixative may not work as well as the final one. Try spraying your artwork with a light coat of final fixative, matte.
- To create your artwork use the colors that appear brighter naturally. Medium light to very light pencils look vibrant on black paper.
- Metallic colored pencils do appear metallic drawn on black paper (Row 4). You can see that they are even more vibrant shaded on black, rather than on black with white pencil (Row 5). The shimmer of the metallics usually disappears if shaded on white paper.
- Draw on smooth, black paper that has just enough texture to grab the pencil.

STEP-BY-STEP INSTRUCTIONS

Drawing on Black Paper

Materials: Prismacolor Premier and Caran d'Ache Pablo colored pencils; Koh-I-Noor black drawing paper pad; white transfer paper; kneaded eraser; Grumbacher final fixative matte

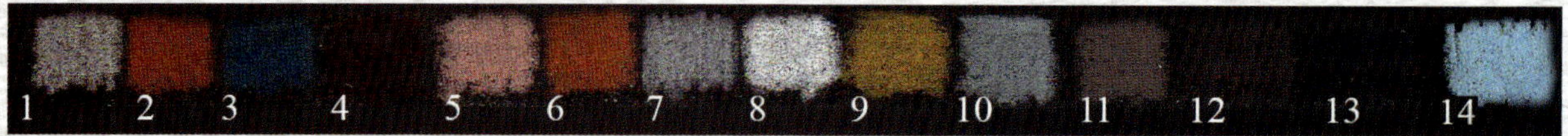

Color Chart: 1. Metallic Silver 2. Burnt Ochre 3. Pablo Malachite Green 4. Black Raspberry 5. Nectar 6. Orange 7. Pablo Silver Grey 8. White 9. Yellowed Orange 10. Jade Green 11. 70% French Grey 12. 90% French Grey 13. 90% Warm Grey 14. Pablo Turquoise Blue Small amounts of other colors may have been used as well.

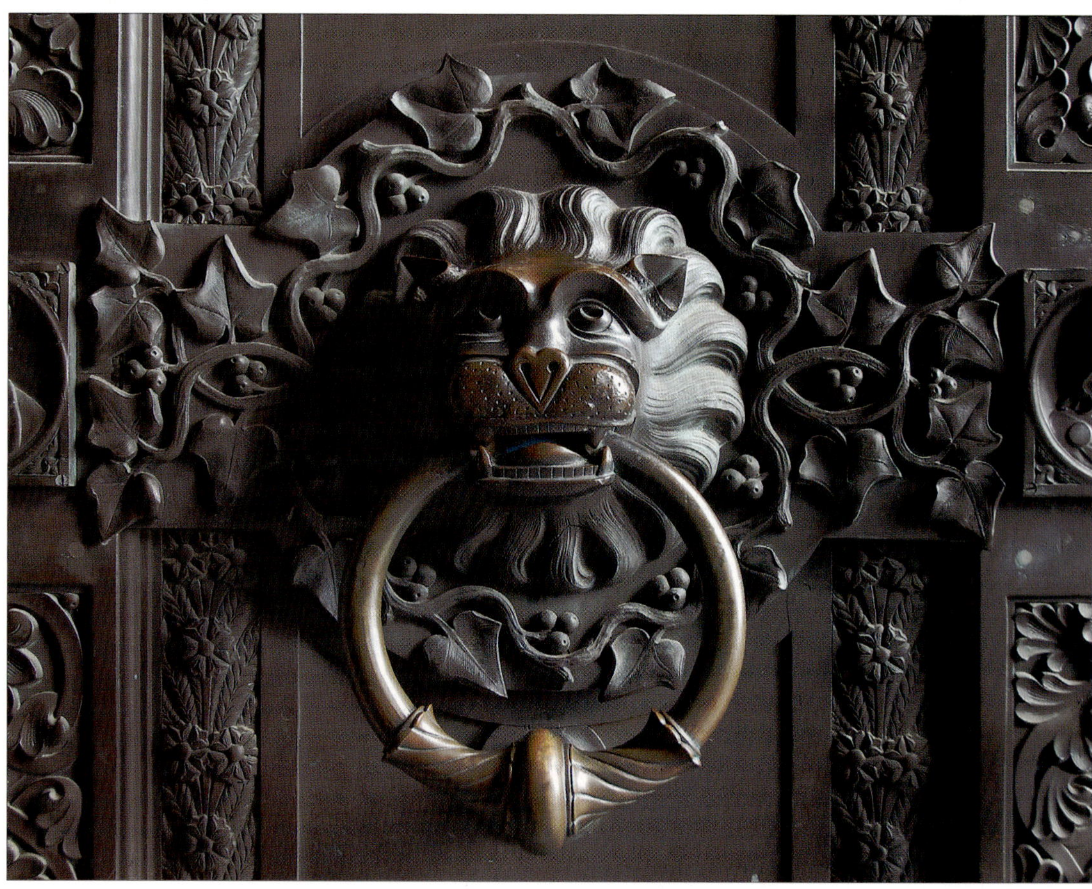

This image has lots of black in it and therefore is a good candidate for drawing on black paper. Also the photo has a limited palette with just a few low-chroma browns and greys. In this project you'll see how the author opens it up to artistic interpretation and sees more color that harmonizes well with browns and greys.

Step 1

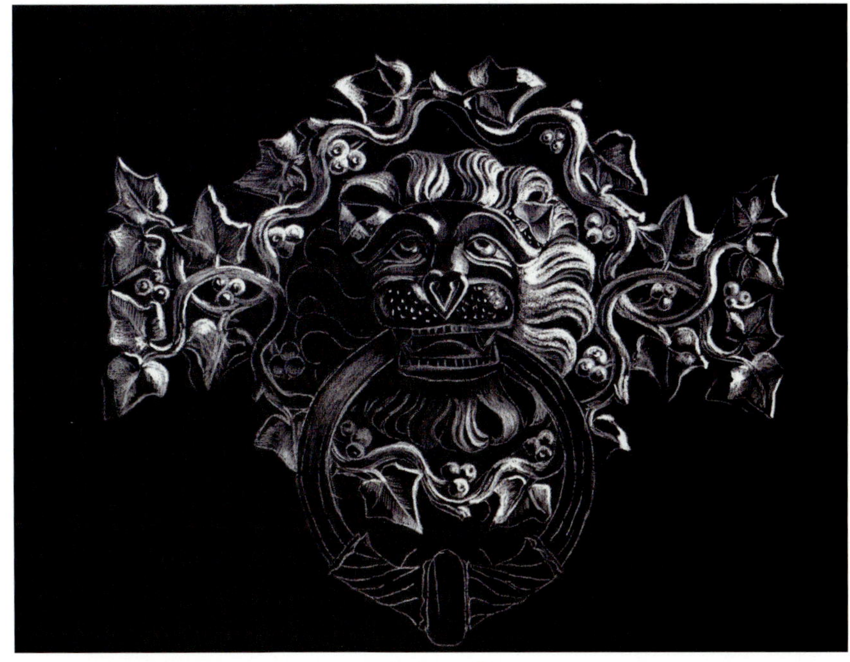

Transfer your outlines with white transfer paper. Separate the warm and cool colors you see in the light. The lion's head, right eye, and leaves have cool lights set against neutral brown-grey hues, while the face and door handle have warm, brown-orange hues. Focus on the cool light and draw it with consistency. Shade with white and Pablo silver grey. (Pablo silver grey doesn't look silvery, it is similar to Prismacolor 10% cool grey and slightly less bright than pure white colored pencil.) Here you can see that it is possible to create an artwork in white only by varying the pencil pressure and stroke direction.

Step 2

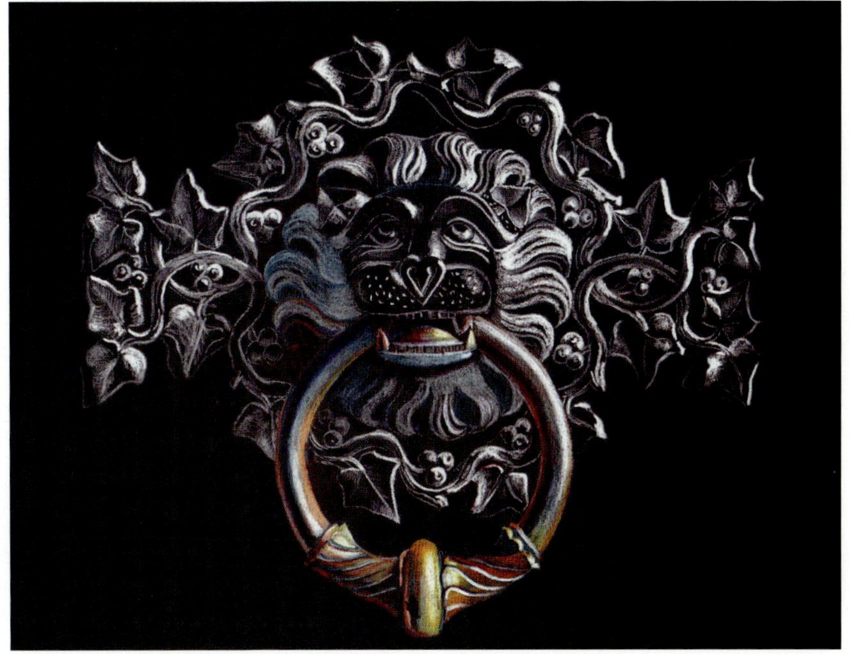

You need to have some color in black to draw out the darkest shapes and shadows, even though they seem to fall in complete darkness and appear black in the image. These areas are the form shadow in the ring, the darks in the handle, the lion's hair on the left side, and under the lion's chin. The artist picks Prismacolor black raspberry and Pablo malachite green to shade these areas in the dark. Any dark color will work instead of black raspberry, but this color has some red in it that harmonizes well with the browns and orange. Pablo malachite green is a much darker version of the same color seen in cool lights on the metal (in the lion's hair on the right side and some leaves). Prismacolor jade green is a light, cool green that makes a nice transition between the darkest shadows and the highlights. Don't be a slave to your camera or a picture: find colors that make a statement and harmonize well with the lights.

Once you place these shadows, create the golden colors in the mouth and handle. It's a misconception to use metallic pencils to depict metal surfaces. The important thing is to see colorful reflections in the metal, noticing its color temperature. To map out the warm golden handle and the lion's mouth, shade with Prismacolor orange, yellowed orange, burnt ochre, nectar, and white. Shade with white using the heaviest pressure. Pay attention to the curvature of the stripes: if you make them linear, the handle will look flat. While you shade, pay attention to the symmetry and evenness of the shapes too. The artist notices mishaps in the handle that will be fixed up in the next step.

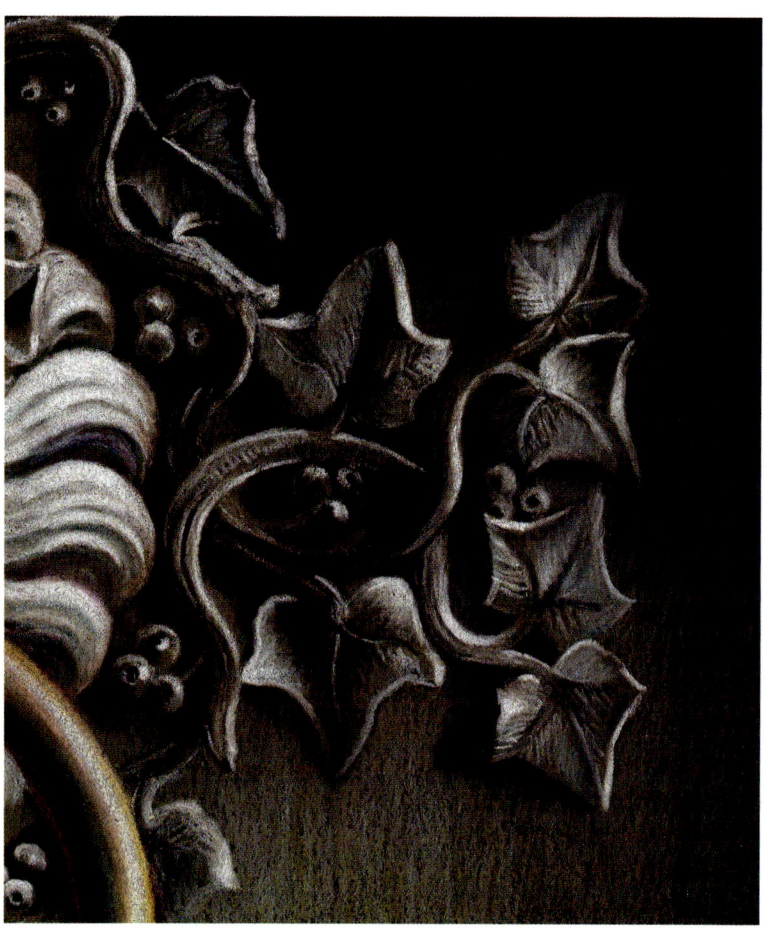

Step 3

Most of the drawing in the leaves and background is done with three greys. Prismacolor 90% warm grey is in the deepest shadows and shapes' outlines that appear very close to being black. Prismacolor 90% French grey is in medium dark values, and 70% French grey is in medium values. White and Pablo silver grey make up the highlights.

Notice how stroke direction rotates each leaf and stem. Also tiny strokes make veins in the leaves and texture in the stems. Once every leaf is done and you have cast shadows under the leaves, shade the background.

In the background you use the same three greys: 70% French grey at the bottom, 90% French grey in the middle, and 90% warm grey at the top. Once again, the stroke direction separates the background from your subject. The artist shades up and down in parallel strokes that go "against" the texture and stroke variation seen in the leaves.

Shade the light blue parts on the face and handle using Pablo turquoise blue. This color may be added to the surrounding leaves as well for color unity.

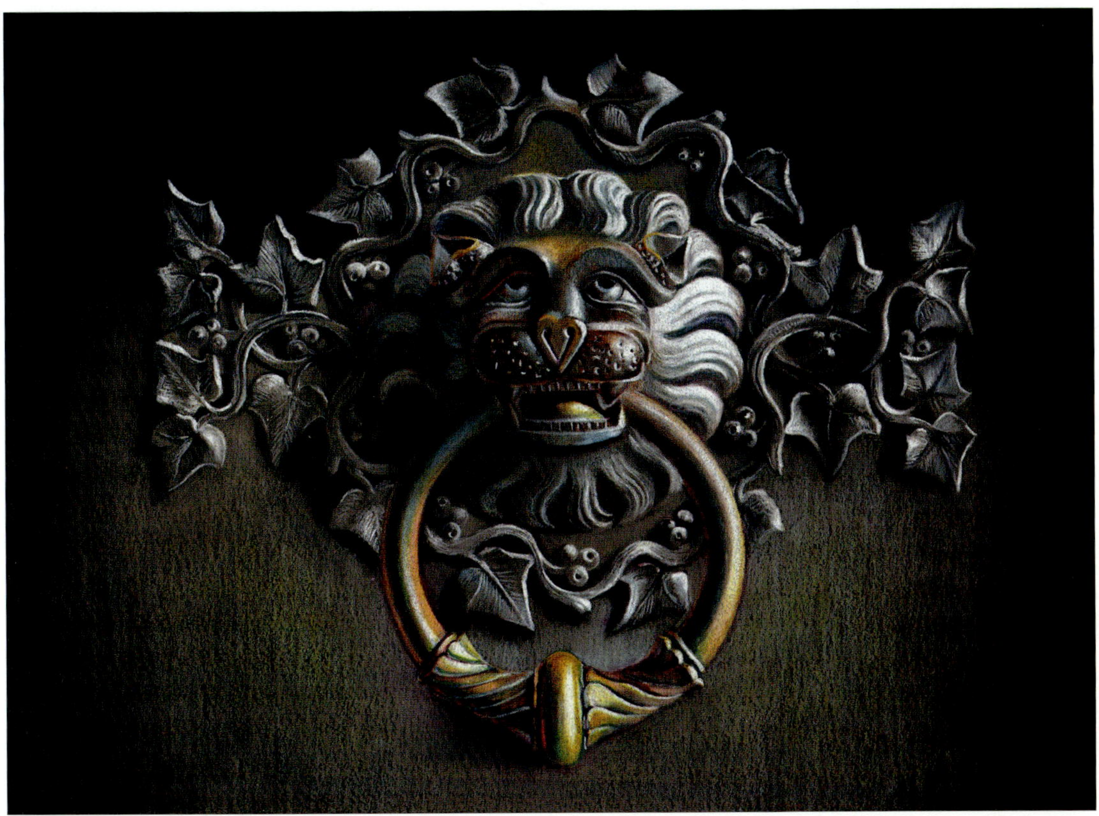

Step 4

Once the entire image is shaded in greys only, you can add fractions of colors previously used in the lion and the handle. For instance the lightest areas in the background can have some yellowed orange in warm lights or jade green in cool light. Some of the petals can have nectar and jade green too.

To shade the face, the artist puts some color underneath the greys. For that use black raspberry in the darks; use burnt ochre, yellowed orange, and a small amount of yellow ochre on the lion's forehead. Overlap the previously used greys (70% French grey and 90% French grey) on the entire face and hair. Use heavy pressure to draw the lightest hair on the right in white.

On the face some areas around the highlights look light blue. The artist uses jade green and white with Pablo silver grey. To add stronger color in the eyes, the artist shades with Pablo turquoise blue very lightly. (You can see a darker version of this turquoise color in the shadow because Pablo malachite green mixes with jade green and greys, giving a similar hue, only darker).

Step back to check the accuracy of your drawing. The artist thinks of the form, its definition, and roundness, which informs her shading method. Are the edges sharp in the face and the handle? Are the edges soft in the cast shadows under the leaves? Do you have enough contrast in the leaves and handle? Spray with a final fixative outdoors. It's ready for framing.

Making highlights on colored paper

When drawing on black and colored papers, you will use the same principles to make highlights as you did on white paper. However, use a white colored pencil (make sure it is sharp) to shade the highlights as opposed to shading around them on white paper. The darker the colored paper, the brighter your highlights will appear on it.

Note that white is a cool color by itself, and often the highlight should be warm. In realist colored pencil drawing, it is best to use some light color placed underneath the white. Therefore, artists often shade with light, warm-colored pencils first and then use white. Usually the application of white requires shading with a very heavy pencil pressure, using the softest colored pencil possible.

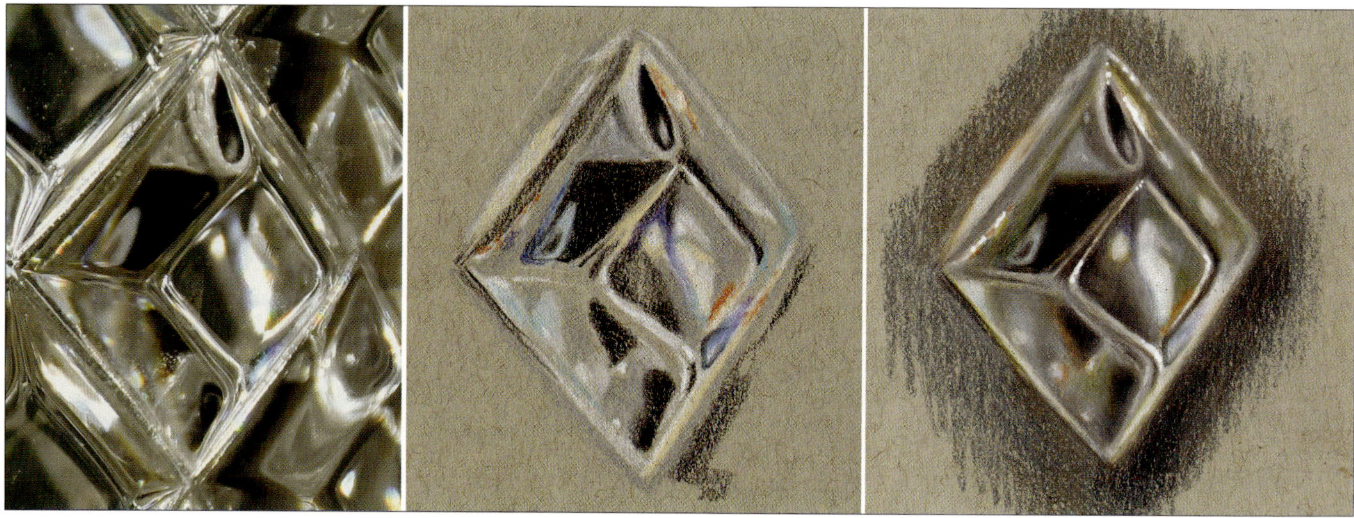

In general glass will look like glass if all transitions between shapes and colors are smooth (well blended) and major highlights are copied well. In this example you see one section taken out from the crystal pitcher. While crystal looks complicated to draw, when you break it down into small sections and copy the big shapes and highlights inside each section, it's doable. If you are a beginner, pick crystal glass with a simple pattern, take pictures to catch the reflections, and begin drawing by observing the pattern of crystal cuts.

STEP-BY-STEP INSTRUCTIONS

Drawing Crystal on Colored Paper

Materials: Prismacolor Premier colored pencils unless noted otherwise, Koh-I-Noor black drawing paper, white transfer paper, kneaded eraser, Grumbacher final fixative, matte, Caran d'Ache full blender

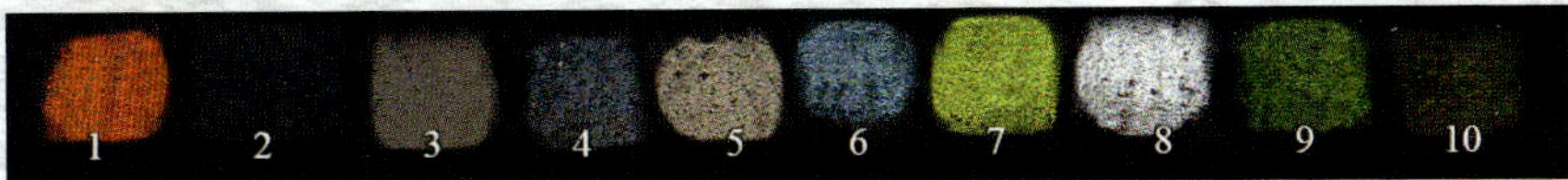

Color Chart: 1. Orange 2. 90% Warm Grey 3. 70% French Grey 4. 70% Cool Grey 5. Beige Sienna 6. Pablo Turquoise Blue 7. Canary Yellow 8. White 9. Koh-I-Noor 62 10. Artichoke Small amounts of other colors may have been used as well.

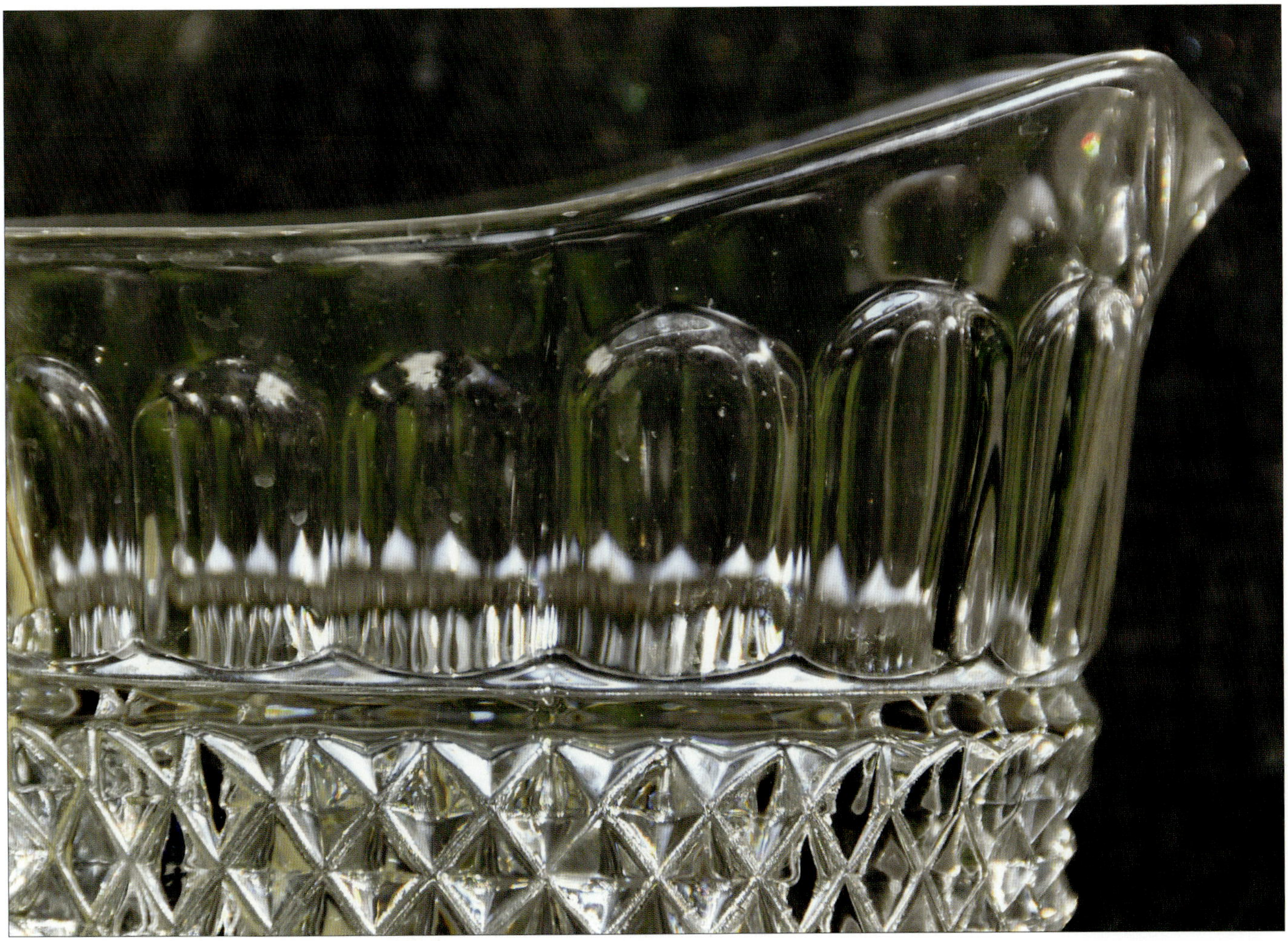

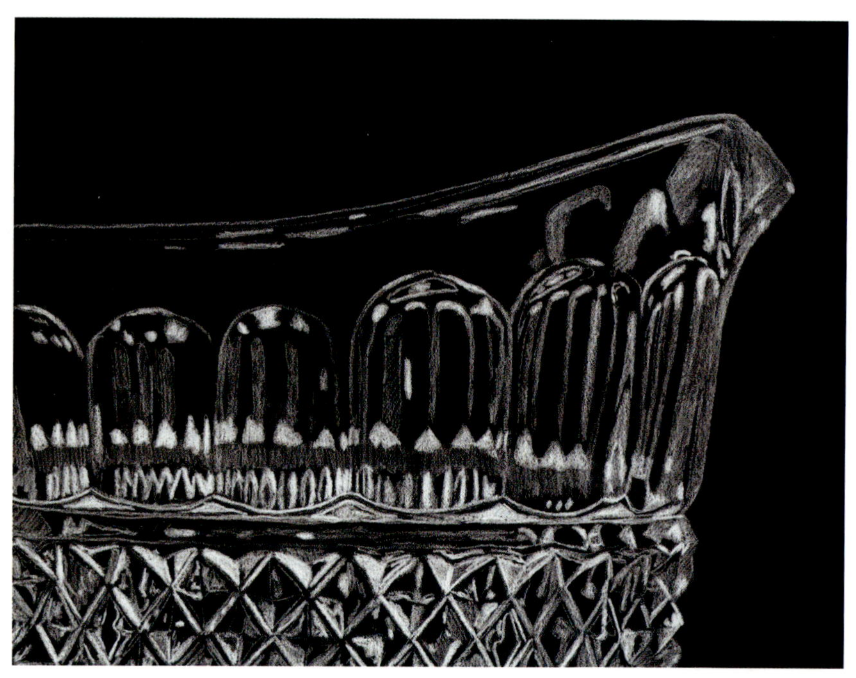

Step 1

Transfer the outlines with a white transfer paper. Spray the paper with a light coat of a final fixative, matte. (It will make the colors appear brighter). Take a sharp soft white pencil and map out all the lights and sparkles you see in the image. Think in terms of pattern design and notice how the crystal rhombs rotate in space and change their shapes on the sides of the pitcher. The top part of the glass pitcher consists of six "domes" that reflect the elongated shapes inside each of them. Use different pressure to make brighter and softer whites, depending on the strength of the reflection. The artist underpaints with white some areas that will be colored green in the next step (green appears brighter shaded over white).

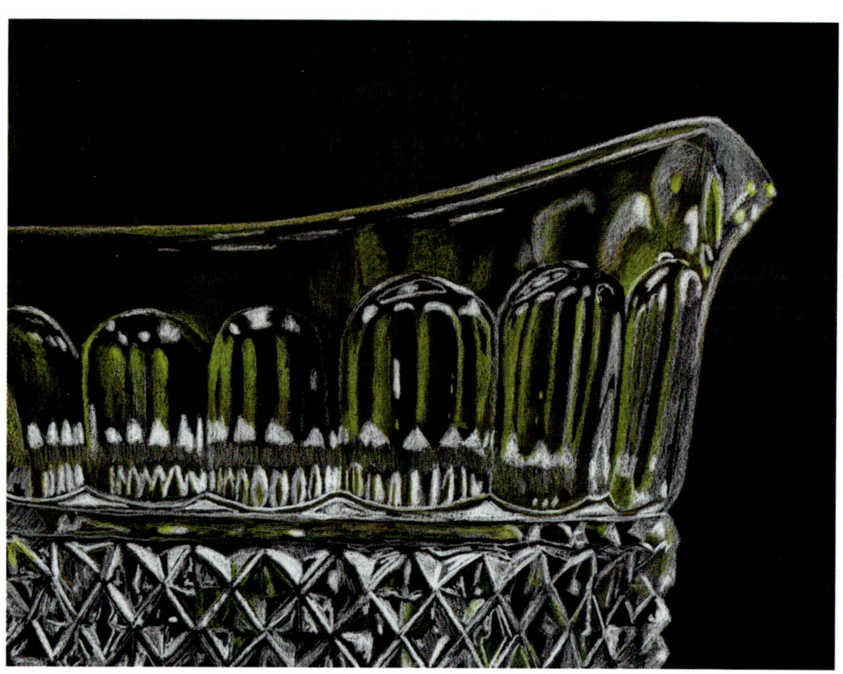

Step 2

Add one color at a time. Here you see the artist work with a single green (Koh-I-Noor 62), and then artichoke with some greys (90% warm grey, 70% French grey, and 70% cool grey). Remember, you can definitely replace the Koh-I-Noor green with one you have in your box. Test it on the side of the page to see if it's warm and bright enough to show up well in your drawing.

Step 3

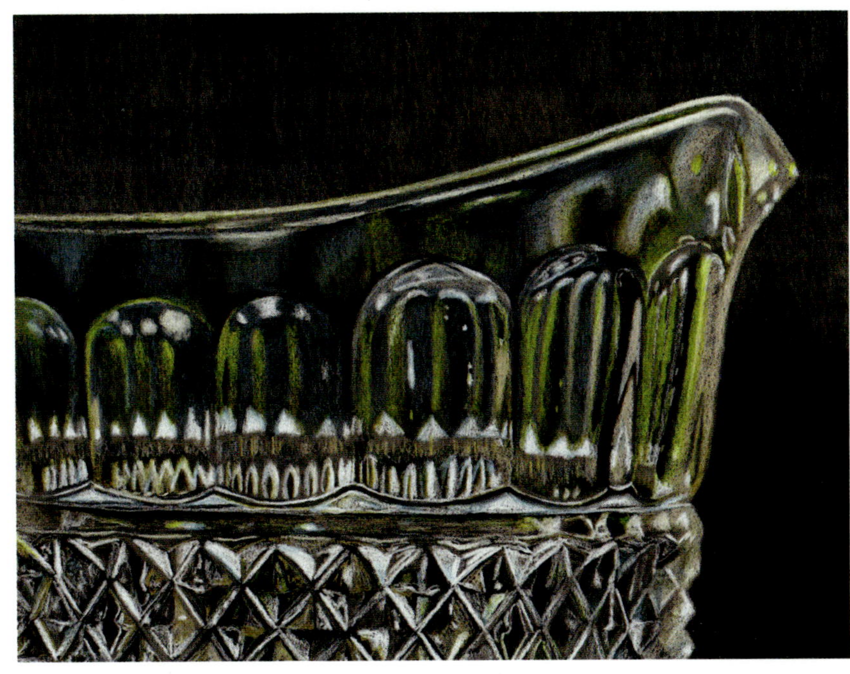

Let's add more color now. Because this paper is so smooth, colors tend to layer very smoothly and blending is not needed at all. However, if you work on paper with a slight texture, you will need to remember to create soft transitions between the colors via layering and blending with a full blender.

Add darker green (artichoke) at the bottom of each green stripe seen in the domes. Overlap it over the lighter green to make a soft transition. You also want to put the darker green into the background, because the pitcher reflects the colors and the background has greyed down greens and blues in it.

Shade softly around the edges of the pyramid-shaped whites in the pitcher with Pablo turquoise blue. (This color can be replaced with almost any light blue). Add touches of this blue into the cut crystal as well.

Use the greys to color the background and to fill in the gaps between the green stripes in the domes. The artist shades with 70% cool grey here. The space that you see on the right edge of the pitcher and the grey stripe under the small white pyramids is filled in with a combination of 70% French grey and beige sienna in parallel, up and down strokes. You will want to keep the edges very soft here.

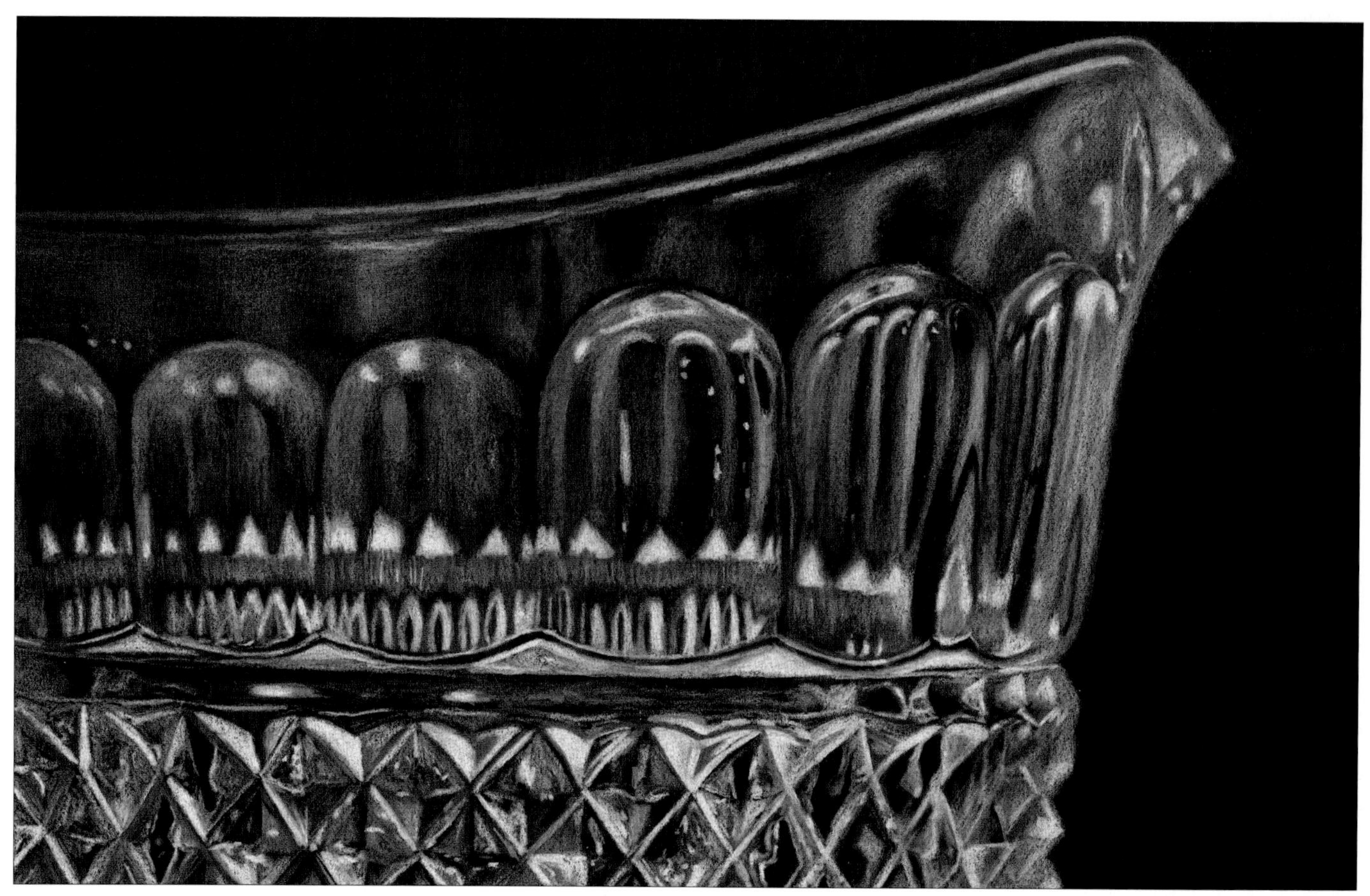

Step 4

Spray the drawing. Let it dry and continue working on strengthening color and details. While the artist darkens the background with 90% warm grey and 70% French grey, you can also shade with 90% cool grey in some parts of the background for variation. Also, use 90% warm grey to define the edges in the cut crystal if the form gets lost. You want to preserve the original shapes of small rhombs. Add tiny, colorful sparkles in canary yellow and orange in the rhombs. You can also add Prismacolor indigo blue into the darkest abstract shapes seen in the rhombs. Strengthen the brightest whites with white colored pencil again, using heavy pressure. Some off-white colors like light peach and eggshell will add warmth to white. A touch of jade green will make nice transitions between the light colors, blending the edges. Unlike in the reference photo, the background is almost black in this drawing. It's a matter of personal preference. You can easily shade with lighter greys over your background to match the lighter values. The artist prefers having more contrast in the final drawing. You may wonder why bother coloring the black background if it is almost black in the end anyway. Black is not a color on its own. It's the absence of it, so pure black paper looks dull uncolored. There is always some light passing through the object, and while the reproduction may not show all the information we see with our eyes, we can definitely see the difference looking at art in person.

Chapter 10

How to Draw Textures

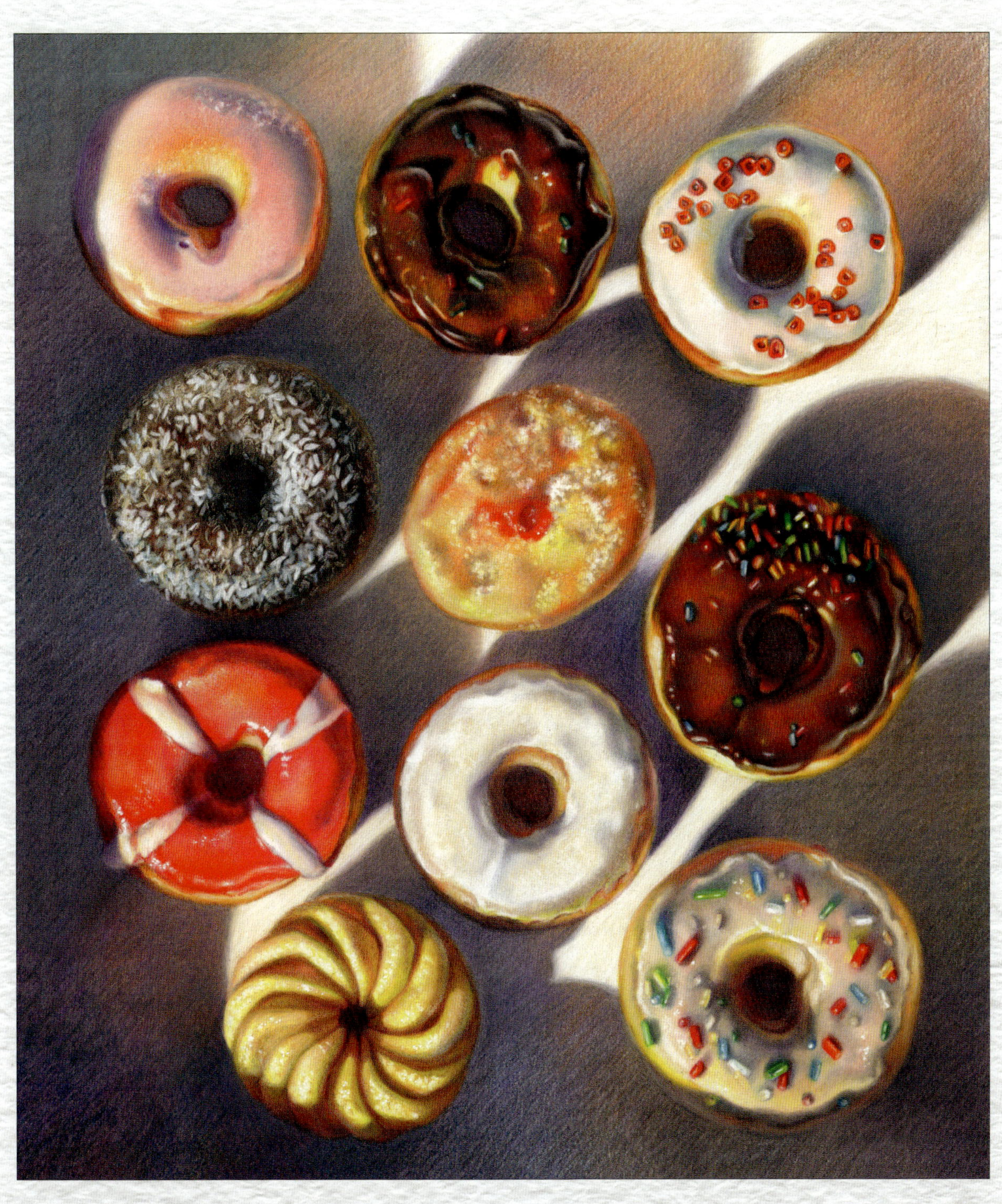

Sometimes you want to go beyond regular crosshatching or burnishing to create fun and unique textures. Three major techniques you can try are rubbing (Chapter 3), paper indenting, and the application of varied directional strokes (shown in this chapter). Before you start shading, you should plan out which parts of your drawing become rubbings and which areas are good for indentations or varied strokes. Rubbings seem to work best on larger areas, while paper indenting is good for working on smaller details. Varied strokes can describe numerous surfaces.

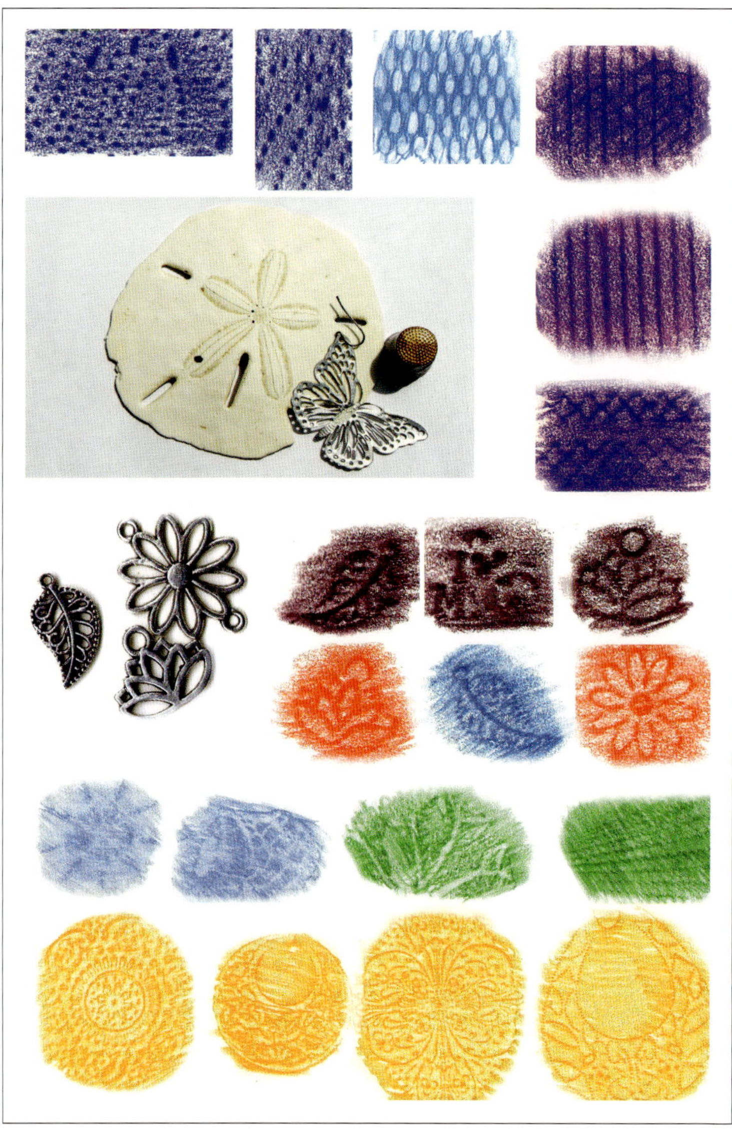

Rubbing

Did you ever place a paper over a coin and rub over it with your graphite pencil to see the design emerge on the paper? That's a great technique to use in colored pencil drawing! In these images you can see examples of textured objects that the artist placed underneath her paper to make rubbings. Charms, trinkets, pieces of wood, and even some earrings can offer you wonderful possibilities.

Make sure you test all the surfaces that you want to use for rubbings on a separate piece of paper before using it in your drawing! You can see the results much better if you rub a fairly large area in your drawing on a rather thin paper. If pencils are soft and paper is not too thick, the rubbings will show up quickly. You can also vary the pencil pressure and adjust it as you keep rubbing the surface.

Paper indenting

Paper indenting is good for adding small details and texture like you see in the image detail of the sea biscuit drawing. This is a great technique to make white whiskers, very thin branches or veins in the leaves, and to make other super fine lines where leaving a thin, neat line would not be possible otherwise. The pen strokes on tracing paper should imitate the real texture of the object, look random, curve, change, and rotate in accordance with the shape and its linear perspective.

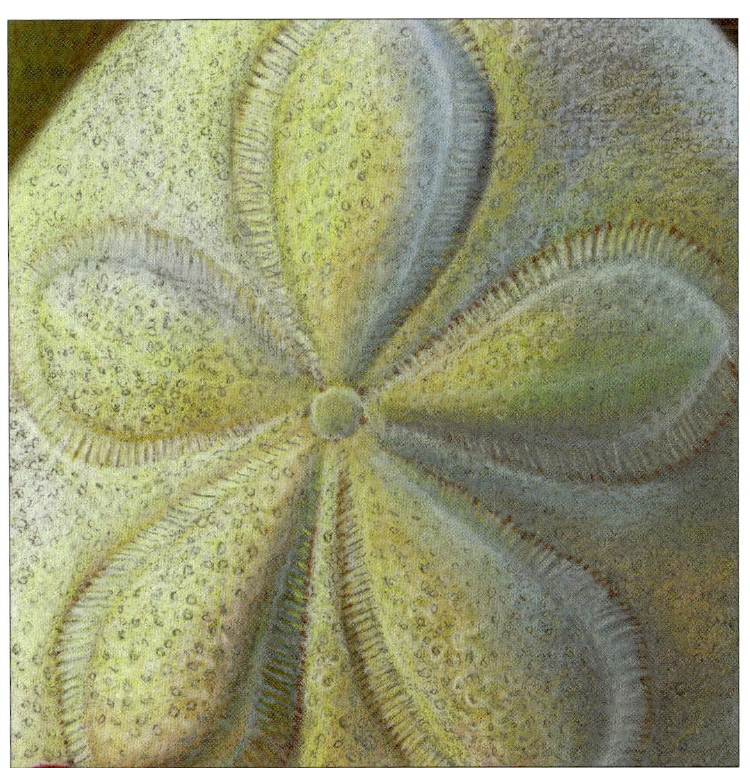

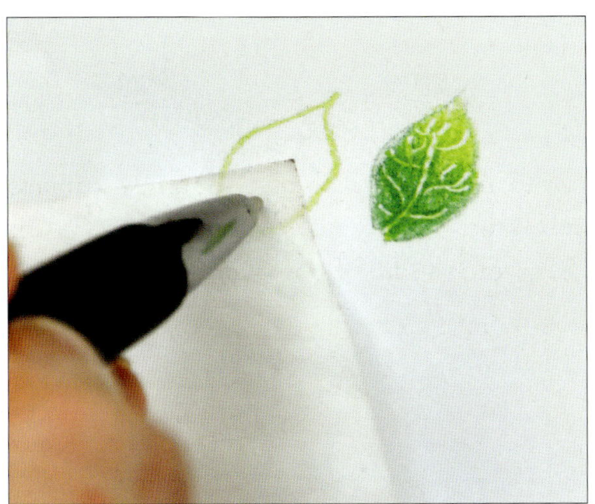

How to use: Plan and indent your paper before you begin shading the drawing. Place a piece of tracing paper over your drawing paper, tape the corners with masking tape, and make indentations over it with a pen. The heavier the pen pressure, the deeper the marks will indent into your paper. Here you see the artist using lines and circular strokes to complete the paper indenting. The pen marks will show up in subsequent shading.

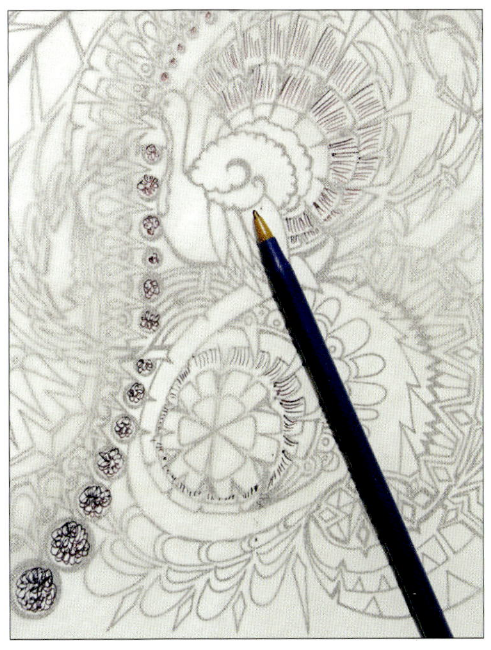

Lifting out

Lifting out is a useful technique that serves the purpose of getting rid of pigment where you don't want it to be. But it's also great at establishing textures with soft edges, such as in backgrounds, grass, feathers, highlights, and more.

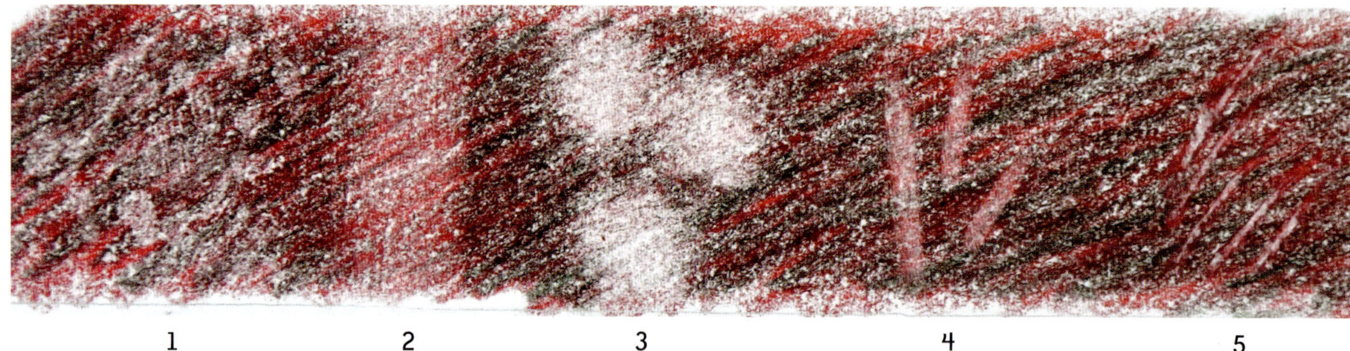

1 2 3 4 5

Colored pencil never lifts out 100%. It is vital to reserve highlights on white paper where you need them; however you can do considerable lifting out using the following methods:

1. Magic tape: for general lifting and specific shapes. You can create specific shapes that you want to lift out by drawing with a ballpoint pen on magic tape and pulling it off the page. You can do this multiple times, creating various textures.
2. Kneaded eraser: for light values and textural effects with soft edges. This eraser produces soft lifting as you can see in the second wide stripe.
3. Mounting putty: for more aggressive erasing and lighting up. Mounting putty is very similar to the kneaded eraser in texture and application, but is more aggressive at lift outs. You can see how bright three dots look being lifted out multiple times. This can be handy at developing textures in backgrounds or subjects that require the preservation of soft edges. Just remember that the putty is not an eraser; therefore you complete the lift outs not by dragging the putty across the surface but by placing the putty down and up.
4. Tombow Mono eraser: for lifting out tiny details. This tiny eraser is irreplaceable because you can fix a lot of your mistakes getting into small areas, where regular erasers just won't work. It makes great lift outs in hard to reach, small areas.
5. Scraping with an X-Acto knife gives you texture and a sharp lift out that you should use with caution. It's best to use it in the end of the drawing process because it can permanently change the paper's surface, depending on the blade's rotation. Sometimes you can make a lift out to reveal the previous hue that was colored by accident, or other times make an incision-like mark that permanently changes the paper's surface (scraping it).

Varied directional strokes

This application gives you numerous textures for almost any subject but glass. The following project explains how you can make textures in fur with varied strokes.

STEP-BY-STEP INSTRUCTIONS

Varied strokes and color development

Materials: Koh- I-Noor Progresso Woodless colored pencils; Prismacolor Premier colored pencils; Canson Colorline fuchsia; Caran-d'Ache full blender; Grumbacher final fixative

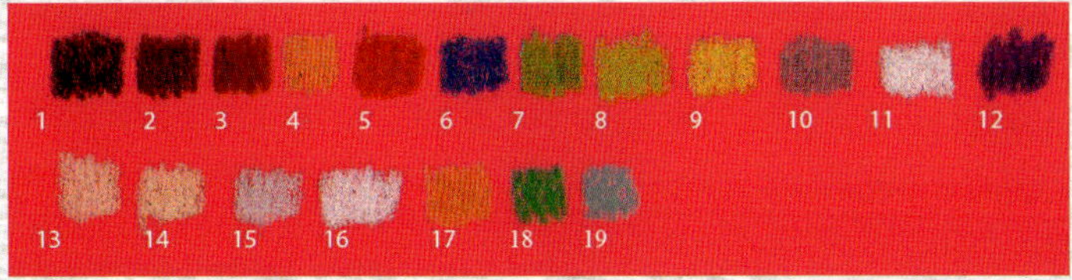

Color Chart: (Note: 1–5 are hues for dark fur, and 6–12 are hues for the eye)
1. Black 2. Koh-I-Noor Natural Sepia (Prismacolor Dark Brown) 3. Koh-I-Noor Brown (Prismacolor Sienna Brown) 4. Koh-I-Noor Light Ochre (Prismacolor Burnt Ochre) 5. Koh-I-Noor Burnt Sienna (Prismacolor Terra Cotta) 6. Koh-I-Noor Paris Blue (Prismacolor Indigo Blue) 7. Koh-I-Noor Light Green (Prismacolor Spring Green) 8. Prismacolor Chartreuse 9. Prismacolor Yellow Chartreuse 10. Koh-I-Noor Light Grey (Prismacolor 30% Warm Grey) 11. Prismacolor White 12. Prismacolor Violet

(**Note:** 13–17 for light fur)

13. Prismacolor Beige 14. Prismacolor Eggshell 15. Prismacolor 10% Warm Grey 16. Prismacolor White 17. Koh-I-Noor Light Ochre (Prismacolor Burnt Ochre) 18. Koh-I-Noor Dark Green (Prismacolor Light Green or Sap Green Light) 19. Prismacolor Jade Green (for the light cool color of the eye).

Note: Koh-I-Noor Woodless pencils are harder than Prismacolor Premier and are similar to Caran d'Ache Pablo in hardness and color intensity. While their dark and medium values are okay for drawing, the lighter colors by Prismacolor show up more on toned paper due to their softness.

Here the color of the eye has warm, light green in the center and a cooler light green around the eye that we are going to enhance by drawing on toned paper. These colors pop on bright drawing papers such as Canson Colorline fuchsia. Also, white and off-white colors get more punch drawn on this paper.

In this project we focus on colored pencil shading with varied strokes and color development, rather than on the technique of drawing shapes correctly (which is fundamental to basic drawing).

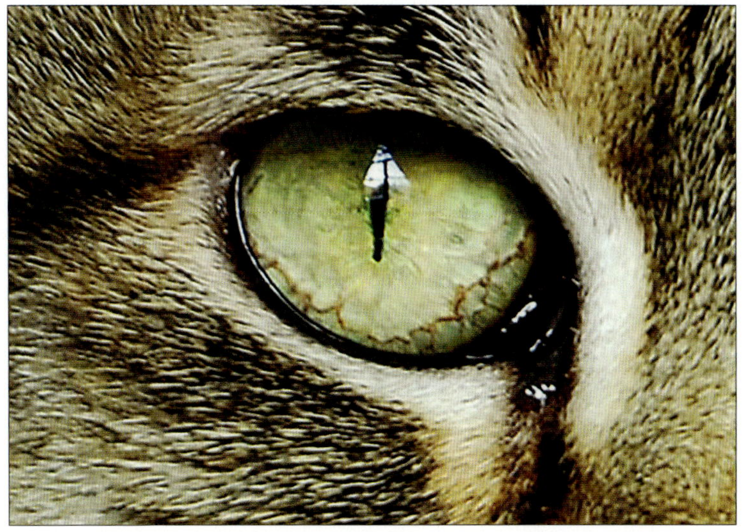

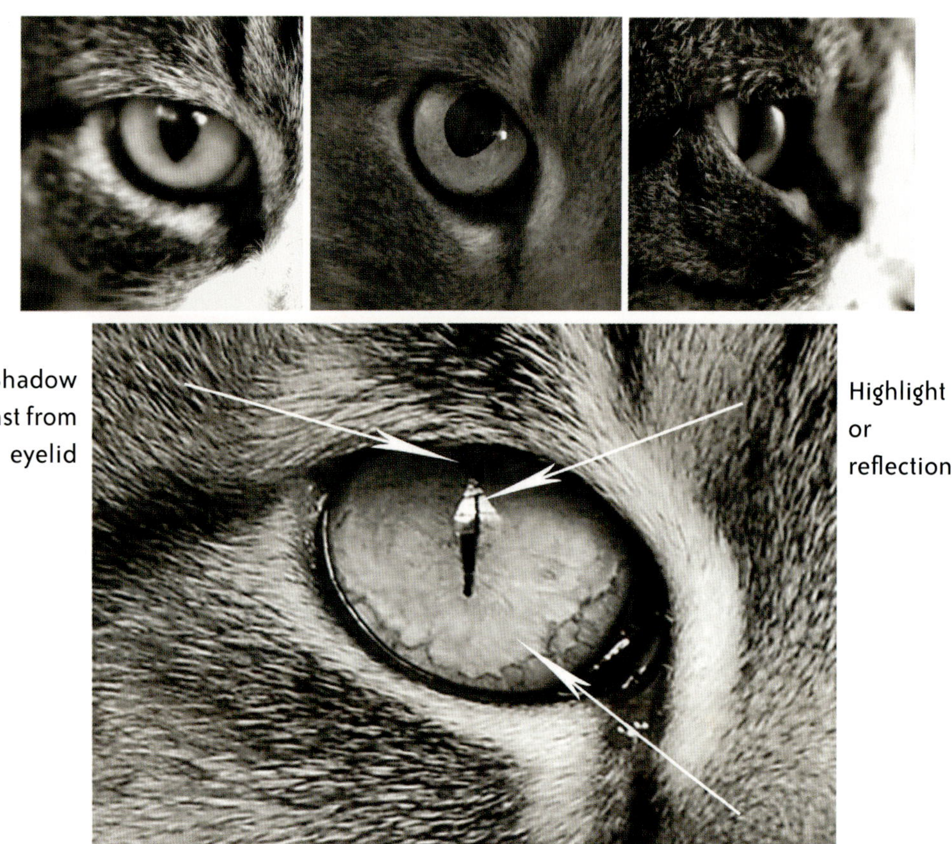

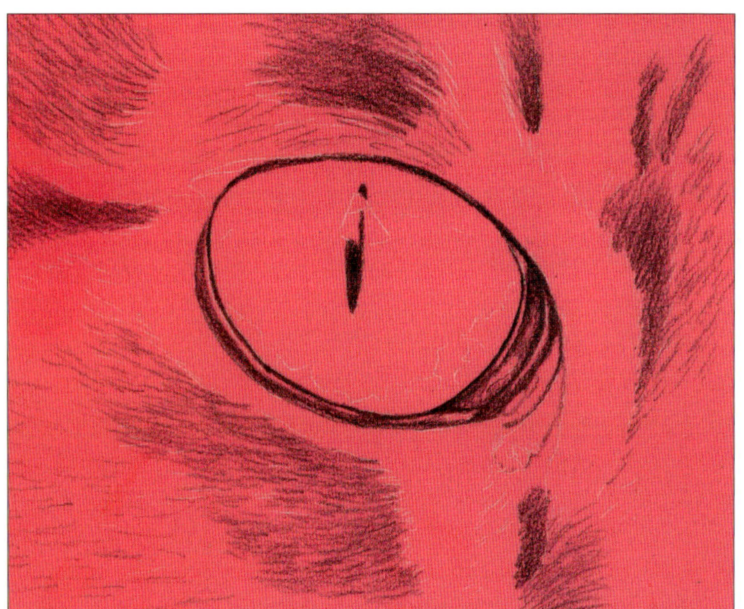

Step 1

To begin establishing the darkest darks, outline and fill in the pupil and the outer rim of the eye with sharp black. Pay attention to how the artist varies pencil pressure to shade slightly lighter values in between the lines there. No strokes go beyond that sharp outline in the rim. After that you map out the fur in black. Notice that the fur hairs have varied lengths and directions. The upper eyelid has long hairs that curve around the eye, while the area between the eyes has very short, tiny hairs. The space under the eye has short and medium length hairs that you define with short and medium length strokes that move around the eye from right to left. In other words, all three areas—the upper eyelid, the under eye area, and space between the eyes—have different pencil direction and length of the stroke. You copy this pattern by rotating your drawing as you move around the eye making individual strokes of varied lengths. All strokes should have soft edges.

Step 2

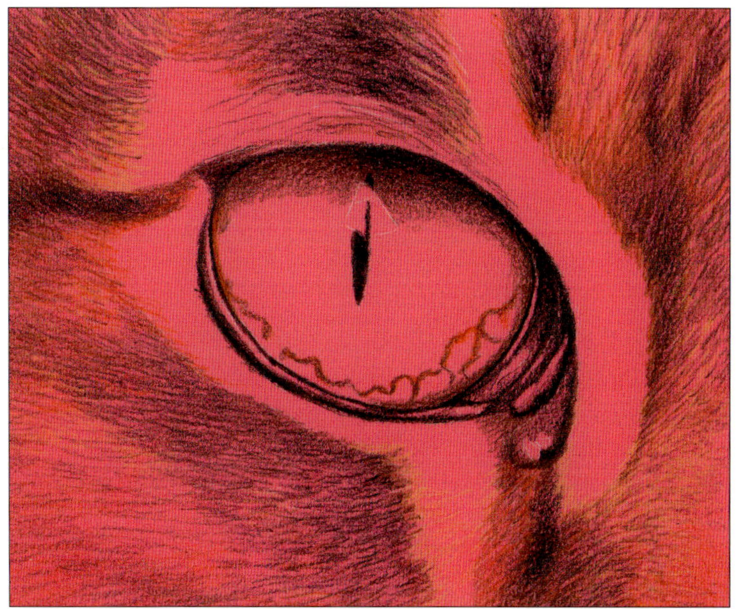

Once you establish all the darks in single black, you can fill in medium dark tones with other colors following the same pencil direction and softness you've just established in black. (Koh-I-Noor natural sepia (or Prismacolor dark brown), Koh-I-Noor brown (or Prismacolor sienna brown), Koh- I-Noor light ochre (or Prismacolor burnt ochre), Koh-I-Noor burnt sienna (or Prismacolor terra cotta). Overlap the hues over black to achieve smooth transitions between the colors.

Shade with Koh-I-Noor natural sepia (or Prismacolor dark brown) at the top of the eye—that's the cast shadow from the eyelid that is crucial to the natural appearance of the eye. Don't outline this shadow but shade softly, rotating your paper to curve it more around the eye rather than making it straight and linear (which would flatten out the form).

Step 3

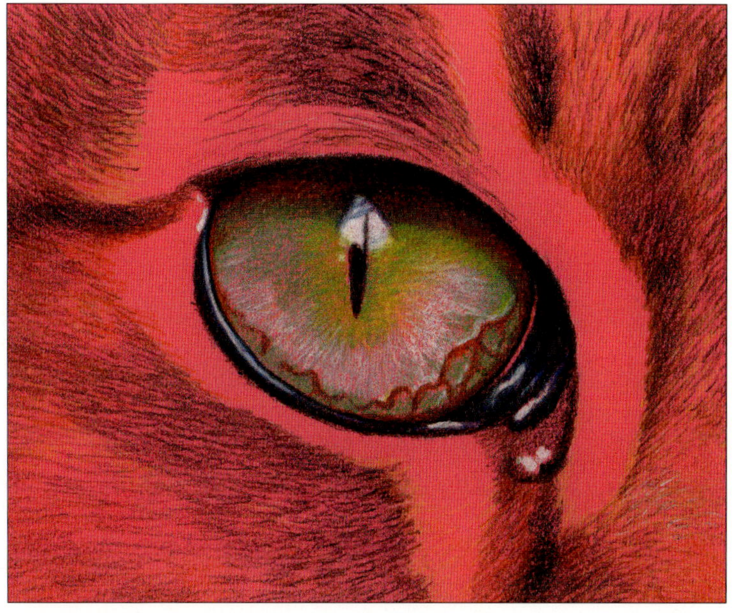

In this step we focus on the color of the eye. Unlike the fur, the end result of layering should be seamless; some blending with a full blender may be necessary if your layering is quite rough. Begin by drawing the triangular reflection in the eye with Koh-I-Noor Paris blue (or Prismacolor indigo blue) and fill it in with white. Add this blue into the deepest black oval rim of the eye, and finish up with Prismacolor violet there—blue and violet add cool color to basic black. Begin shading the eye with strokes that move away from the pupil radially. Color with these warm colors: Koh-I-Noor light green (Prismacolor spring green), Prismacolor chartreuse, and Prismacolor yellow chartreuse. Overlap over the cast shadow to avoid leaving tiny, uncolored gaps.

Transition into the cooler green of the eye with Koh-I-Noor light grey (or Prismacolor 30% warm grey), Koh-I-Noor dark green, which is actually a light cool green (or Prismacolor light green or sap green light), and Prismacolor jade green. Shade with Prismacolor white with light pressure in the lightest area of the eye. To make a warm brown curve set close to the eye's rim, the artist uses Koh-I-Noor burnt sienna, which can be replaced with any similar color such as Prismacolor terra cotta or sienna brown.

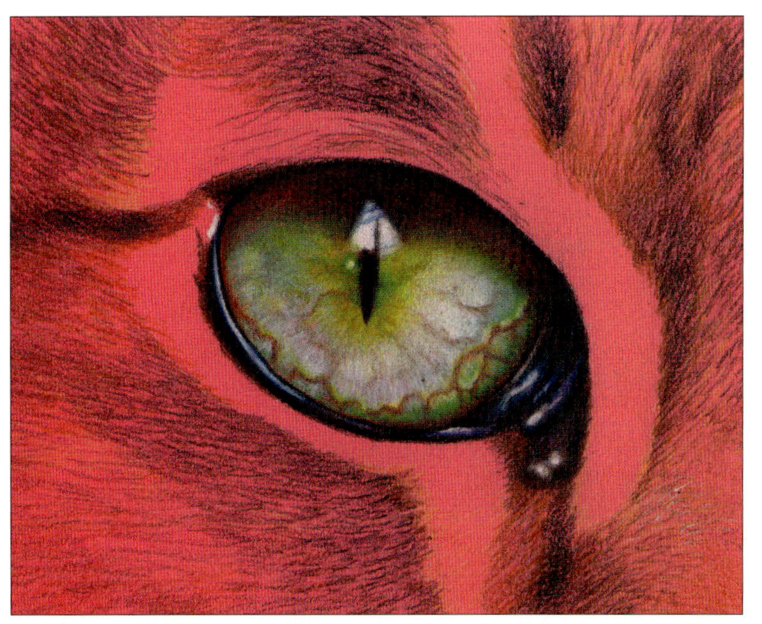

Step 4

In this step you see a repetition of layering with the same colors where they begin to "melt" one into another because of heavier pressure. The artist adds curving, light brown lines into the eye that must remain soft and not too linear.

Use Prismacolor yellow chartreuse and white to add a few lightert spots set next to the brown curves in the eye. Add more white into the highlight only so it is your brightest light. Blend the eye, if you haven't achieved burnishing via layering.

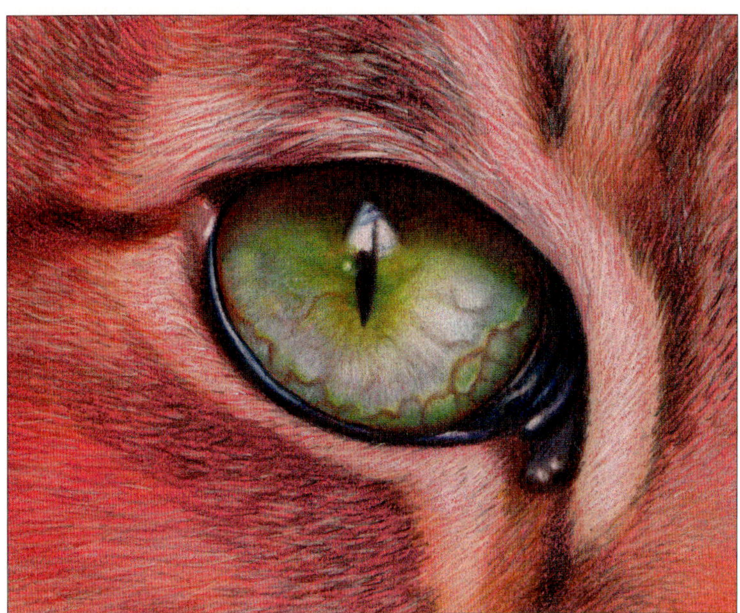

Step 5

Here you shade the lightest patterns in fur, observing hair length and direction. It's crucial to overlap the colors in soft strokes. Shade with Prismacolor beige, Prismacolor eggshell, Prismacolor 10% warm grey, Koh-I-Noor light ochre (Prismacolor burnt ochre). Add Prismacolor white in the lightest area of the fur moving around the eye. Spray it lightly with a fixative.

Step 6

In the final step you layer the same colors in the fur again without working with the full blender. Because you have sprayed it in the previous step, the drawing paper can accept more pigment so that you can intensify all the colors, especially black and white. Some blending in the fur occurs because of multiple layering in single, directional strokes. Notice how smooth the eye is and how much texture we see in the fur. Spray the artwork again once done.

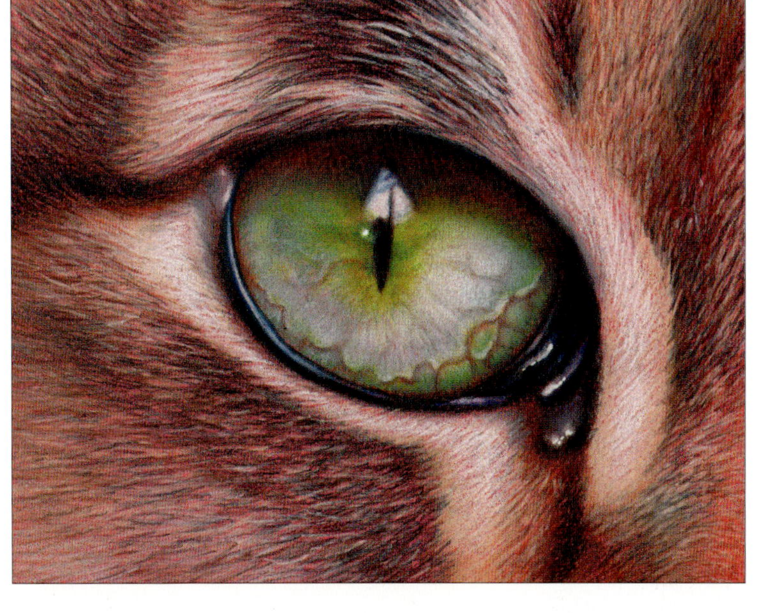

In this drawing you see a very similar process of color layering where the lightest texture of the fur is achieved with Winsor & Newton white marker and Sakura pen-touch marker. This marker has a very soft white that makes it possible to layer the lightest hairs with some caution (if you draw small, strokes may appear too thick). The Sakura pen gives very bright highlights that you can see here as dots. They have hard edges and should be used sparingly. As a result, the fur gets a rougher appearance with brighter whites in comparison to a more natural appearance present in the previous drawing.

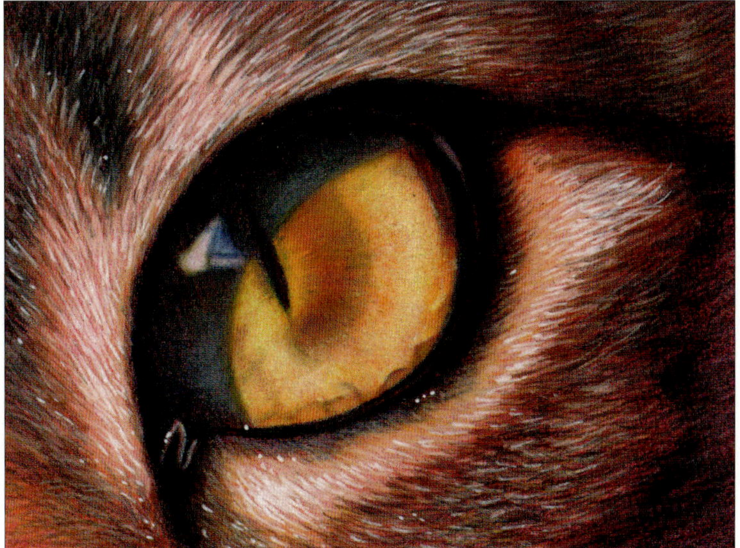

STEP-BY-STEP INSTRUCTIONS

Adding Texture with Paper Indenting

Materials: Prismacolor Premier Colored Pencils; Koh-I-Noor Bristol Vellum, 9 x 12; kneaded eraser, transfer paper, Grumbacher final fixative matte or gloss

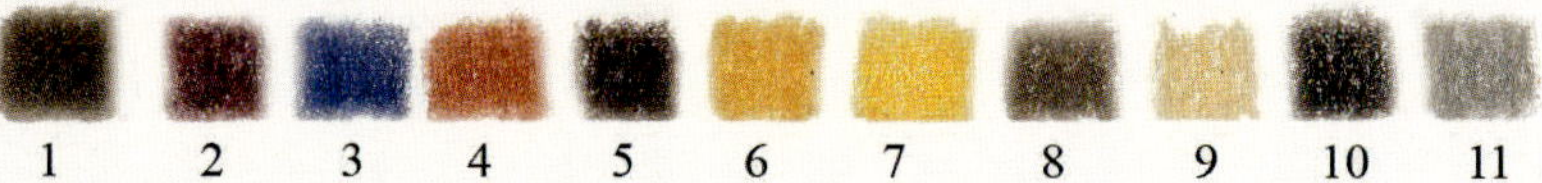

Color Chart: 1. Dark Brown 2. Black Raspberry 3. Indigo Blue 4. Burnt Ochre 5. Dark Umber 6. Yellow Ochre 7. Spanish Orange 8. 70% French Grey 9. Eggshell 10. 90% Warm Grey 11. 20% Cool Grey

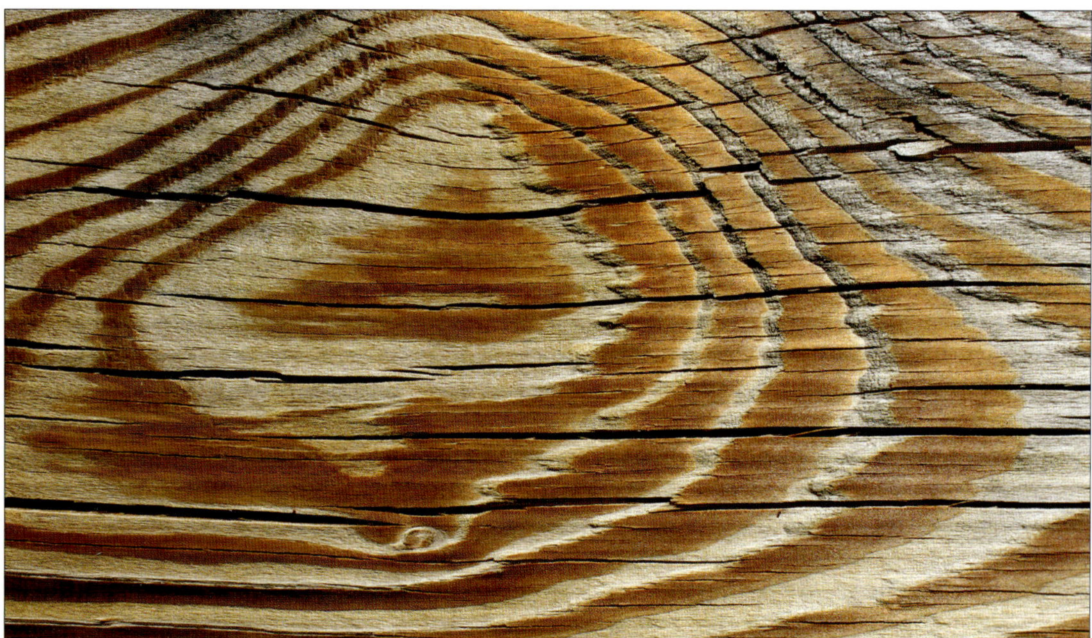

When you browse through wood images, pick those that have interesting patterns occurring around the wood knot or there is something fun going on with color and stripes. If you see a branch or other object sitting on the wood, that object casts a shadow onto the wood and you will need to place it to make the drawing even more realistic.

In this project you'll create texture of wood with shading, directional strokes, and some paper indenting rather than the rubbings, although it is also possible to create texture when you draw on a rather thin paper. Depending on your photo, drawing on textured paper may be an option too, if the surface of the wood looks rugged. When you shade over textured papers, the paper's surface gives you a very uneven application.

To simplify, either draw half the image or capture fewer stripes by making them a bit wider.

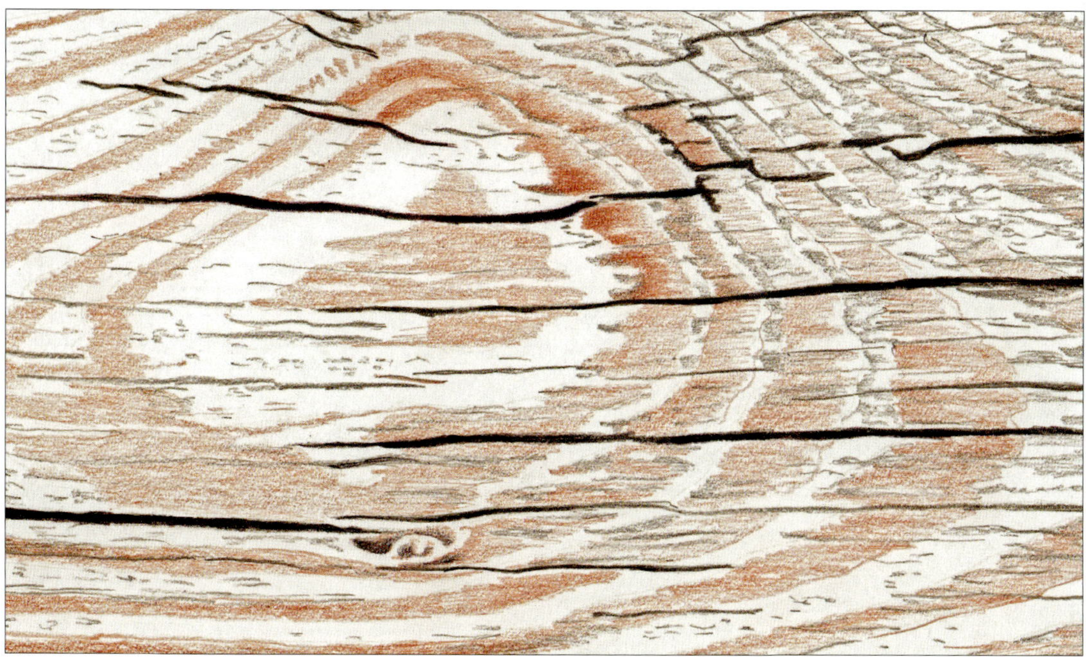

Step 1

Study the pattern of the wood. There are two major patterns happening in the wood: black cracks and brown stripes. They have different flow—the overall rotation and direction of soft, golden-brown lines is not the same as for the cracks with their sharp edges.

It is hard to copy everything that is here; that is why you should define the major cracks and stripes. If you make a mistake by placing fewer lines or making some of them wider or narrower, no one would ever know as long as you keep the general pattern correct.

Cracks: There are many ways to color the deepest cracks in the wood. You can use a combination of black and dark brown. The artist outlines the edges with dark brown (or dark raspberry) and mixes this color with indigo blue/dark umber for the deepest cracks in the wood. Pay attention to the width of each crack: some look like thin lines while others are pretty wide—you will need to create this variation.

Stripes: Mark the radial lines with burnt ochre and shade softly between the lines. It is best to keep these strokes horizontal at all times. Rotate your drawing paper so it is easier to place them horizontally. Lines found in nature never repeat themselves although they are arranged in a pattern; therefore keep the brown lines fluid and avoid making parallel lines! Their edges stay soft, while the cracks should be defined.

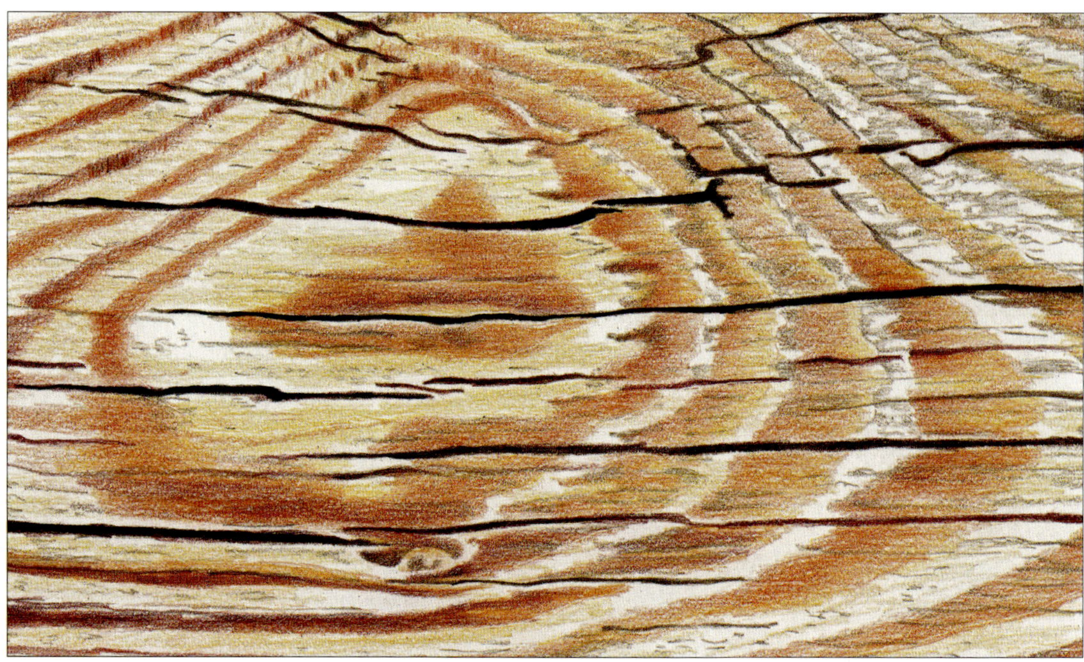

Step 2

White area: Because you work on white paper, saving the highlights and white areas by not coloring them is essential to realistic drawing here. Therefore, you need to work around your light areas with care. You can always shade over the lights later, but you can't erase them once colored. Indent your paper for tiny lights and texture. In the third step you can see where the artist indents her paper as the marks reveal themselves after shading (bottom part of the drawing). These are small, short lines in the lightest stripes and longer lines in brown lines.

Although you add more color in this step, the majority of work is done in just two hues—burnt ochre and dark umber—by varying pressure. Therefore develop values in the brown stripes with these colors further before adding more. Use sharp black to harden the edges in the cracks. Vary their width and length.

To get darker, reddish brown color in brown stripes, use a combination of black raspberry and burnt ochre, working in horizontal strokes darkening the pattern. Add Spanish orange in warm brown stripes.

Shade with yellow ochre and eggshell in the light stripes unevenly (in between the brown stripes), skipping over the paper to leave some white paper untouched. Map out the wood pattern in the top right corner with 70% French grey.

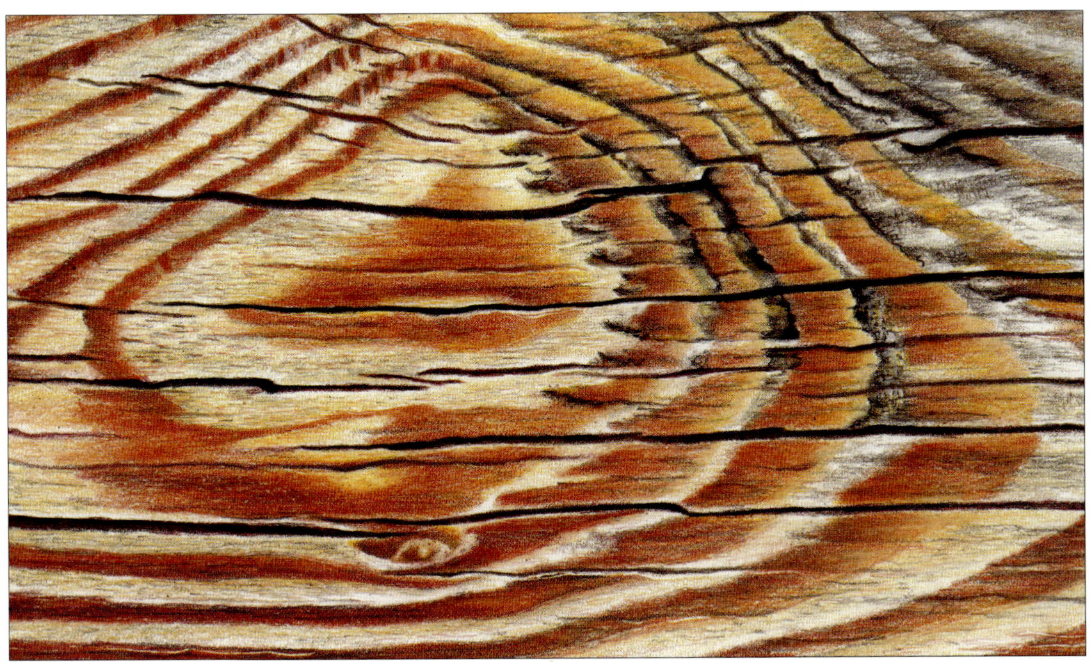

Step 3

Here you darken the values and work on textural details that vary in every corner of the drawing. The artist creates more focus in the center and right center of the drawing, blurring out the rest slightly. To make dark texture on the right, use a combination of greys: 20% cool grey for the lightest areas, 70% French grey for the mid values, and 90% warm grey for the sharp details. You must outline one edge only to make it the darkest. You can also make tiny sharp lines for texture in the bark on the right. Intensify colors in the warm brown stripes by layering yellow ochre, burnt ochre, and Spanish orange.

Light stripes: Layer more eggshell and use 20% cool grey in the light stripes at the bottom left corner. The bottom left corner becomes a little bit darker than the right. Make sure that the stripes are curving and uneven so they look natural. If your stripes look too straight or too parallel to each other, the wood would look like a striped shirt. Use a very light pressure in 70% French grey and burnt ochre to make tiny lines in the light stripes for texture. They should "mingle" with the previously indented tiny white stripes.

Cracks: To make an illusion of a crack, study how it catches the light. The darkest value is the crack itself. Next you have the highlight right below each crack and a darker value at the top of the crack.

No blending is necessary in this project due to the subject. Bristol vellum is a pretty smooth paper with a slight texture that works well here. Step back to look at your drawing from a distance to check the contrast. Make adjustments and use a spray varnish outdoors to fix your drawing against the smudges and UV light.

STEP-BY-STEP INSTRUCTIONS

Focusing on Color, Shading, and Texture

Materials: Prismacolor Premier colored pencils unless noted; kneaded eraser; magic tape; pen; tracing paper; Grumbacher final fixative; a large sheet of printmaking paper that is very light grey in color (it can be replaced with either Stonehenge light grey or tan)

Note: The Color Chart is given next to each donut example to simplify the process of drawing.

To simplify, draw one or two donuts instead of all of the donuts. The artist spent roughly five hours drawing each donut and more than eight hours shading the background for this 12" x 14" drawing!

Once again, in this project we don't discuss basic drawing techniques but focus on color, shading, and texture. While the artist lays out the drawing sequence of every donut, the artwork is completed by filling in the background first and then layering one color at a time while working on all donuts simultaneously. By shading the background first, the artist creates instant contrast to work against in coloring the donuts.

It took a considerable creative effort to make this arrangement of donuts. The artist aimed at balancing out every texture, color, and shape, which required multiple rotations, changes of place, as well as shooting at different times of the day to capture strong shadows with lots of color.

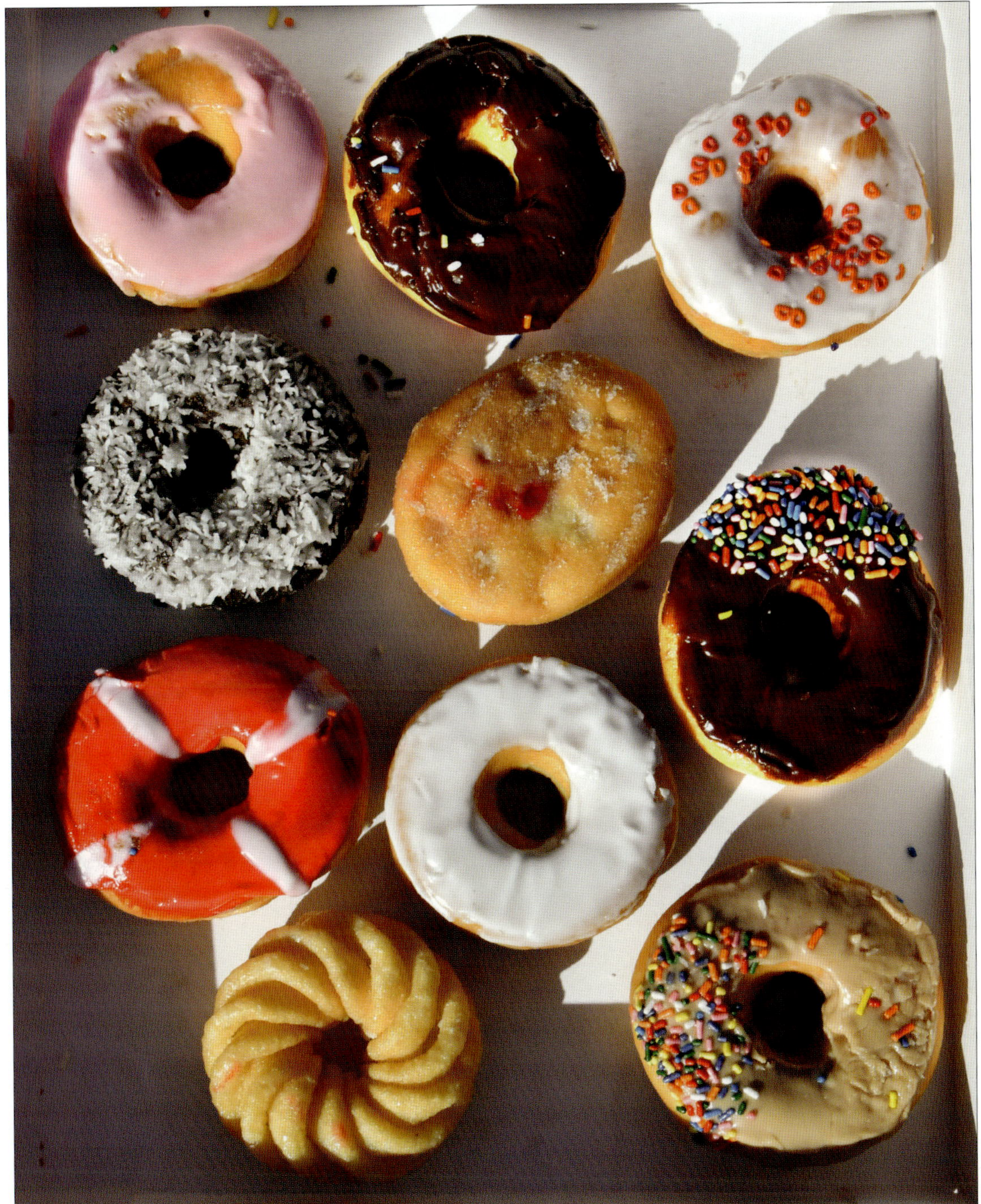

Photo reference

This project was completed on a very light grey printmaking paper that often doesn't read as such in photography. It has minimal texture and the colors tend to blend on their own without employing additional blending techniques. For the artwork examples, some of the textures have been created with magic tape, varied stroke applications, and Sakura Pen-touch marker.

DONUT 1

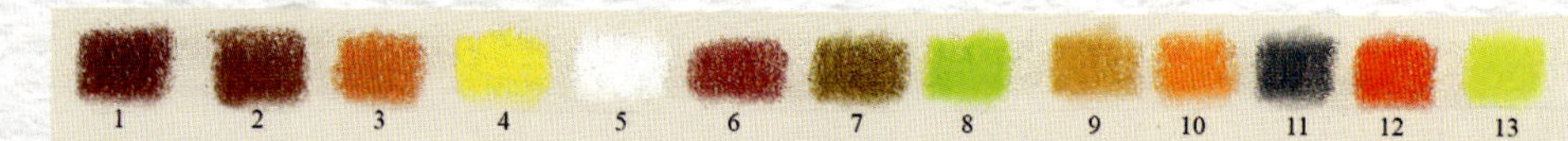

Color Chart: 1. Terra Cotta 2. Sienna Brown 3. Mineral Orange 4. (Pablo) Yellow 5. White 6. Henna 7. Artichoke 8. Chartreuse 9. Yellow Ochre 10. Yellow Orange 11. 70% Cool Grey 12. Pumpkin Orange 13. Yellow Chartreuse

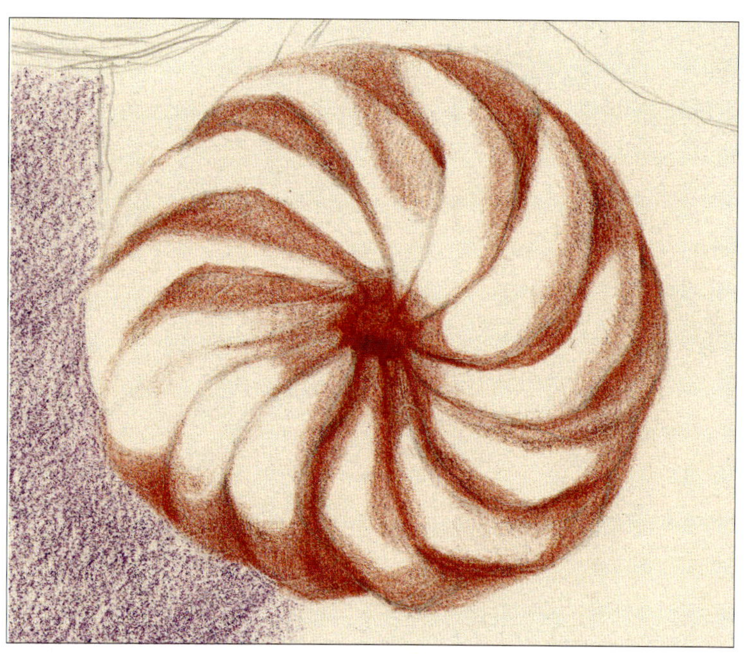

Step 1

Tap all graphite lines with the kneaded eraser. It's a light donut and graphite will show up once you begin shading.

Begin drawing out the rotation of each fold with either terra cotta or sienna brown. While the color looks reddish here, it's actually a warm brown that the author suggests you use for shading.

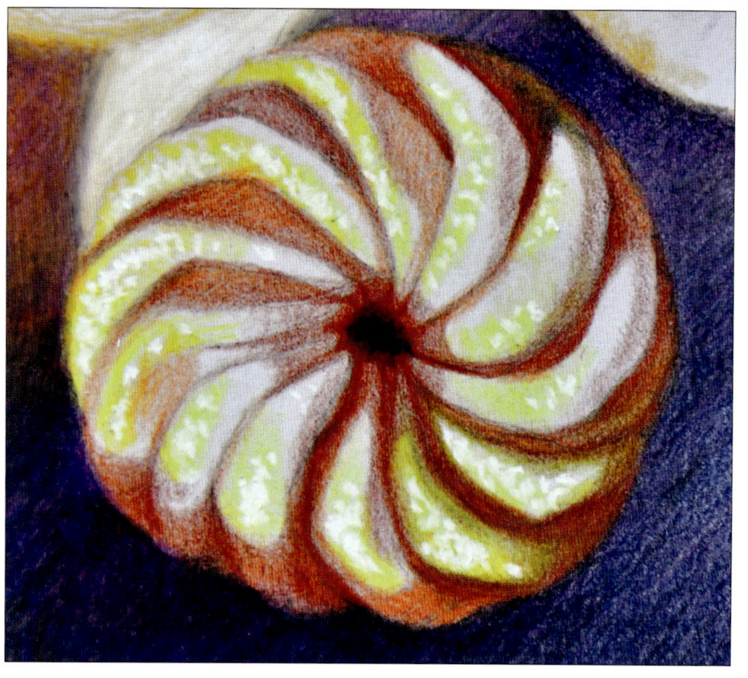

Step 2

Once you place the background colors, you set the contrast to begin working on the donut. With a sharp point, place random white spots and shade around them with Pablo yellow. Add mineral orange into the brown to warm up the color.

Step 3

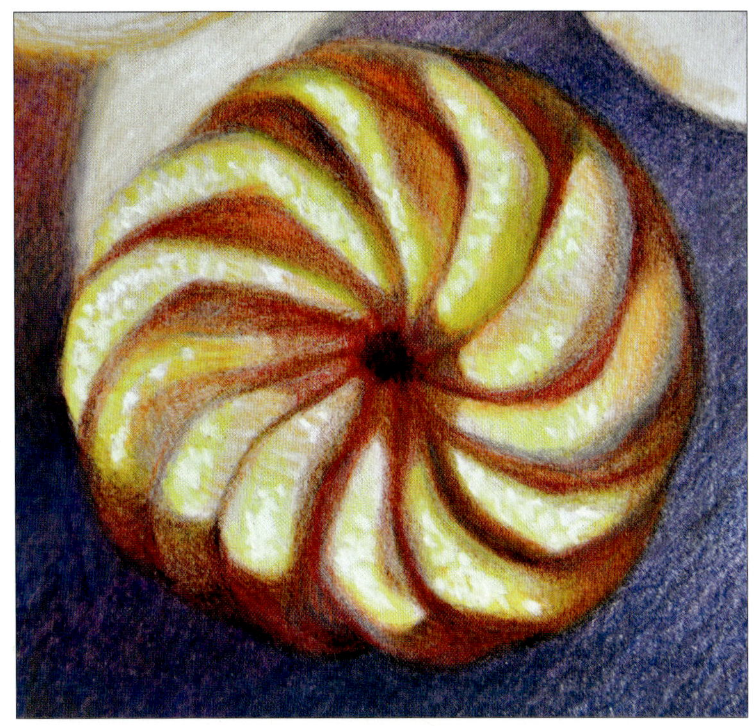

With every new step, you keep defining the edges to preserve the correct rotation and clarity in each section. You also work in short, directional strokes on every section to create volume. For that you need to keep rotating your drawing paper as you shade, so the strokes wrap around the forms and don't become too linear.

Define the brown edges with henna and fill them in with this color in light pressure. Add warm, light greens—chartreuse and artichoke—shading around the yellow to create value transitions between the dark (browns) and the light (white). You shade from white to yellow to chartreuse to artichoke. After that the shapes turn to orange-brown shadows (that you've already done).

Step 4

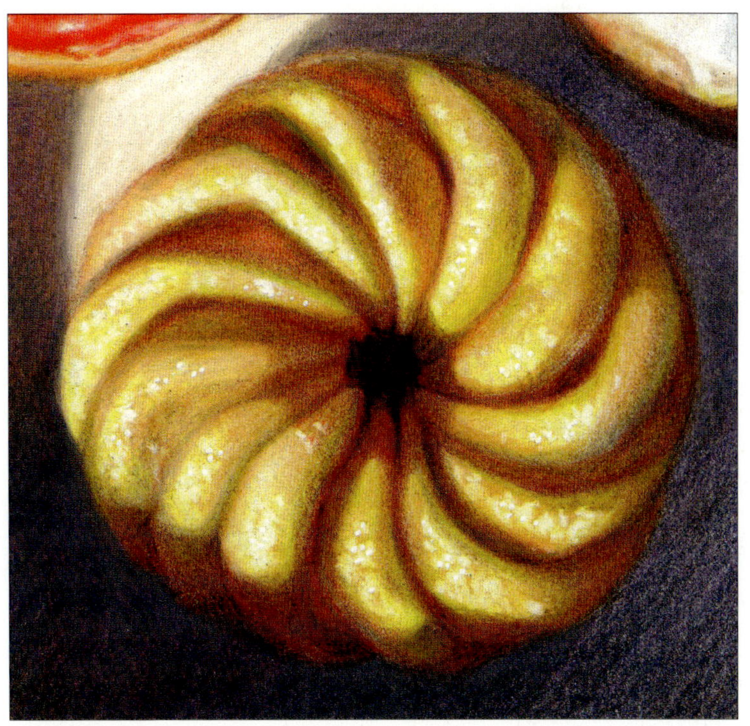

Once the basic pattern of light and shade is in place, you can add variations to the colors seen in the light. The artist shades with yellow ochre, yellow orange, pumpkin orange, chartreuse, and Pablo yellow. Most of the time it is simply layering the same colors over and over again until the right contrast and volume are achieved. Add 70% cool grey into the form shadow in every section.

Texture: Reinforce the texture with white for small dots in the light and add just a few tiny highlights on the left side with the Sakura Pen-Touch.

DONUT 2

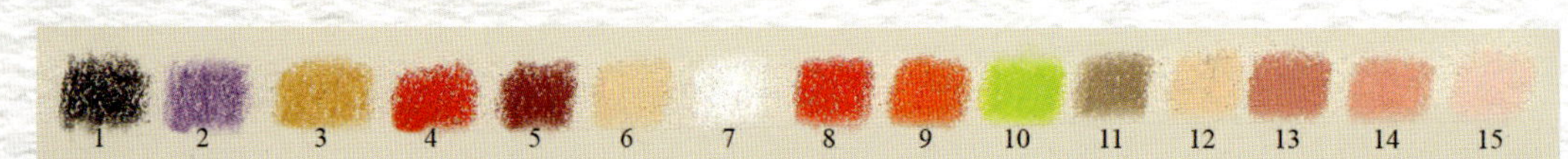

Color Chart: 1. 70% Warm Grey 2. Pablo Periwinkle Blue 3. Yellow Ochre 4. Crimson Red 5. Henna 6. Eggshell 7. White 8. Permanent Red 9. Pumpkin Orange 10. Chartreuse 11. Beige Sienna 12. Beige 13. Nectar 14. Peach 15. Light Peach

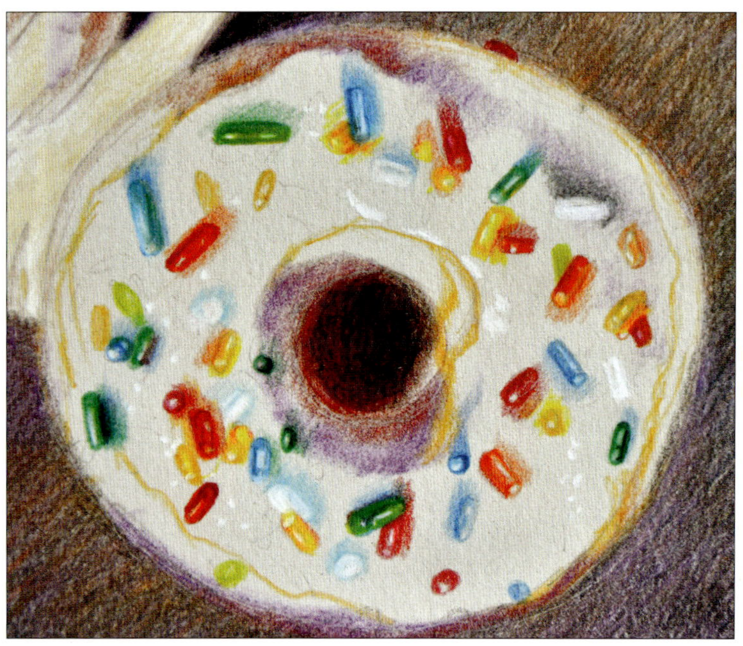

Step 1

You always begin shading from your shadows. The artist colors with Pablo periwinkle blue (lilac hue) in the shadow of every donut. Feel free to pick your own colors for the rainbow sprinkles.

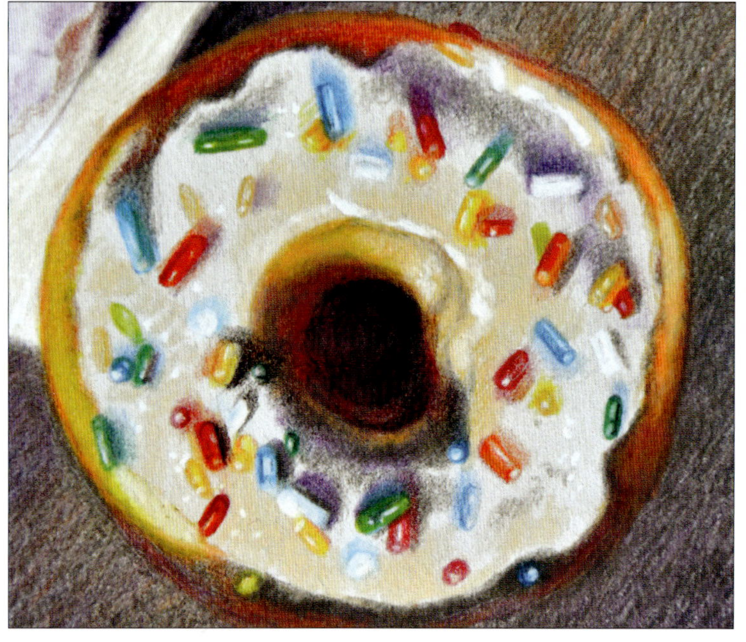

Step 2

Think how you can turn the form with values (light/dark) rather than focusing on colors only. Begin developing the darks in the center and the outer edge of the donut with 70% warm grey, yellow ochre, crimson red, and henna to create depth. When the donut turns to light that you see as the top, these dark colors will change to much lighter values such as yellows, warm white (eggshell), and light peaches, which you'll color in the next step. As of now, you see the paper's light grey color in the light.

With heavy pressure, draw with white to place the lights, and soften the white edges with eggshell by shading around the white.

Step 3

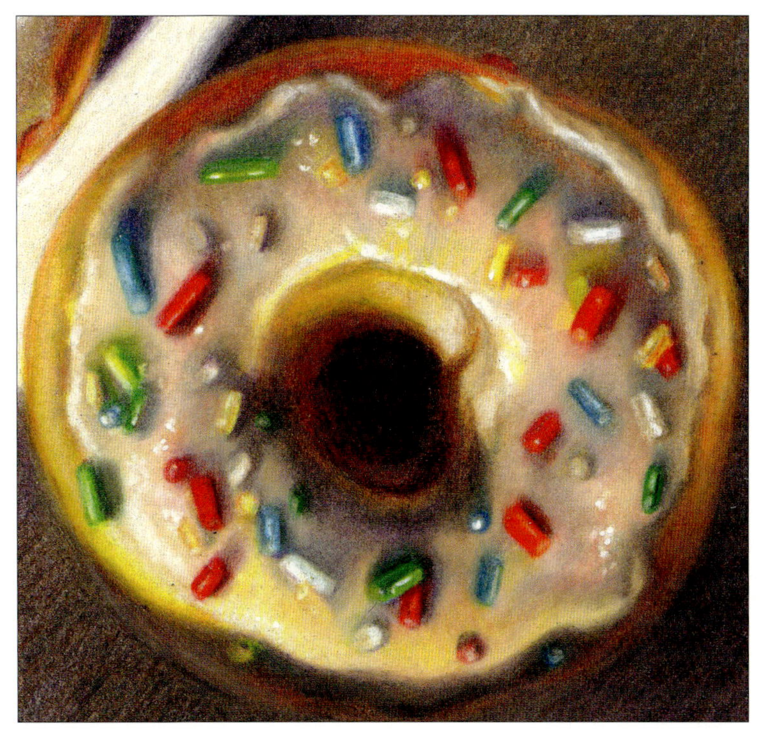

Let's work on the glaze with these colors: yellow ochre, eggshell and white, beige sienna, beige (looks light pink on this paper), chartreuse, nectar, peach, and light peach.

With light pressure, deepen the shadows on the donut's sides in henna, permanent red, and pumpkin orange. Shade with chartreuse on the left (where you see light yellow-green).

To create texture in this donut, you draw the sprinkles one by one. Pick your favorite colors. To make some of them stand out more than others, you place a shadow under the sprinkle with Pablo periwinkle blue (lilac), 70% warm grey, and the local color of the sprinkle. Outline under the sprinkle for clarity.

Once you have established color for the cast shadows under the sprinkles, shade over them with beige sienna. Beige sienna is a greyed-down pink that unifies and blends the colors nicely as well as creates soft transitions into the light hues in the glaze.

Step back to see if you want to reinforce the whites and if the glaze appears well blended. If not, shade with the full blender to achieve a similar result.

DONUT 3

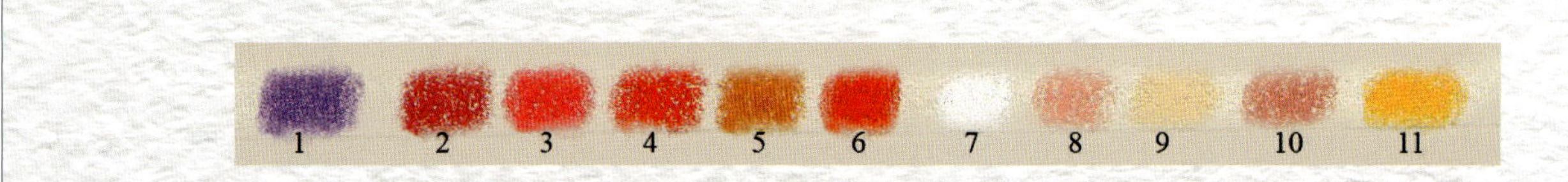

Color Chart: 1. Pablo Periwinkle Blue 2. Pomegranate 3. Carmine Red 4. Permanent Red 5. Mineral Orange 6. Pablo Scarlet 7. White 8. Peach 9. Eggshell 10. Nectar 11. Spanish Orange

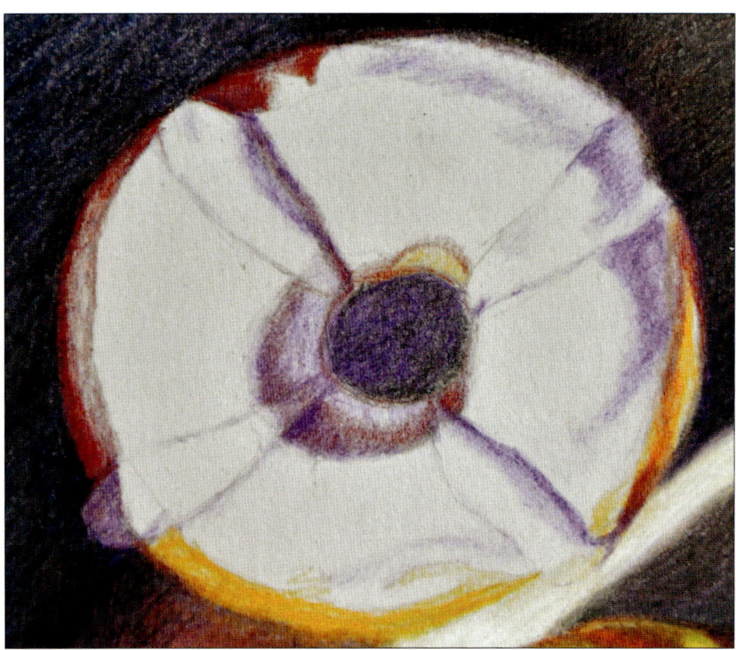

Step 1

Mix Pablo periwinkle blue (lilac) with pomegranate to map out the shadow in the center and on the left side. Both are cool colors that harmonize well with each other. Add mineral orange and Spanish orange into the yellow side of the donut.

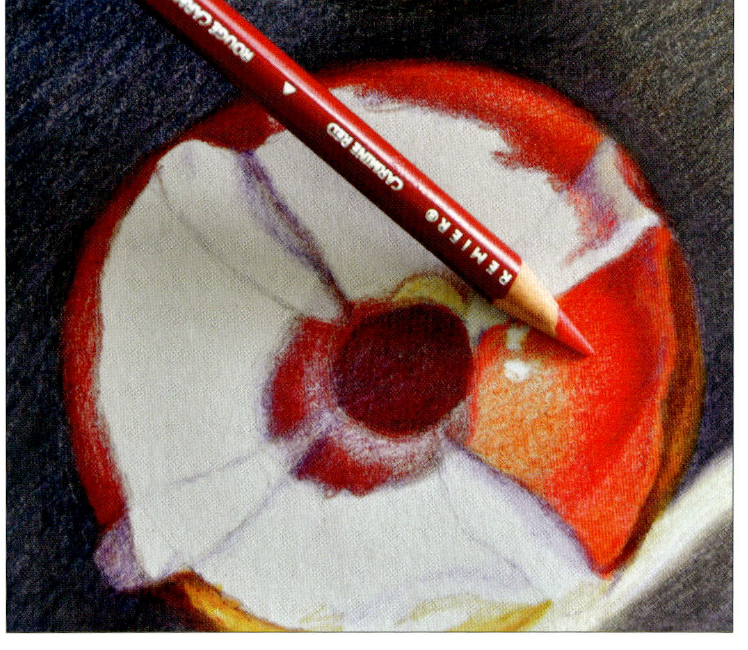

Step 2

Outline the edge inside the hole with pomegranate and fill it in with medium pressure because red from the donut gets cast into the background around it. In this and in the next steps, carmine red will take the most work because you will alternate pencil pressures to make a variety of values in one color. For that you should constantly think how light or dark you want to shade and vary the pressure to fill in the donut, going around the highlights.

Step 3

Mark the highlights with white pencil.

Mix permanent red with mineral orange to get the lighter, warmer reds you see at the top of the red glaze. Shade with eggshell over this color with medium pressure to lighten up the values even more in the middle of each section. Another way of doing the same thing is to layer Spanish orange as a base in the light and shade with permanent red, Pablo scarlet (warm red such as Prismacolor poppy red), and carmine red over it, adjusting the pressure, depending on the area.

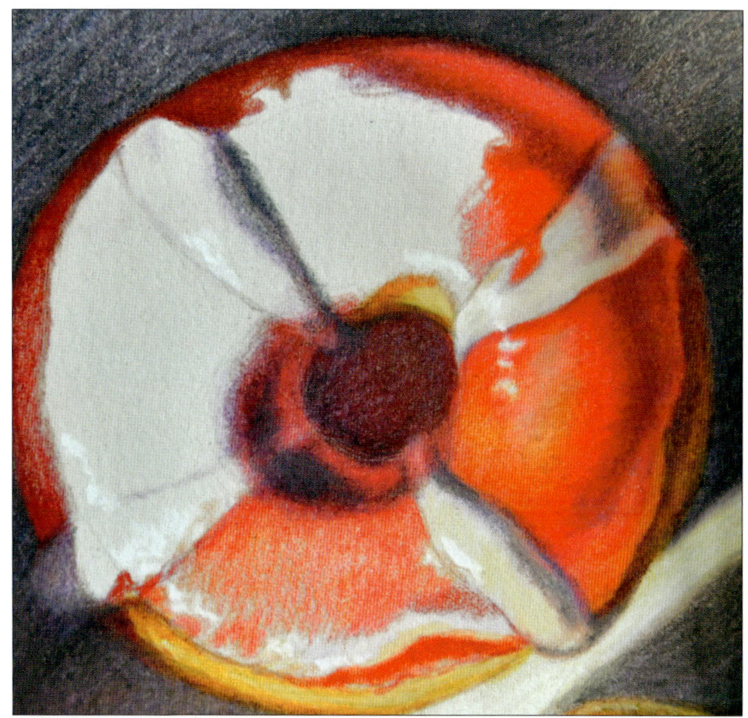

Step 4

To color the white cream, use white, peach, eggshell, nectar, and Spanish orange. Nectar blends reds in the areas around the orange light. You should use white pencil to make highlights in the white cream, and to add the brightest highlights draw a few dots in the light with the Sakura pen. Blend with a full blender, if needed. The glaze must look smooth.

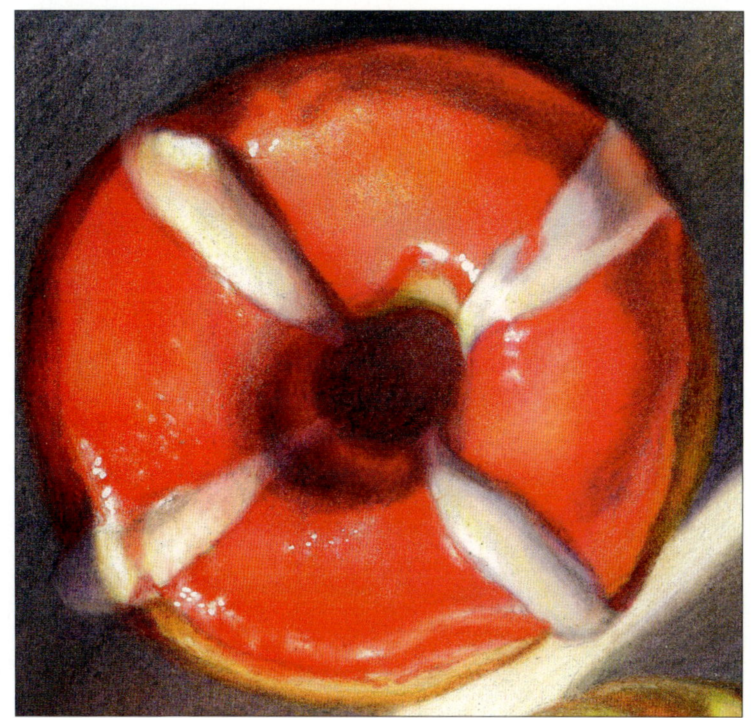

DONUT 4

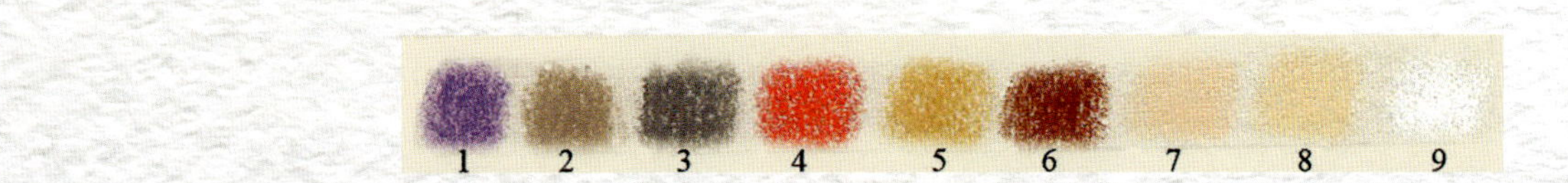

Colors: 1. Pablo Periwinkle Blue 2. Burnt Sienna 3. 50% French Grey 4. Permanent Red 5. Yellow Ochre 6. Terra Cotta 7. Beige 8. Eggshell 9. White

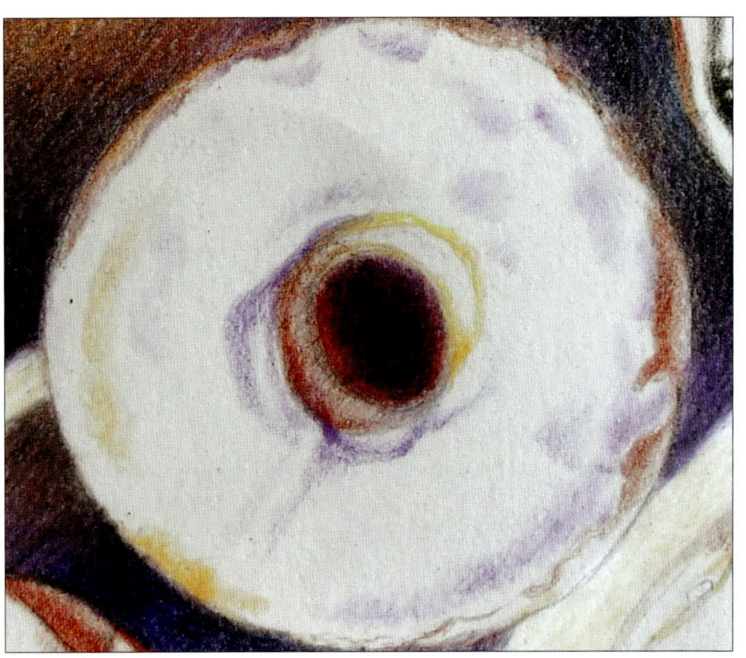

Step 1

Once the contrast is set against the background, you can begin mapping out the shadows with Pablo periwinkle blue. (Use a single color throughout for color unity.)

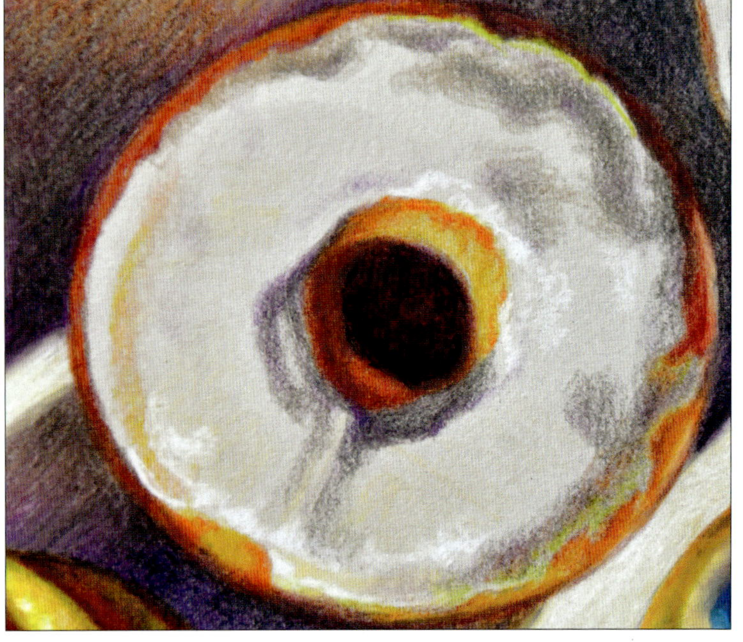

Step 2

Mark the highlights with white in random circular strokes. Shade the outer rim of the donut with chartreuse, yellow ochre, permanent red, and terra cotta. Place a colorful grey shadow in the glaze by mixing Pablo periwinkle blue (lilac) with 50% French grey and beige sienna.

Step 3

For the white glaze, use beige, eggshell, and white. You apply white with heavy pressure, going over these colors to create strong, colorful whites at the top. To create this light texture in the white sugar glaze, aim for random, little circular strokes applied with heavy pressure.

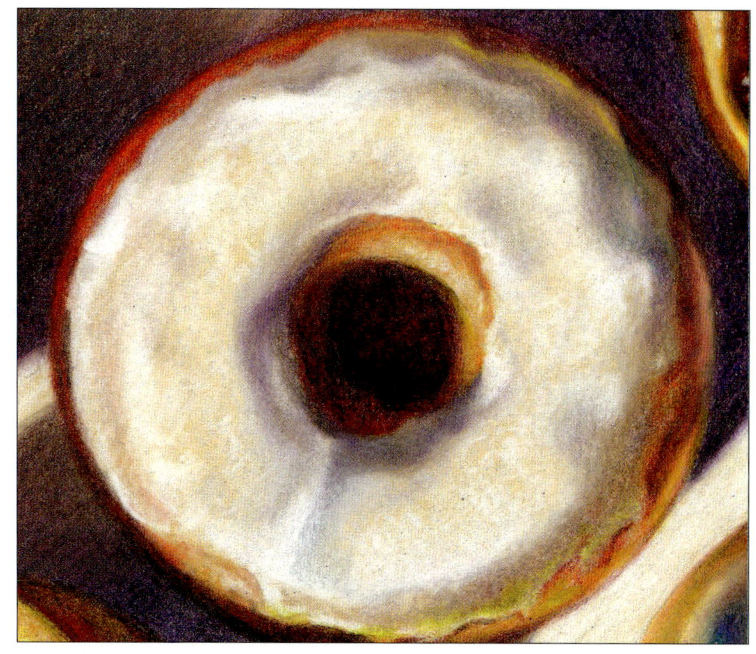

DONUT 5

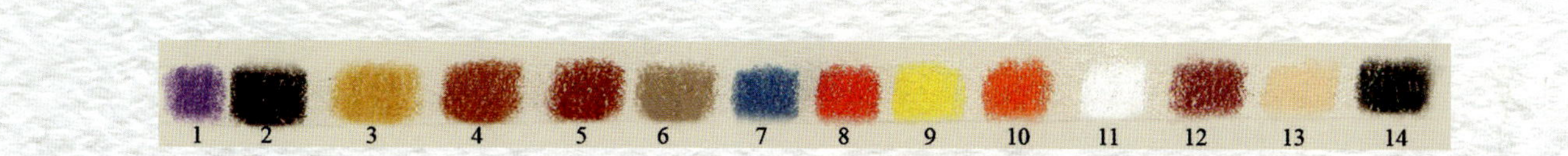

Colors: 1. Pablo Periwinkle Blue 2. Dark Umber 3. Yellow Ochre 4. Burnt Ochre 5. Terra Cotta 6. Beige Sienna 7. Pablo Cobalt Blue 8. Crimson Red 9. Pablo Yellow 10. Pumpkin Orange 11. White 12. Henna 13. Eggshell 14. Sepia

Step 1

Map out the donut's chocolate glaze in a single color—dark umber with a touch of Pablo periwinkle blue (lilac). You start shading from dark to light, skipping the lightest areas and shading around them with light pressure. Make your choice for colors in the rainbow sprinkles. The artist draws with Pablo cobalt blue, Pablo yellow, and Prismacolor crimson red.

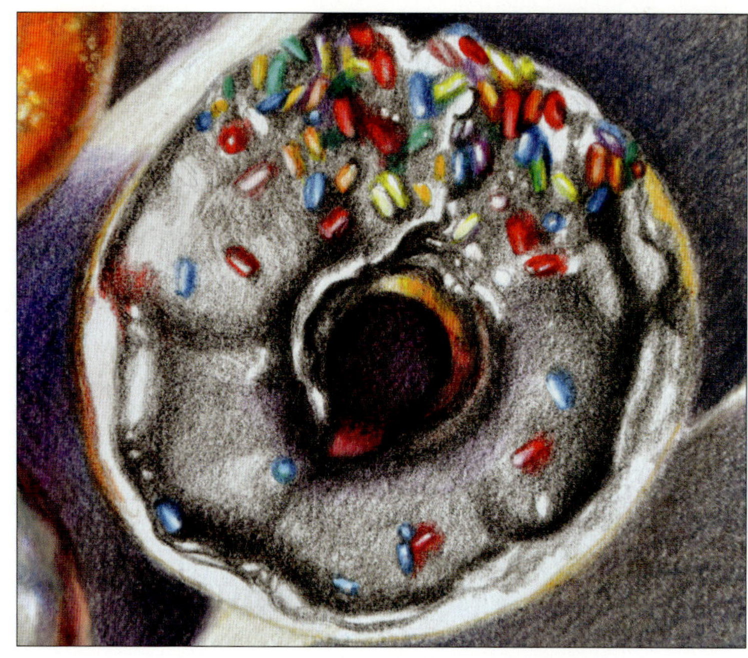

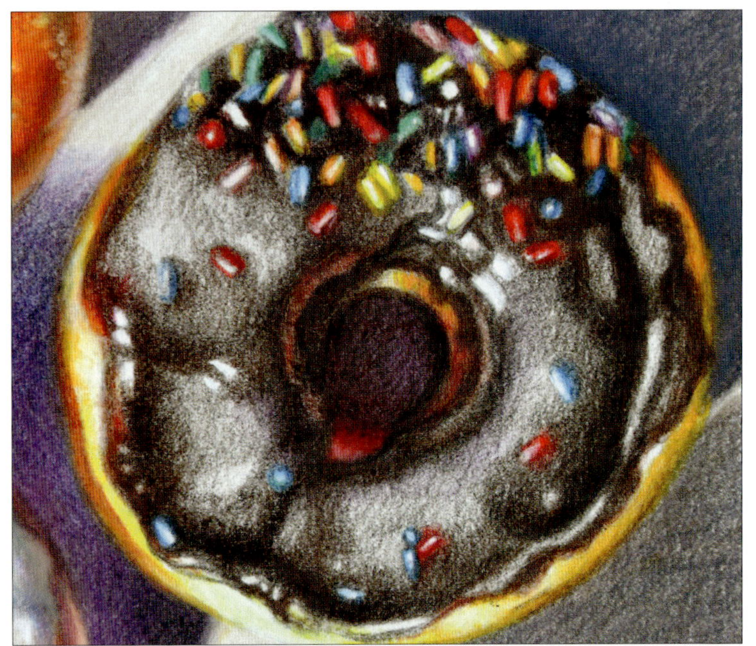

Step 2

Shade the outer edge with burnt ochre, terra cotta, yellow ochre, and Pablo yellow. Begin layering the second color over dark brown in the chocolate glaze by applying sepia and burnt ochre. Use the Tombow Mono Eraser to softly erase small, curving shapes in the glaze.

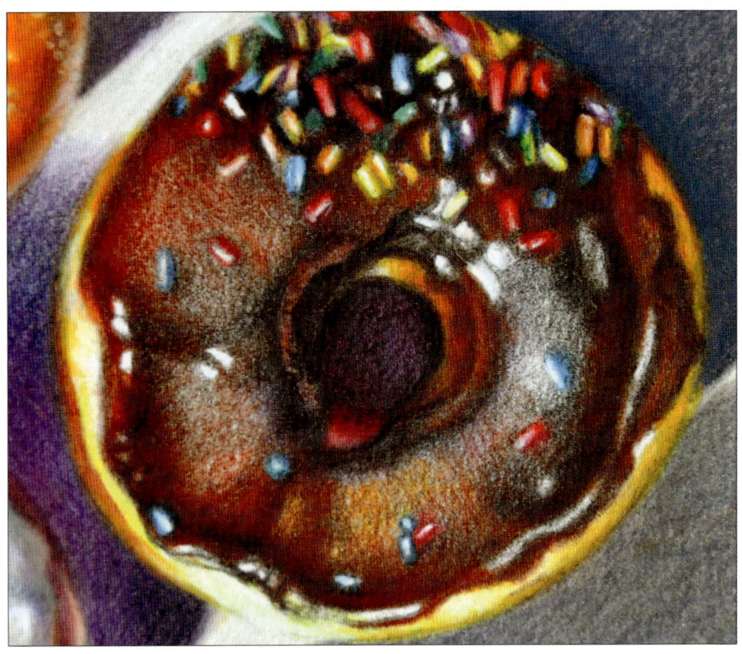

Step 3

Once you have placed the darkest values and marked the highlights, you begin working on bridging these values with lighter tones.

Chocolate glaze in the light: Shade with pumpkin orange and burnt ochre with heavy pressure.

Chocolate glaze in the dark and medium dark: crimson red, henna and terra cotta.

Step 4

Use beige sienna to grey down the lighter passages you see in the chocolate glaze that are going around the outer rim of the donut. This color blends the dark edges, creating reflected light seen in brown.

Add eggshell with white in the lightest parts of the yellow rim.

Texture for sprinkles: You need to outline sharply under the sprinkles with dark umber. This will create definition. Use white with heavy pressure to make individual highlights on top of each sprinkle in the light.

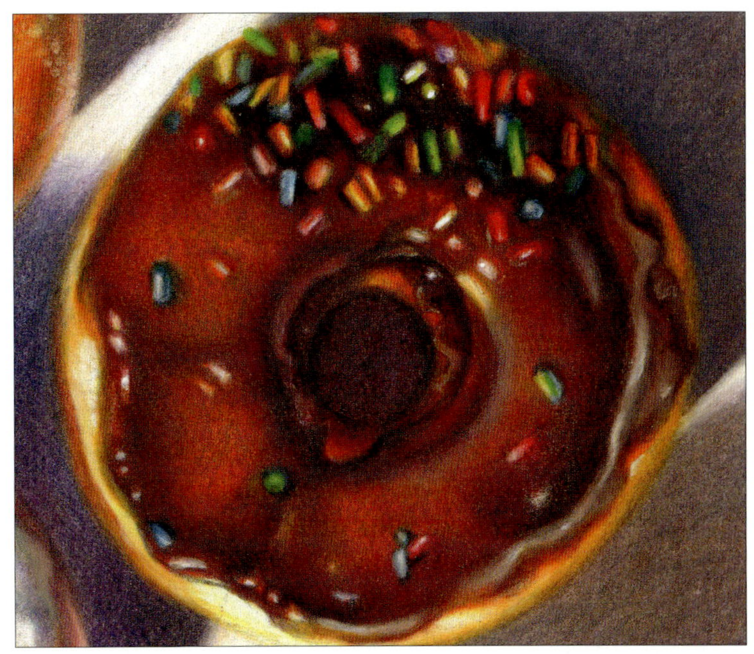

DONUT 6

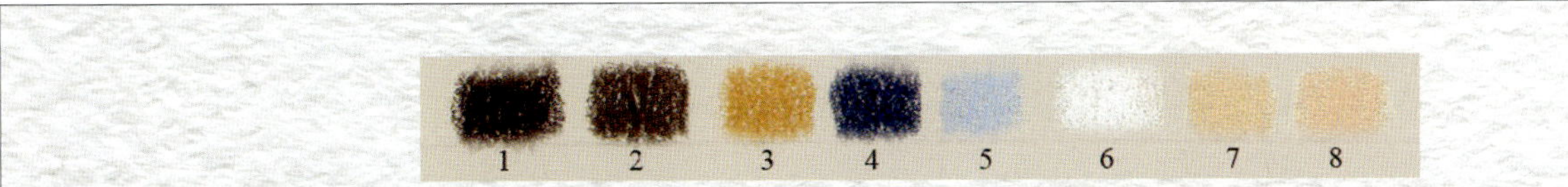

Colors: 1. Dark Umber 2. Dark Brown 3. Yellow Ochre 4. Indigo Blue 5. Luminance Light Cobalt Blue (Prismacolor Powder Blue) 6. White 7. Eggshell 8. Beige

Step 1

Shade the darkest darks on the rim and in the hole with dark umber and dark brown with medium pressure. Transition these colors to make lighter values in the entire donut with light pressure. Add yellow ochre in the light and overlap it over the browns.

Texture: Once you've shaded the entire donut, put a piece of magic tape onto your drawing and draw the coconut sprinkles with a ballpoint pen, indenting the paper. Pay attention to length, width, overlapping, and curvature of the sprinkles. They repeat the curving shape of the donut and should be placed to match with their rotation in space.

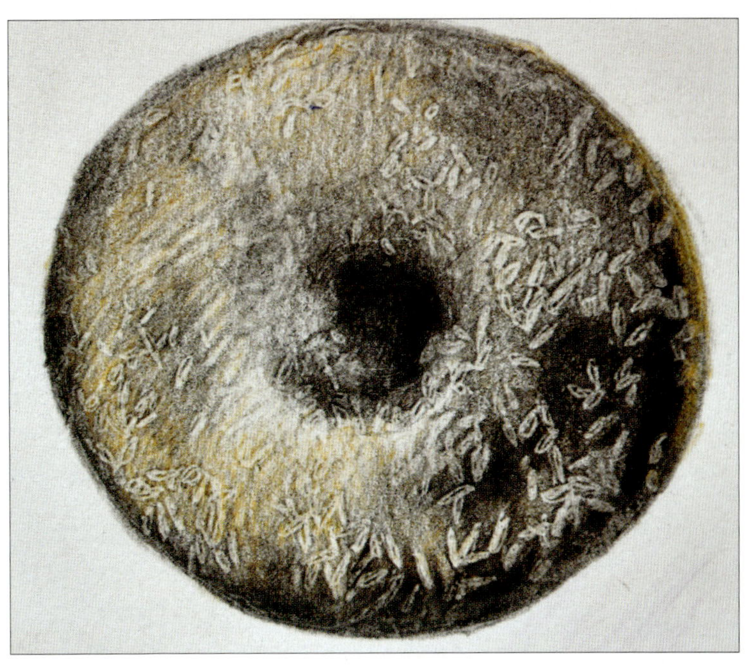

Pull off the tape, move it to the next section, and repeat the process until you cover the entire donut with texture. When you lift off the magic tape you expose the paper's original color, which is a very light grey here. Once you color the donut more, you'll see that the coconut sprinkles appear brighter set against the shaded browns.

Deepen the values: Repeat the coloring with dark umber, dark brown, and yellow ochre. The coconut sprinkles become noticeable as pencil skips through the paper indentations.

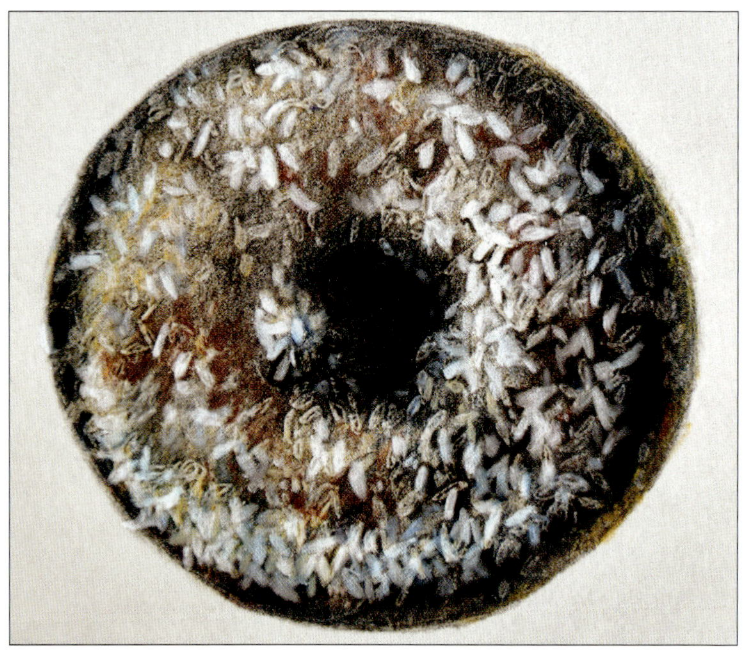

Step 2

You repeat the process of paper indenting and lifting out with magic tape 2–3 times to build texture. But in subsequent steps you not only shade through the pencil skips but also around some of them to outline the edges with indigo blue for better definition in the dark (right side).

Coconut flakes: With heavy pressure begin coloring over some indentations with Luminance light cobalt blue (Prismacolor powder blue), eggshell, beige, and white. Not every coconut flake is white; some are light blue, others are grey or ochre-grey. You see white only in the lightest areas. Therefore, you color the flakes and then add the purest white only on a few of them.

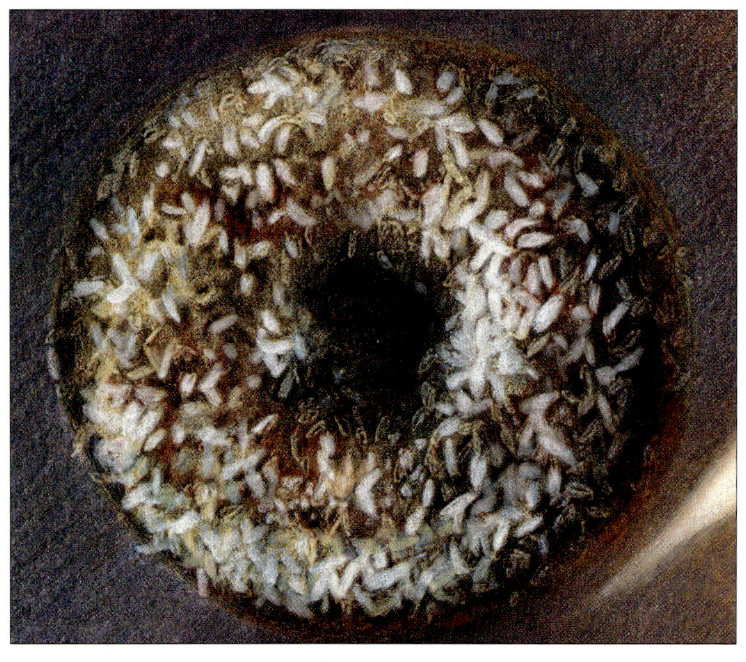

Step 3

Once the background is established, the coconut sprinkles read even lighter because they are set against the dark browns on a dark background.

It is important to blend the donut's outer edge into the background for a natural appearance. If you haven't achieved this with shading, blend the edge with the full blender. Notice that there are no light skips or white spaces around the donut; it fuses with the background completely. Beginning students often leave tiny, uncolored areas around their subjects, making the background look like it sits next to or around an object, instead of under it.

DONUT 7

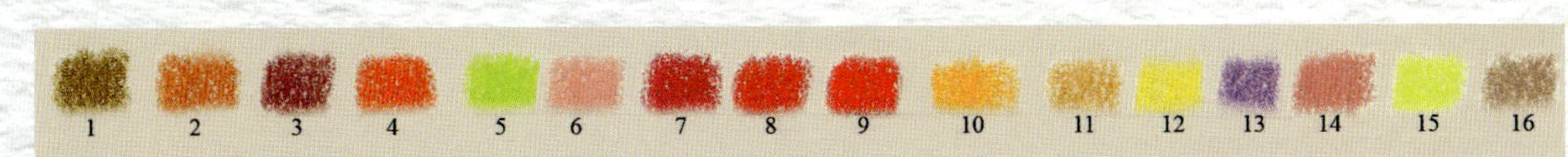

Colors: 1. Artichoke 2. Mineral Orange 3. Henna 4. Orange 5. Chartreuse 6. Peach 7. Pomegranate 8. Crimson Red 9. Permanent Red 10. Spanish Orange 11. Yellow Orange 12. Pablo Yellow 13. Pablo Periwinkle Blue 14. Nectar 15. Yellow Chartreuse 16. Beige Sienna

Step 1

In this step you focus on the form shadow, defining it with artichoke and henna and adding mineral orange (or orange) in the reflected light. It creates volume.

To shade the red center, make dots with a very sharp white. Shade with the reds around the tiny white dots (crimson red, pomegranate, permanent red). The left inner side of the red center is darker than the right.

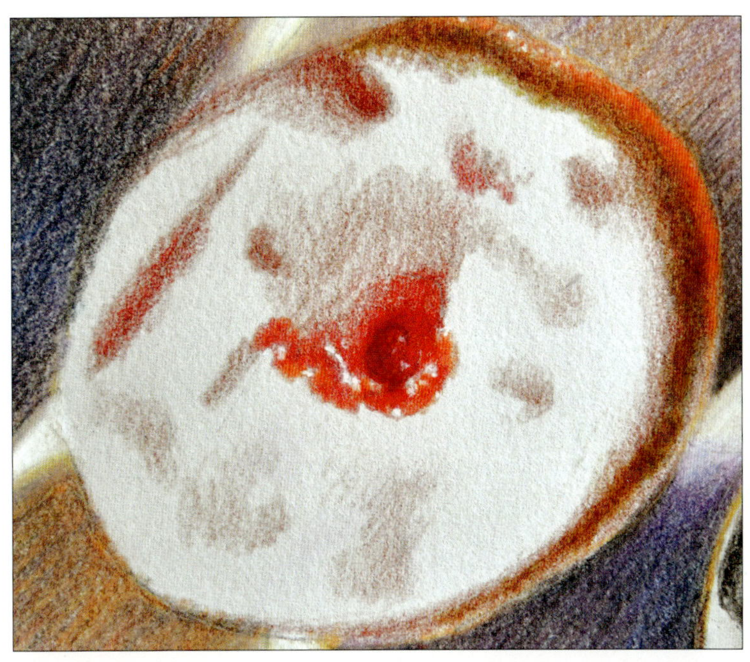

Step 2

Lay in the foundation for texture by placing white specks on the donut that will represent tiny sugar granules.

Shade the donut's top with chartreuse (light, greenish yellow). Add peach in the reflected light on the right side of the donut so that orange transitions to peach.

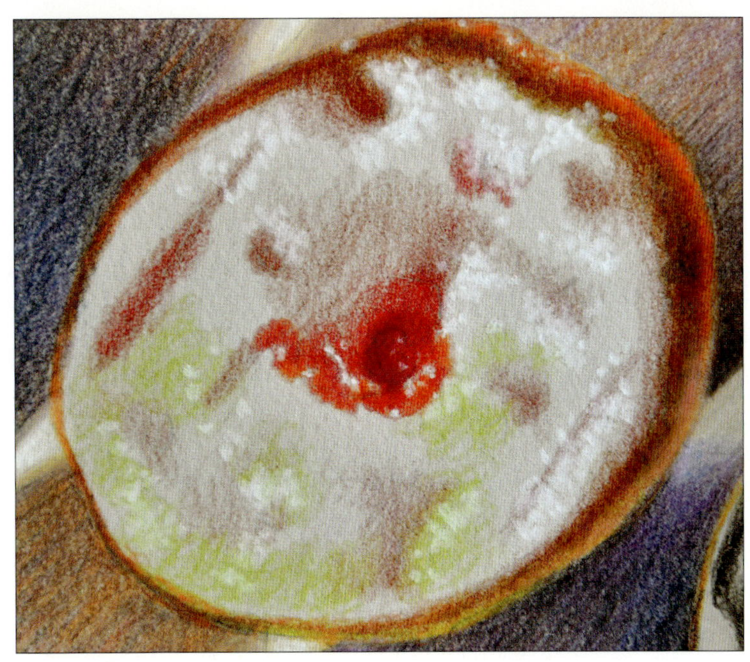

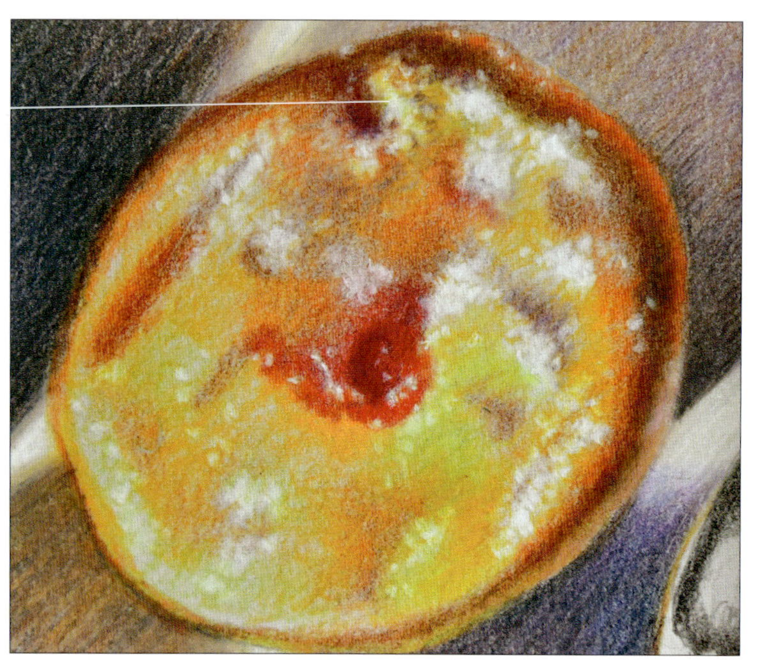

Step 3

Enhance the form shadow at the top of the donut with overlapping strokes of artichoke. Vary pressure to blend the colors and to transition artichoke into the light (yellow).

Enhance the colors of the donut in the light, using these yellows: Spanish orange, Pablo yellow, yellow ochre, yellow chartreuse. Add warm red, Prismacolor permanent red, to make the jam brighter. Keep the red edge very soft to create the illusion and flow. Outlined edges and lines flatten out the form!

To make the whites brighter, it's not just about shading with white using heavy pressure; it's more about shading with darker colors around the whites. Apply 30% warm grey, henna, and Pablo periwinkle blue in the areas around the white sugar granules. Move in small, soft circles to create colorful shadows. Edges must look uneven and irregular to imitate the sugar clusters.

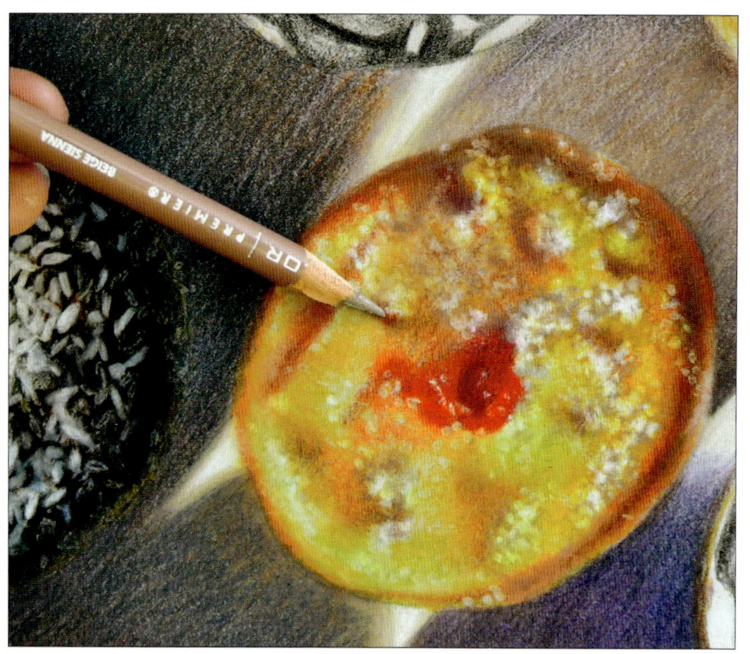

Step 4

Beige sienna softens the edges between these newly created shadows and bright yellows. You need to overlap beige sienna over all the colors applied in the shadow and extend its shading into the yellow to create subtle value transitions. This is a unifying color that blends and lightens up the shadows, greying them down further.

To increase the appearance of texture, you can make magic tape lift outs on the donut and then color them with white pencil. When you lift out on the sides of the donut, revealing the paper's light grey color, it looks like sugar granules in the shadow without additional coloring.

Step 5

Step back to look at your work from a distance and see if your color application remains very soft and the brightest sugar granules are the whitest in the light.

The artist doesn't blend the surface; but if you work on a different paper that has some texture, blend it with a full blender, not the solvents, because these are light colors. Once again see how the donut's outer rim blends into the background seamlessly.

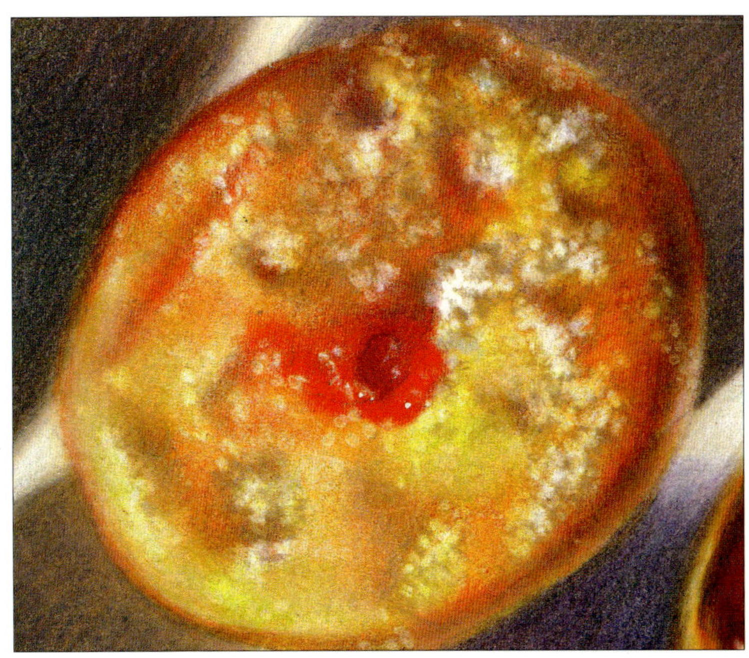

DONUT 8

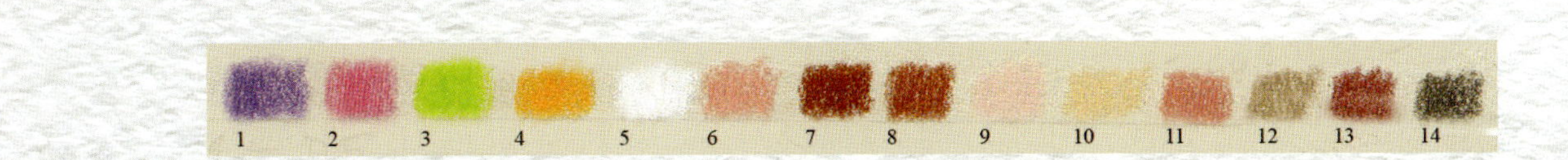

Colors: 1. Pablo Periwinkle Blue 2. Pablo Purple 3. Chartreuse 4. Spanish Orange 5. White 6. Peach 7. Terra Cotta 8. Burnt Ochre 9. Light Peach 10. Eggshell 11. Nectar 12. Beige Sienna 13. Henna 14. 70% French Grey

Step 1

Just like in previous donuts, map out the shadow with Pablo periwinkle blue (lilac), Pablo purple (or Prismacolor magenta), and 70% French grey.

Use a combination of chartreuse, Spanish orange, terra cotta, and burnt ochre to shade the donut from dark to light on its sides. Remember to blend the outer edge into the background. Once all the darks are in place you can proceed to the next step where you work on shading in the light (pink glaze).

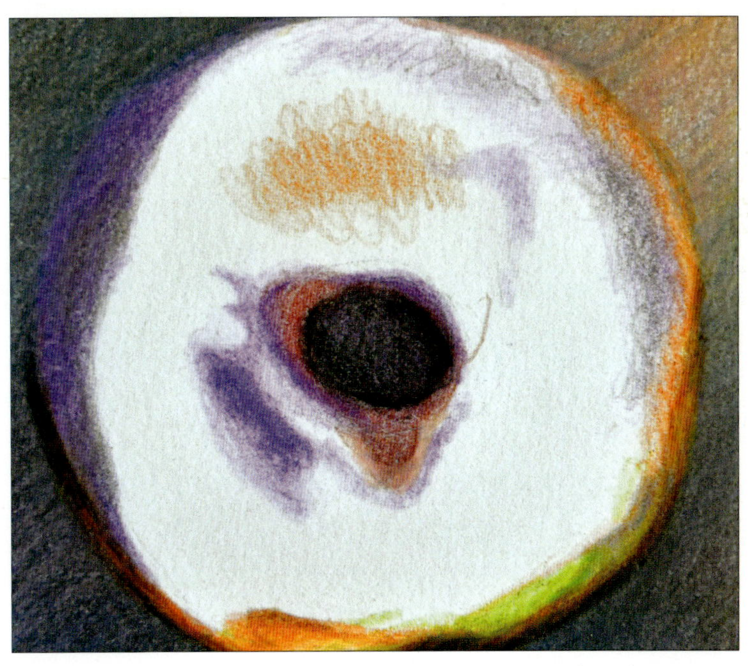

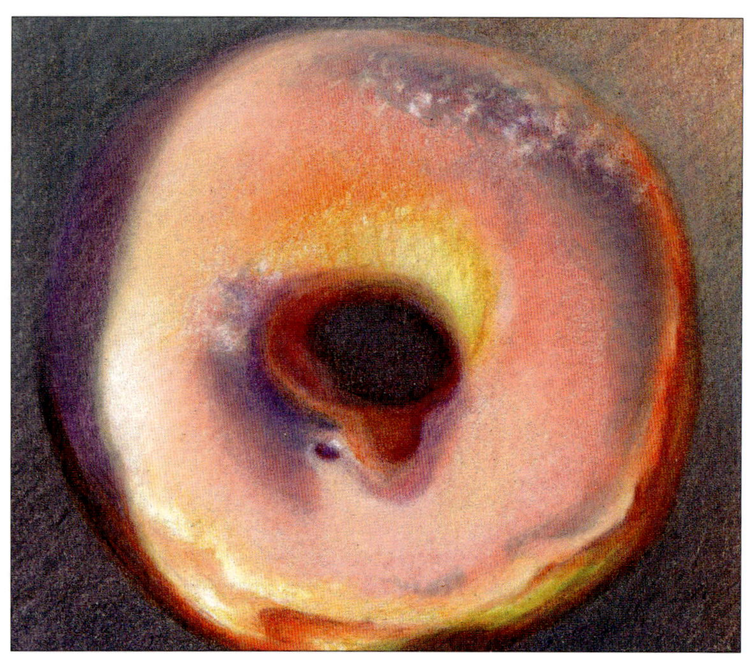

Step 2

Shade the pink glaze with henna, nectar, and peach to create medium tones at the donut's top, and light peach, eggshell, beige sienna, and white to create the lightest areas on the left and bottom. Use magic tape to complete lift outs for the sugar speck at the top side. Step back to check on the softness of edges and values. Use henna and 70% French grey with light pressure to define dark edges inside the hole and on the donut's outer edge to blend it into the background. Apply a mix of light peach and white with heavy pressure over the pinks to blend and to brighten up the colors seen in the light. Use white with heavy pressure for the highlights only. They will seem brighter when you place darker values around the white.

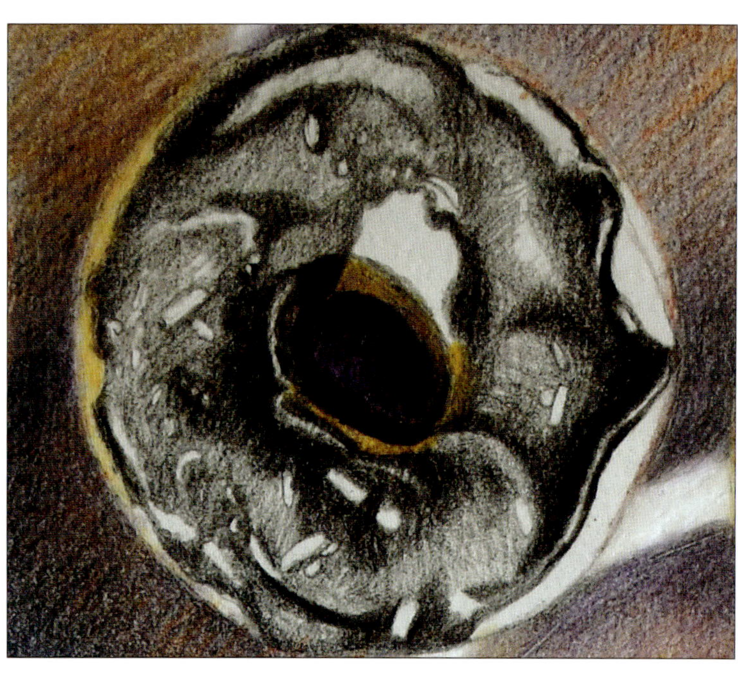

DONUT 9

Step 1

Note: This donut is very similar to drawing Donut 5, only the colors for sprinkles may differ. Therefore the color chart is the same as for Donut 5 on page 157. Refer to the color chart and the instructions for Donut 5. While the colors are similar, the shape of the chocolate glaze is different.

Begin shading from dark to light. Map out the donut's chocolate glaze in a single color—dark umber. Skip the lightest areas and shade around them with light pressure.

Step 2

Fill in colors for the sprinkles. Shade the outside edge with burnt ochre, terra cotta, yellow ochre, and Pablo yellow. Layer the second color in the glaze by shading with sepia and burnt ochre. Softly erase the small, curving shapes and fill in with light grey. Chocolate glaze in the light: Shade with pumpkin orange and burnt ochre with heavy pressure. Chocolate glaze in the dark and medium dark: crimson red, henna and terra cotta. Use beige sienna to grey down the lighter passages on the outer rim to blend the edges, creating reflected light. Add yellow, eggshell, and white in the brightest yellow light near the hole.

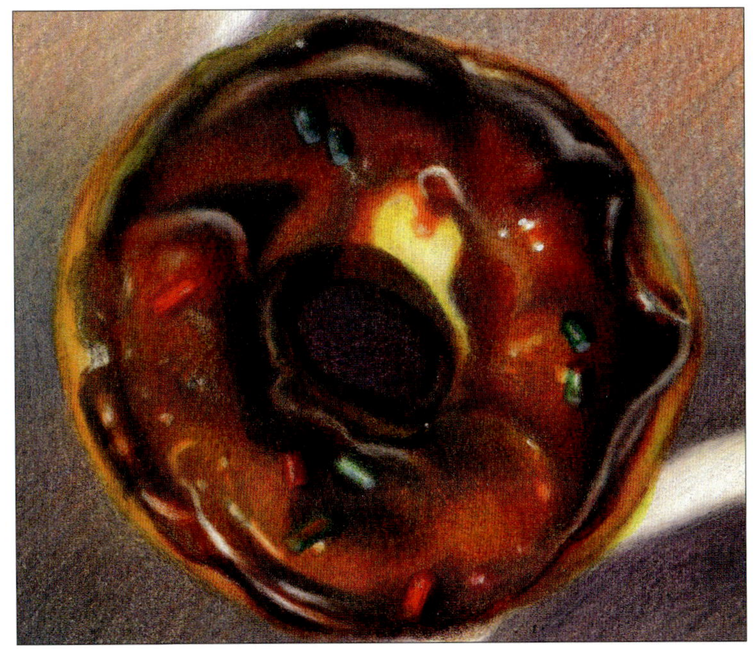

DONUT 10

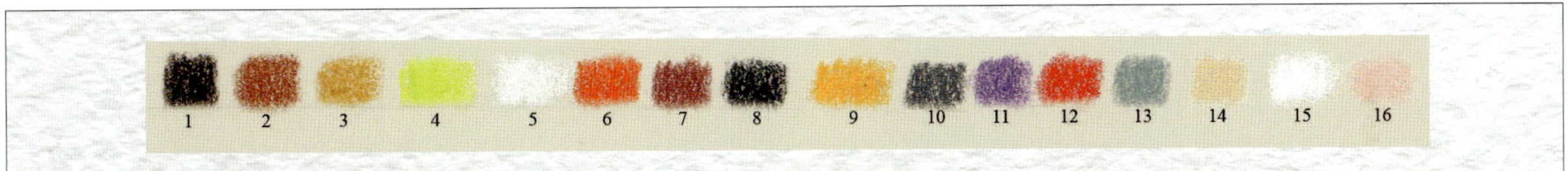

Color Chart: 1. Dark Umber 2. Burnt Ochre 3. Yellow Ochre 4. Yellow Chartreuse 5. White 6. Orange 7. Henna 8. 90% Warm Grey 9. Spanish Orange 10. 70% Cool Grey 11. Pablo Periwinkle Blue 12. Permanent Red 13. Jade Green 14. Eggshell 15. White 16. Light Peach

Step 1

Outline and fill in the hole with dark umber and 70% cool grey. Shade lightly with this color on the inner sides of the donut. Shade the outer side and the rim with burnt ochre, yellow ochre, and orange.

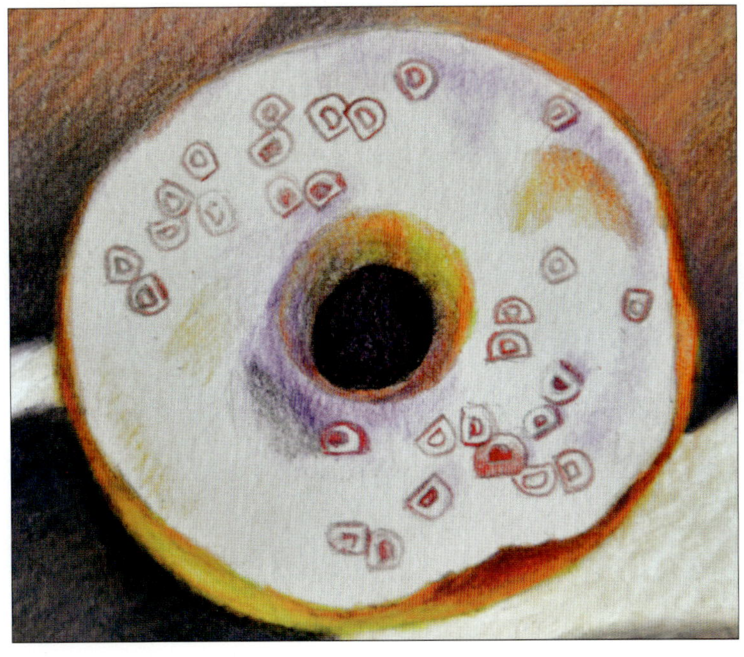

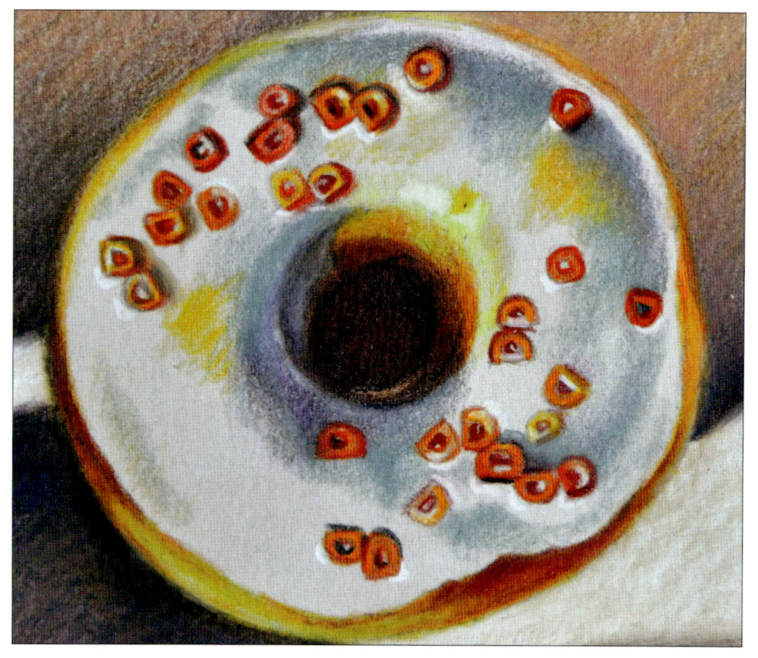

Step 2

In this step you develop the shadows on the glaze and draft the letters.

Letters: Define and fill in parts of the letters with a sharp point of henna. Mix it with permanent red, orange, and yellow to vary values (light/dark). Use a sharp point and heavy pressure to make the lightest strokes in the white present around the Ds.

Shadow in the glaze: Mix jade green, 70% cool grey, and Pablo periwinkle blue (lilac).

Add Spanish orange in lighter areas of the glaze. Add 90% warm grey with light pressure to grey down the hole further. Blend the outer rim of the donut into the background.

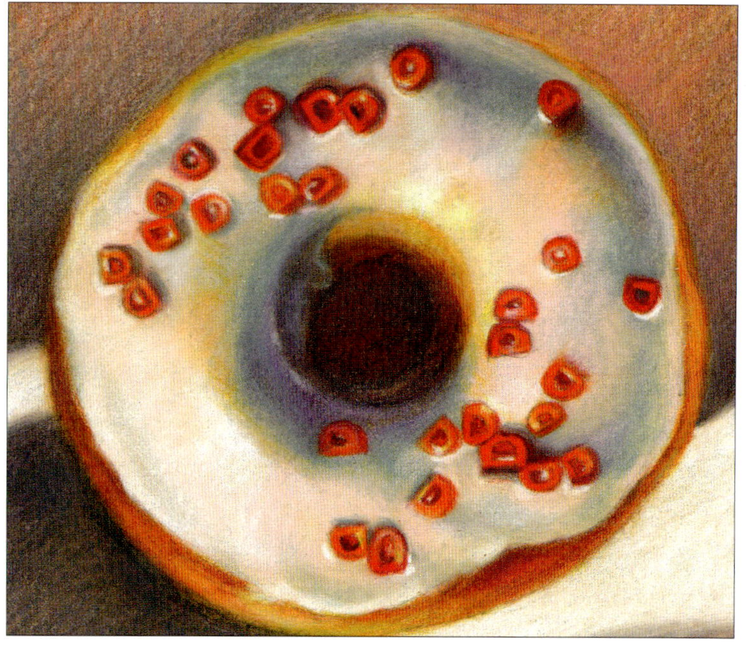

Step 3

Here you work on the light in the glaze. For that, use a combination of eggshell, light peach, and white in heavy pressure to fill in the light glaze around the letters. Press hard on the white to make the brightest whites (highlights). Blend the donut with a full blender, if needed.

BACKGROUND

Step 1

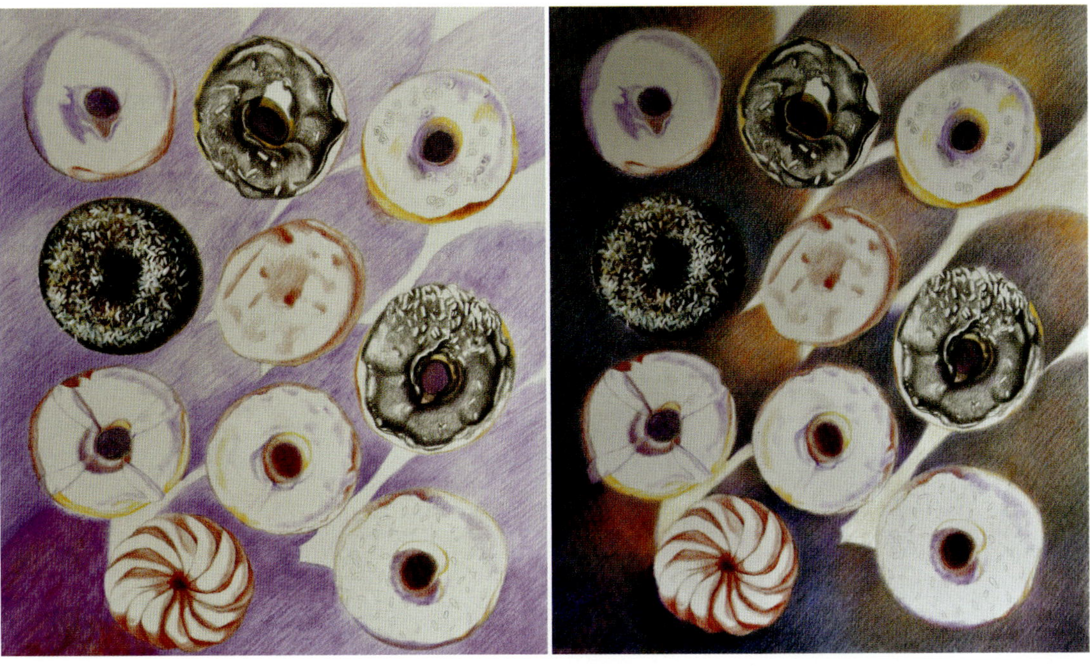

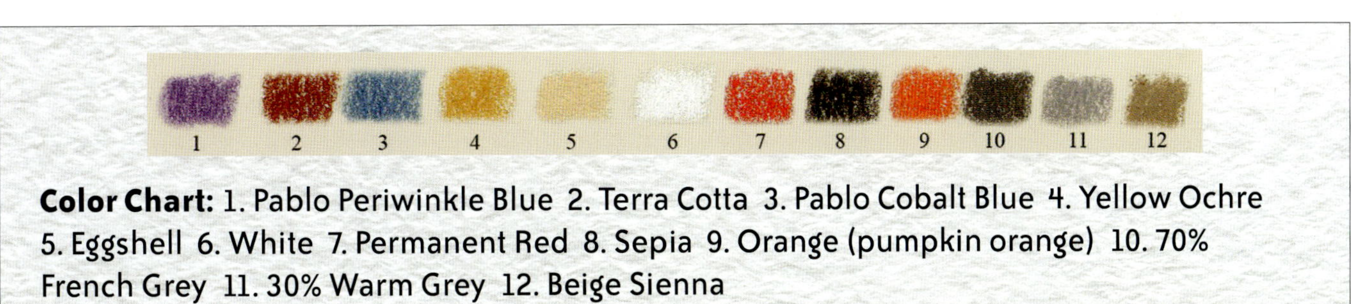

Color Chart: 1. Pablo Periwinkle Blue 2. Terra Cotta 3. Pablo Cobalt Blue 4. Yellow Ochre 5. Eggshell 6. White 7. Permanent Red 8. Sepia 9. Orange (pumpkin orange) 10. 70% French Grey 11. 30% Warm Grey 12. Beige Sienna

While the background shares some basic colors with the entire drawing, there are major color variations happening due to changes in reflected light and cast shadows seen next to every donut. The individual donuts "throw" their local color into their cast shadows in the background, which makes the shadows look colorful. Therefore, you begin to block in with two or three basic colors that are common for the entire image, and later add additional hues based on the local color of each donut.

The first color to layer is Pablo periwinkle blue (lilac), which is also present in the form shadow of almost every donut you've done (see the left image above). Block in with this color and add Pablo cobalt blue, terra cotta, and sepia (almost any dark brown will work here) to darken the values, especially on the left. Block in with yellow ochre in large mid-value areas. Overlap this color over the browns.

You will now begin adding the local colors of the donuts into the cast shadows (shadows underneath each donut). For that you add permanent red, orange, or Spanish orange, depending on the color of the donut. It is important to let all these colors overlap each other. You will unify and blend them more with greys in the last step.

It is important to make a choice for your directional strokes for the background and stick to it. While these strokes can vary in approach (circles, horizontal, vertical, crosshatching), they mustn't go around every donut, or they will flatten out the form. The background must stay behind the objects, not next to it. Therefore resist the temptation to place marks going around each donut. Eliminate these strokes so not to compete with the textures of the donuts achieved by layering and blending.

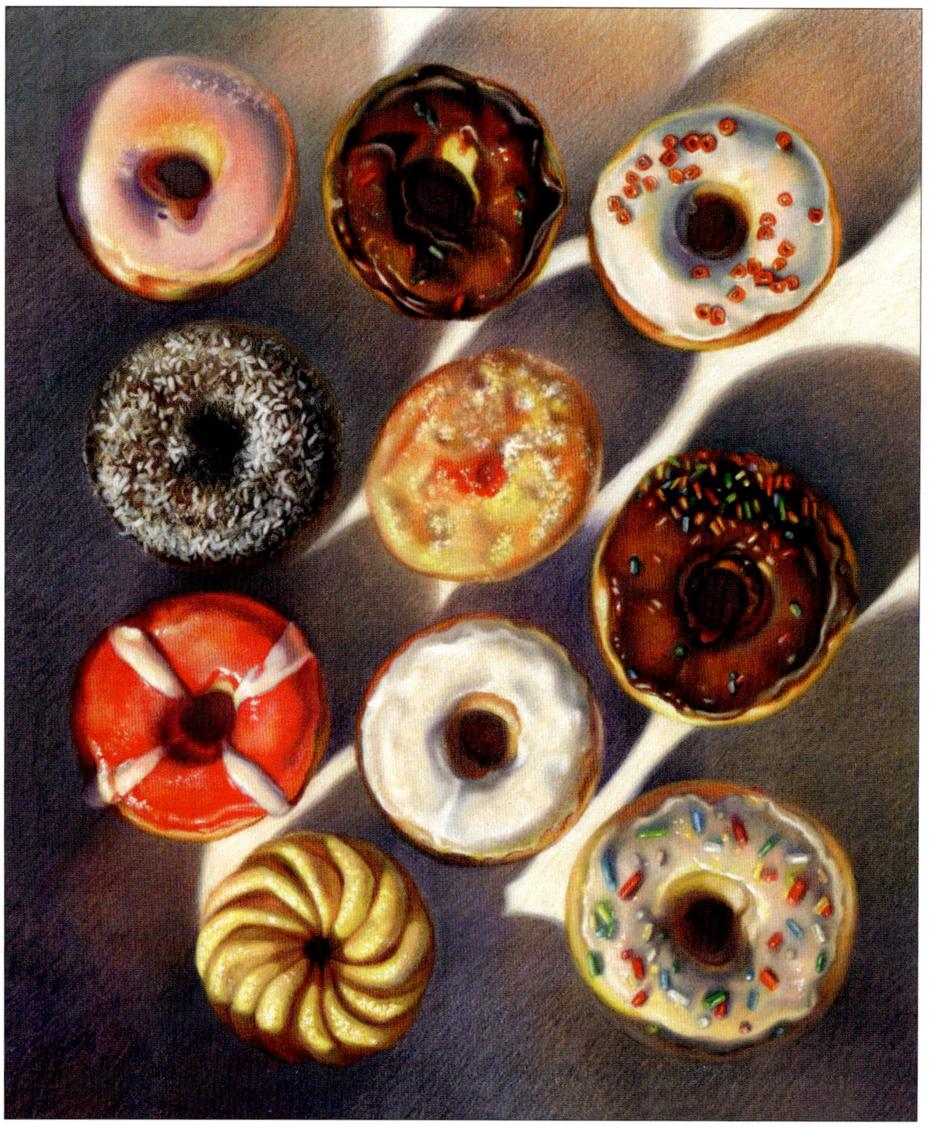

Step 2

The light passages in the background are shaded with eggshell and white over them. It is important to keep the edges very soft while simultaneously preserving the shape of every cast shadow. For that, shading and overlapping lighter color over the dark is crucial.

Grey down and darken the entire background with 70% French grey in the deepest dark, 30% warm grey and beige sienna in medium dark. Spray with a final fixative twice outdoors. Frame.

TROUBLESHOOTING PROBLEMS

Solvents

PROBLEM: I'm applying the solvent, but it doesn't do anything.

SOLUTION: The technique of blending colored pencils with solvents (see Chapter 5) works well with the wax-based colored pencils only. Either change the brand of your pencils or try using a bit more solvent on your brush. Also, some artists are timid in their shading, not applying enough pigment. If you have used light colors in your drawing, the solvent doesn't have much information to work with, and therefore the blending is not noticeable.

PROBLEM: I'm applying the solvent, but it is smearing all over the place.

SOLUTION: You're using too much solvent. Tap your brush against a paper towel before applying it to your image.

PROBLEM: I'm applying the solvent, but the colors are smearing and I am seeing exaggerated pencil strokes.

SOLUTION: Paint over your colors slowly, making sure you go from light to dark. This way you can't drag the dark colors into the light colors. Rarely, exaggerated strokes will appear depending on the color used in the drawing. Most colors blend in the same way; however, a few colors—Prismacolor Mulberry (cool red) for example—tend to react differently to solvent.

Wax Bloom

Wax bloom is a white, waxy haze that may appear on some colored pencil drawings that have been saturated with color and the surface becomes so waxy it cannot accept any additional layering. Sometimes it appears a few weeks after the work is finished. Because pencils such as Prismacolor and Pablo contain wax, wax bloom may occur occasionally. Normally, the spraying of professional final fixative will prevent the bloom. To prevent wax bloom from occurring in your drawings, follow these steps:

- Test each one of the steps in the instructions as you go through them on a scrap piece of paper that is the same type of paper you are using for your project.
- Spray fixative in a low-humidity environment, holding the can about a foot away from your drawing. Follow the directions on the can.
- If wax bloom does occur, wipe off the bloom gently with a soft tissue or a soft cotton fabric rag. Be careful not to smudge the pigment.

Using Fixatives

Final Fixative: A final fixative is used to protect drawings from smudging, moisture, and UV light. It comes in several finishes, including glossy and matte. The artist prefers using matte final fixative so the surface becomes uniform, yet doesn't reflect the colors at different angles. Test your fixative on a scrap paper before applying it over your artwork. Sometimes a fixative can darken the colors or it will layer unevenly if it is not a good one. Always spray fixative outdoors or in a well-ventilated space with low humidity levels. Extreme conditions such as high humidity and temperature may affect the layering of the spray. Don't allow children to use a fixative and be sure to store it in a cool and dry place because it's flammable.

Shake the can before every use for a minute or so. Spray onto a butcher paper first and then onto your artwork about 20 inches away from it. The artist usually sprays the artwork twice, giving each coat time to dry completely for about 10 minutes.

Workable Fixative: A workable fixative works very similar to a final one but has a much thinner coat of resin, allowing for rework and easy lift outs. Usually, artists use this fixative in between layers. Follow the same instructions as written for the final fixative.

Students can download a complete pdf file with full-page images and outlines for every project on the artist's website: **www.veronicasart.com**